Shojo Beat

Sweet Rein

3

Story & Art by Sakura Tsukuba

Sweet Rein

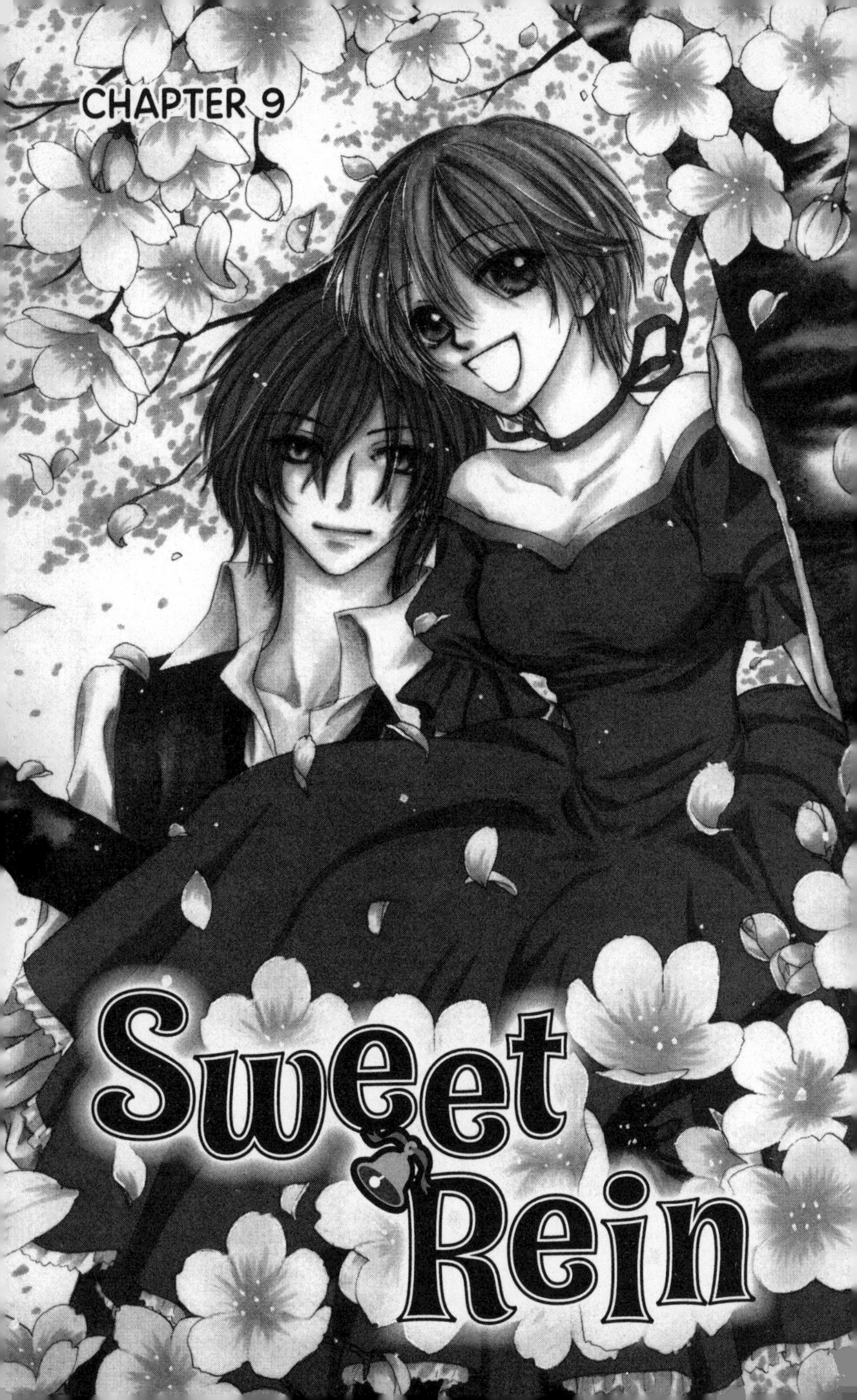
CHAPTER 9
Sweet Rein

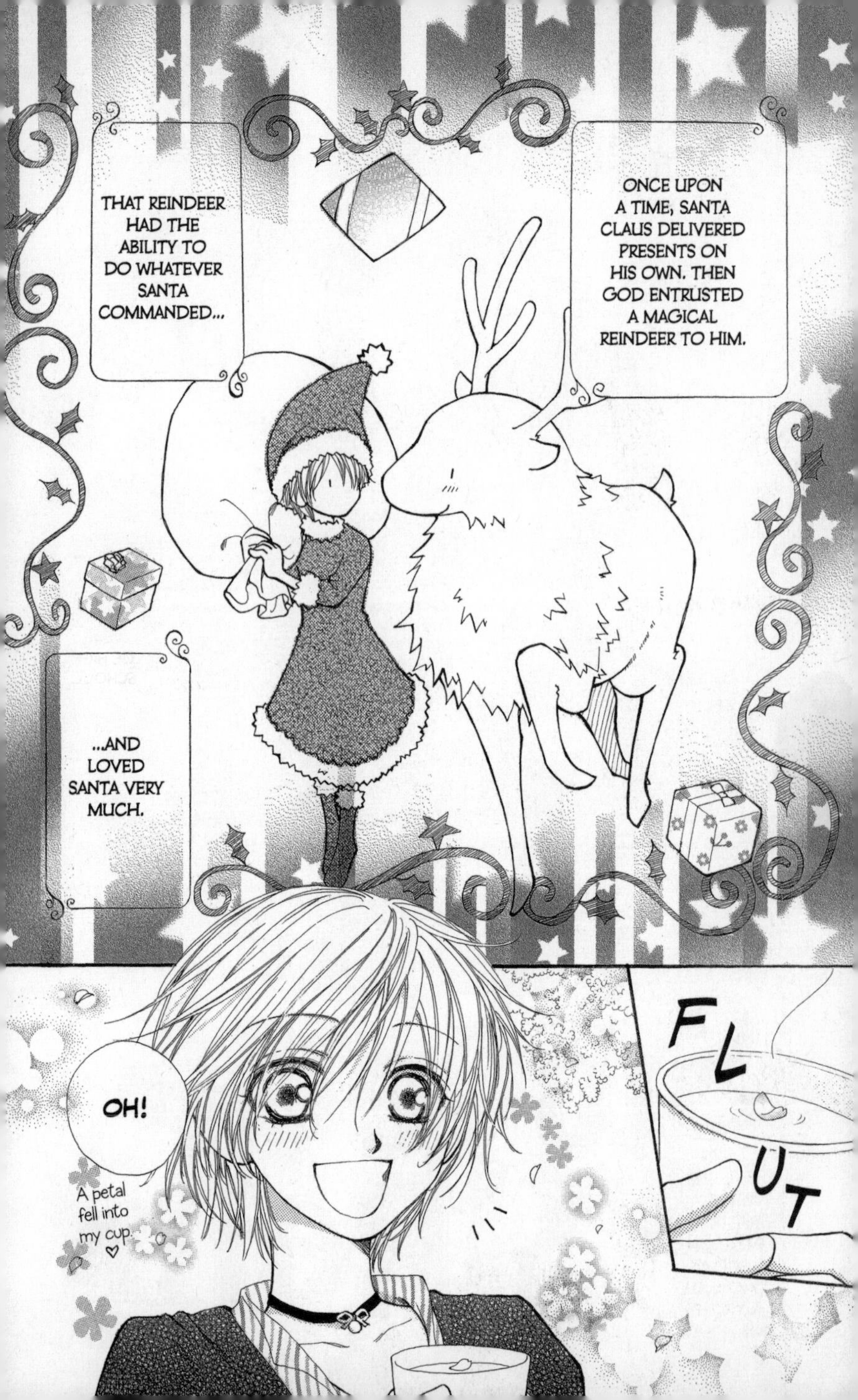

ONCE UPON A TIME, SANTA CLAUS DELIVERED PRESENTS ON HIS OWN. THEN GOD ENTRUSTED A MAGICAL REINDEER TO HIM.
THAT REINDEER HAD THE ABILITY TO DO WHATEVER SANTA COMMANDED...
...AND LOVED SANTA VERY MUCH.
FLUT
OH!
A petal fell into my cup. ♥

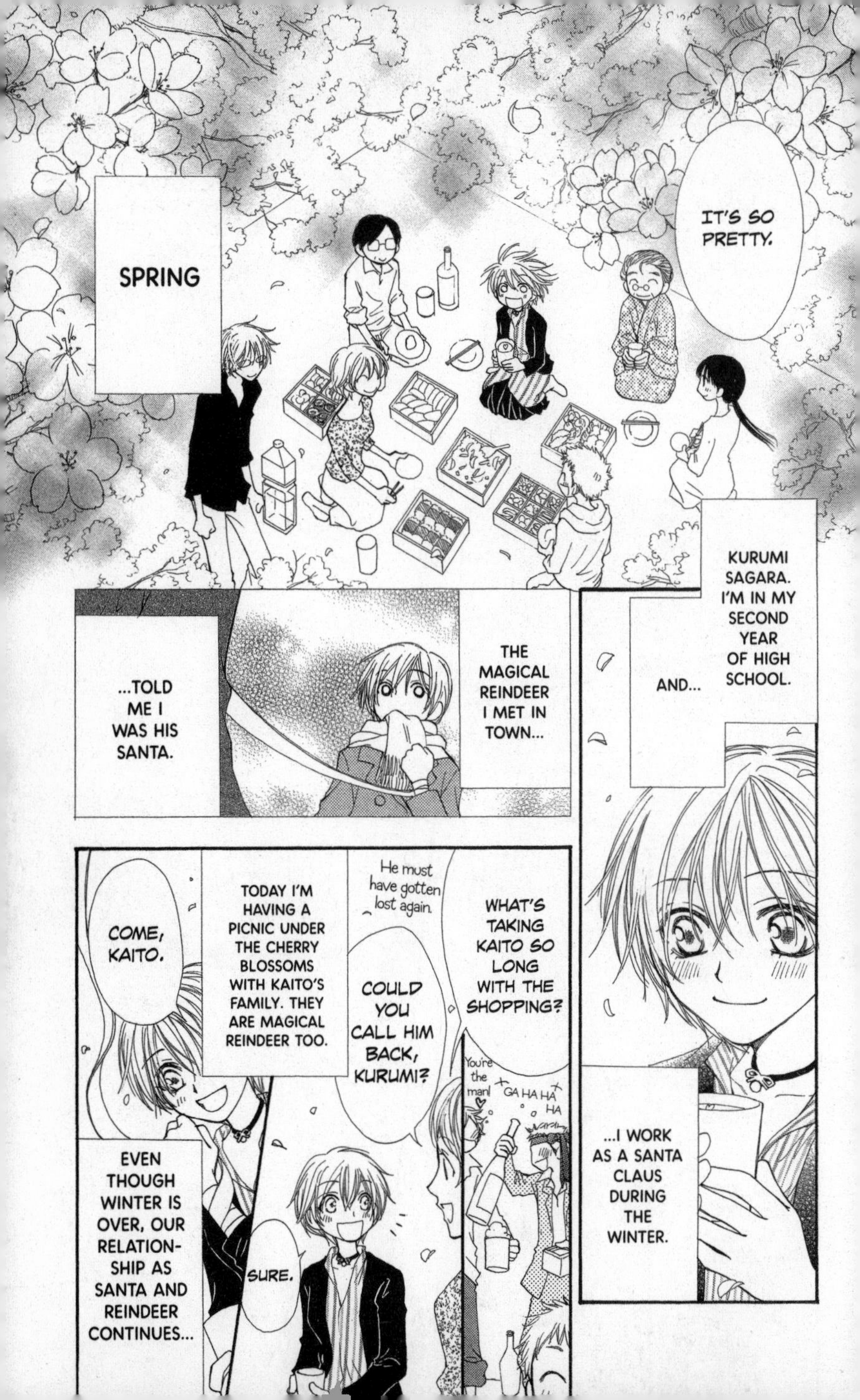
IT'S SO PRETTY.
SPRING
KURUMI SAGARA. I'M IN MY SECOND YEAR OF HIGH SCHOOL.
AND...
...I WORK AS A SANTA CLAUS DURING THE WINTER.
THE MAGICAL REINDEER I MET IN TOWN...
...TOLD ME I WAS HIS SANTA.
WHAT'S TAKING KAITO SO LONG WITH THE SHOPPING?
He must have gotten lost again.
COULD YOU CALL HIM BACK, KURUMI?
TODAY I'M HAVING A PICNIC UNDER THE CHERRY BLOSSOMS WITH KAITO'S FAMILY. THEY ARE MAGICAL REINDEER TOO.
COME, KAITO.
You're the man!
GA HA HA HA
SURE.
EVEN THOUGH WINTER IS OVER, OUR RELATION-SHIP AS SANTA AND REINDEER CONTINUES...

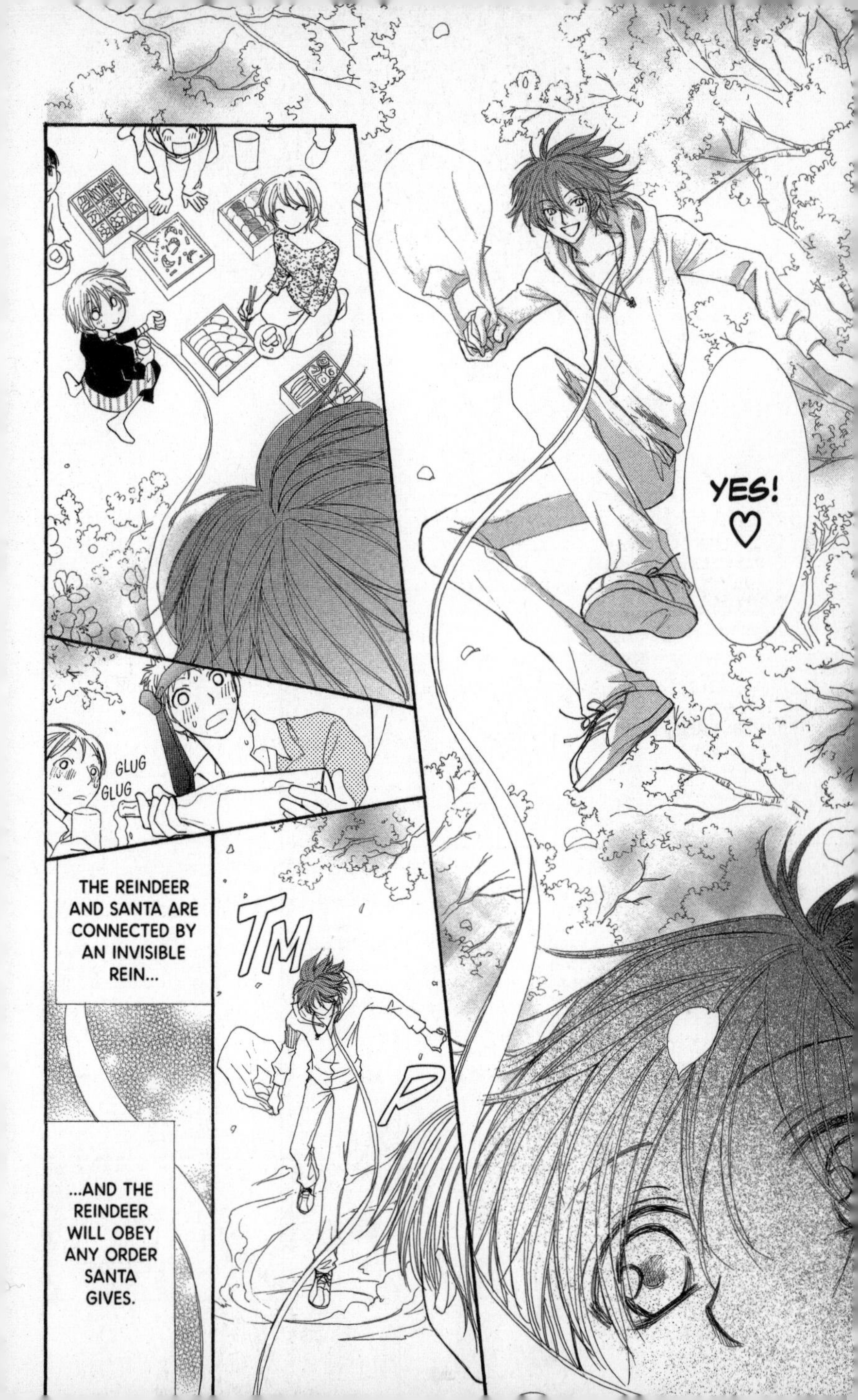
YES! ♡
GLUG GLUG
THE REINDEER AND SANTA ARE CONNECTED BY AN INVISIBLE REIN...
TMP
...AND THE REINDEER WILL OBEY ANY ORDER SANTA GIVES.

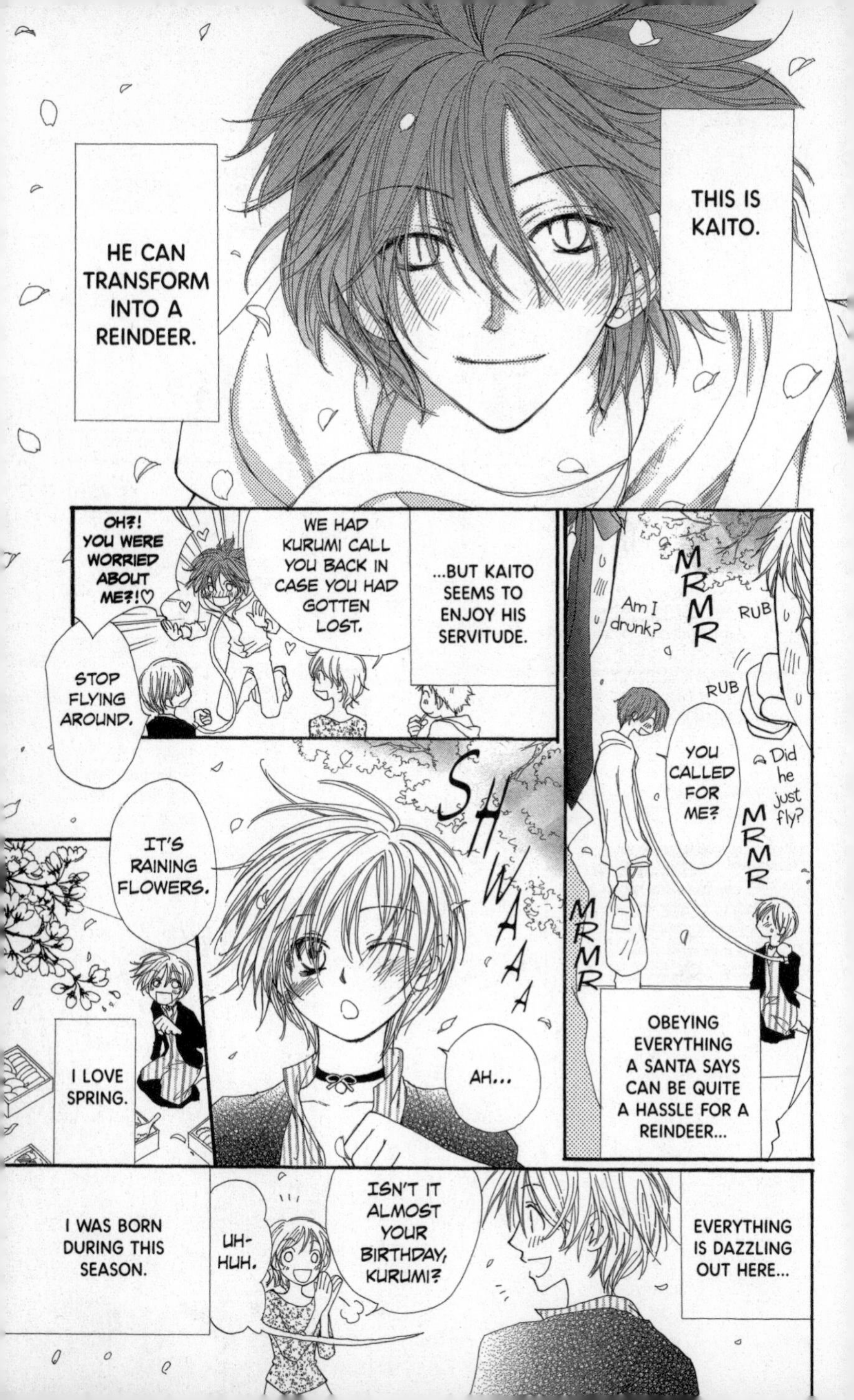
THIS IS KAITO.
HE CAN TRANSFORM INTO A REINDEER.
MRMR
RUB
Am I drunk?
RUB
YOU CALLED FOR ME?
Did he just fly?
MRMR
MRMR
OBEYING EVERYTHING A SANTA SAYS CAN BE QUITE A HASSLE FOR A REINDEER...
...BUT KAITO SEEMS TO ENJOY HIS SERVITUDE.
WE HAD KURUMI CALL YOU BACK IN CASE YOU HAD GOTTEN LOST.
OH?! YOU WERE WORRIED ABOUT ME?!♡
STOP FLYING AROUND.
SHWAAA
AH...
IT'S RAINING FLOWERS.
I LOVE SPRING.
EVERYTHING IS DAZZLING OUT HERE...
ISN'T IT ALMOST YOUR BIRTHDAY, KURUMI?
UH-HUH.
I WAS BORN DURING THIS SEASON.

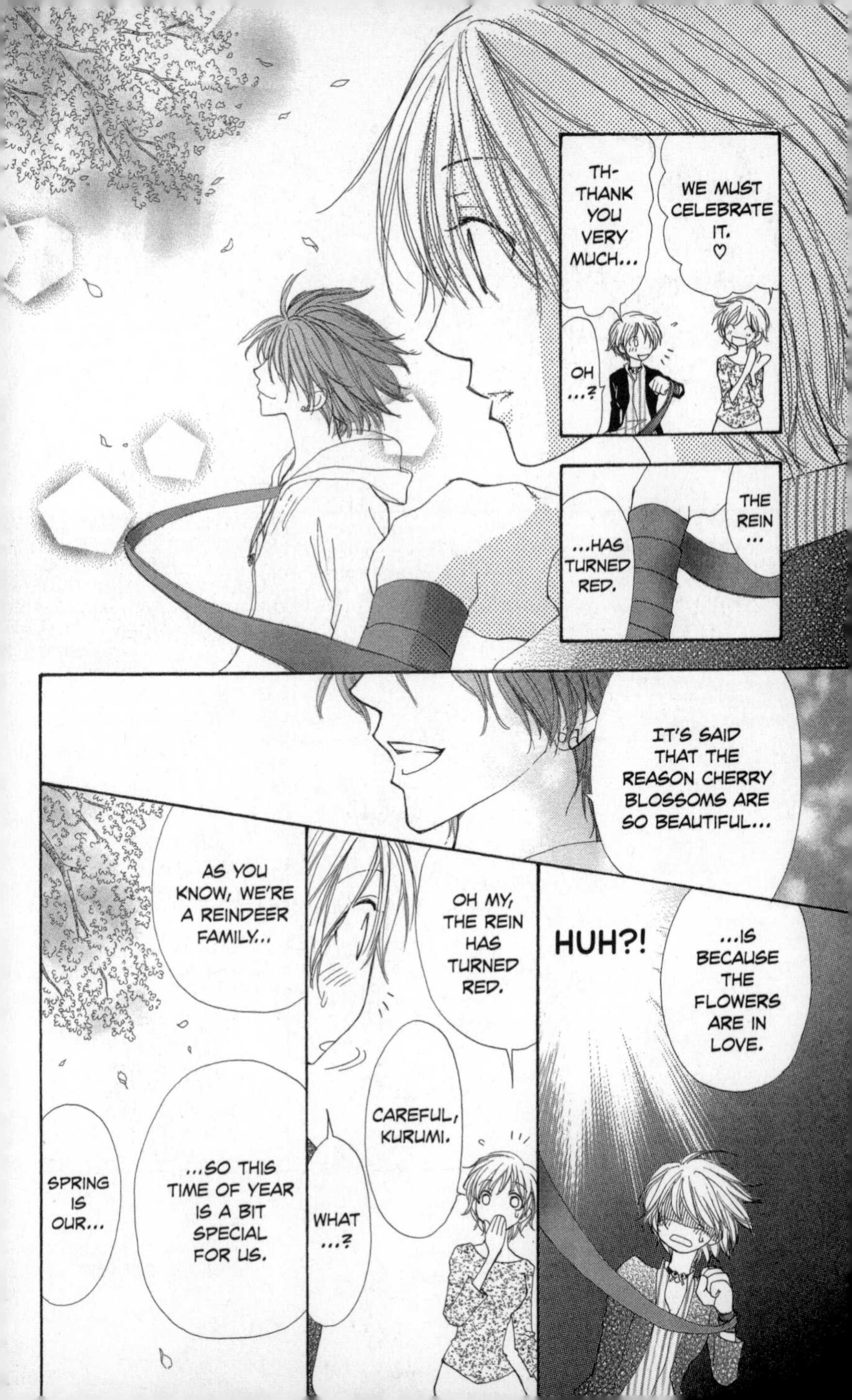
WE MUST CELEBRATE IT. ♡
TH-THANK YOU VERY MUCH...
OH ...?
THE REIN ...
...HAS TURNED RED.
IT'S SAID THAT THE REASON CHERRY BLOSSOMS ARE SO BEAUTIFUL...
...IS BECAUSE THE FLOWERS ARE IN LOVE.
HUH?!
OH MY, THE REIN HAS TURNED RED.
CAREFUL, KURUMI.
WHAT ...?
AS YOU KNOW, WE'RE A REINDEER FAMILY...
...SO THIS TIME OF YEAR IS A BIT SPECIAL FOR US.
SPRING IS OUR...

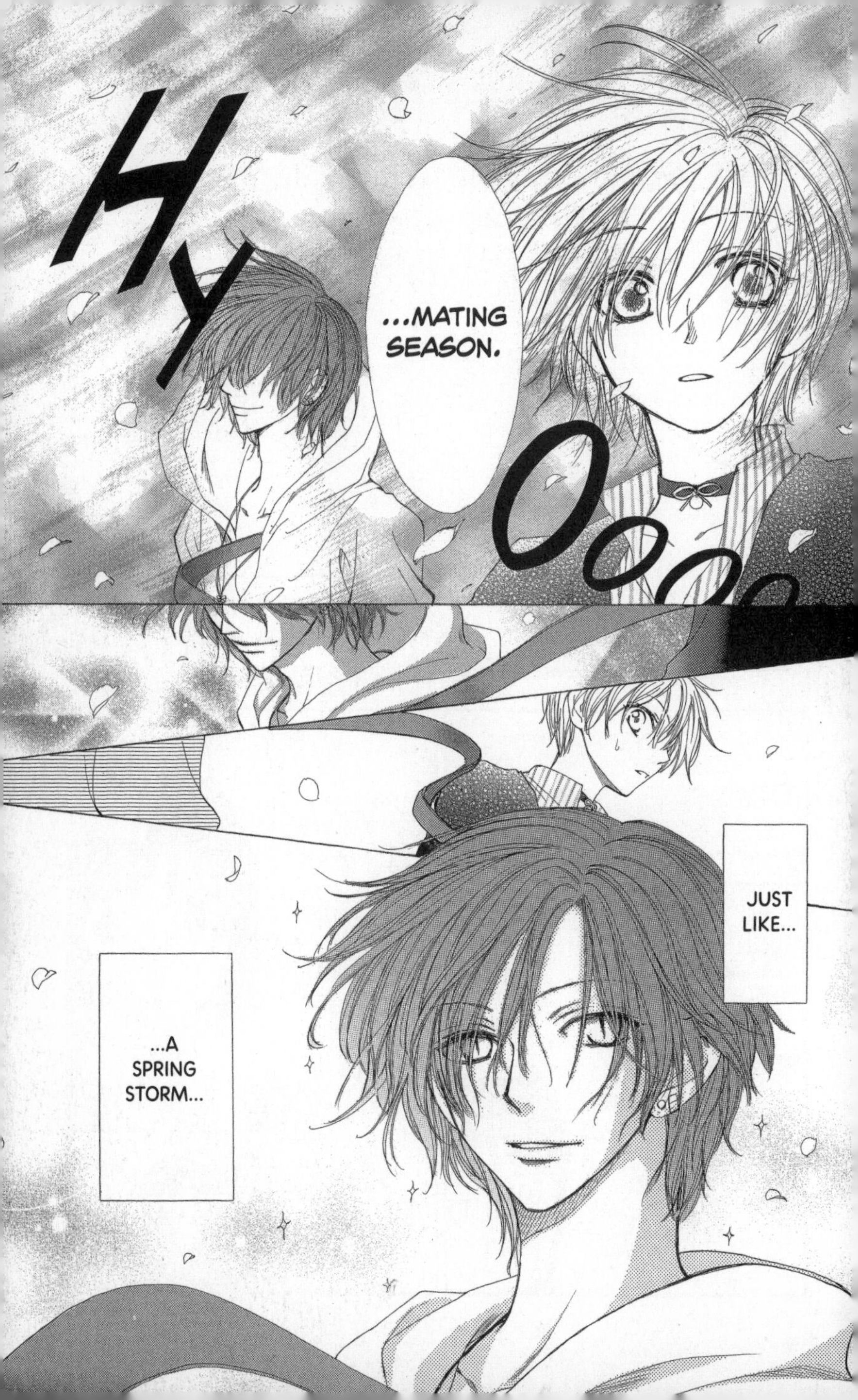
...MATING SEASON.
HYOOOO
JUST LIKE...
...A SPRING STORM...

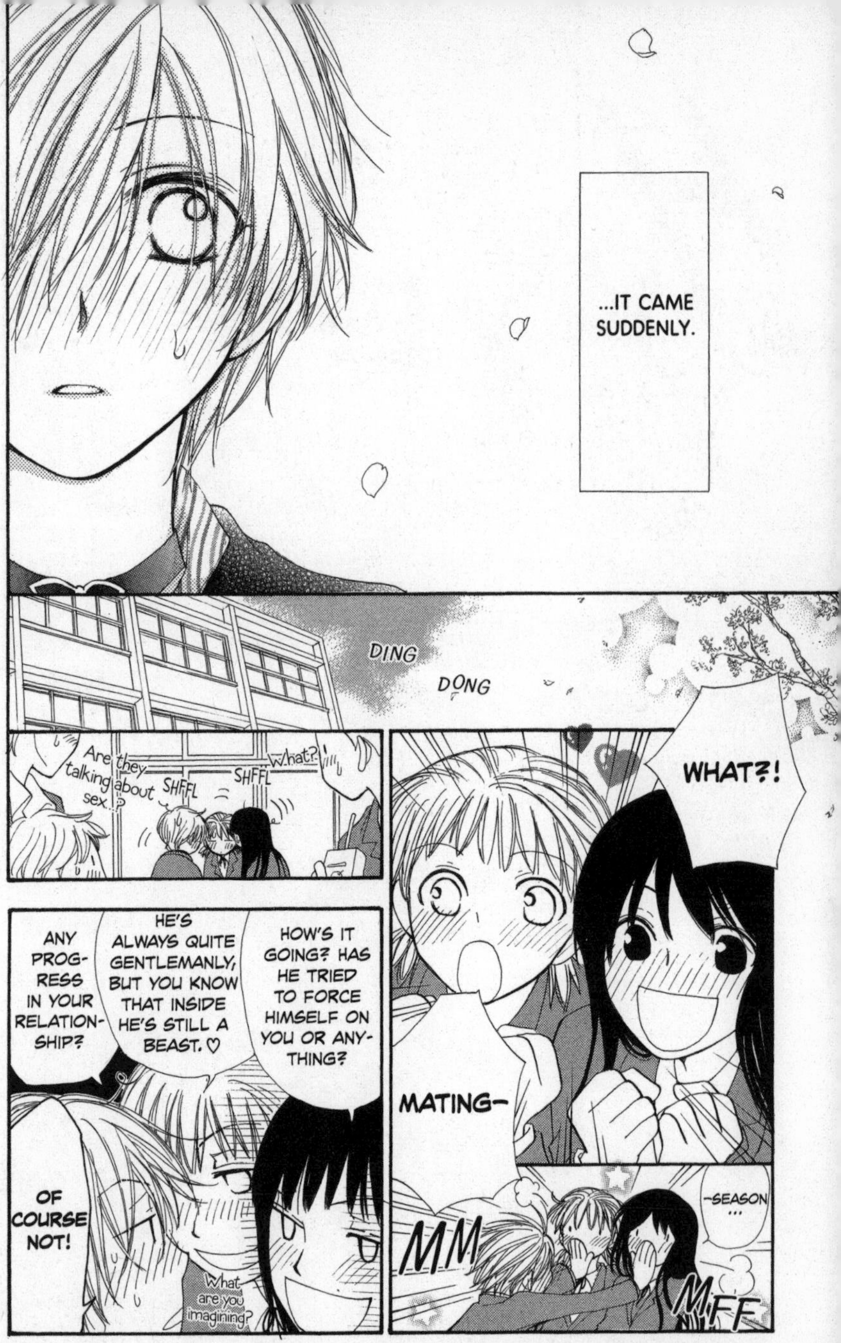
...IT CAME SUDDENLY.
DING
DONG
WHAT?!
MATING–
–SEASON ...
MM
MFF
What?
SHFFL
SHFFL
Are they talking about sex..?
HOW'S IT GOING? HAS HE TRIED TO FORCE HIMSELF ON YOU OR ANYTHING?
HE'S ALWAYS QUITE GENTLEMANLY, BUT YOU KNOW THAT INSIDE HE'S STILL A BEAST. ♡
ANY PROGRESS IN YOUR RELATIONSHIP?
What are you imagining?
OF COURSE NOT!

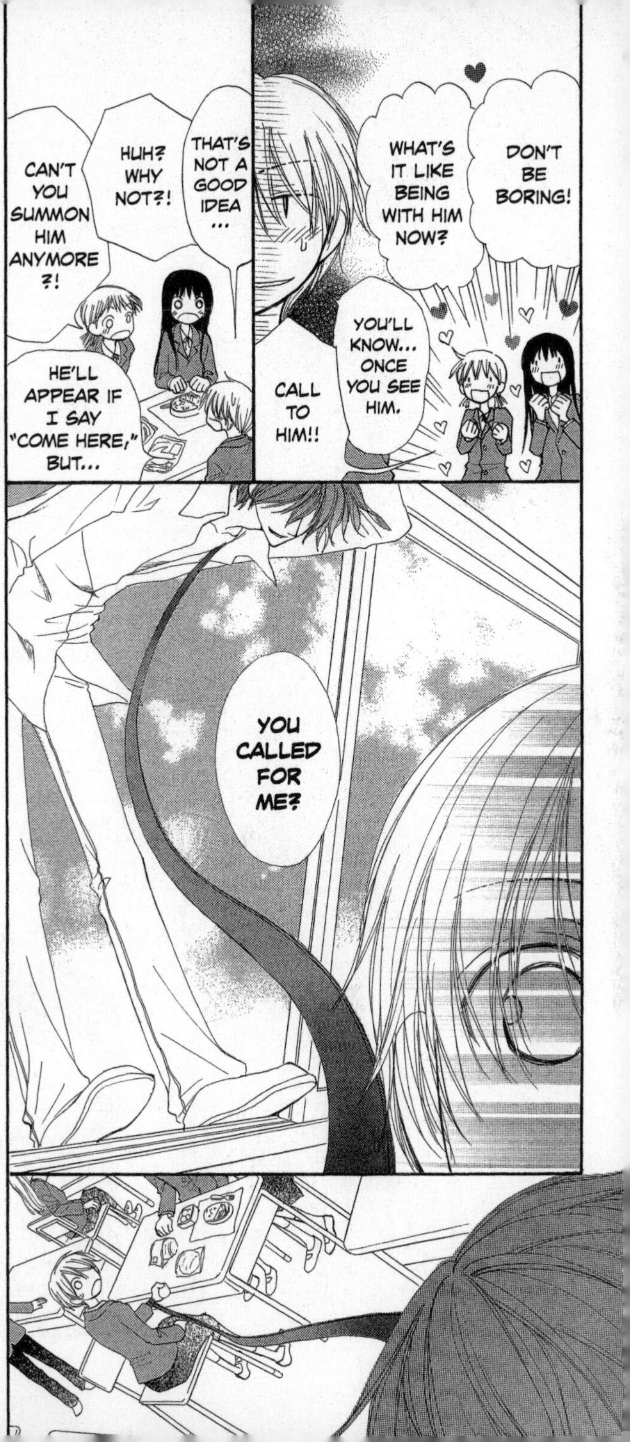
DON'T BE BORING!
WHAT'S IT LIKE BEING WITH HIM NOW?
YOU'LL KNOW... ONCE YOU SEE HIM.
CALL TO HIM!!
THAT'S NOT A GOOD IDEA...
HUH? WHY NOT?!
CAN'T YOU SUMMON HIM ANYMORE?!
HE'LL APPEAR IF I SAY "COME HERE," BUT...
YOU CALLED FOR ME?

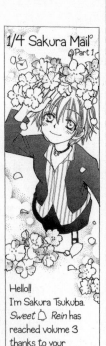

1/4 Sakura Mail
Part 1

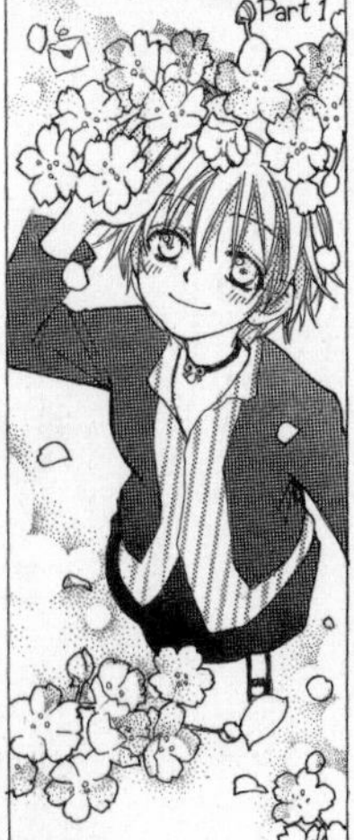

Hello!! I'm Sakura Tsukuba. *Sweet* 🔔 *Rein* has reached volume 3 thanks to your support. ♡ Hurray, hurray! ♡ Um, I'm drawing this series 🔔 using strong seasonal colors, and this chapter was for the spring issue of the magazine. I really enjoyed working on it. I realized I hadn't yet written a chapter that takes place in spring. Of course I should be writing about Christmas, but there are many chapters that take place in summer for some reason... Many chapters with swimsuits. ♡

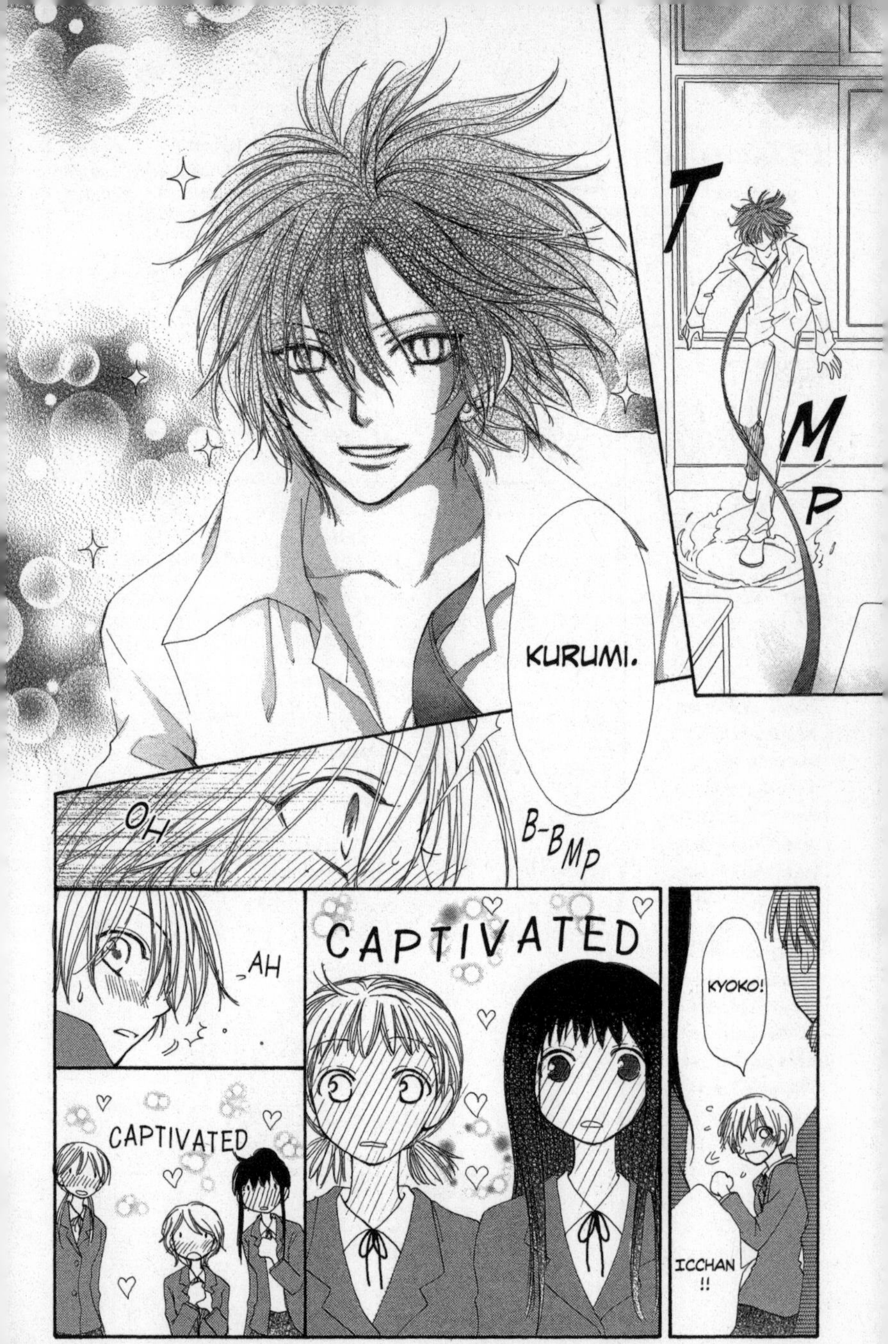

TMP
KURUMI.
B-BMP
OH
KYOKO!
ICCHAN !!
CAPTIVATED
AH
CAPTIVATED

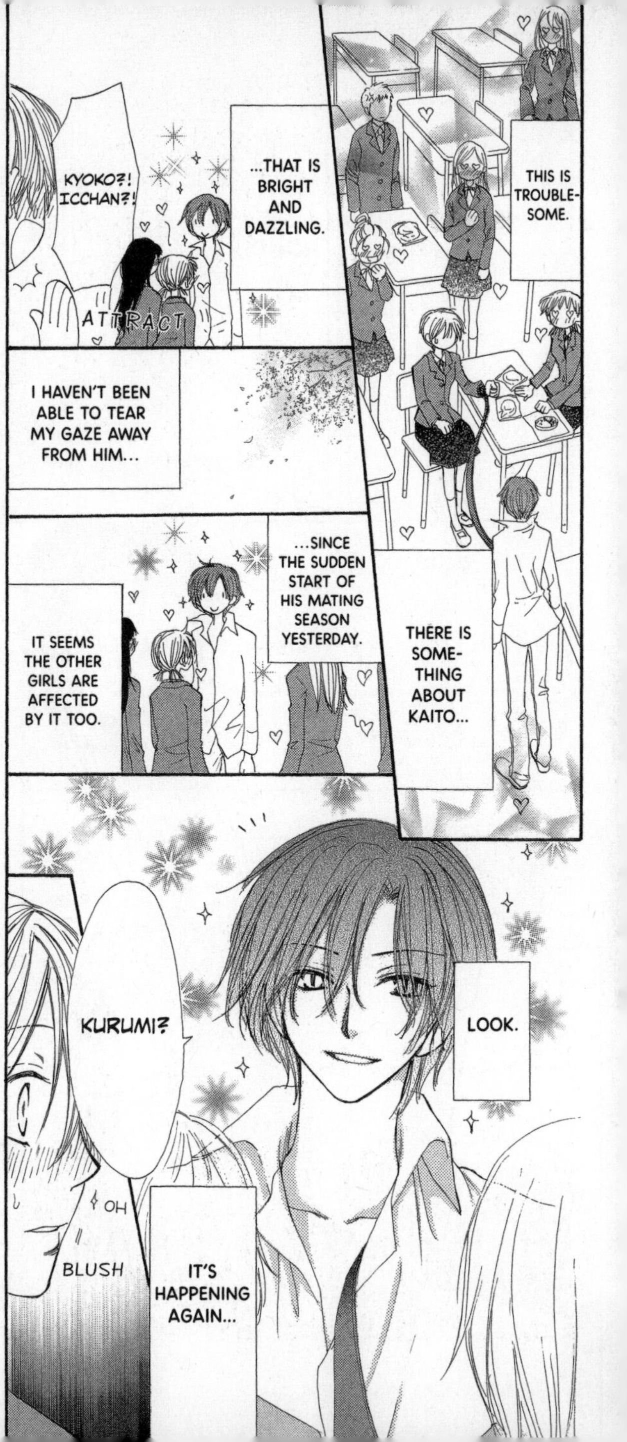
THIS IS TROUBLESOME.
THERE IS SOMETHING ABOUT KAITO...
...THAT IS BRIGHT AND DAZZLING.
KYOKO?! ICCHAN?!
ATTRACT
I HAVEN'T BEEN ABLE TO TEAR MY GAZE AWAY FROM HIM...
...SINCE THE SUDDEN START OF HIS MATING SEASON YESTERDAY.
IT SEEMS THE OTHER GIRLS ARE AFFECTED BY IT TOO.
LOOK.
KURUMI?
IT'S HAPPENING AGAIN...
OH
BLUSH

1/4 Sakura Mail
Part 2

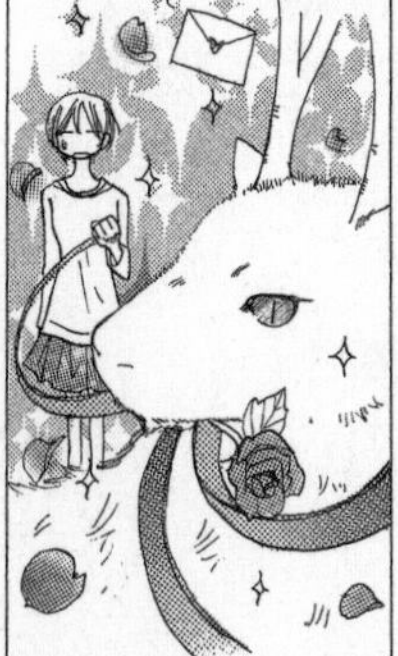

So it's spring. And spring is the season of cherry blossoms! It's the season of love!! Mating season!!! I've drawn Santa's reindeer differently from an actual reindeer, by the way. Well, they do fly after all! These reindeer are a present from God, so I've added all sorts of unique characteristics to them. I enjoy coming up with those. Kaito is a good-looking guy, so the girls are attracted to him. But he's a total airhead in front of Kurumi, so she tends to forget that he's handsome.

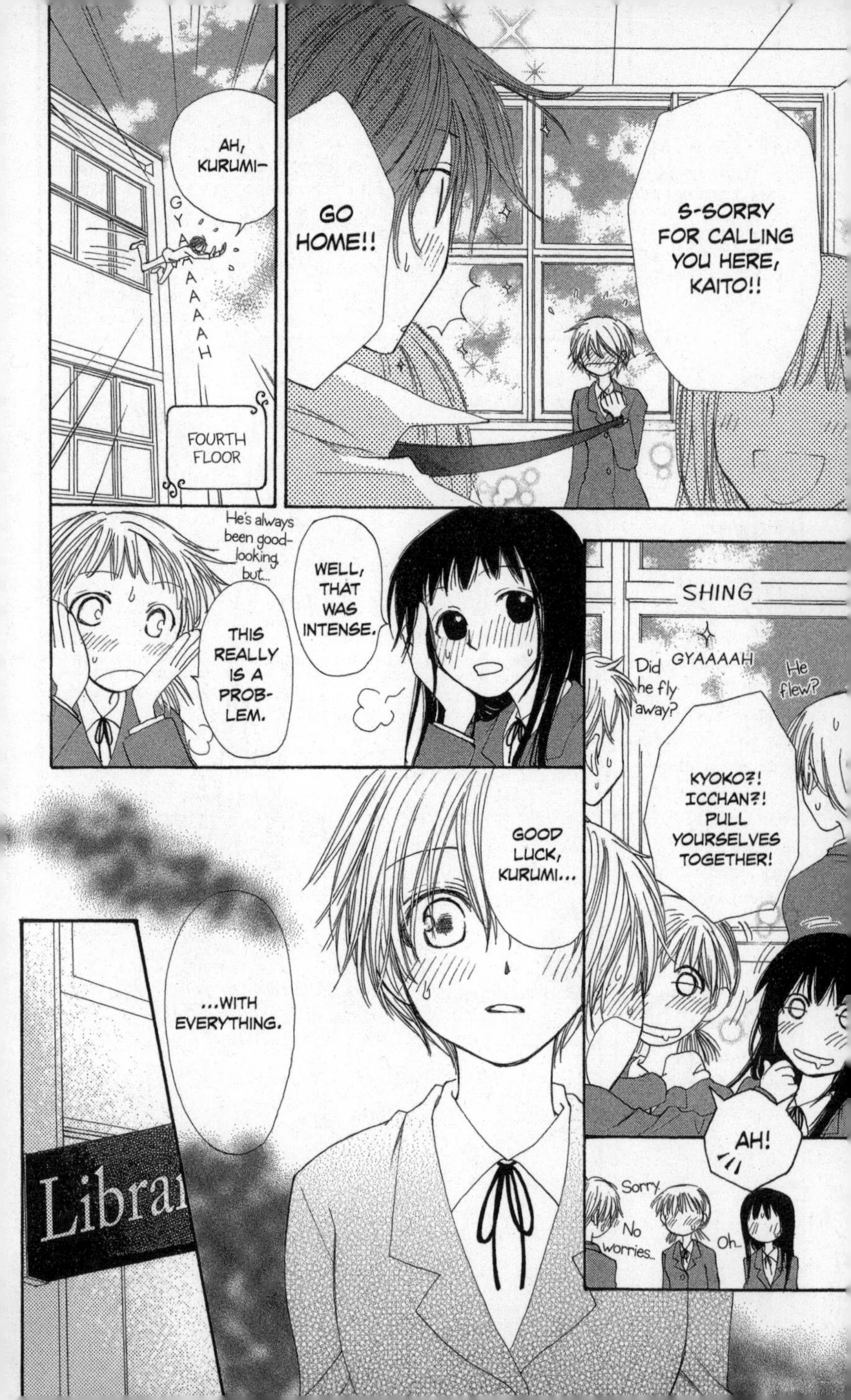
S-SORRY FOR CALLING YOU HERE, KAITO!!
GO HOME!!
AH, KURUMI–
GYAAAAAAAH
FOURTH FLOOR
SHING
He flew?
GYAAAAH
Did he fly away?
WELL, THAT WAS INTENSE.
He's always been good-looking, but...
THIS REALLY IS A PROBLEM.
KYOKO?! ICCHAN?! PULL YOURSELVES TOGETHER!
AH!
Oh...
No worries...
Sorry.
GOOD LUCK, KURUMI...
...WITH EVERYTHING.
Librar

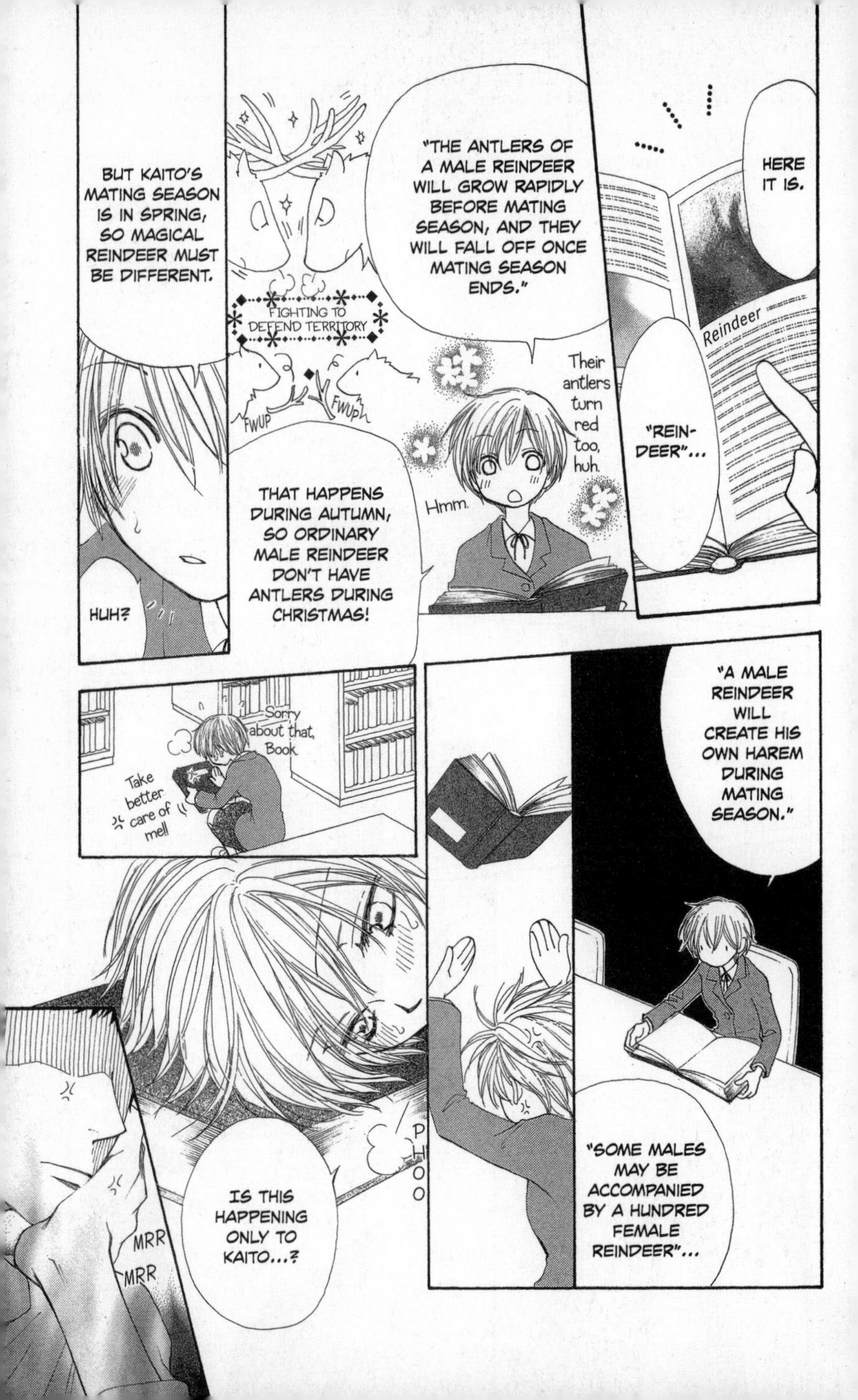

HERE IT IS.
.....
.....
.....
Reindeer
"REIN-DEER"...
"THE ANTLERS OF A MALE REINDEER WILL GROW RAPIDLY BEFORE MATING SEASON, AND THEY WILL FALL OFF ONCE MATING SEASON ENDS."
FIGHTING TO DEFEND TERRITORY
FWUP
FWUP
Their antlers turn red too, huh.
Hmm.
THAT HAPPENS DURING AUTUMN, SO ORDINARY MALE REINDEER DON'T HAVE ANTLERS DURING CHRISTMAS!
BUT KAITO'S MATING SEASON IS IN SPRING, SO MAGICAL REINDEER MUST BE DIFFERENT.
HUH?
"A MALE REINDEER WILL CREATE HIS OWN HAREM DURING MATING SEASON."
"SOME MALES MAY BE ACCOMPANIED BY A HUNDRED FEMALE REINDEER"...
Sorry about that, Book.
Take better care of me!!
PHOO
IS THIS HAPPENING ONLY TO KAITO...?
MRR
MRR

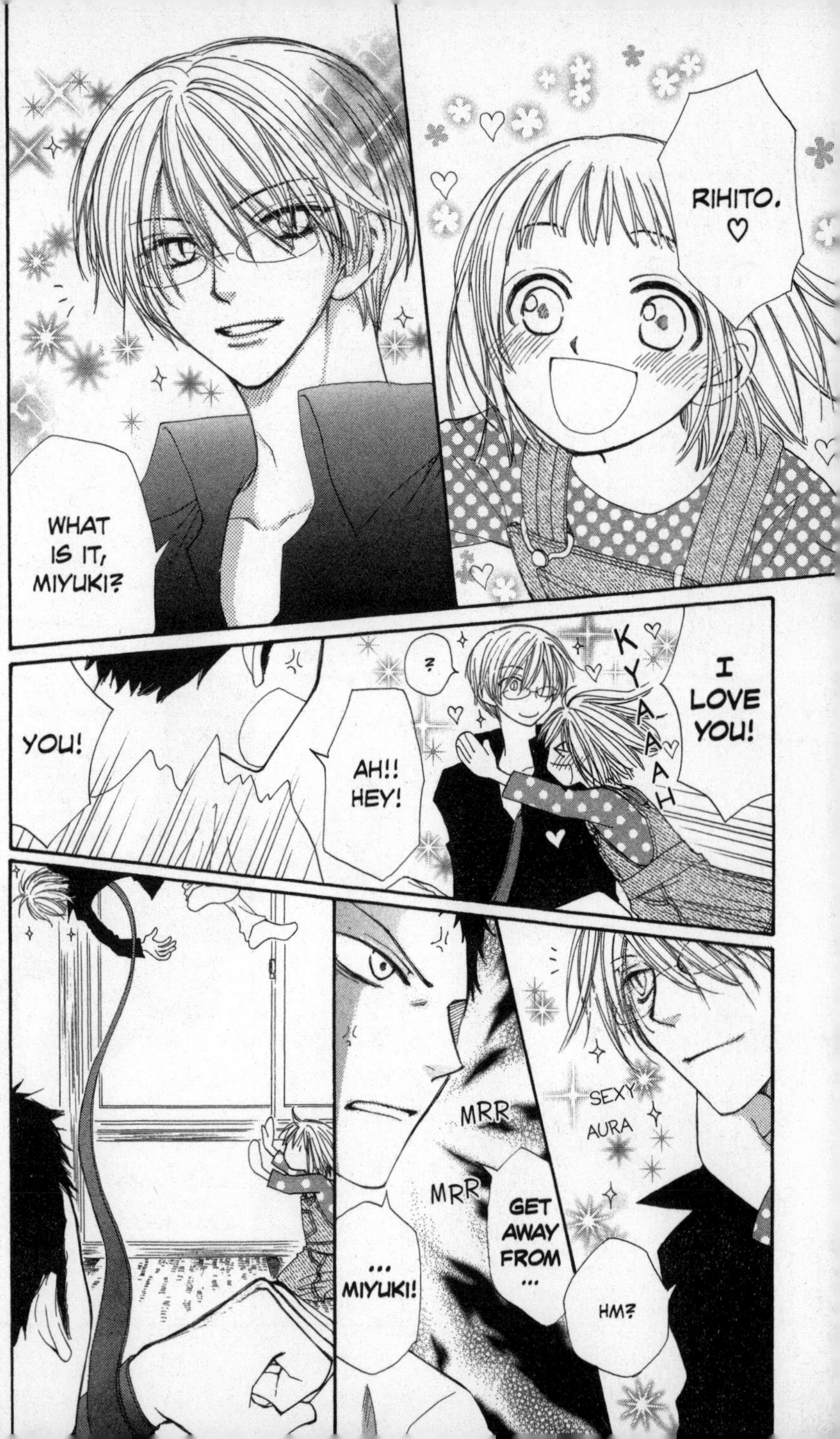
RIHITO. ♡
WHAT IS IT, MIYUKI?
I LOVE YOU!
KYAAAH
?
AH!! HEY!
YOU!
SEXY AURA
HM?
MRR
MRR
GET AWAY FROM ...
... MIYUKI!

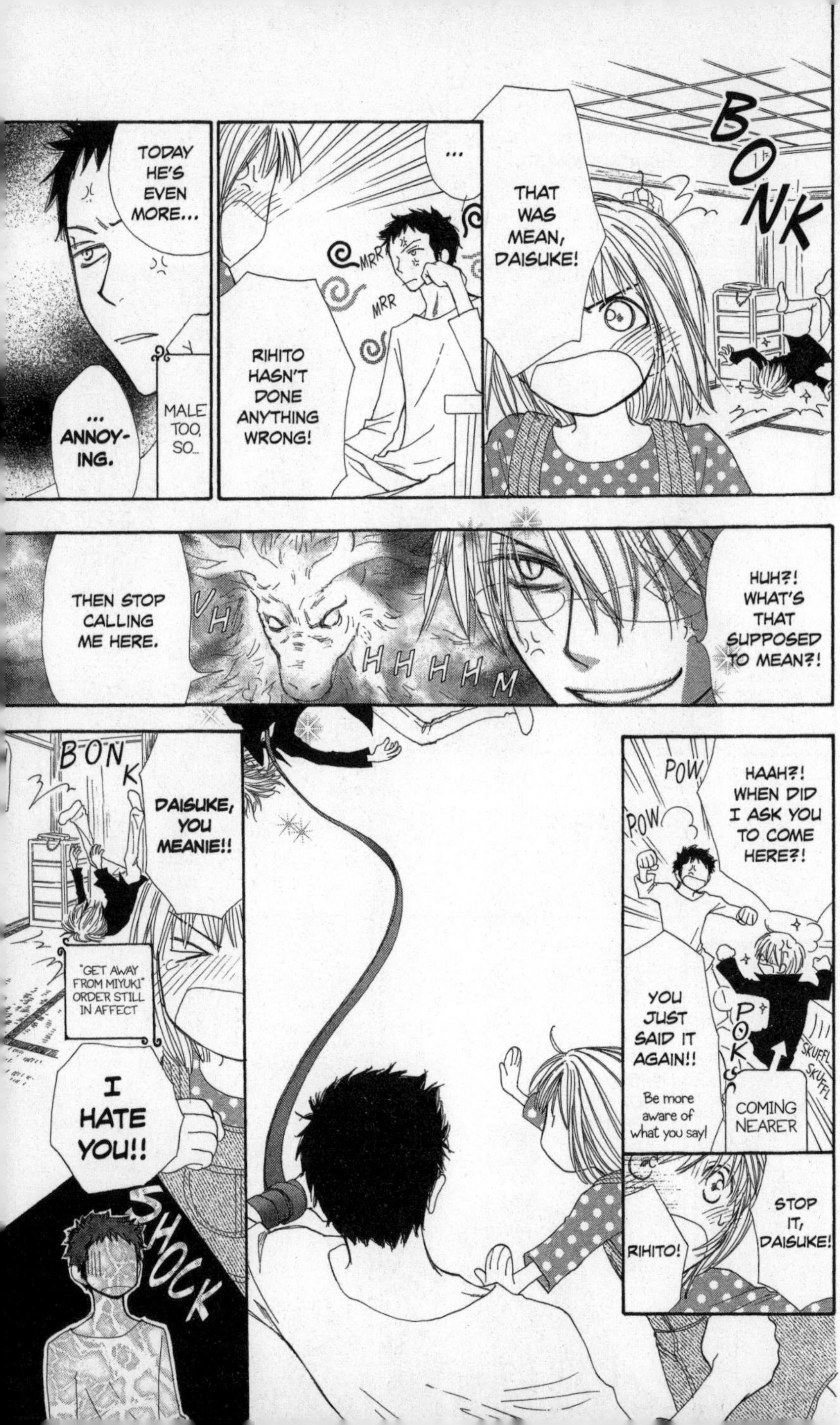
BONK
...
THAT WAS MEAN, DAISUKE!
MRR
MRR
RIHITO HASN'T DONE ANYTHING WRONG!
TODAY HE'S EVEN MORE...
MALE TOO, SO...
... ANNOY-ING.
HUH?! WHAT'S THAT SUPPOSED TO MEAN?!
VHHHHHM
THEN STOP CALLING ME HERE.
POW
POW
HAAH?! WHEN DID I ASK YOU TO COME HERE?!
YOU JUST SAID IT AGAIN!!
Be more aware of what you say!
POKE
SKUFFL
SKUFFL
COMING NEARER
STOP IT, DAISUKE!
RIHITO!
BONK
DAISUKE, YOU MEANIE!!
"GET AWAY FROM MIYUKI" ORDER STILL IN AFFECT
I HATE YOU!!
SHOCK

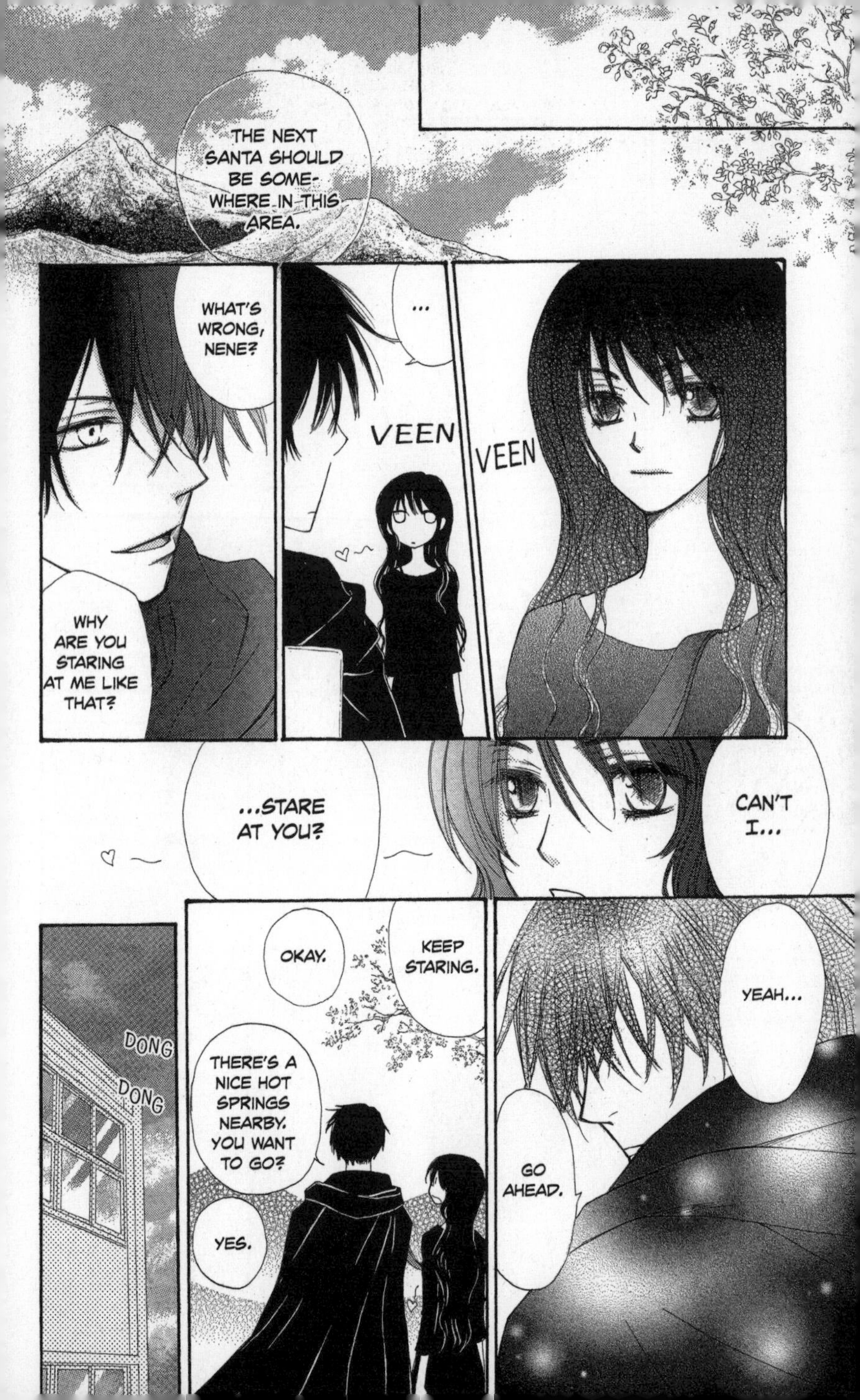
THE NEXT SANTA SHOULD BE SOME-WHERE IN THIS AREA.
VEEN
...
VEEN
WHAT'S WRONG, NENE?
WHY ARE YOU STARING AT ME LIKE THAT?
CAN'T I...
...STARE AT YOU?
YEAH...
GO AHEAD.
KEEP STARING.
OKAY.
THERE'S A NICE HOT SPRINGS NEARBY. YOU WANT TO GO?
YES.
DONG
DONG

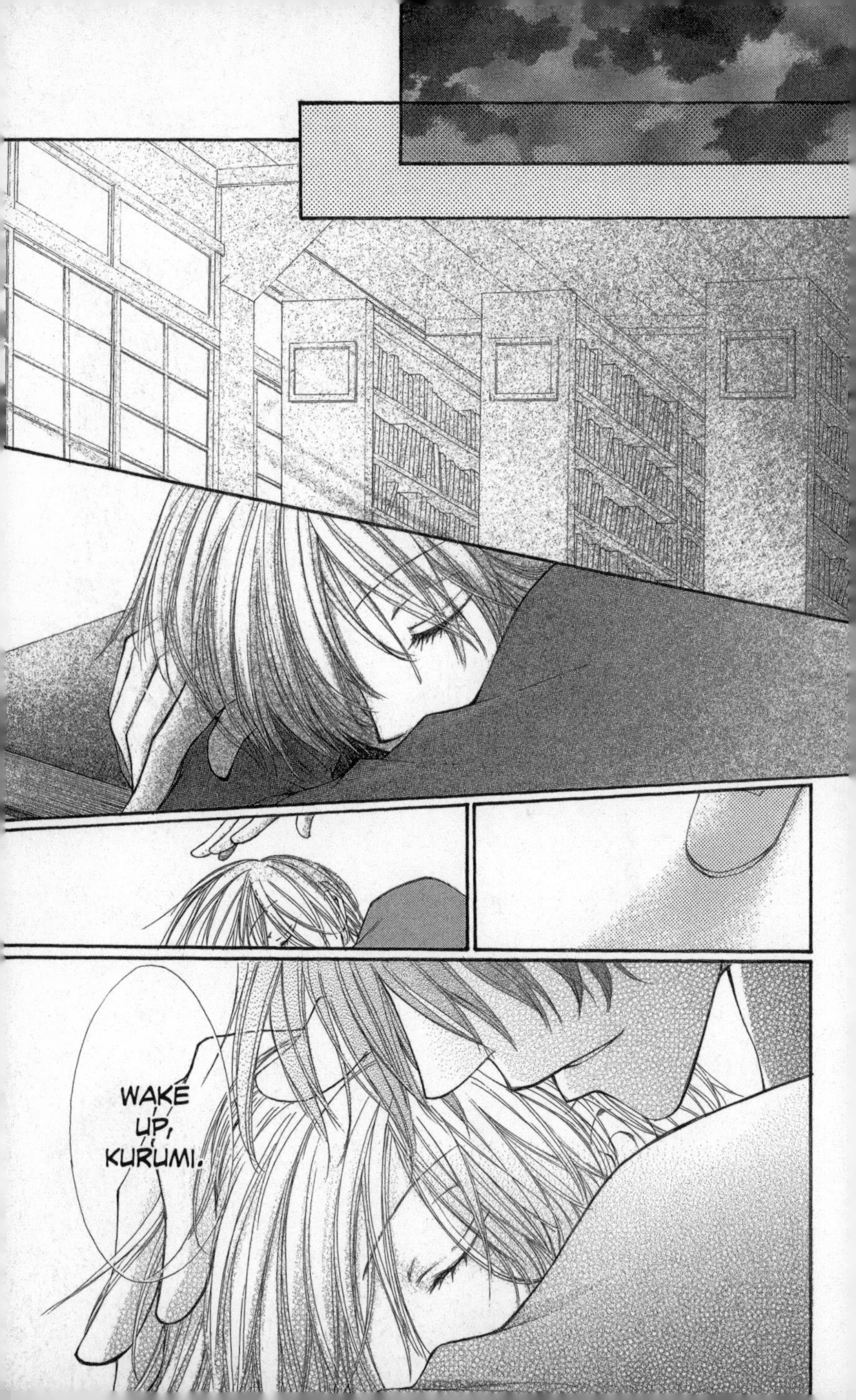
WAKE UP, KURUMI.

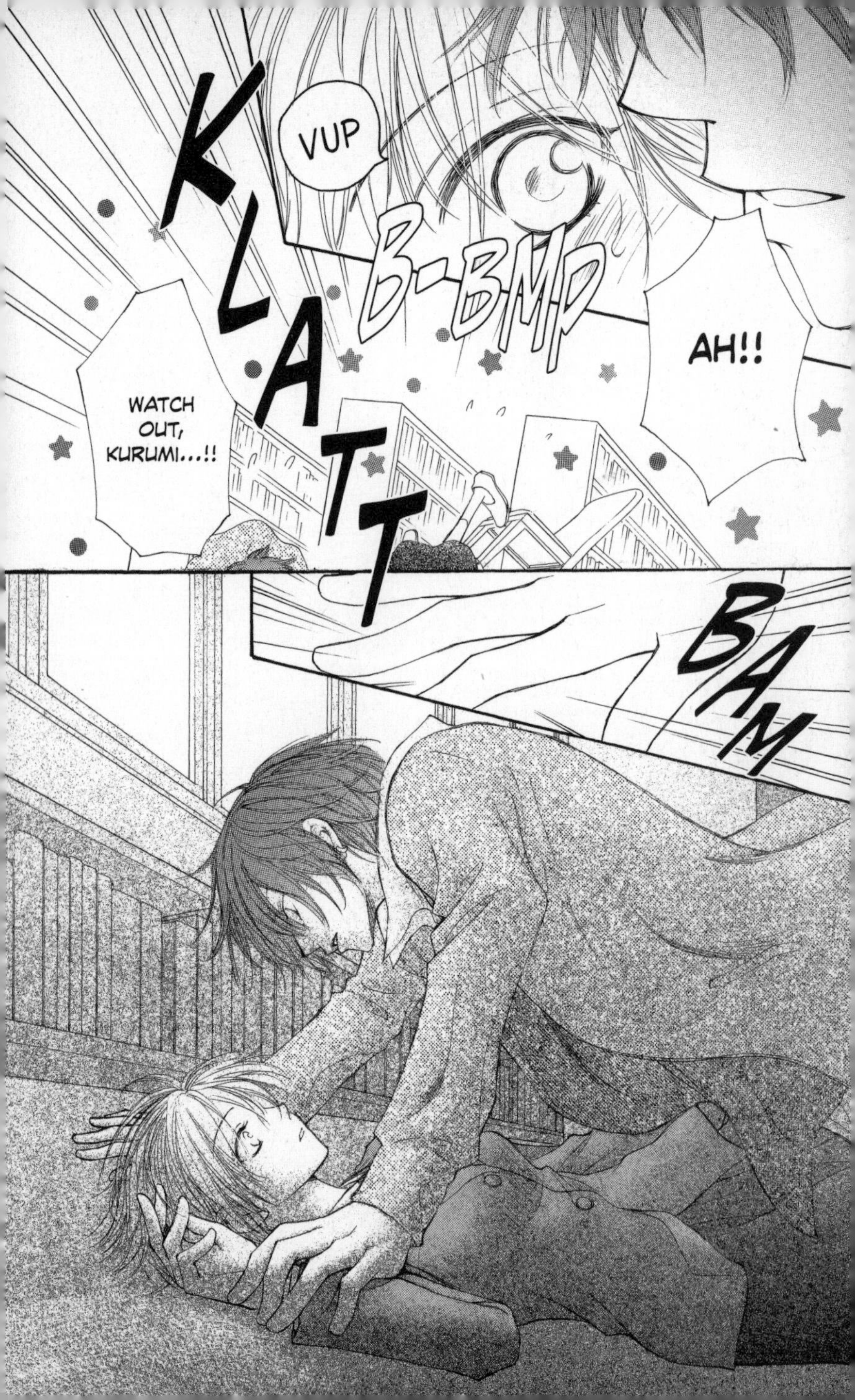
VUP
AH!!
B-BMP
KLATTT
WATCH OUT, KURUMI...!!
BAM

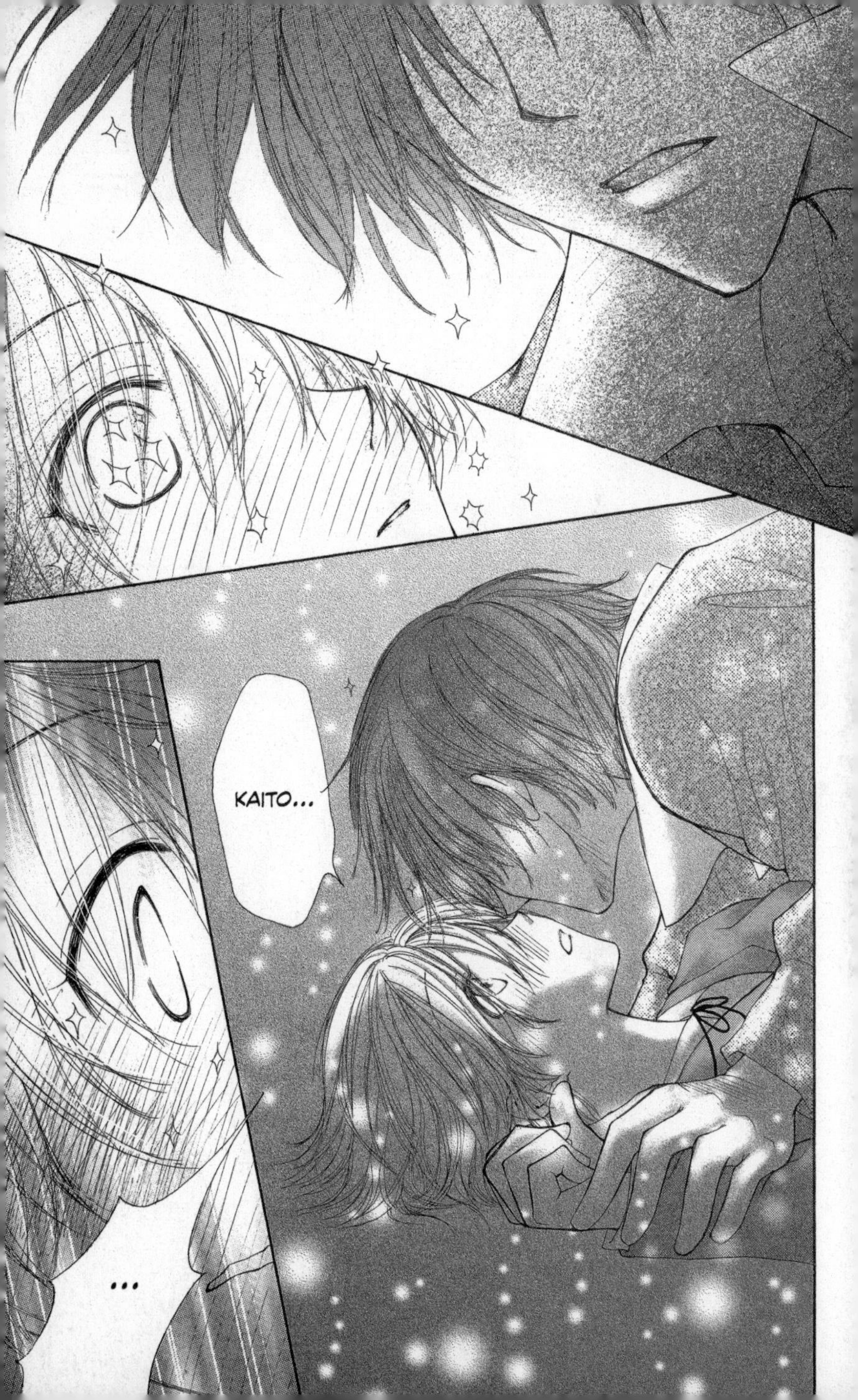
KAITO...
...

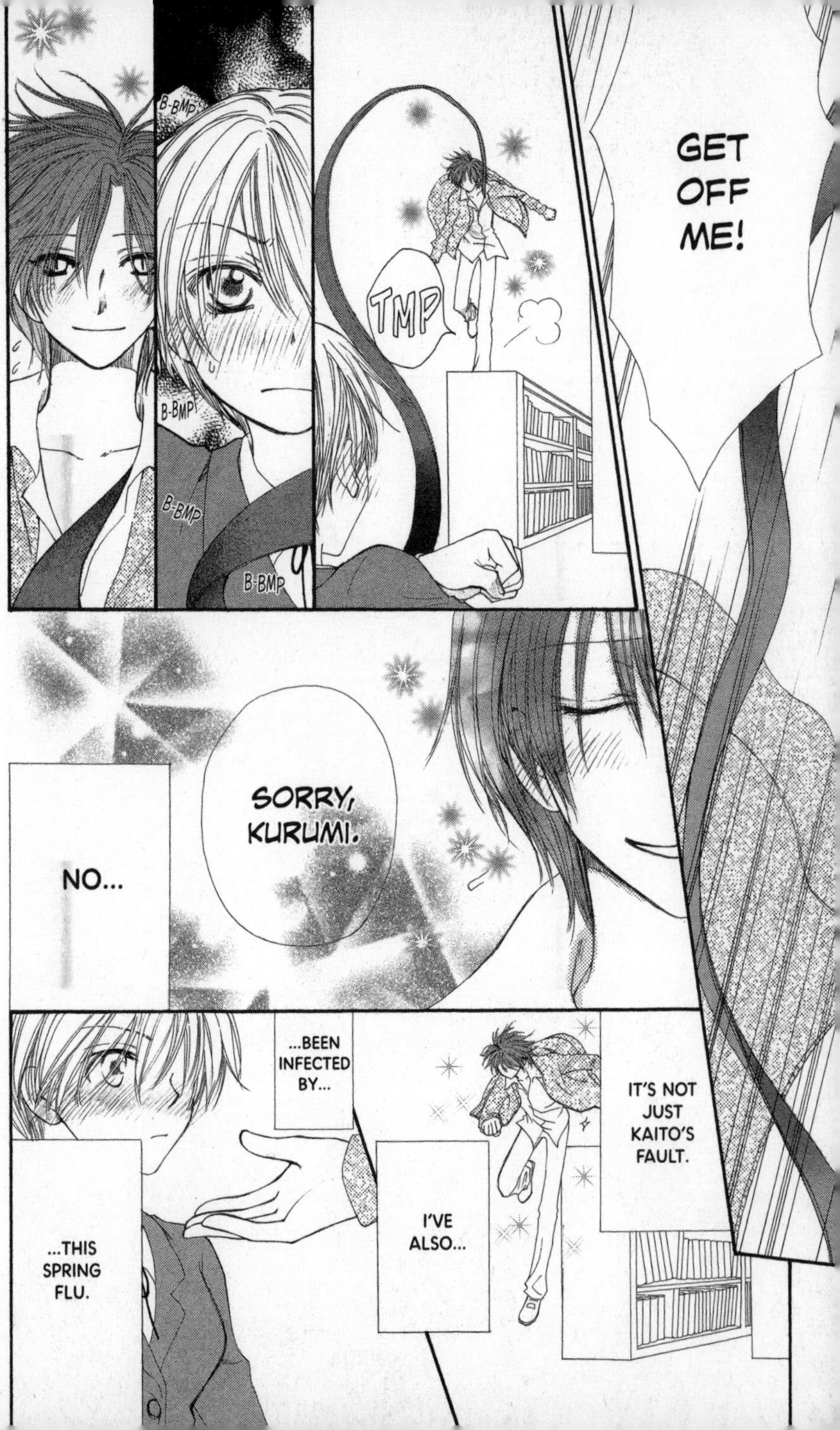
GET OFF ME!
TMP
B-BMP
B-BMP
B-BMP
B-BMP
SORRY, KURUMI.
NO...
IT'S NOT JUST KAITO'S FAULT.
I'VE ALSO...
...BEEN INFECTED BY...
...THIS SPRING FLU.

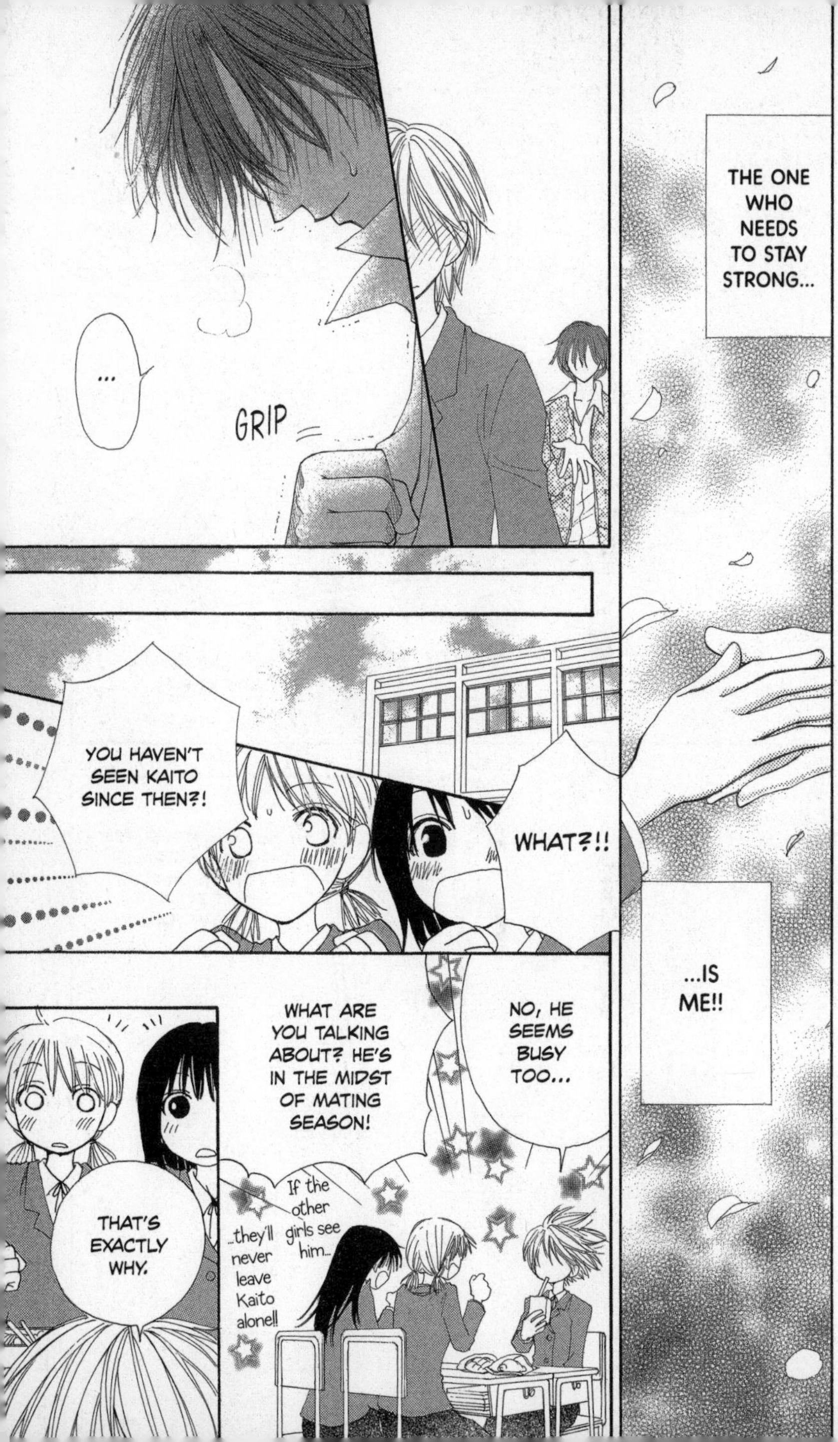
THE ONE WHO NEEDS TO STAY STRONG...
...IS ME!!
...
GRIP
WHAT?!!
YOU HAVEN'T SEEN KAITO SINCE THEN?!
NO, HE SEEMS BUSY TOO...
WHAT ARE YOU TALKING ABOUT? HE'S IN THE MIDST OF MATING SEASON!
If the other girls see him...
...they'll never leave Kaito alone!!
THAT'S EXACTLY WHY.

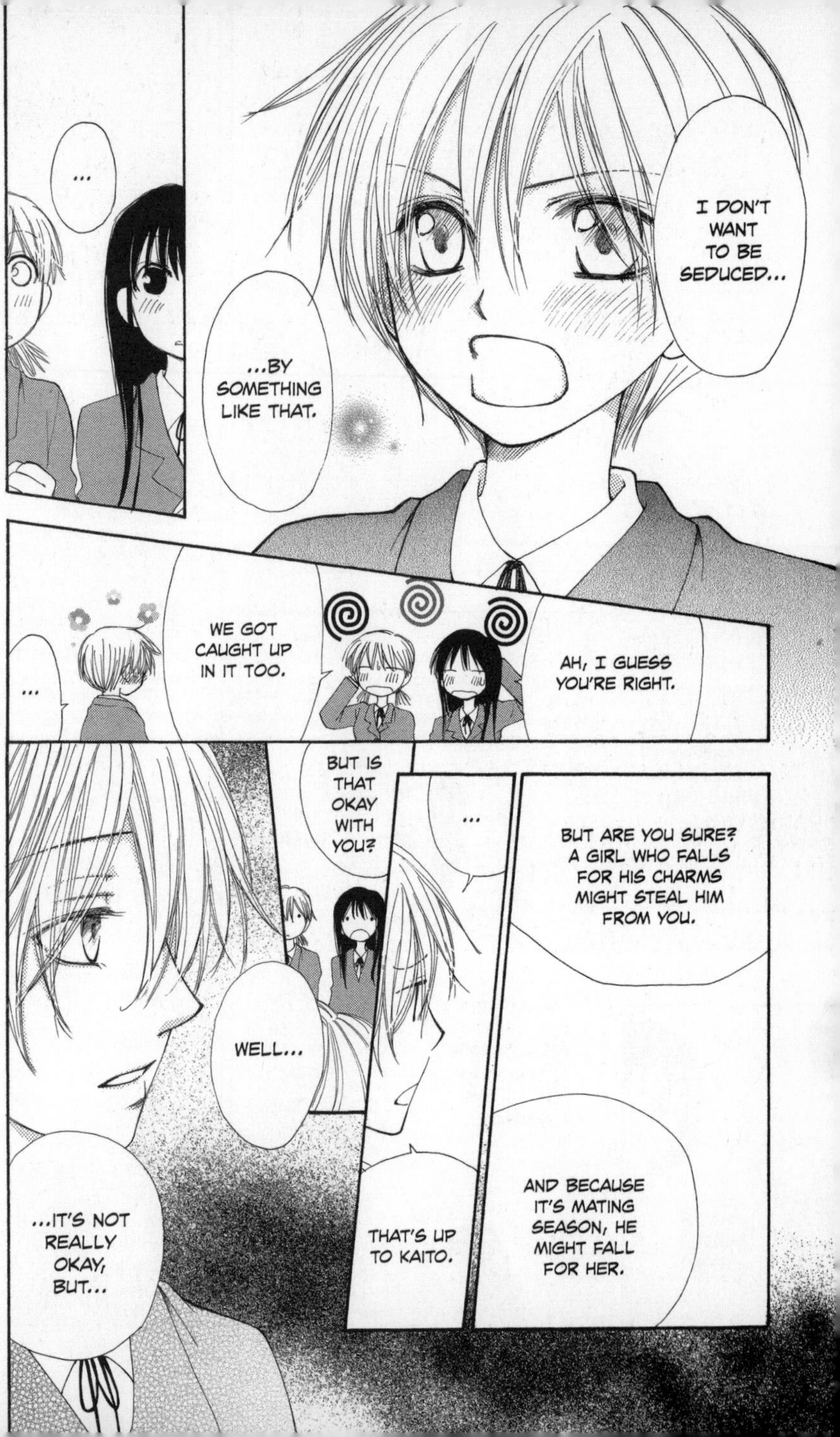
I DON'T WANT TO BE SEDUCED...
...BY SOMETHING LIKE THAT.
...
AH, I GUESS YOU'RE RIGHT.
WE GOT CAUGHT UP IN IT TOO.
...
BUT ARE YOU SURE? A GIRL WHO FALLS FOR HIS CHARMS MIGHT STEAL HIM FROM YOU.
AND BECAUSE IT'S MATING SEASON, HE MIGHT FALL FOR HER.
...
THAT'S UP TO KAITO.
BUT IS THAT OKAY WITH YOU?
WELL...
...IT'S NOT REALLY OKAY, BUT...

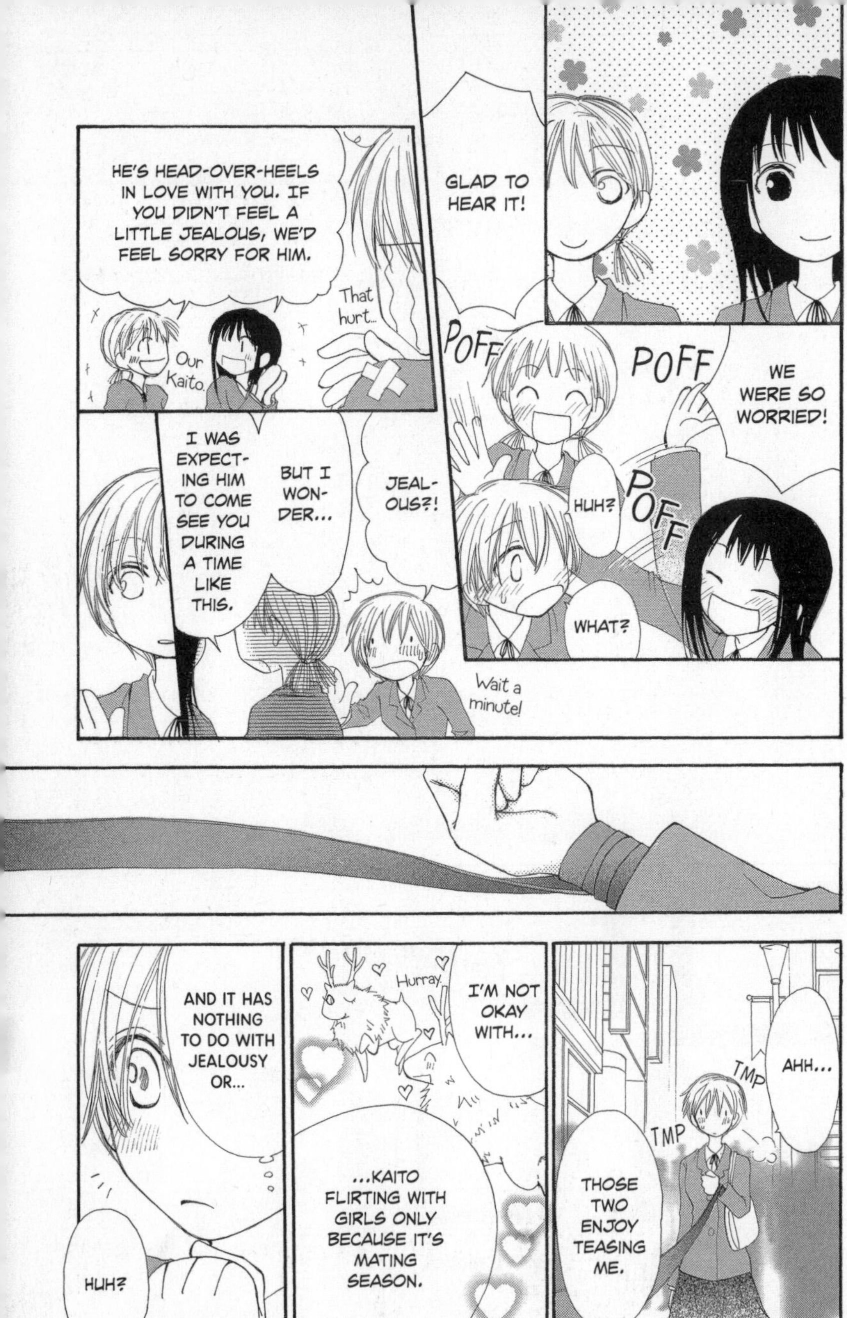
GLAD TO HEAR IT!
HE'S HEAD-OVER-HEELS IN LOVE WITH YOU. IF YOU DIDN'T FEEL A LITTLE JEALOUS, WE'D FEEL SORRY FOR HIM.
That hurt...
Our Kaito.
WE WERE SO WORRIED!
POFF
POFF
POFF
HUH?
WHAT?
JEAL-OUS?!
BUT I WON-DER...
I WAS EXPECT-ING HIM TO COME SEE YOU DURING A TIME LIKE THIS.
Wait a minute!
AHH...
TMP
TMP
THOSE TWO ENJOY TEASING ME.
I'M NOT OKAY WITH...
Hurray.
...KAITO FLIRTING WITH GIRLS ONLY BECAUSE IT'S MATING SEASON.
AND IT HAS NOTHING TO DO WITH JEALOUSY OR...
HUH?

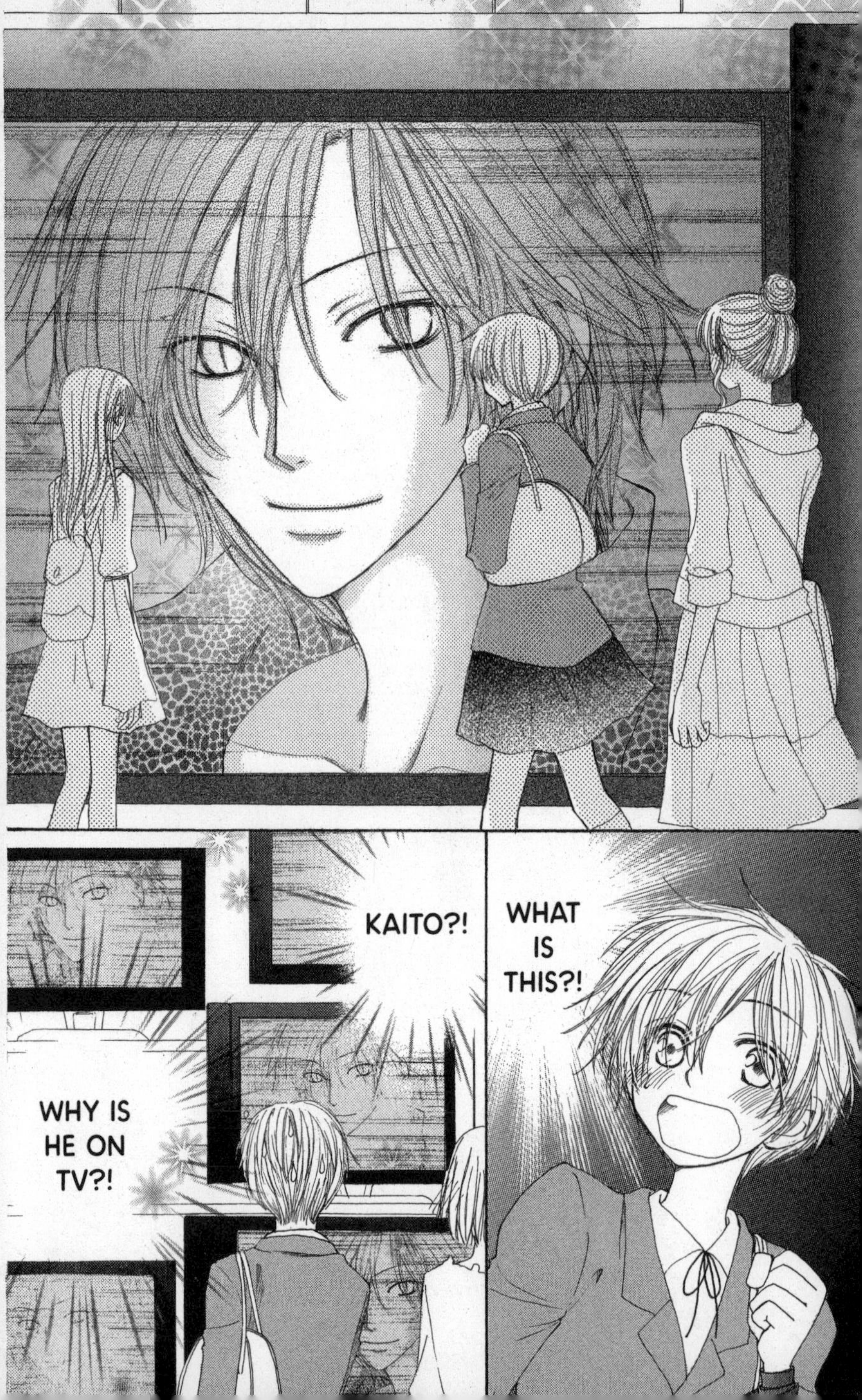
WHAT IS THIS?!
KAITO?!
WHY IS HE ON TV?!

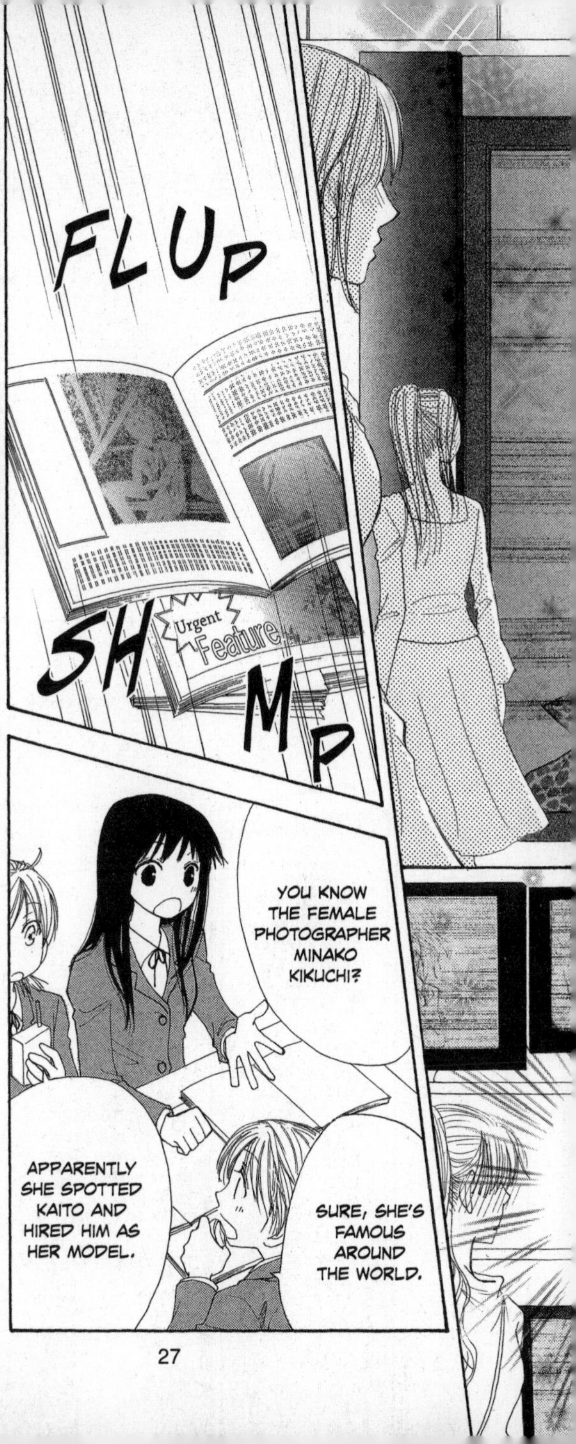
FLUP
Urgent Feature
SHMP
YOU KNOW THE FEMALE PHOTOGRAPHER MINAKO KIKUCHI?
SURE, SHE'S FAMOUS AROUND THE WORLD.
APPARENTLY SHE SPOTTED KAITO AND HIRED HIM AS HER MODEL.

1/4 Sakura Mail

Part 3

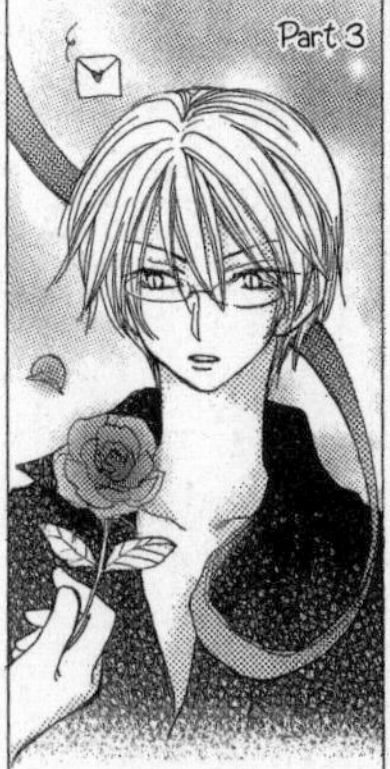

Male reindeer are highly sought after. It's even said that their antlers are used for energy enhancement. Rihito is popular too. Miyuki likes him, but he hasn't noticed. He isn't as open as Kaito, so I decided he wouldn't attract as many girls. Kaito is a bit too open, and I wanted Kurumi to be unnerved by it.

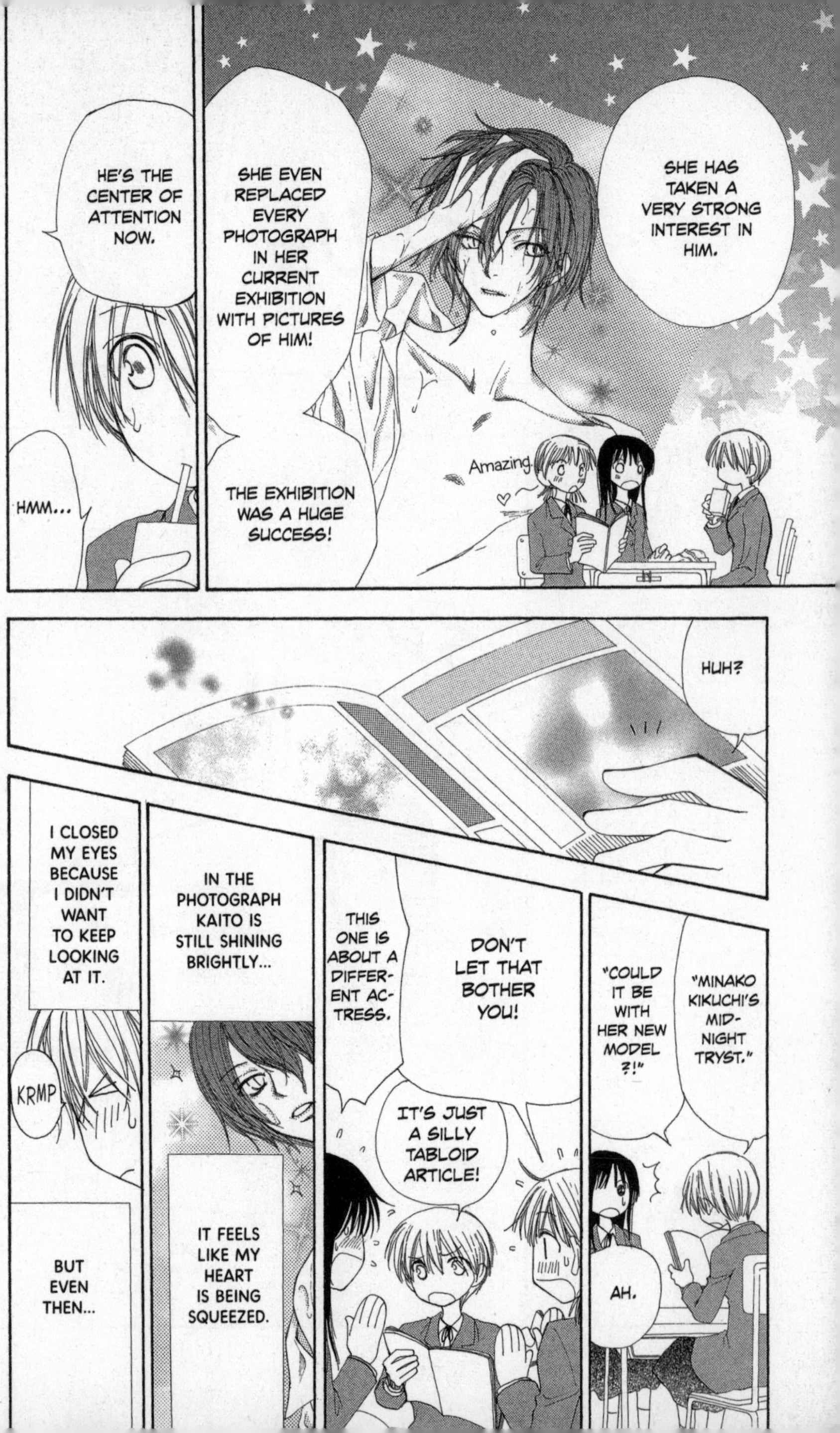
SHE HAS TAKEN A VERY STRONG INTEREST IN HIM.
SHE EVEN REPLACED EVERY PHOTOGRAPH IN HER CURRENT EXHIBITION WITH PICTURES OF HIM!
Amazing
THE EXHIBITION WAS A HUGE SUCCESS!
HE'S THE CENTER OF ATTENTION NOW.
HMM...
HUH?
"MINAKO KIKUCHI'S MID-NIGHT TRYST."
"COULD IT BE WITH HER NEW MODEL ?!"
AH.
DON'T LET THAT BOTHER YOU!
THIS ONE IS ABOUT A DIFFER-ENT AC-TRESS.
IT'S JUST A SILLY TABLOID ARTICLE!
IN THE PHOTOGRAPH KAITO IS STILL SHINING BRIGHTLY...
IT FEELS LIKE MY HEART IS BEING SQUEEZED.
I CLOSED MY EYES BECAUSE I DIDN'T WANT TO KEEP LOOKING AT IT.
KRMP
BUT EVEN THEN...

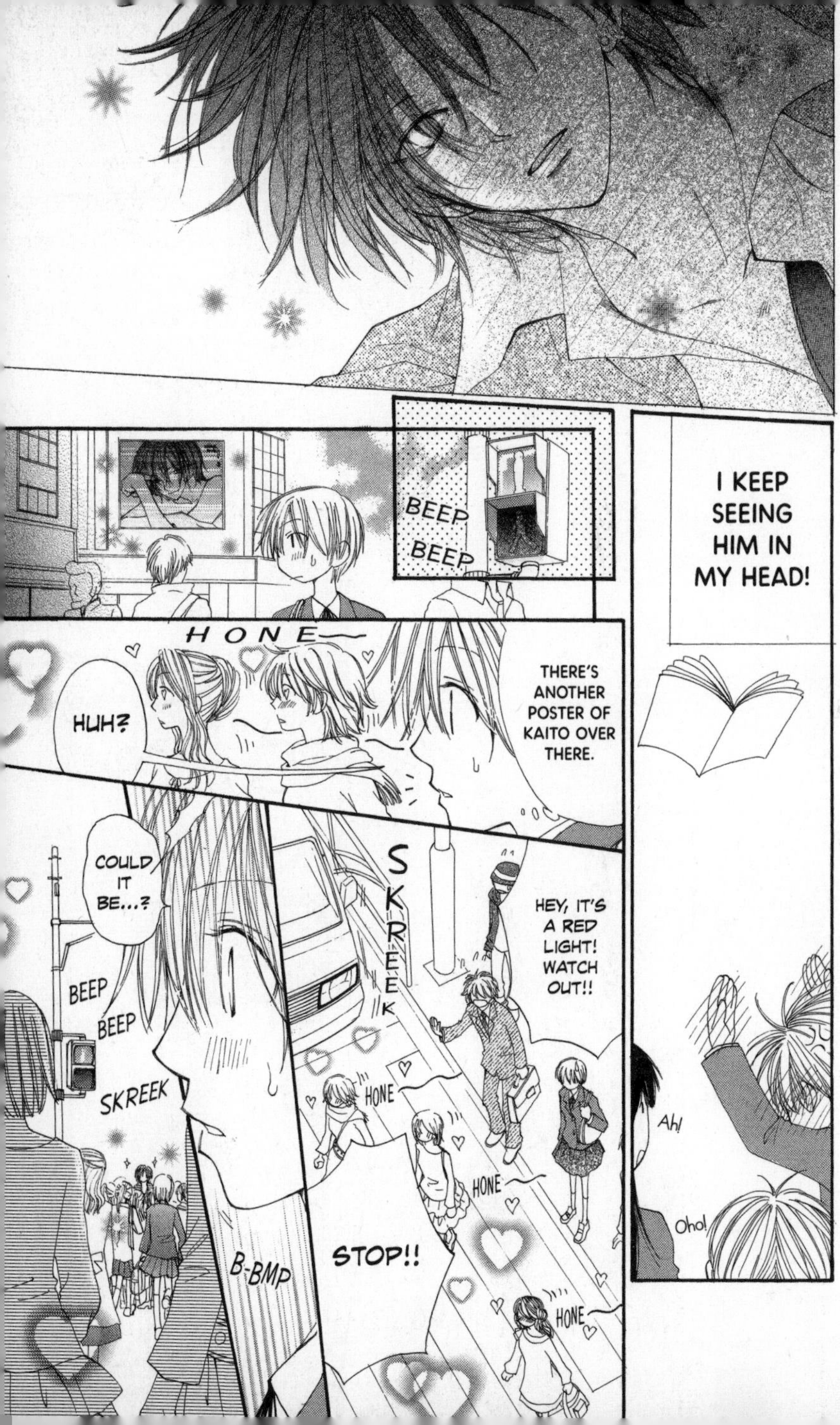
I KEEP SEEING HIM IN MY HEAD!
BEEP BEEP
HONE
THERE'S ANOTHER POSTER OF KAITO OVER THERE.
HUH?
Ah!
Oho!
HEY, IT'S A RED LIGHT! WATCH OUT!!
SKREEEK
HONE
HONE
STOP!!
HONE
COULD IT BE...?
BEEP
BEEP
SKREEK
B-BMP

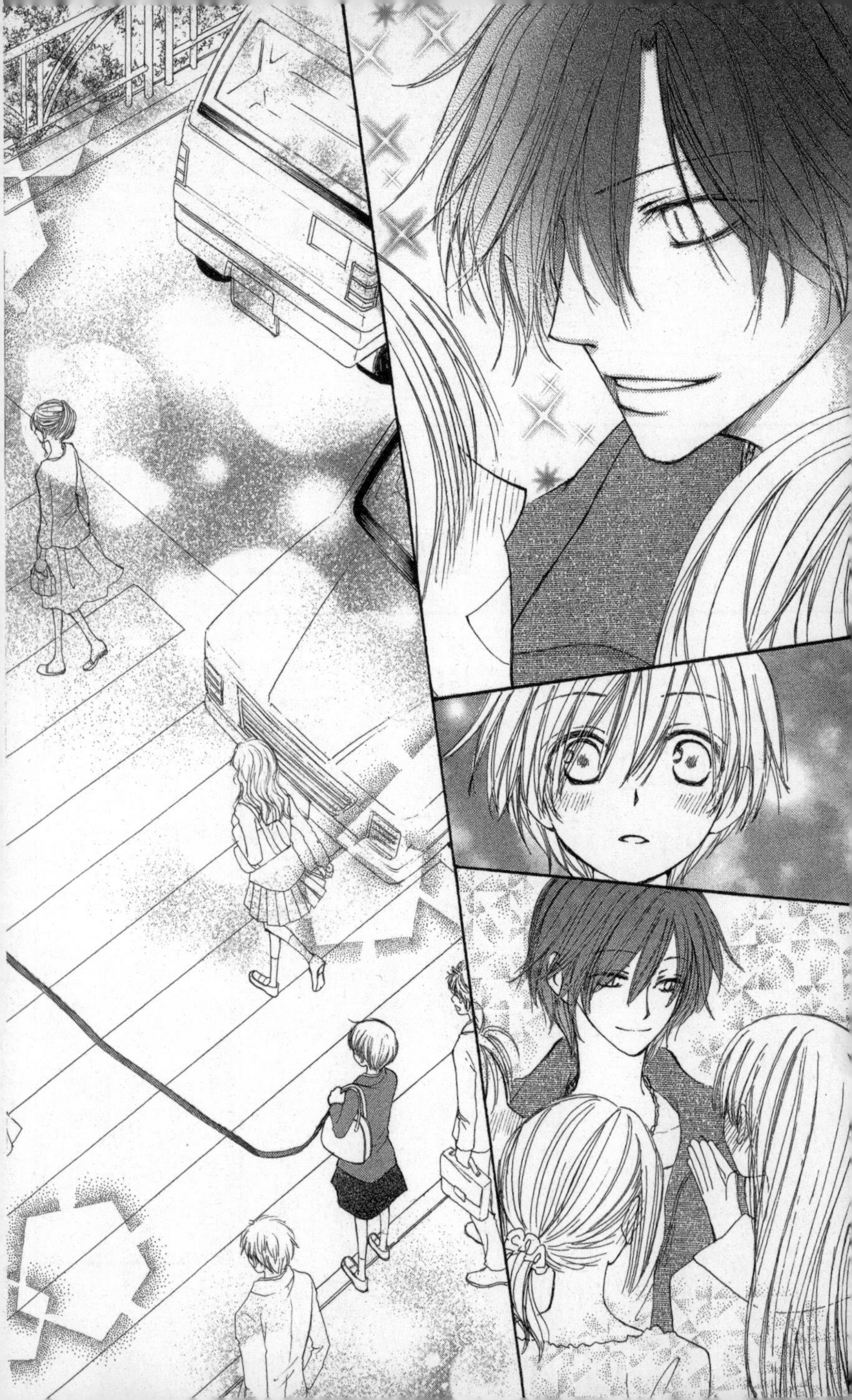

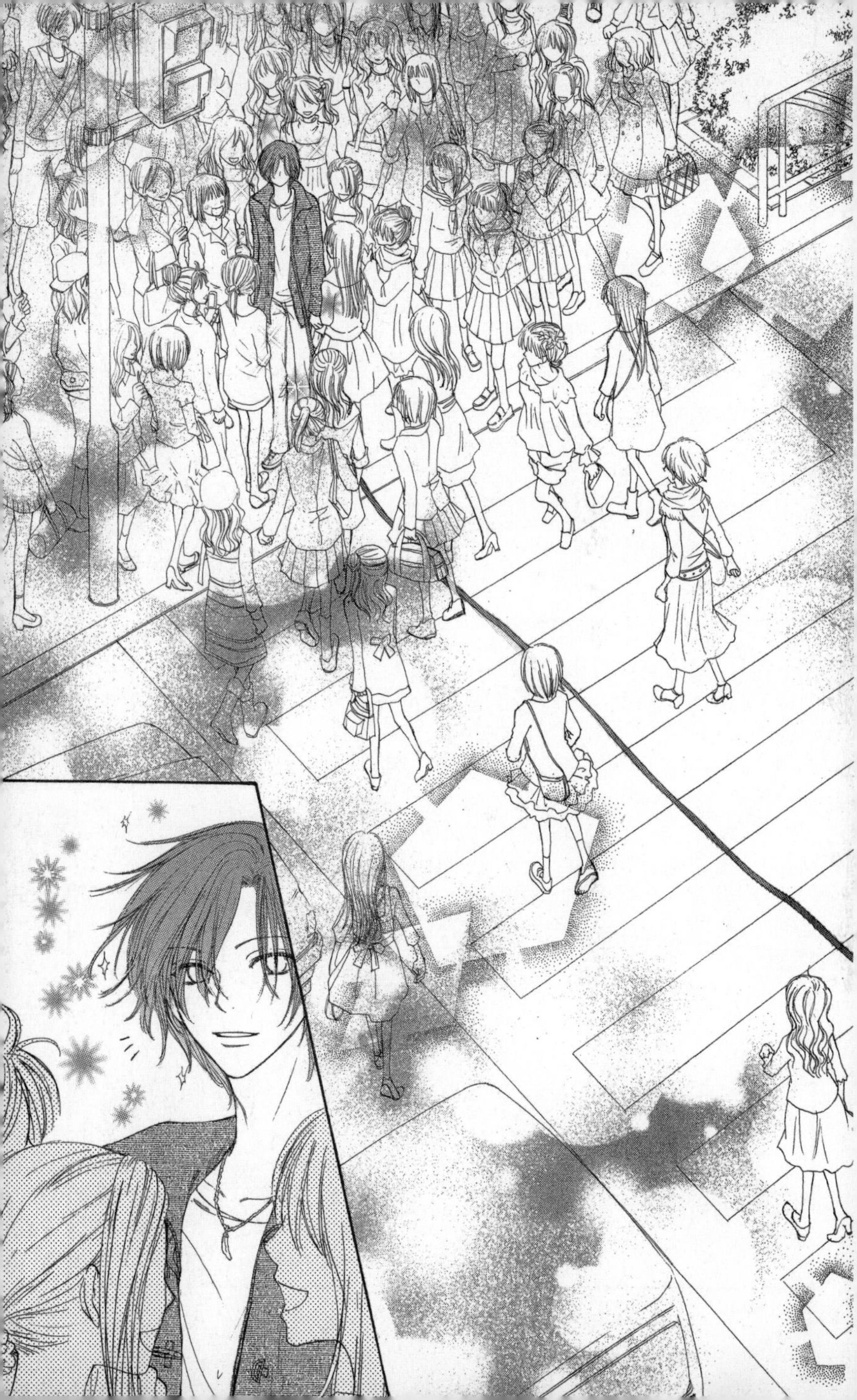

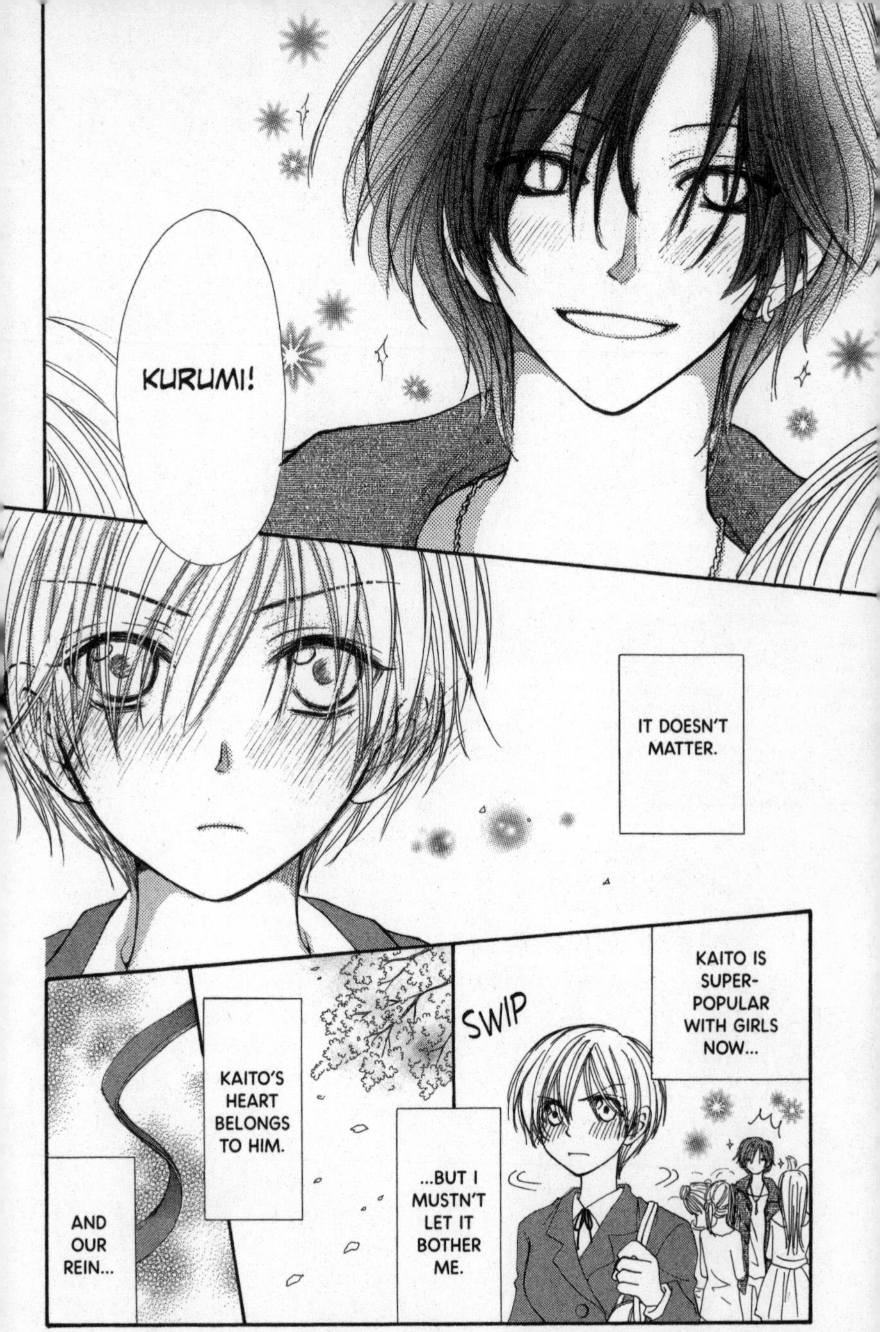
KURUMI!
IT DOESN'T MATTER.
KAITO IS SUPER-POPULAR WITH GIRLS NOW...
SWIP
...BUT I MUSTN'T LET IT BOTHER ME.
KAITO'S HEART BELONGS TO HIM.
AND OUR REIN...

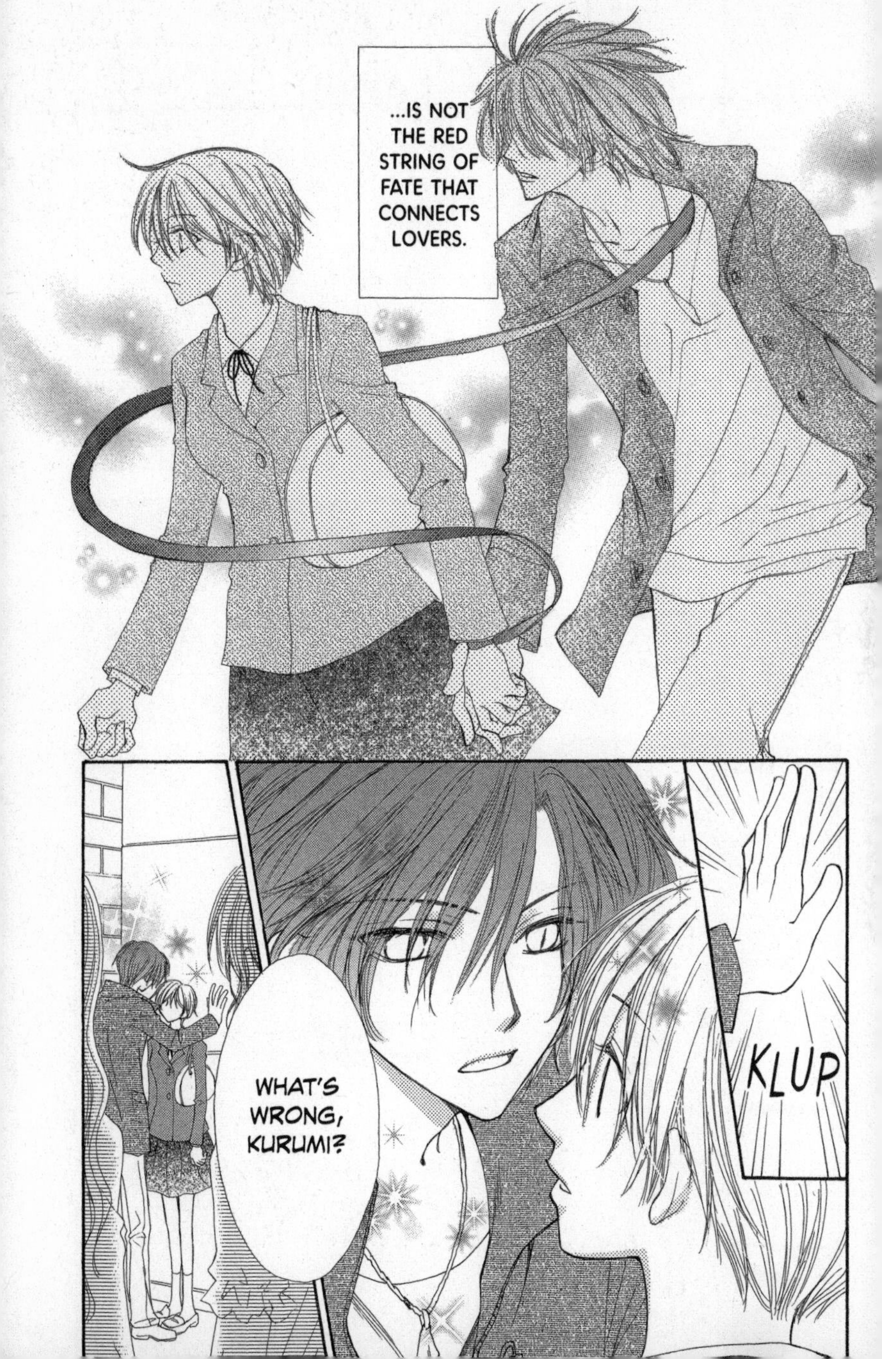
...IS NOT THE RED STRING OF FATE THAT CONNECTS LOVERS.
KLUP
WHAT'S WRONG, KURUMI?

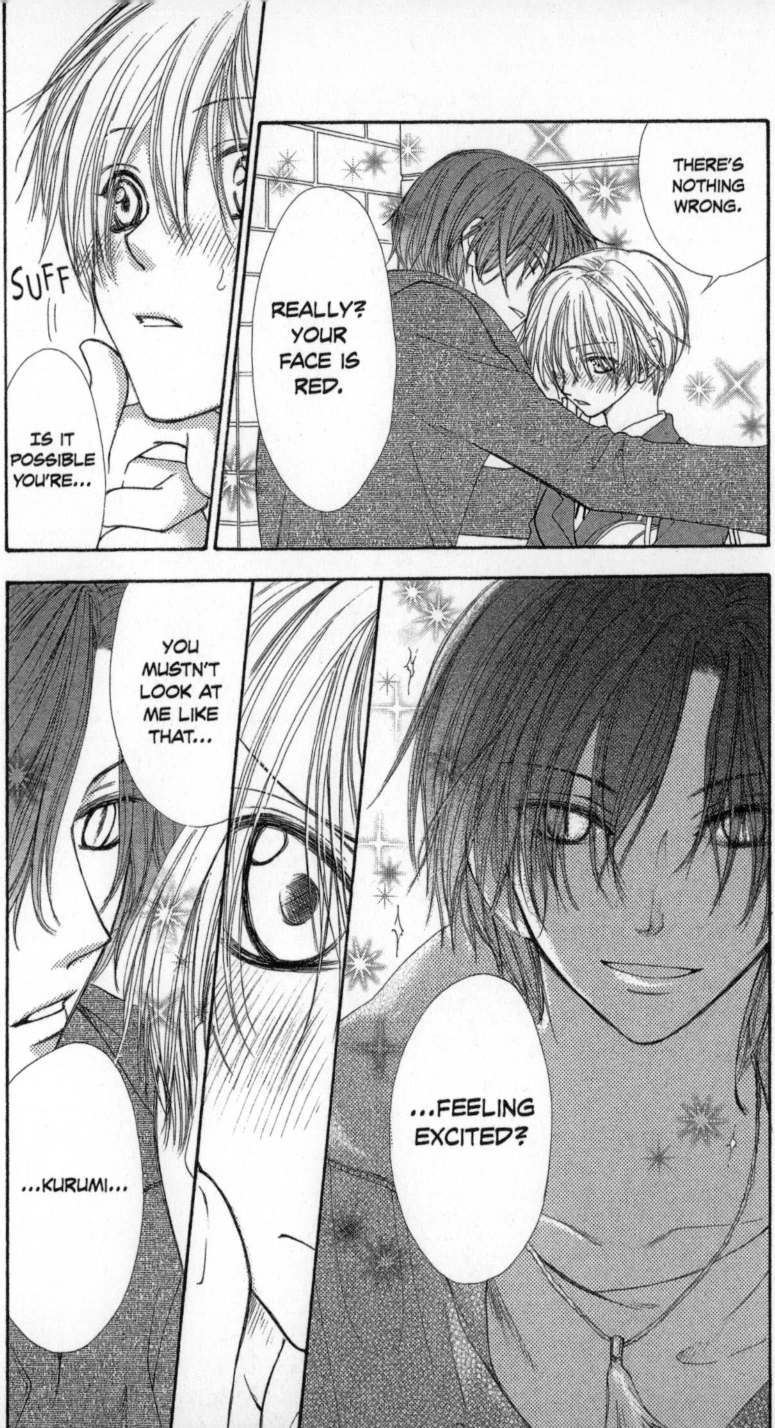
THERE'S NOTHING WRONG.
REALLY? YOUR FACE IS RED.
SUFF
IS IT POSSIBLE YOU'RE...
...FEELING EXCITED?
YOU MUSTN'T LOOK AT ME LIKE THAT...
...KURUMI...

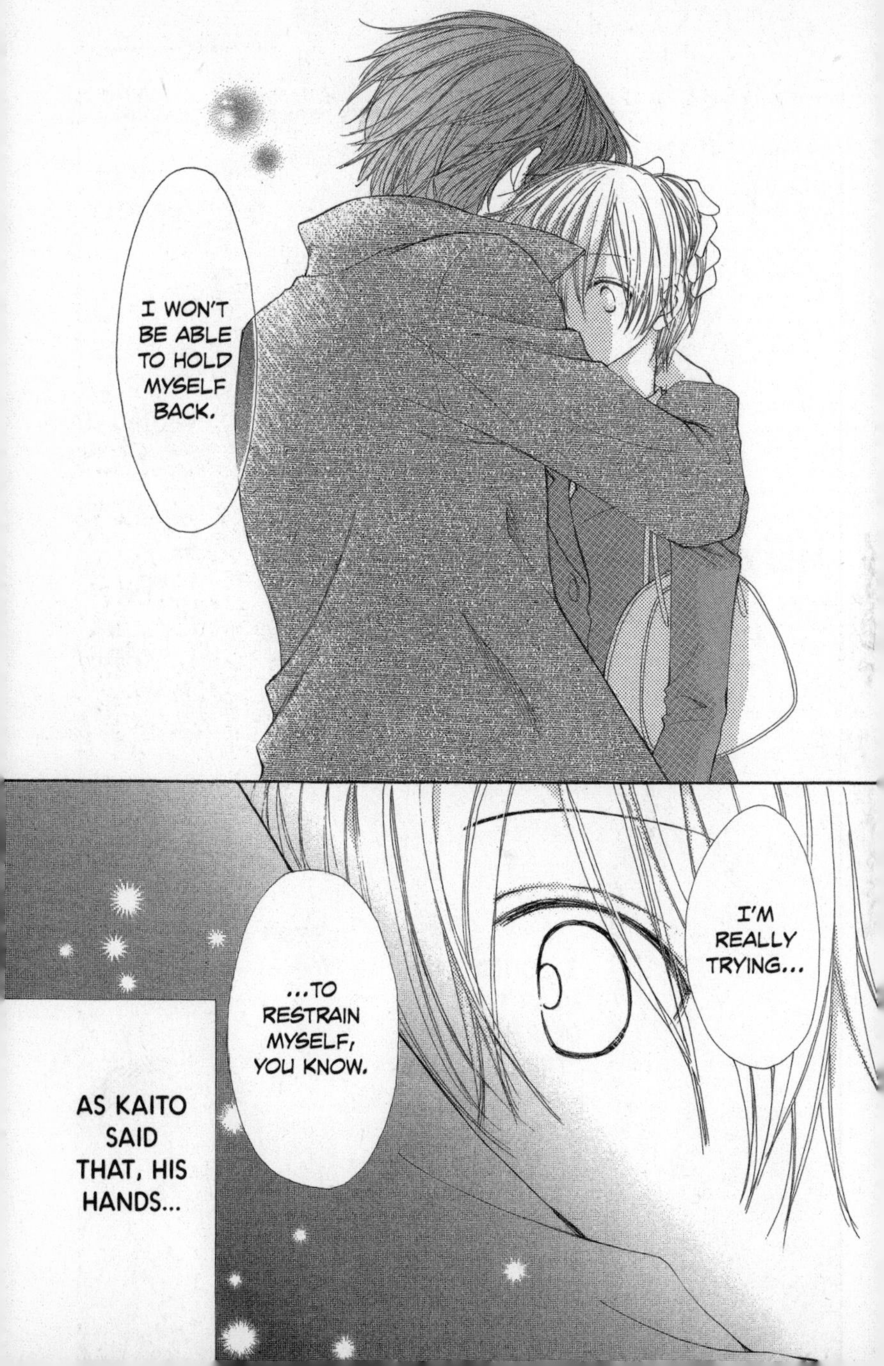
I WON'T BE ABLE TO HOLD MYSELF BACK.
I'M REALLY TRYING...
...TO RESTRAIN MYSELF, YOU KNOW.
AS KAITO SAID THAT, HIS HANDS...

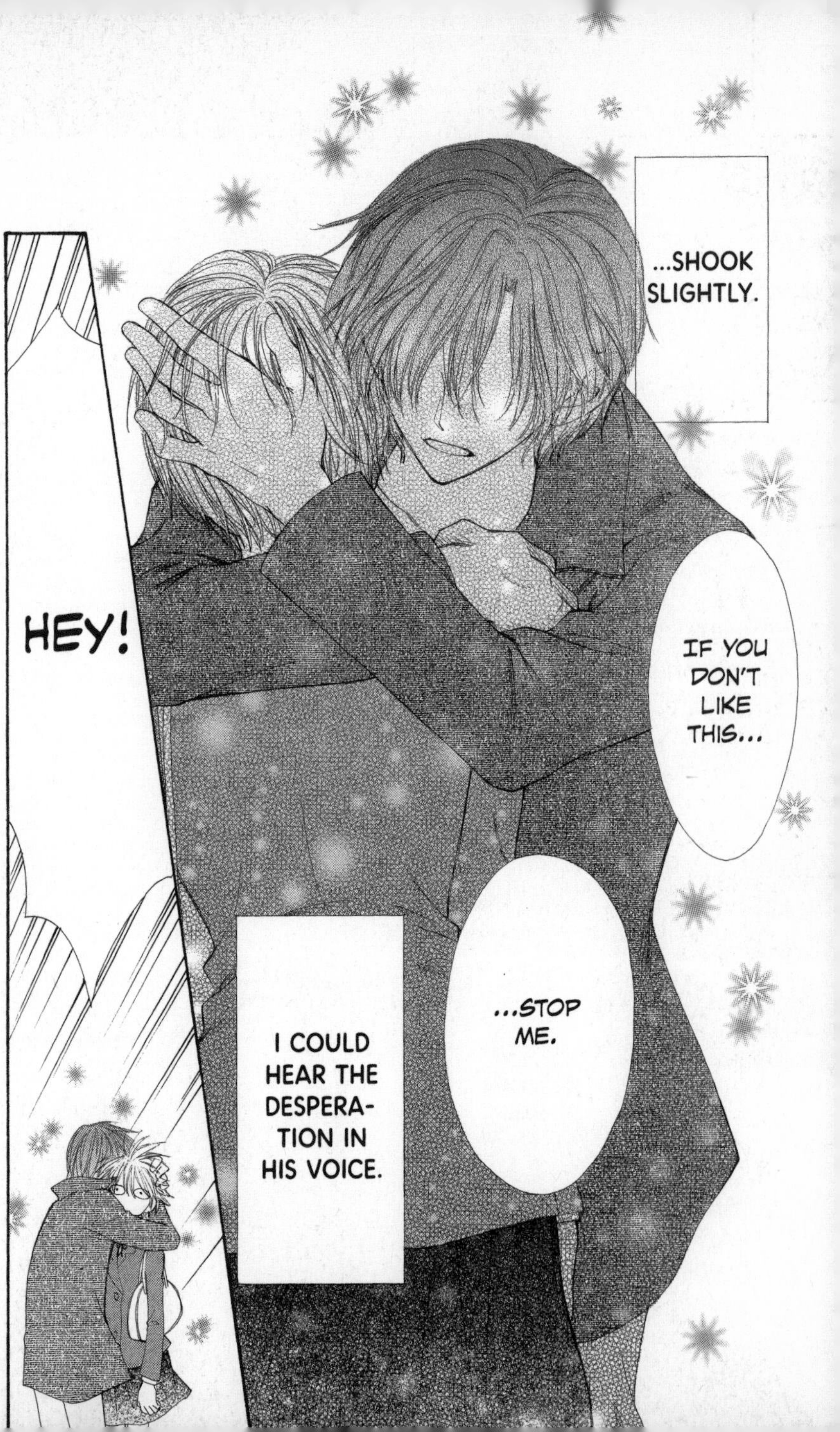
...SHOOK SLIGHTLY.
IF YOU DON'T LIKE THIS...
...STOP ME.
I COULD HEAR THE DESPERATION IN HIS VOICE.
HEY!

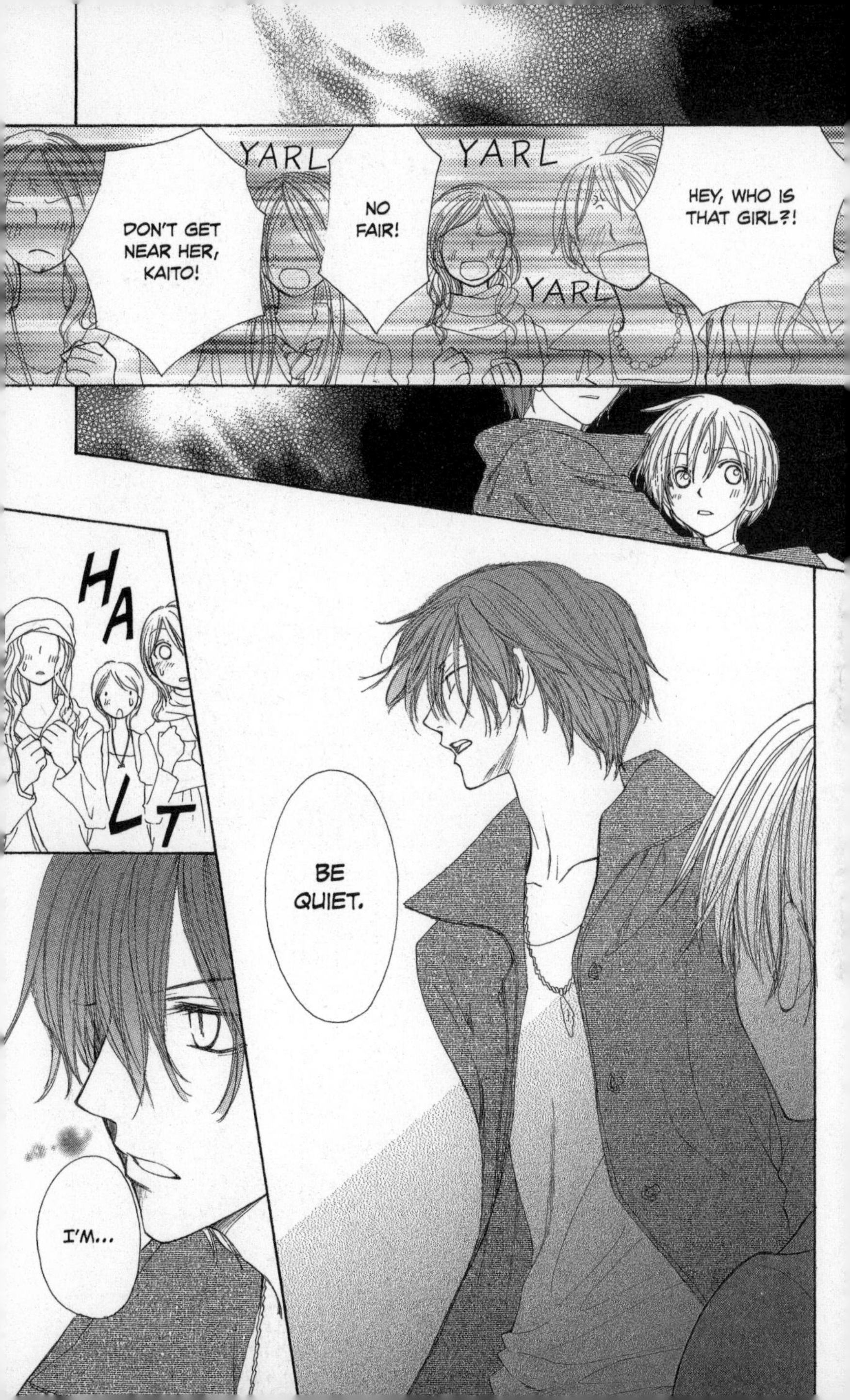
HEY, WHO IS THAT GIRL?!
YARL
NO FAIR!
YARL
DON'T GET NEAR HER, KAITO!
YARL
BE QUIET.
HALT
I'M...

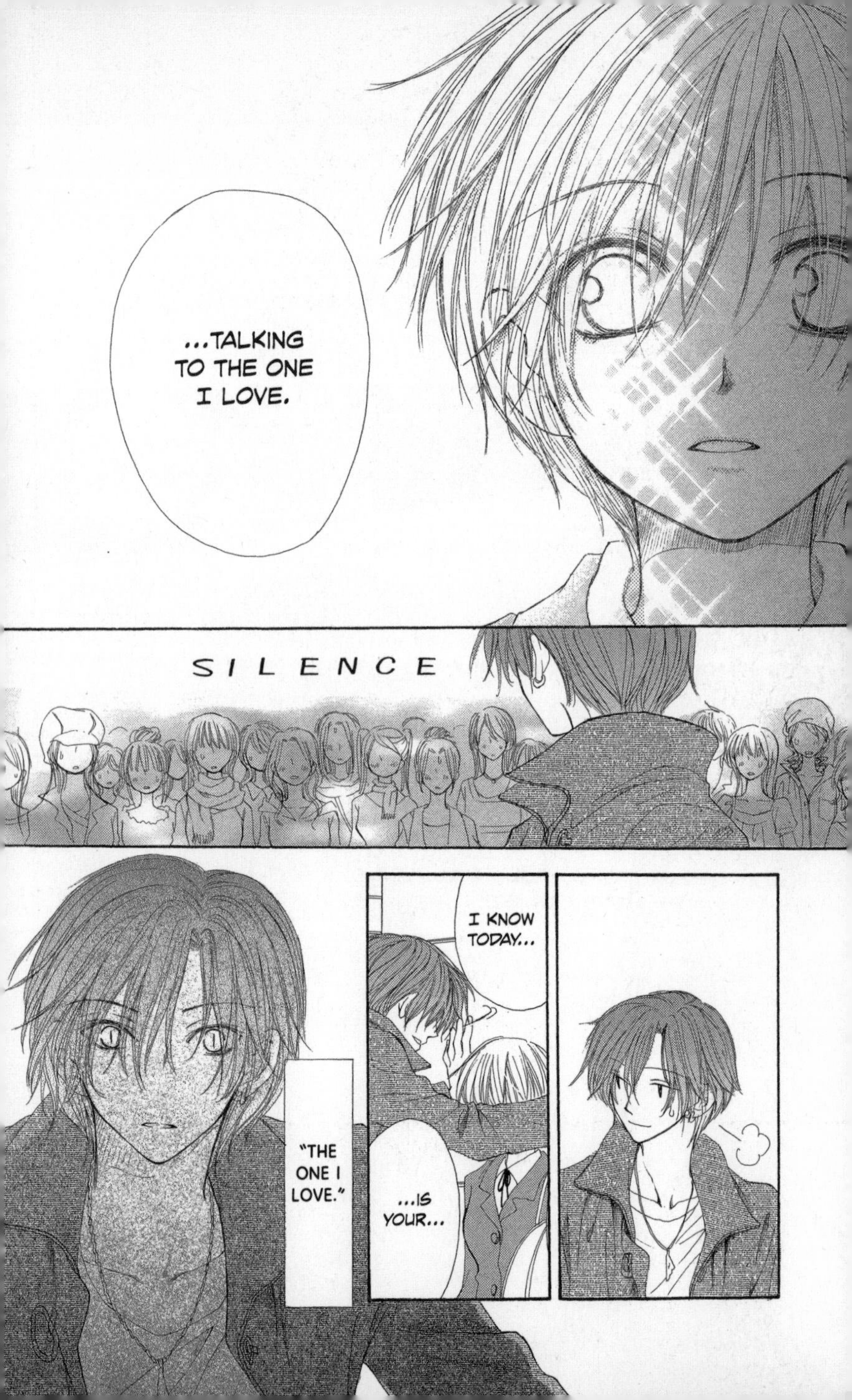
...TALKING TO THE ONE I LOVE.
SILENCE
I KNOW TODAY...
...IS YOUR...
"THE ONE I LOVE."

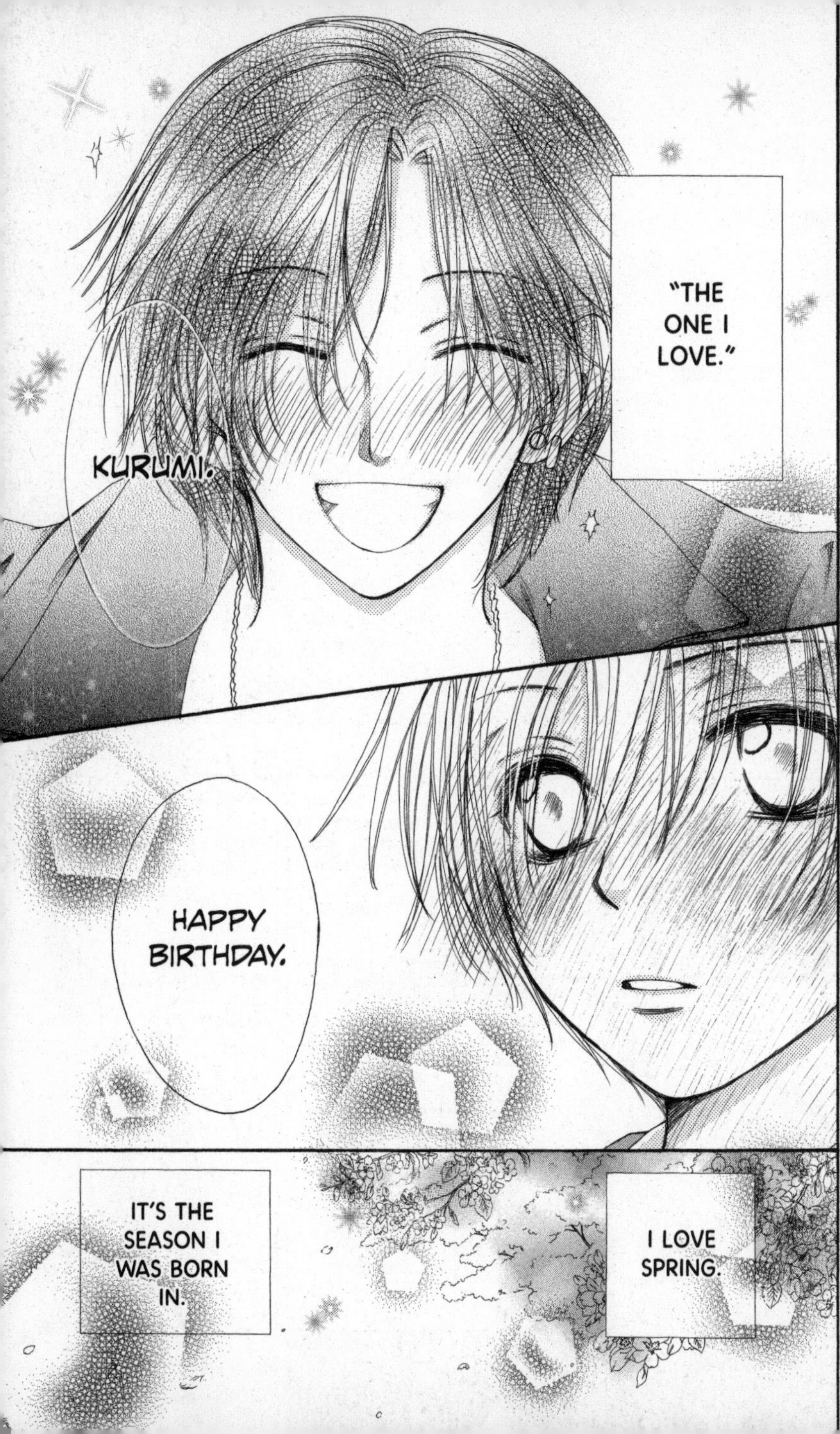
"THE ONE I LOVE."
KURUMI.
HAPPY BIRTHDAY.
I LOVE SPRING.
IT'S THE SEASON I WAS BORN IN.

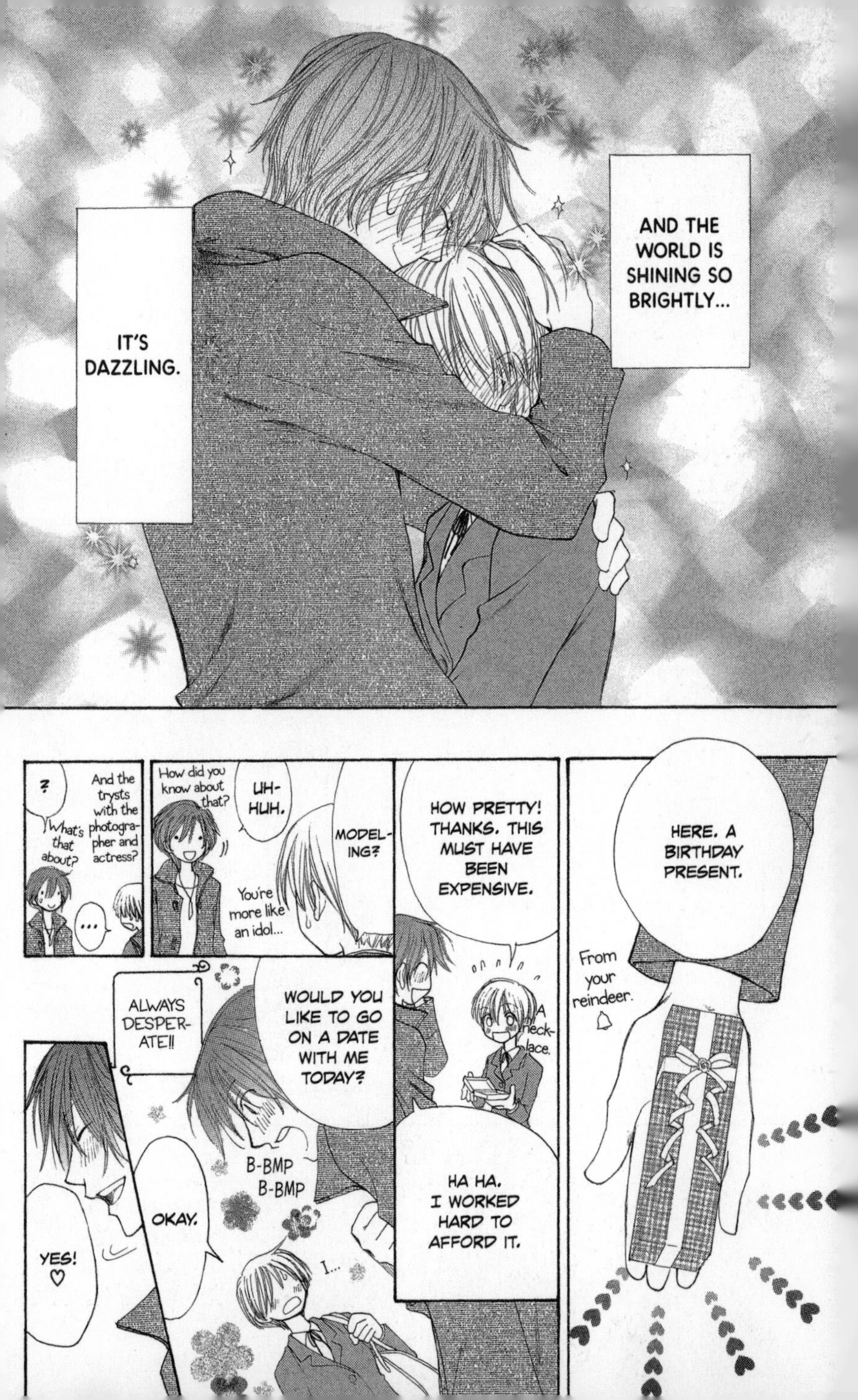
AND THE WORLD IS SHINING SO BRIGHTLY...
IT'S DAZZLING.
HERE. A BIRTHDAY PRESENT.
From your reindeer.
HOW PRETTY! THANKS. THIS MUST HAVE BEEN EXPENSIVE.
A neck-lace.
HA HA. I WORKED HARD TO AFFORD IT.
MODEL-ING?
You're more like an idol...
UH-HUH.
How did you know about that?
And the trysts with the photogra-pher and actress?
?
What's that about?
...
WOULD YOU LIKE TO GO ON A DATE WITH ME TODAY?
B-BMP B-BMP
I...
ALWAYS DESPER-ATE!!
OKAY.
YES! ♡

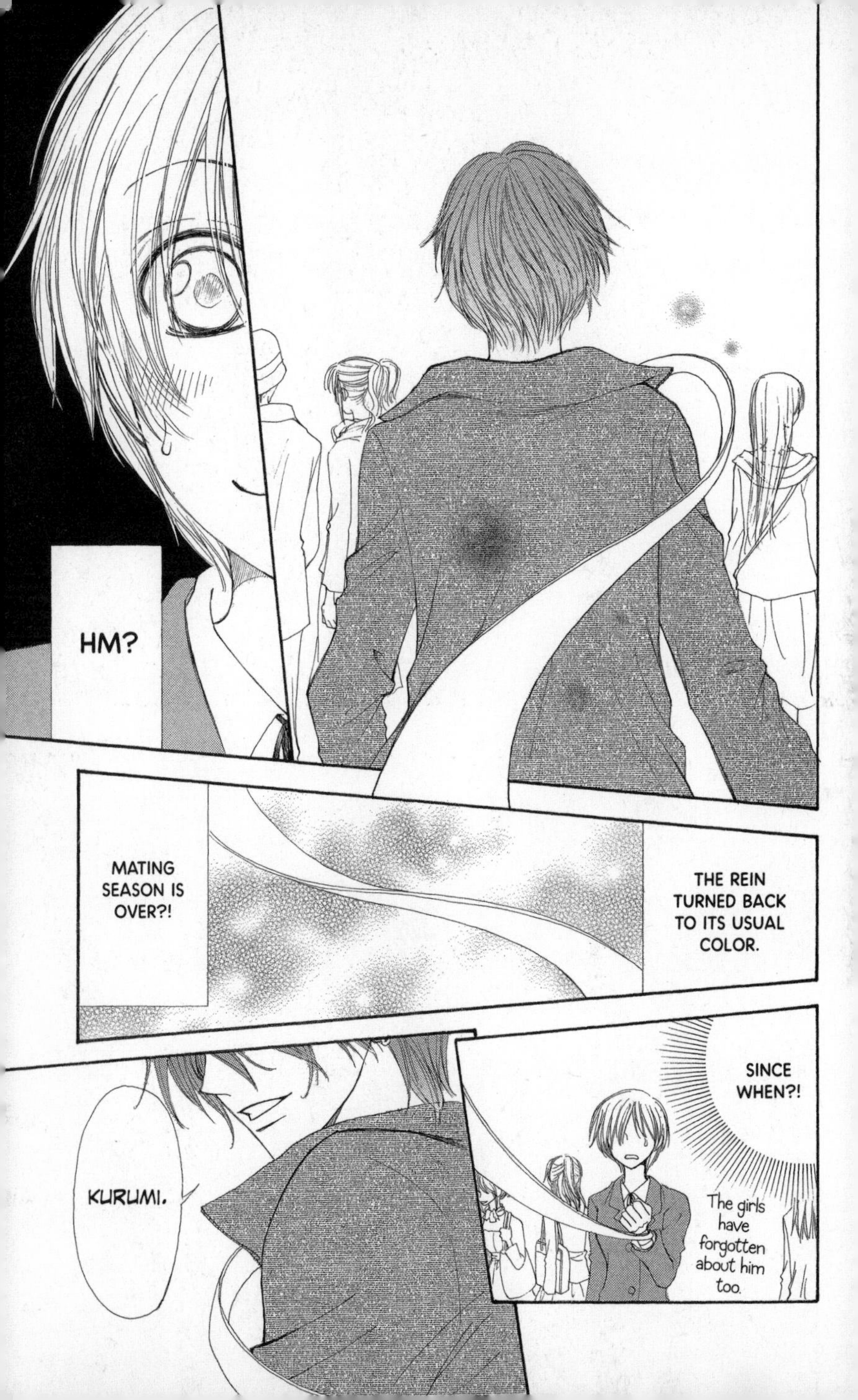
HM?
THE REIN TURNED BACK TO ITS USUAL COLOR.
MATING SEASON IS OVER?!
SINCE WHEN?!
The girls have forgotten about him too.
KURUMI.

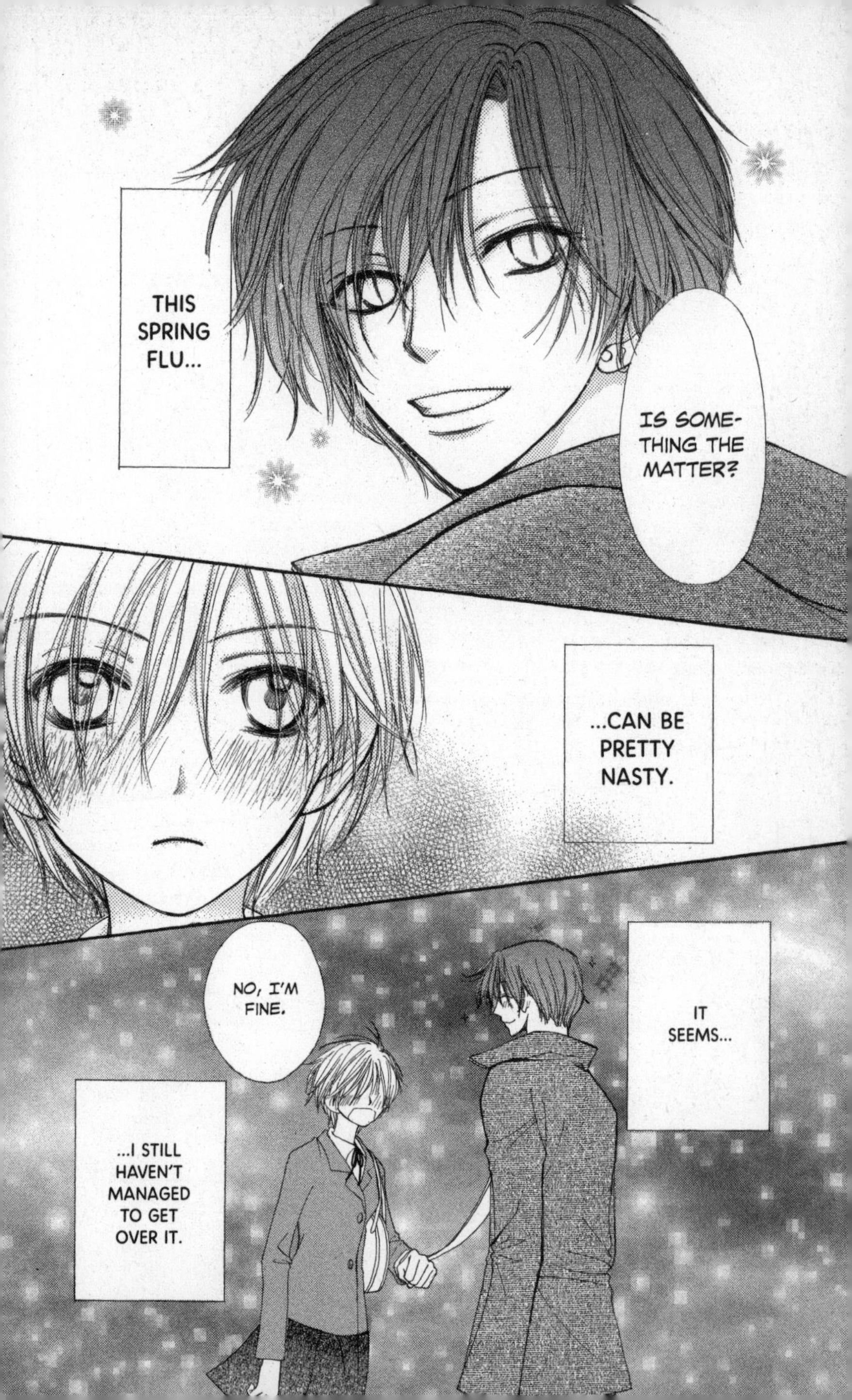
IS SOMETHING THE MATTER?
THIS SPRING FLU...
...CAN BE PRETTY NASTY.
IT SEEMS...
NO, I'M FINE.
...I STILL HAVEN'T MANAGED TO GET OVER IT.

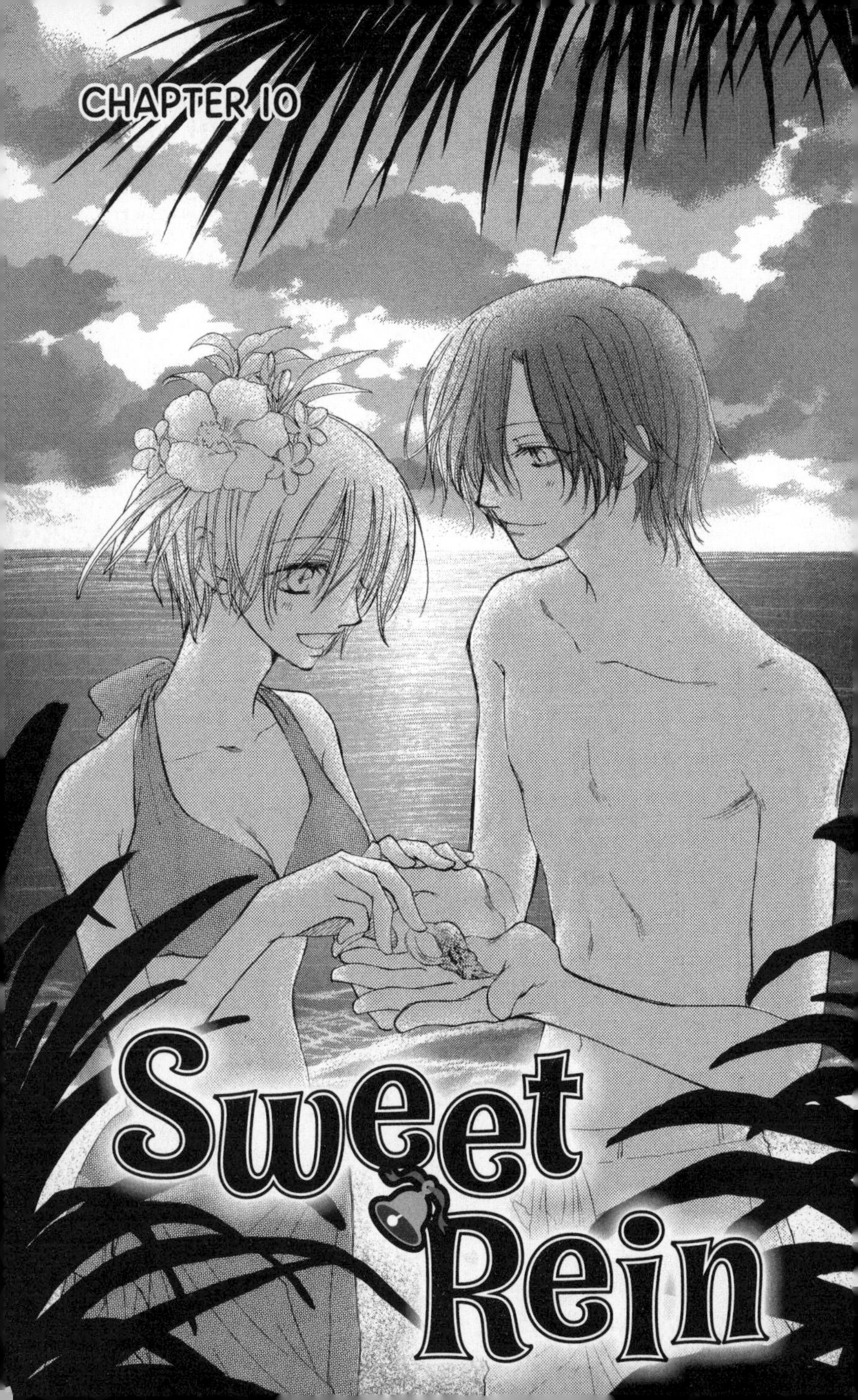
CHAPTER 10
Sweet Rein

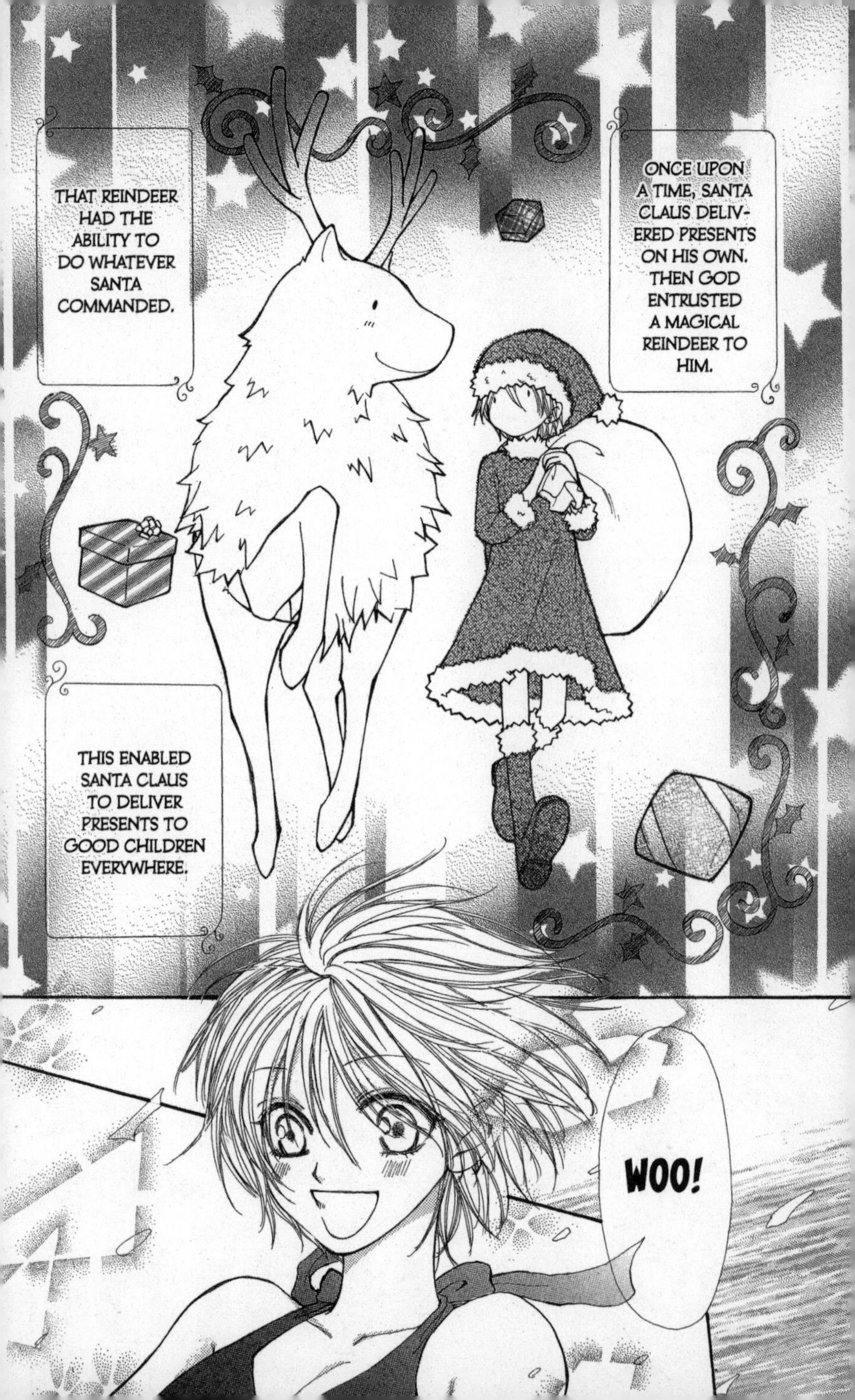
ONCE UPON A TIME, SANTA CLAUS DELIVERED PRESENTS ON HIS OWN. THEN GOD ENTRUSTED A MAGICAL REINDEER TO HIM.
THAT REINDEER HAD THE ABILITY TO DO WHATEVER SANTA COMMANDED.
THIS ENABLED SANTA CLAUS TO DELIVER PRESENTS TO GOOD CHILDREN EVERYWHERE.
WOO!

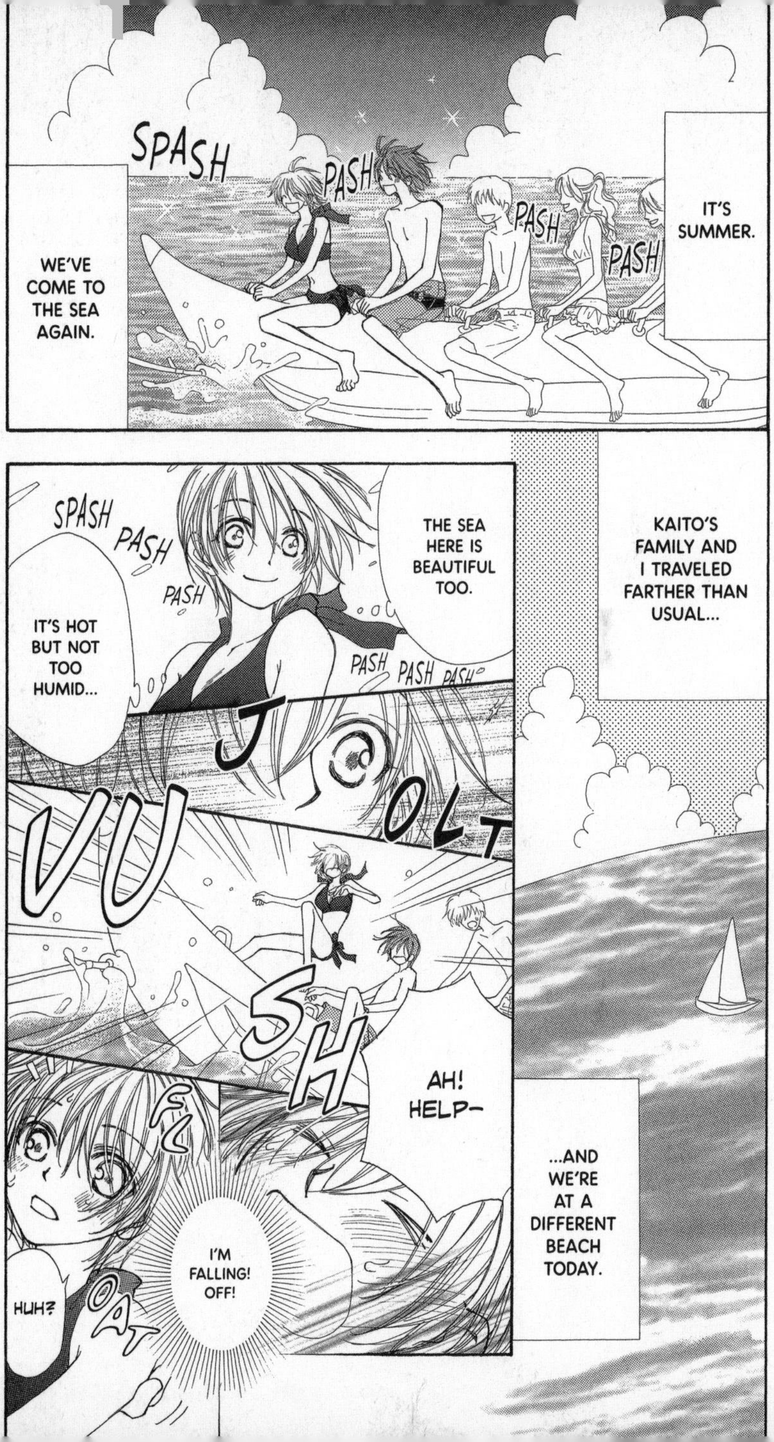
IT'S SUMMER.
PASH
PASH
PASH
SPASH
WE'VE COME TO THE SEA AGAIN.
KAITO'S FAMILY AND I TRAVELED FARTHER THAN USUAL...
...AND WE'RE AT A DIFFERENT BEACH TODAY.
THE SEA HERE IS BEAUTIFUL TOO.
SPASH
PASH
PASH
IT'S HOT BUT NOT TOO HUMID...
PASH PASH PASH
JOLT
VUSH
AH! HELP-
FL
I'M FALLING! OFF!
HUH?
OAT

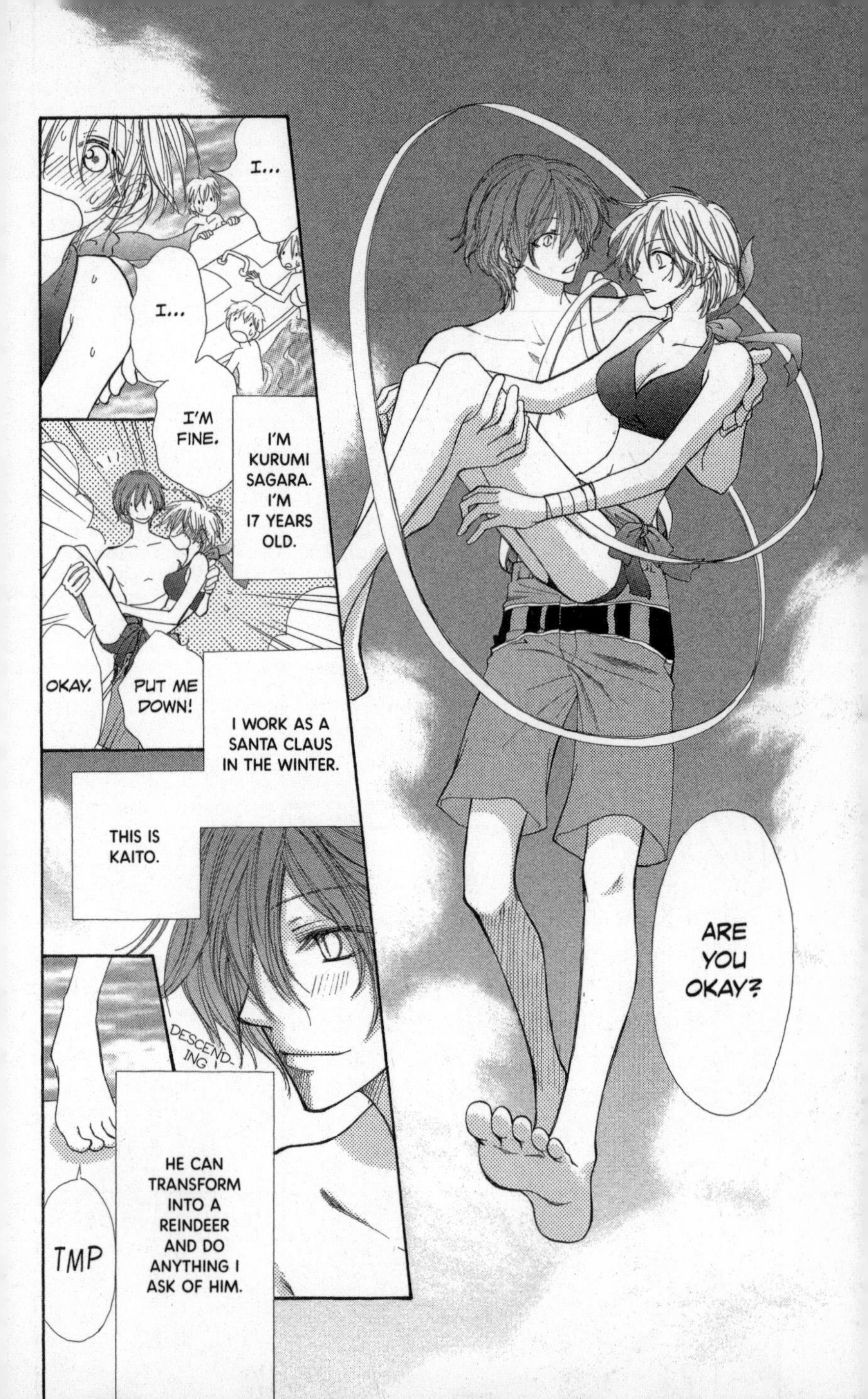
ARE YOU OKAY?
I...
I...
I'M KURUMI SAGARA. I'M 17 YEARS OLD.
I'M FINE.
PUT ME DOWN!
OKAY.
I WORK AS A SANTA CLAUS IN THE WINTER.
THIS IS KAITO.
DESCENDING
HE CAN TRANSFORM INTO A REINDEER AND DO ANYTHING I ASK OF HIM.
TMP

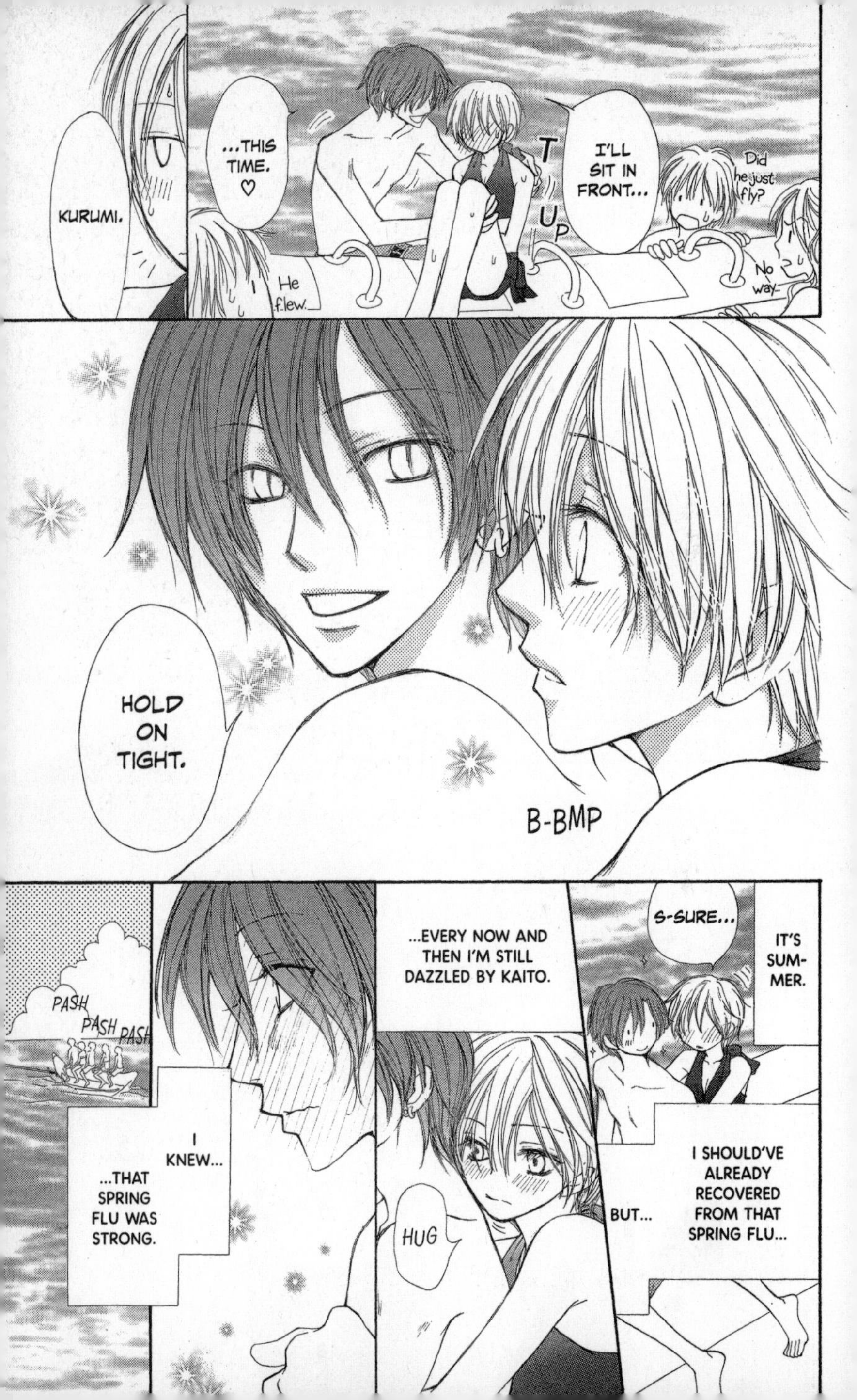
Did he just fly?
No way.
I'LL SIT IN FRONT...
TUP
...THIS TIME. ♡
He flew.
KURUMI.
HOLD ON TIGHT.
B-BMP
IT'S SUMMER.
S-SURE...
I SHOULD'VE ALREADY RECOVERED FROM THAT SPRING FLU...
BUT...
...EVERY NOW AND THEN I'M STILL DAZZLED BY KAITO.
HUG
I KNEW...
...THAT SPRING FLU WAS STRONG.
PASH PASH PASH

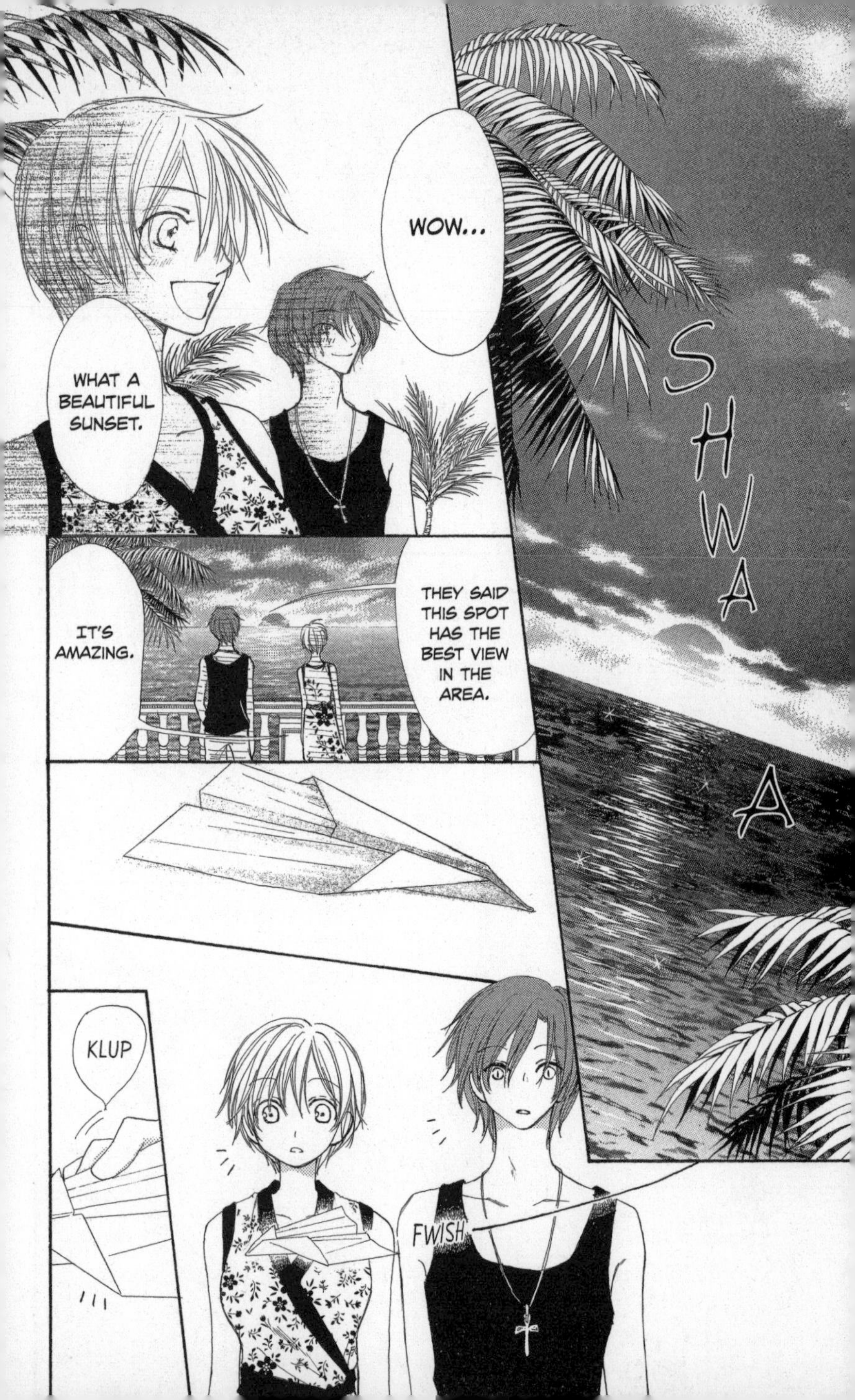
SHWA
A
WOW...
WHAT A BEAUTIFUL SUNSET.
THEY SAID THIS SPOT HAS THE BEST VIEW IN THE AREA.
IT'S AMAZING.
FWISH
KLUP

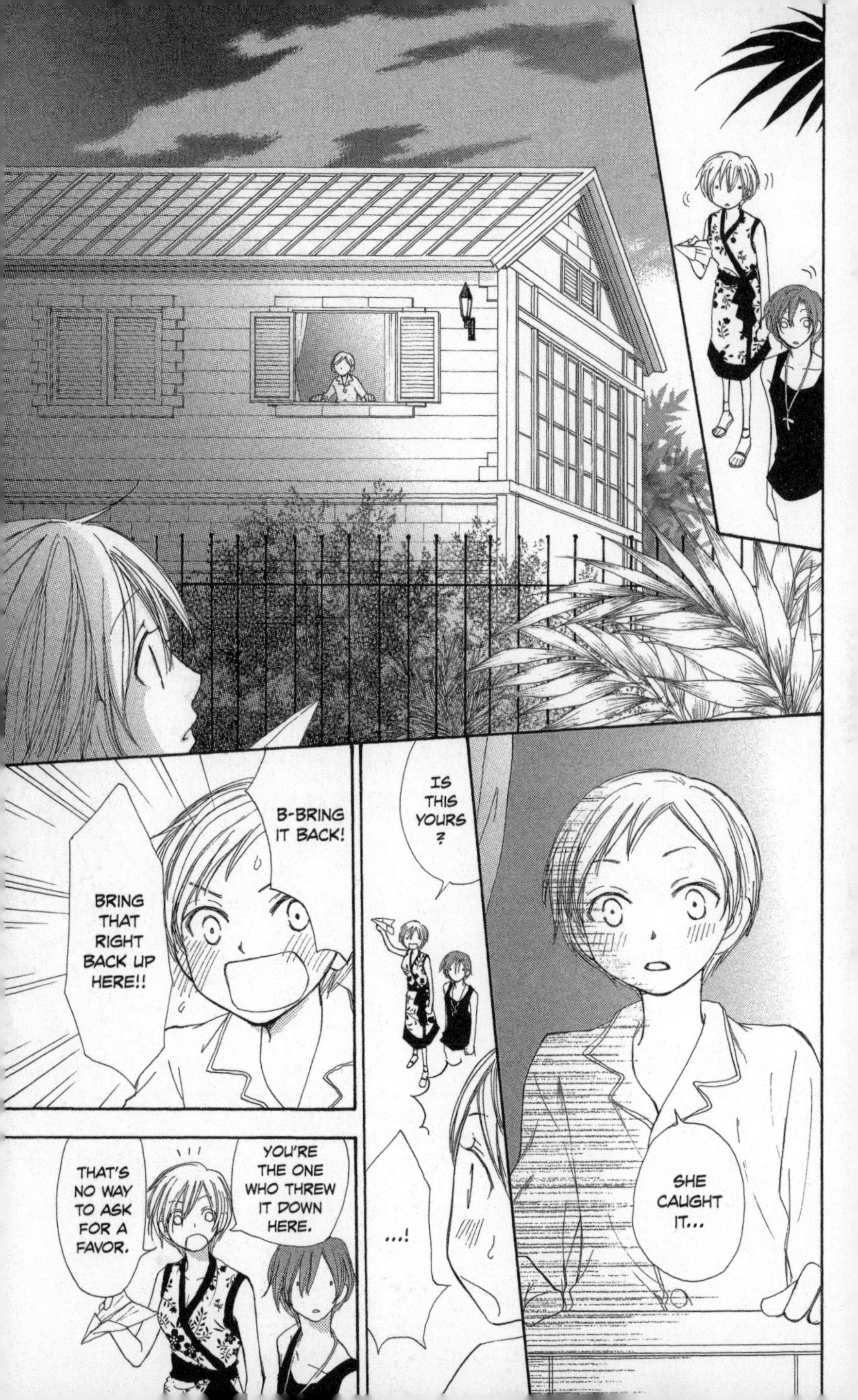
IS THIS YOURS?
...!
SHE CAUGHT IT...
B-BRING IT BACK!
BRING THAT RIGHT BACK UP HERE!!
YOU'RE THE ONE WHO THREW IT DOWN HERE.
THAT'S NO WAY TO ASK FOR A FAVOR.

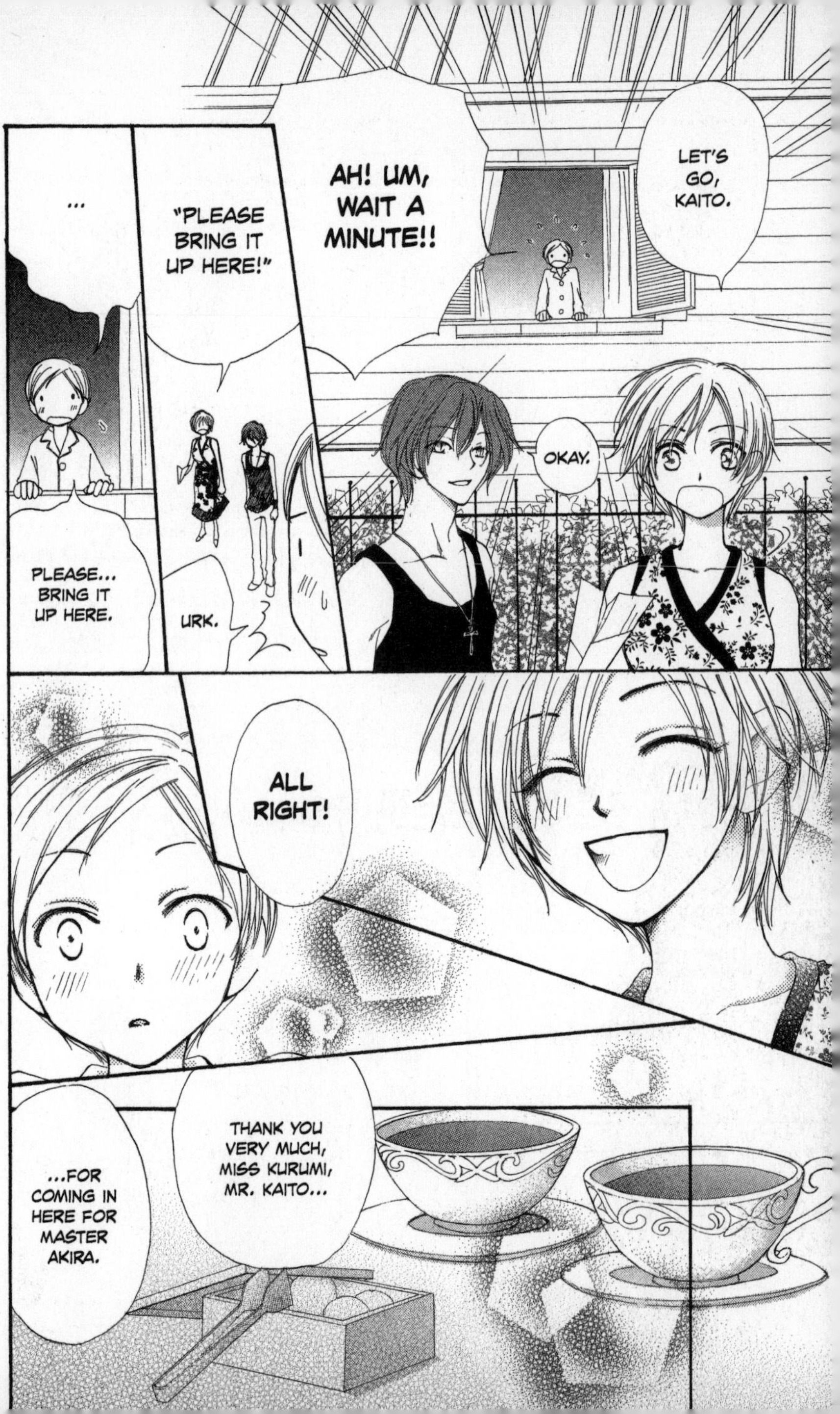
LET'S GO, KAITO.
AH! UM, WAIT A MINUTE!!
OKAY.
"PLEASE BRING IT UP HERE!"
URK.
...
PLEASE... BRING IT UP HERE.
ALL RIGHT!
THANK YOU VERY MUCH, MISS KURUMI, MR. KAITO...
...FOR COMING IN HERE FOR MASTER AKIRA.

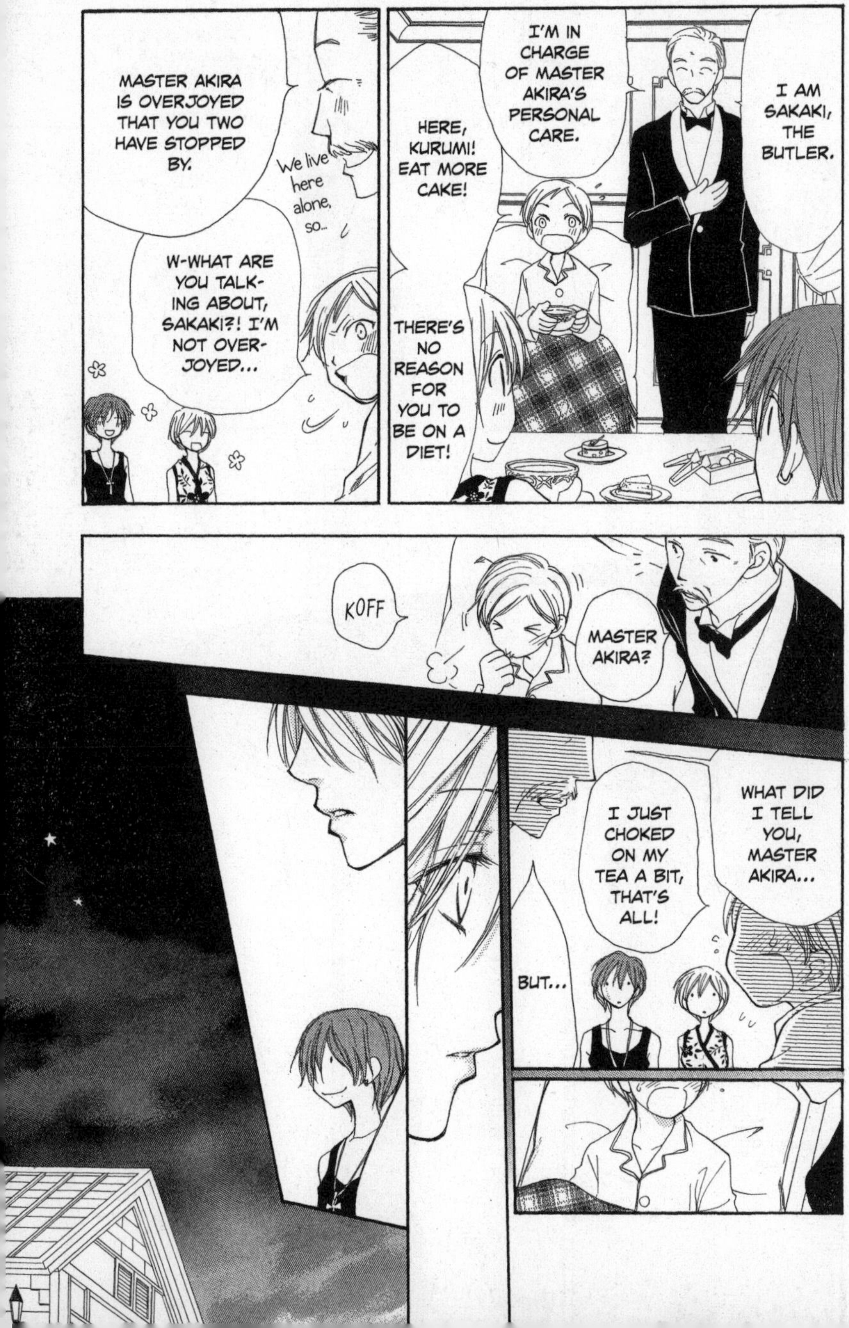
I AM SAKAKI, THE BUTLER.
I'M IN CHARGE OF MASTER AKIRA'S PERSONAL CARE.
HERE, KURUMI! EAT MORE CAKE!
THERE'S NO REASON FOR YOU TO BE ON A DIET!
MASTER AKIRA IS OVERJOYED THAT YOU TWO HAVE STOPPED BY.
We live here alone, so...
W-WHAT ARE YOU TALKING ABOUT, SAKAKI?! I'M NOT OVERJOYED...
MASTER AKIRA?
KOFF
WHAT DID I TELL YOU, MASTER AKIRA...
I JUST CHOKED ON MY TEA A BIT, THAT'S ALL!
BUT...

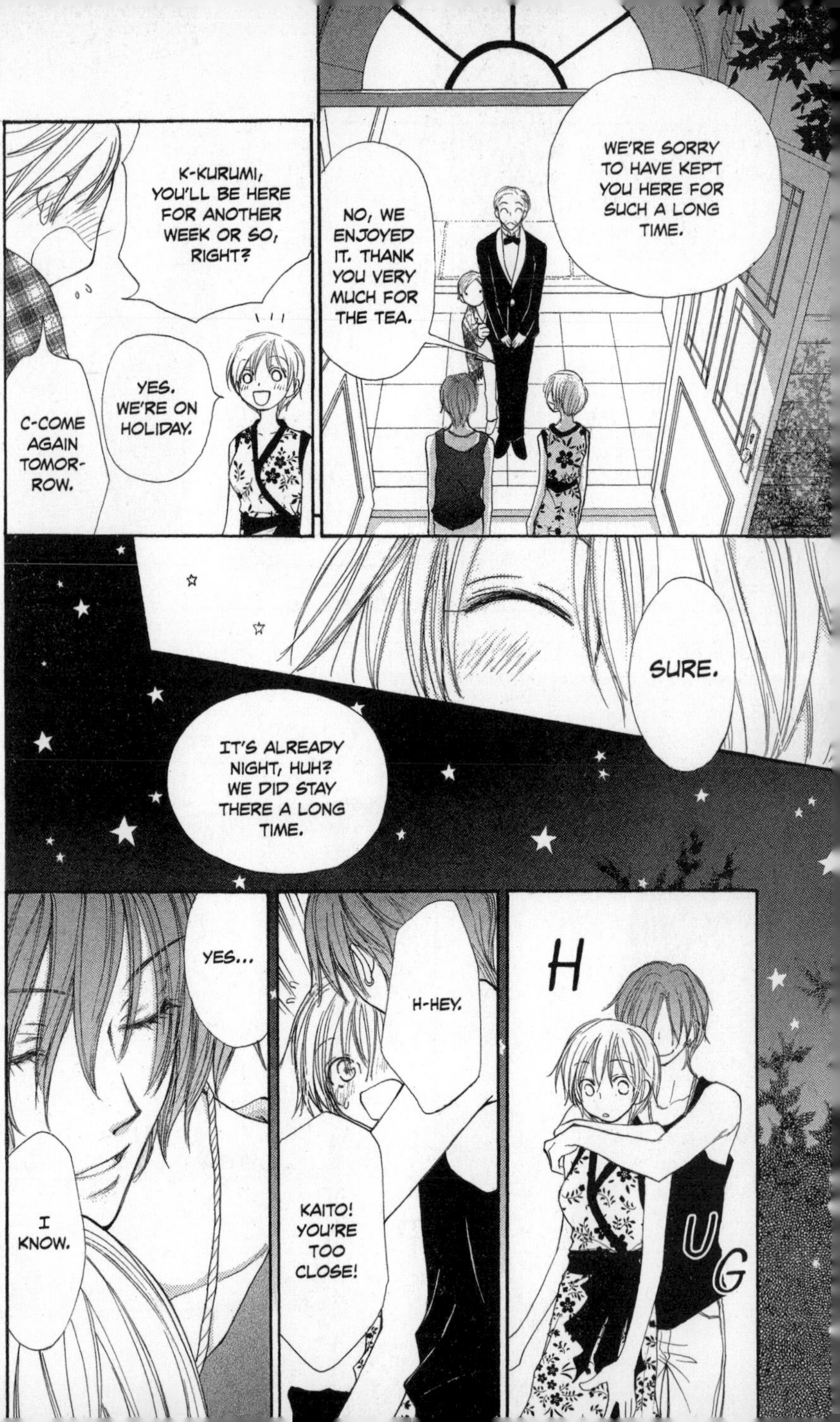
WE'RE SORRY TO HAVE KEPT YOU HERE FOR SUCH A LONG TIME.
NO, WE ENJOYED IT. THANK YOU VERY MUCH FOR THE TEA.
K-KURUMI, YOU'LL BE HERE FOR ANOTHER WEEK OR SO, RIGHT?
YES. WE'RE ON HOLIDAY.
C-COME AGAIN TOMORROW.
SURE.
IT'S ALREADY NIGHT, HUH? WE DID STAY THERE A LONG TIME.
HUG
H-HEY.
KAITO! YOU'RE TOO CLOSE!
YES...
I KNOW.

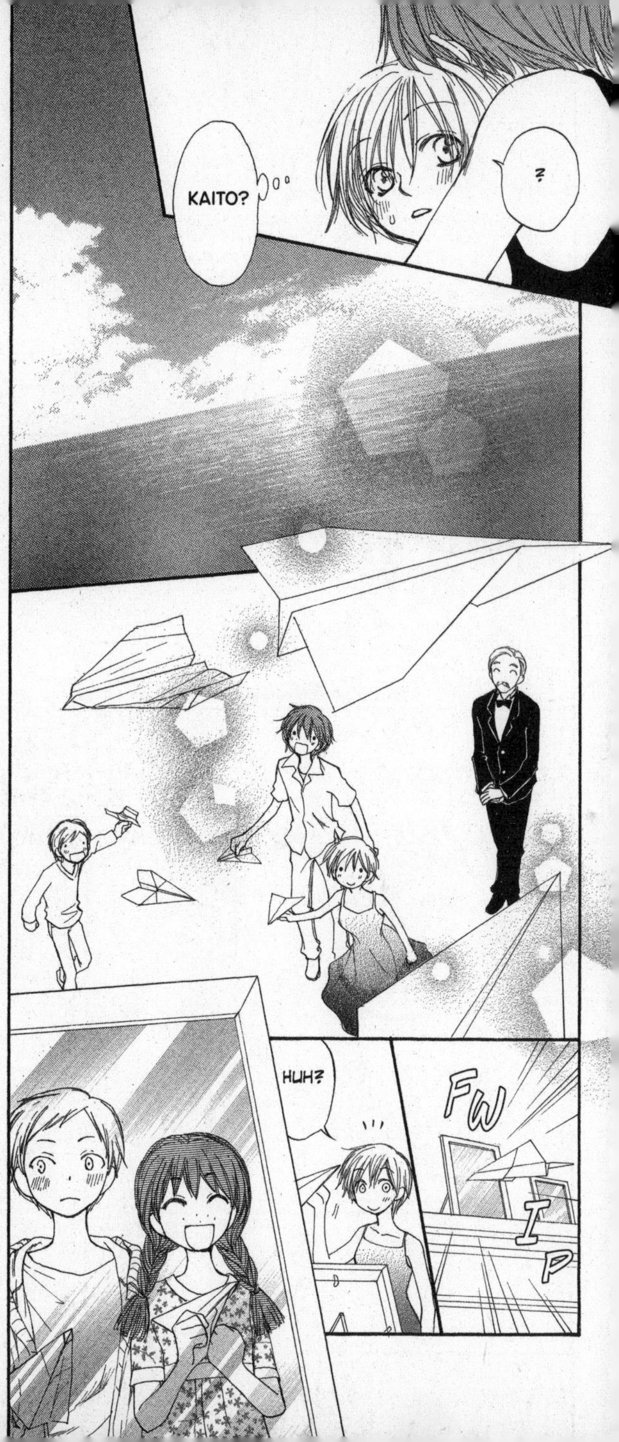
?
KAITO?
HUH?
FWIP

1/4 Sakura Mail

Part 4

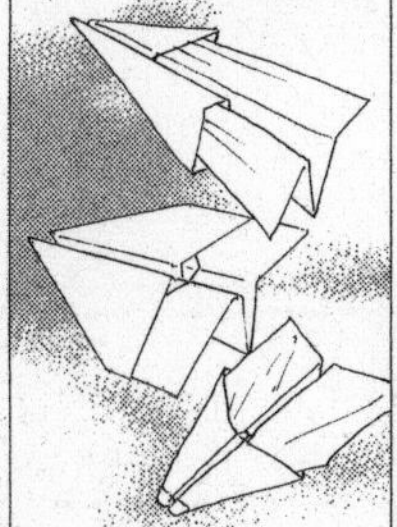

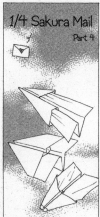

It's another summer chapter for our Santa. It's a tradition for Kaito's family to go to the sea on vacation every year. This year they're on holiday at a seaside resort for about a week. They're relaxing and enjoying their time at the beach. Many paper planes appear in this chapter. I used to make them all the time as a child, but I had forgotten how to fold them. ? My assistants and I went through a lot of trouble making various paper planes to use for reference. In the end my office was filled with all sorts of paper planes.

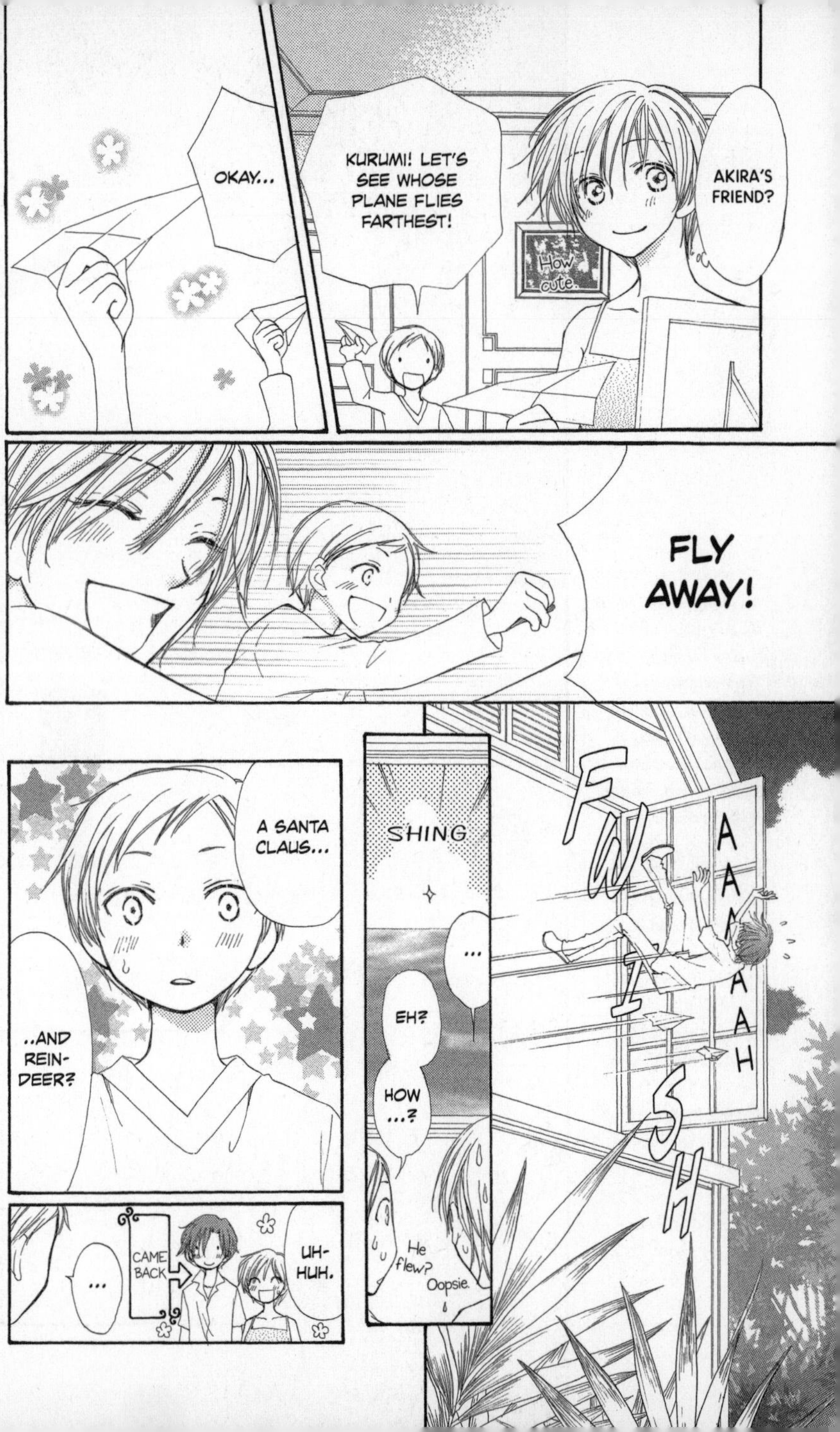
AKIRA'S FRIEND?
How cute.
KURUMI! LET'S SEE WHOSE PLANE FLIES FARTHEST!
OKAY...
FLY AWAY!
FWISH
AAAAAH
SHING
...
EH?
HOW ...?
He flew?
Oopsie.
A SANTA CLAUS...
..AND REIN-DEER?
UH-HUH.
CAME BACK
...

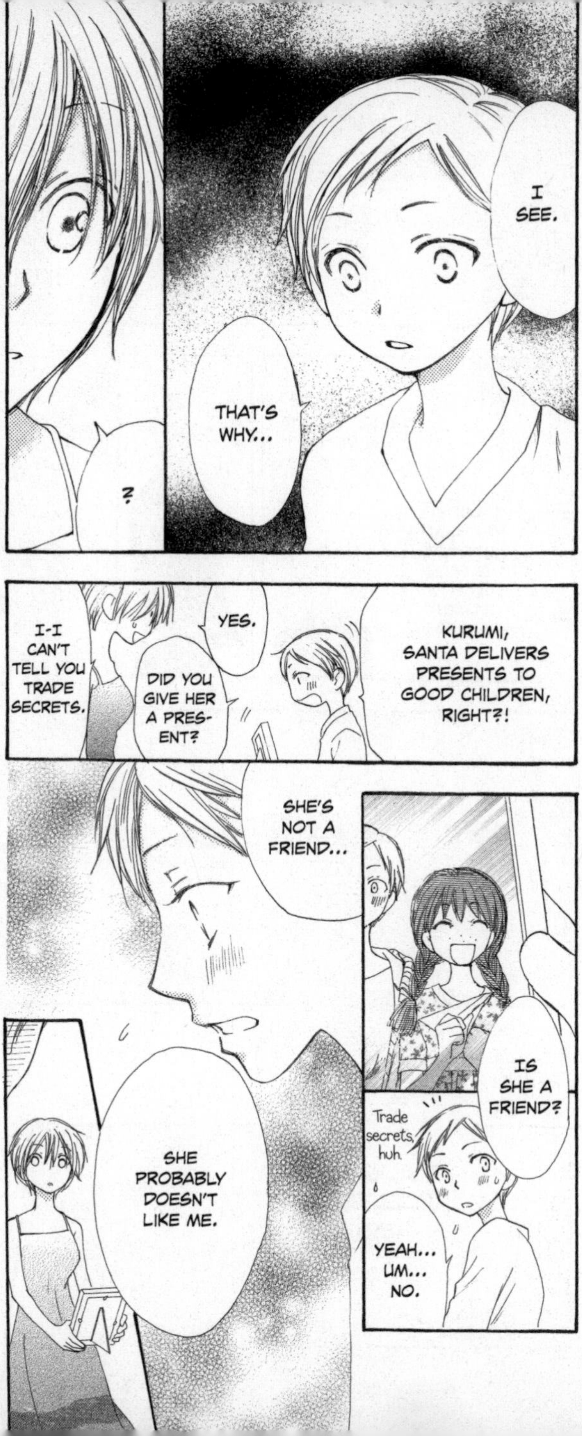
I SEE.
THAT'S WHY...
?
KURUMI, SANTA DELIVERS PRESENTS TO GOOD CHILDREN, RIGHT?!
YES.
DID YOU GIVE HER A PRESENT?
I-I CAN'T TELL YOU TRADE SECRETS.
IS SHE A FRIEND?
Trade secrets, huh.
YEAH... UM... NO.
SHE'S NOT A FRIEND...
SHE PROBABLY DOESN'T LIKE ME.

1/4 Sakura Mail

Part 5

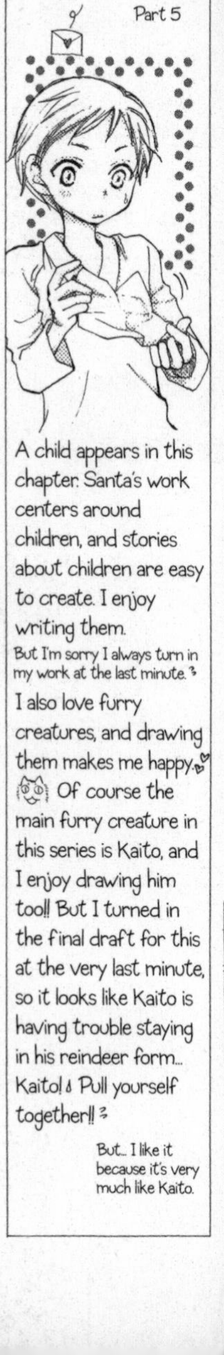

A child appears in this chapter. Santa's work centers around children, and stories about children are easy to create. I enjoy writing them.

But I'm sorry I always turn in my work at the last minute.

I also love furry creatures, and drawing them makes me happy. Of course the main furry creature in this series is Kaito, and I enjoy drawing him too!! But I turned in the final draft for this at the very last minute, so it looks like Kaito is having trouble staying in his reindeer form... Kaito! Pull yourself together!!

But... I like it because it's very much like Kaito.

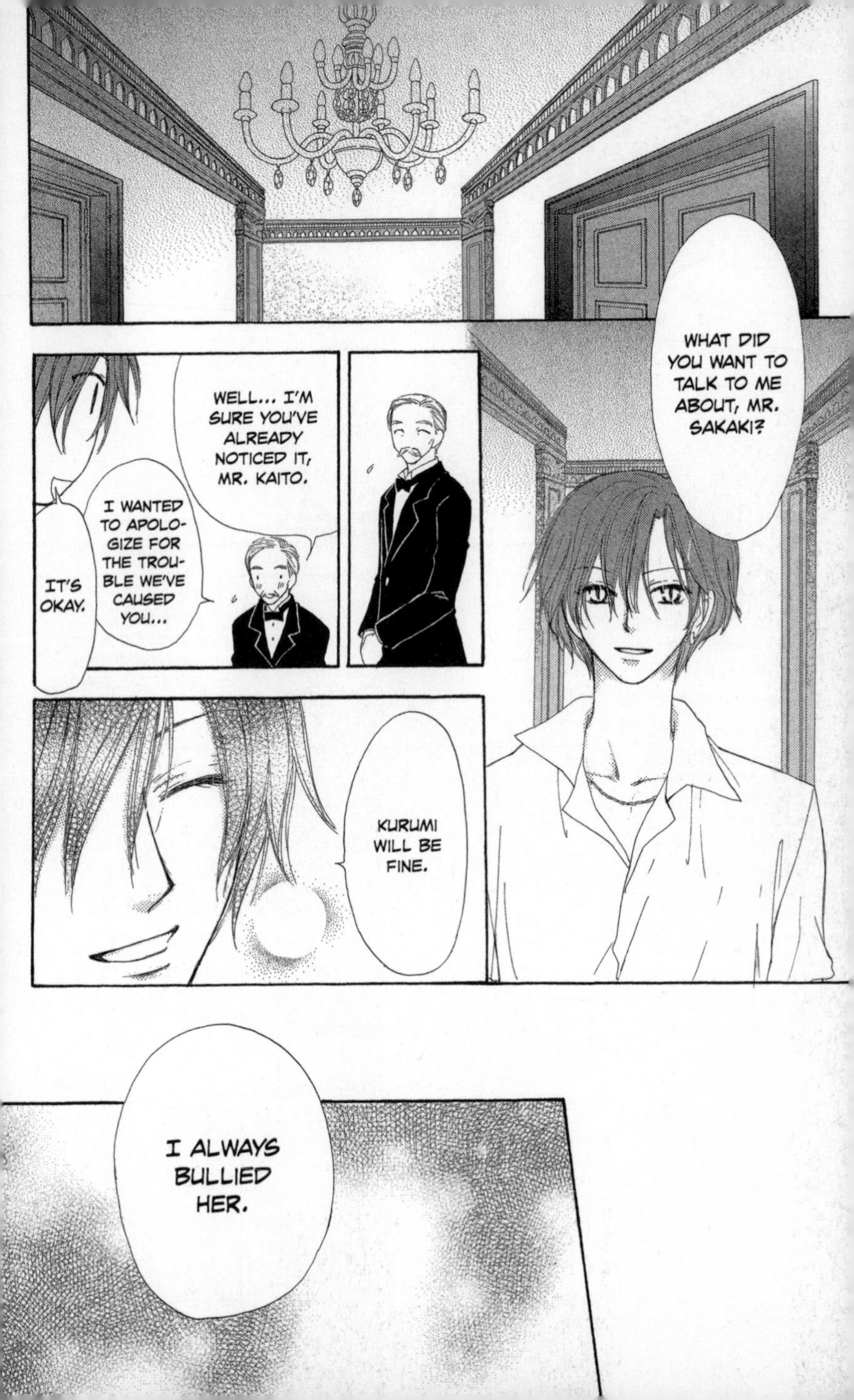
WHAT DID YOU WANT TO TALK TO ME ABOUT, MR. SAKAKI?
WELL... I'M SURE YOU'VE ALREADY NOTICED IT, MR. KAITO.
I WANTED TO APOLOGIZE FOR THE TROUBLE WE'VE CAUSED YOU...
IT'S OKAY.
KURUMI WILL BE FINE.
I ALWAYS BULLIED HER.

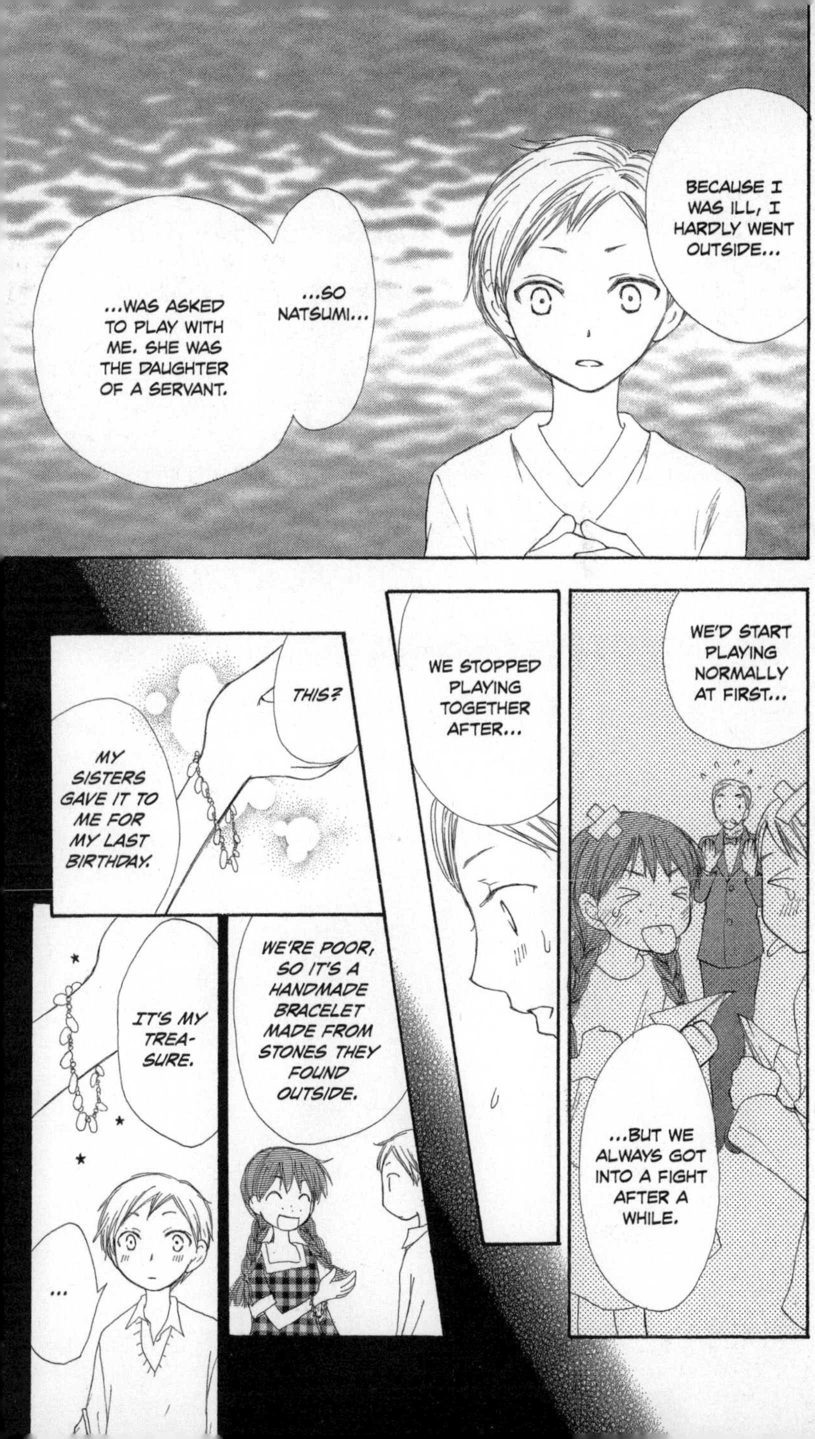
BECAUSE I WAS ILL, I HARDLY WENT OUTSIDE...
...SO NATSUMI...
...WAS ASKED TO PLAY WITH ME. SHE WAS THE DAUGHTER OF A SERVANT.
WE'D START PLAYING NORMALLY AT FIRST...
...BUT WE ALWAYS GOT INTO A FIGHT AFTER A WHILE.
WE STOPPED PLAYING TOGETHER AFTER...
THIS?
MY SISTERS GAVE IT TO ME FOR MY LAST BIRTHDAY.
WE'RE POOR, SO IT'S A HANDMADE BRACELET MADE FROM STONES THEY FOUND OUTSIDE.
IT'S MY TREASURE.
...

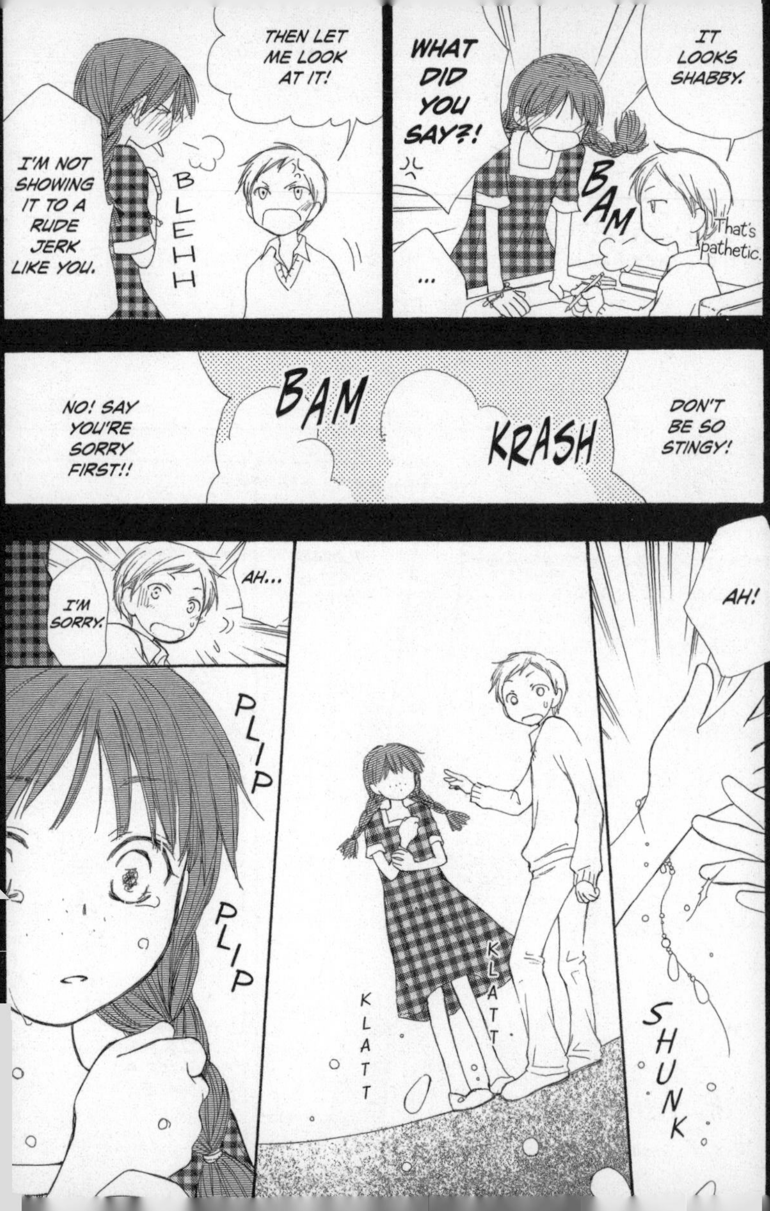
IT LOOKS SHABBY.
WHAT DID YOU SAY?!
...
BAM
That's pathetic.
THEN LET ME LOOK AT IT!
I'M NOT SHOWING IT TO A RUDE JERK LIKE YOU.
BLEHH
DON'T BE SO STINGY!
KRASH
BAM
NO! SAY YOU'RE SORRY FIRST!!
AH!
SHUNK
KLATT
KLATT
AH...
I'M SORRY.
PLIP
PLIP

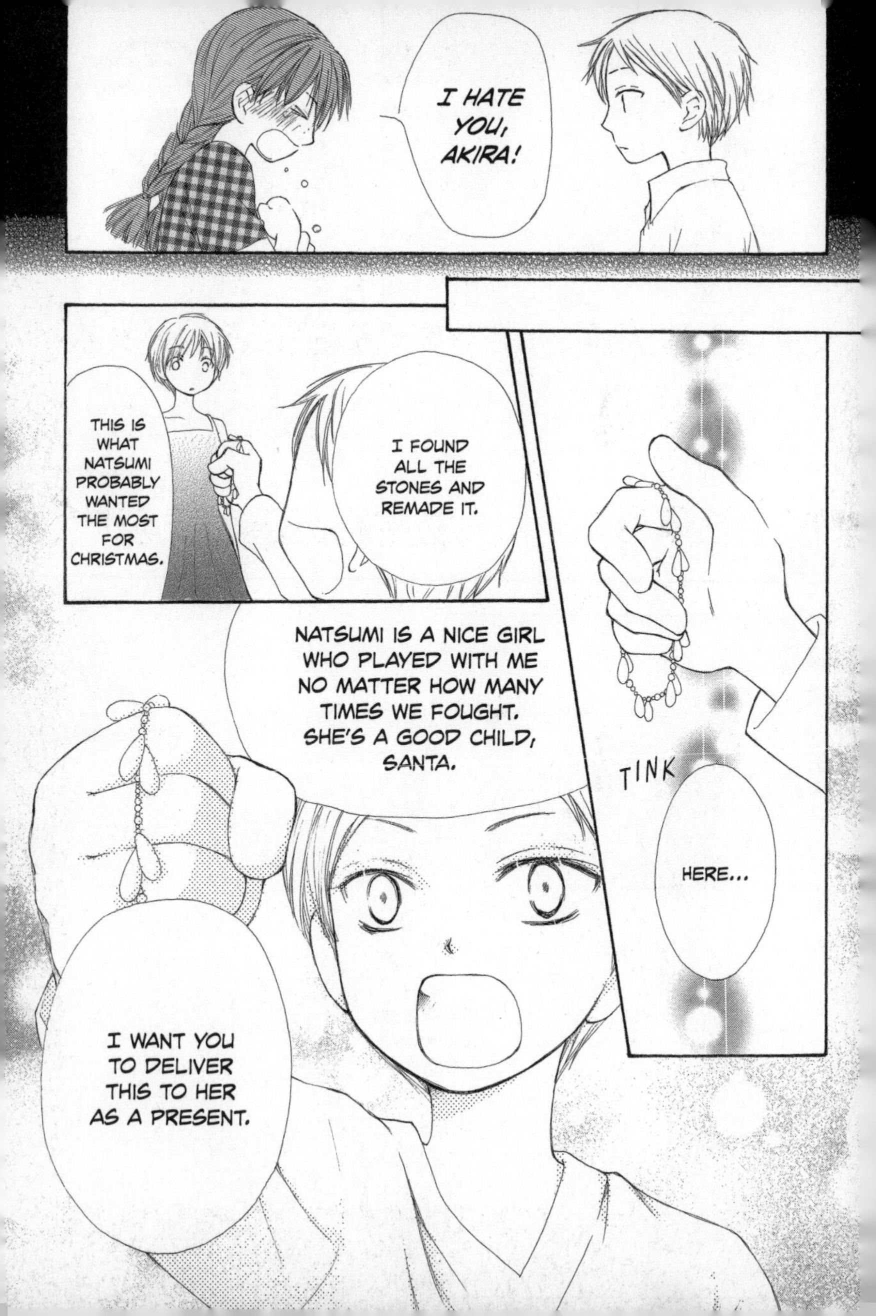
I HATE YOU, AKIRA!
TINK
HERE...
I FOUND ALL THE STONES AND REMADE IT.
THIS IS WHAT NATSUMI PROBABLY WANTED THE MOST FOR CHRISTMAS.
NATSUMI IS A NICE GIRL WHO PLAYED WITH ME NO MATTER HOW MANY TIMES WE FOUGHT. SHE'S A GOOD CHILD, SANTA.
I WANT YOU TO DELIVER THIS TO HER AS A PRESENT.

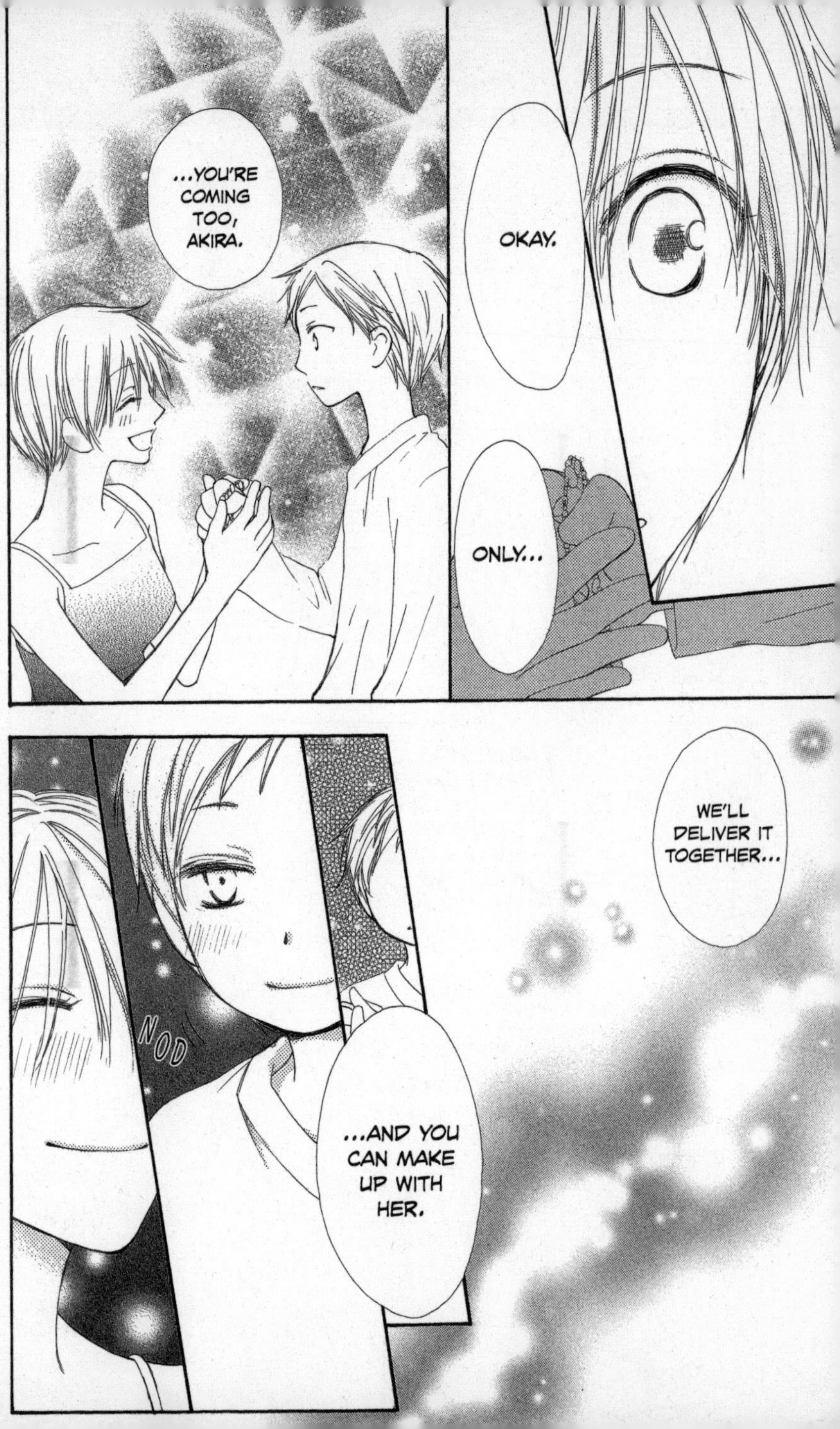
OKAY.
ONLY...
...YOU'RE COMING TOO, AKIRA.
WE'LL DELIVER IT TOGETHER...
...AND YOU CAN MAKE UP WITH HER.
NOD

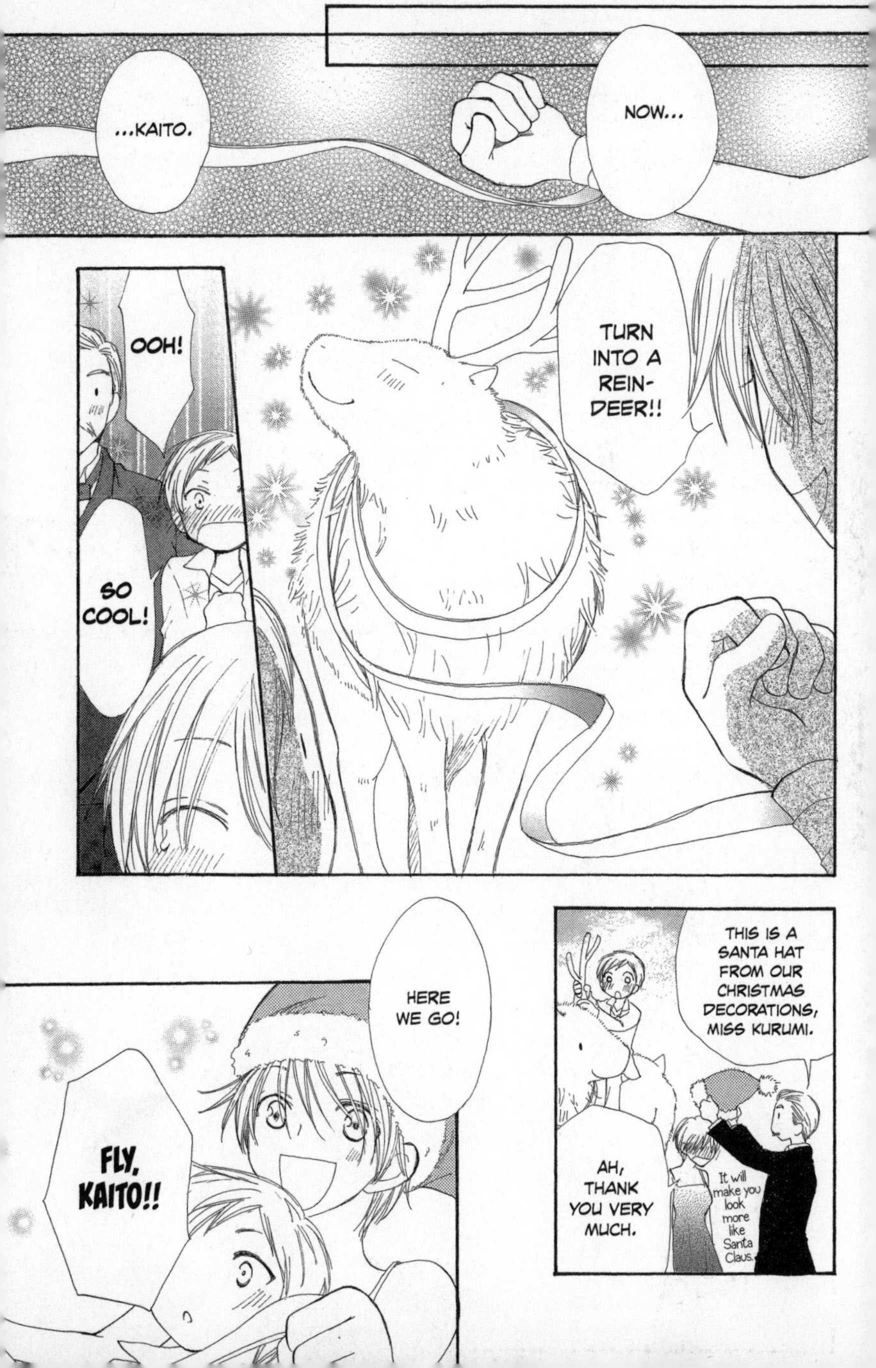
NOW...
...KAITO.
TURN INTO A REIN-DEER!!
OOH!
SO COOL!
THIS IS A SANTA HAT FROM OUR CHRISTMAS DECORATIONS, MISS KURUMI.
It will make you look more like Santa Claus.
AH, THANK YOU VERY MUCH.
HERE WE GO!
FLY, KAITO!!

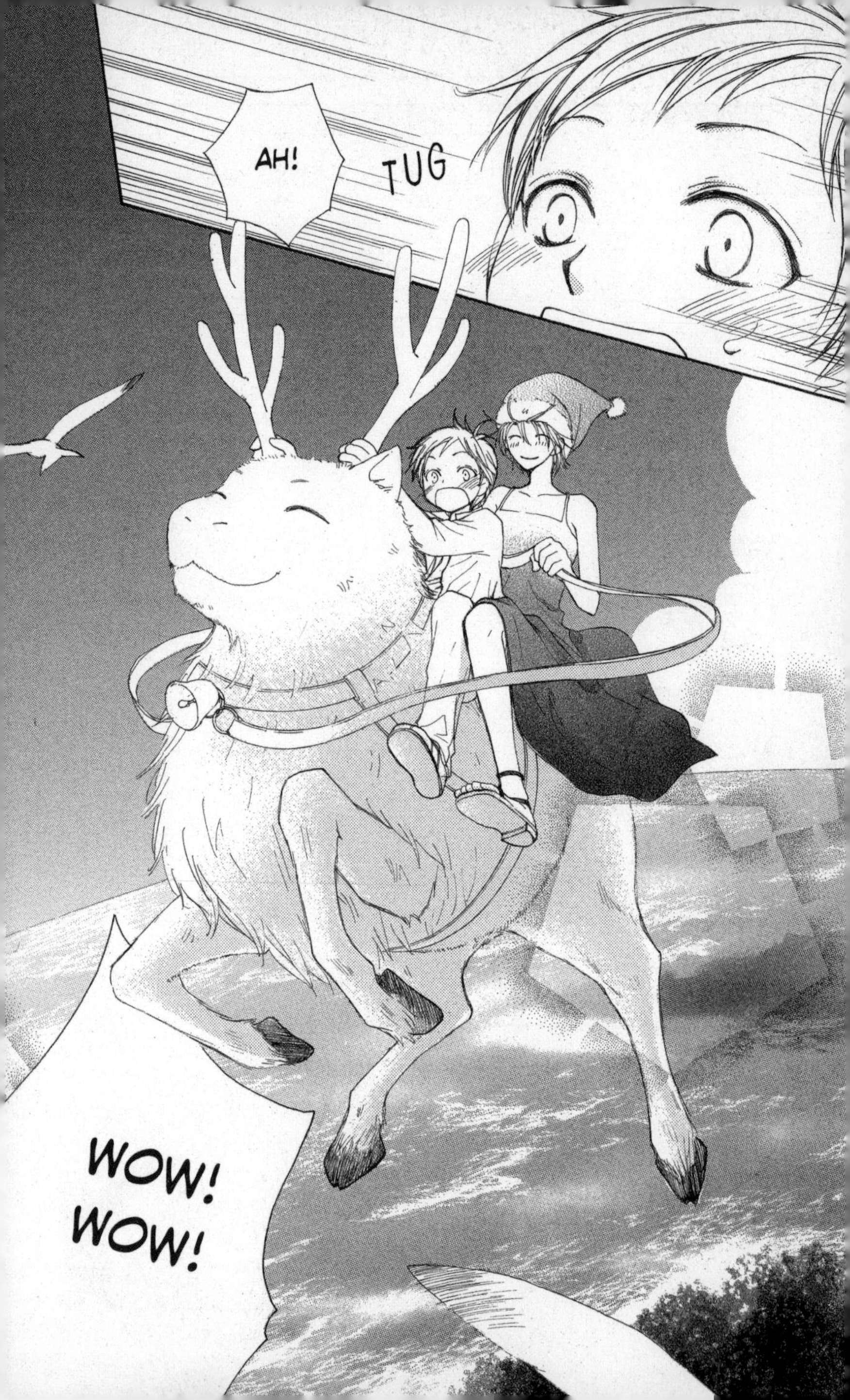
TUG
AH!
WOW! WOW!

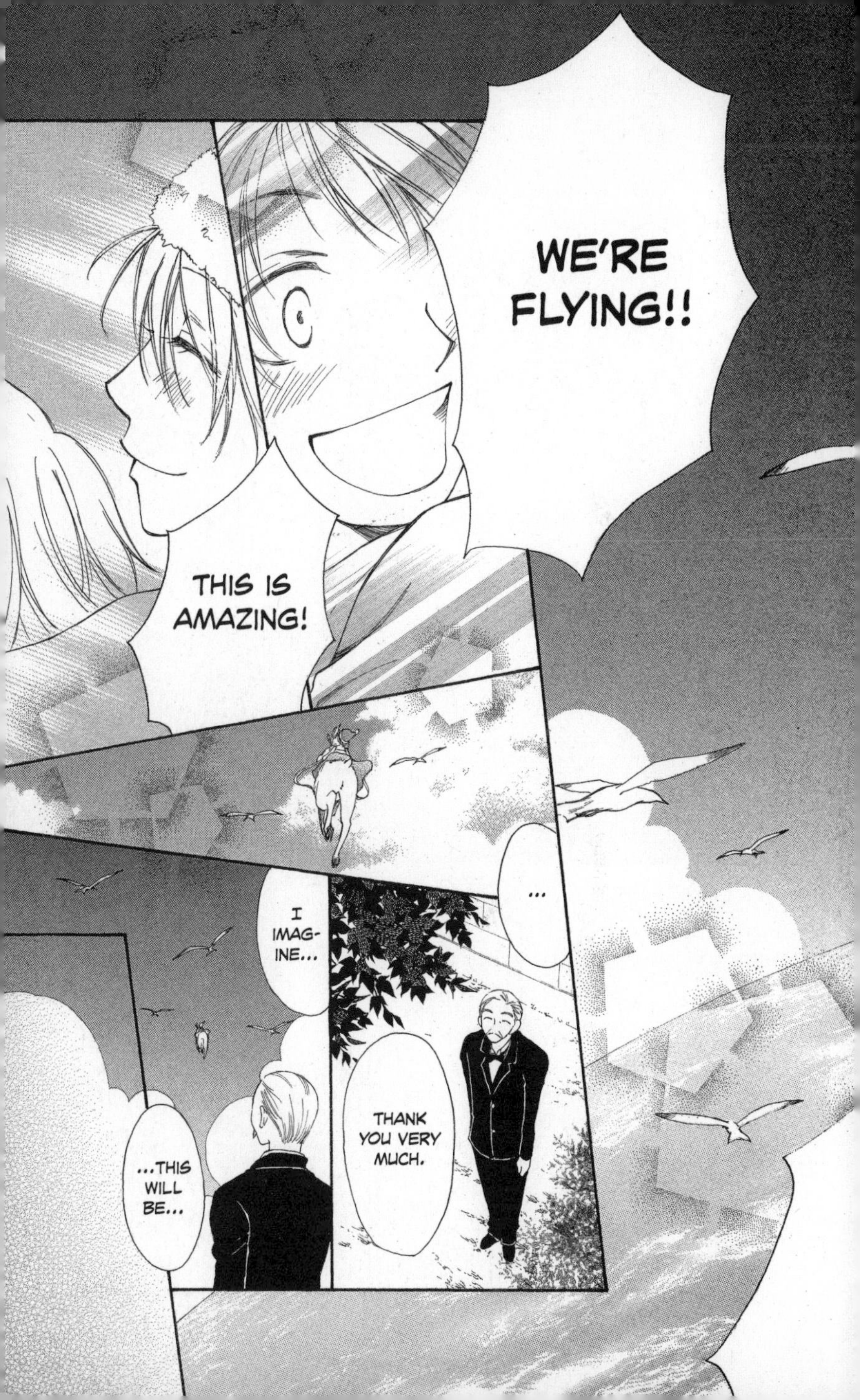
WE'RE FLYING!!
THIS IS AMAZING!
...
I IMAGINE...
THANK YOU VERY MUCH.
...THIS WILL BE...

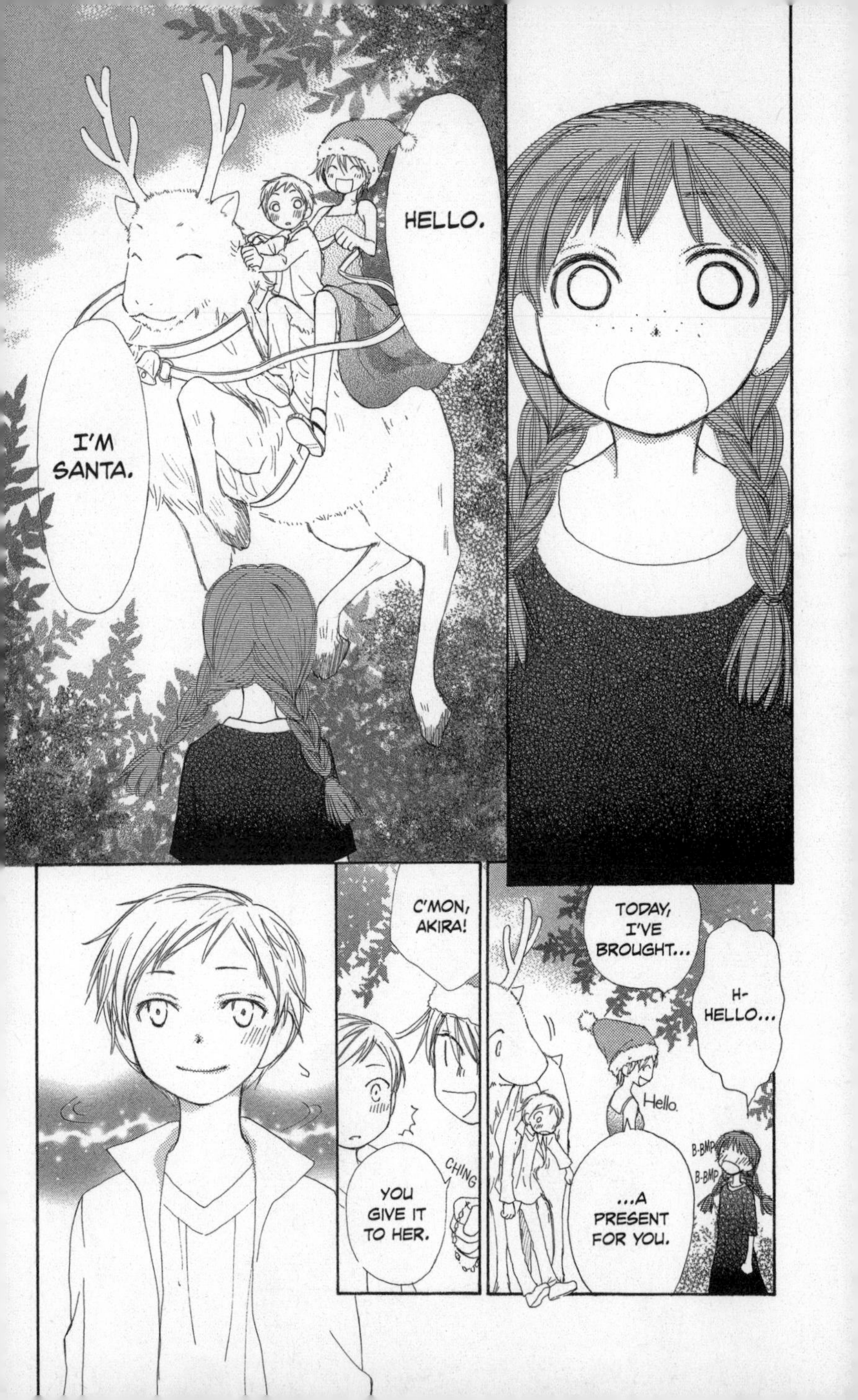
HELLO.
I'M SANTA.
TODAY, I'VE BROUGHT...
H- HELLO...
Hello.
B-BMP B-BMP
...A PRESENT FOR YOU.
C'MON, AKIRA!
CHING
YOU GIVE IT TO HER.

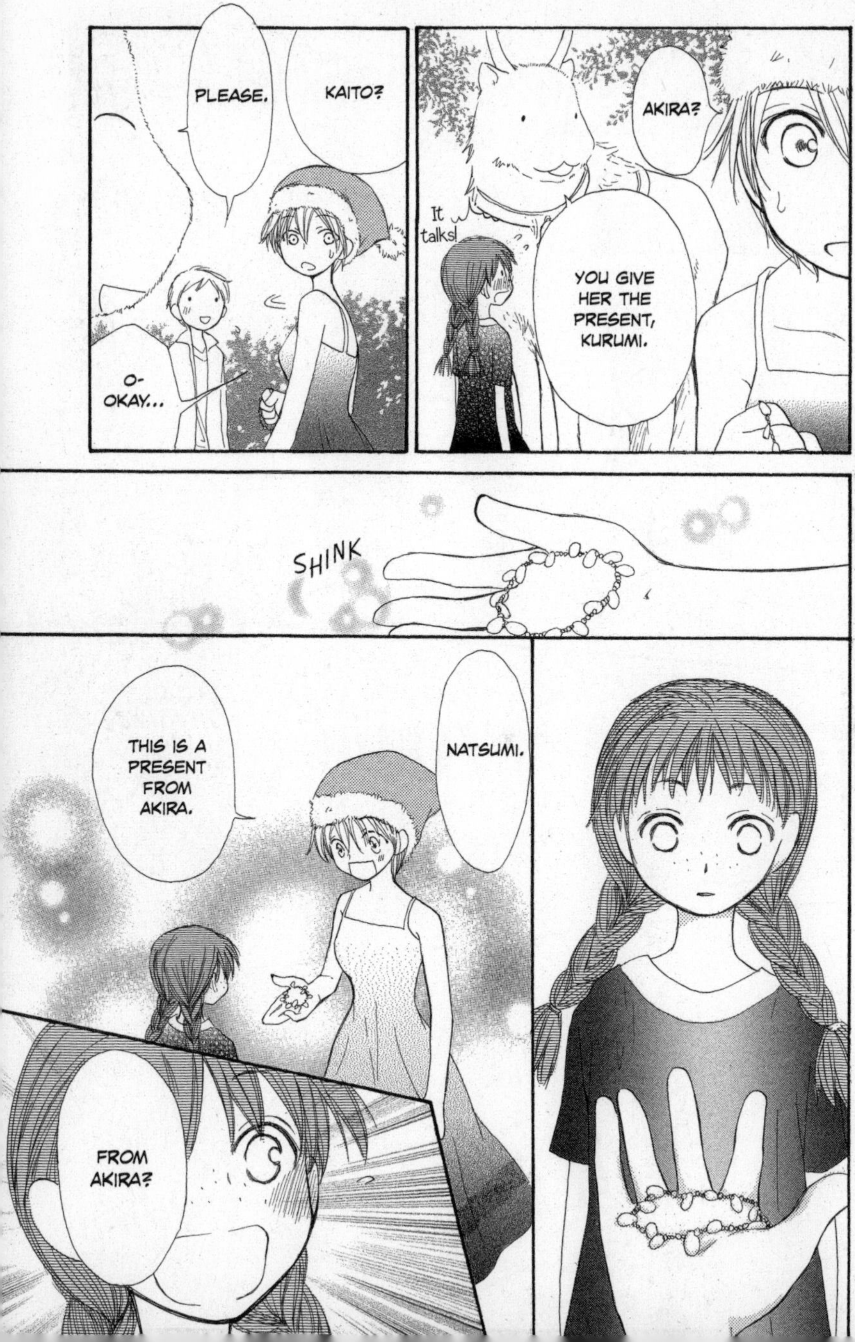
AKIRA?
YOU GIVE HER THE PRESENT, KURUMI.
It talks!
KAITO?
PLEASE.
O-OKAY...
SHINK
NATSUMI.
THIS IS A PRESENT FROM AKIRA.
FROM AKIRA?

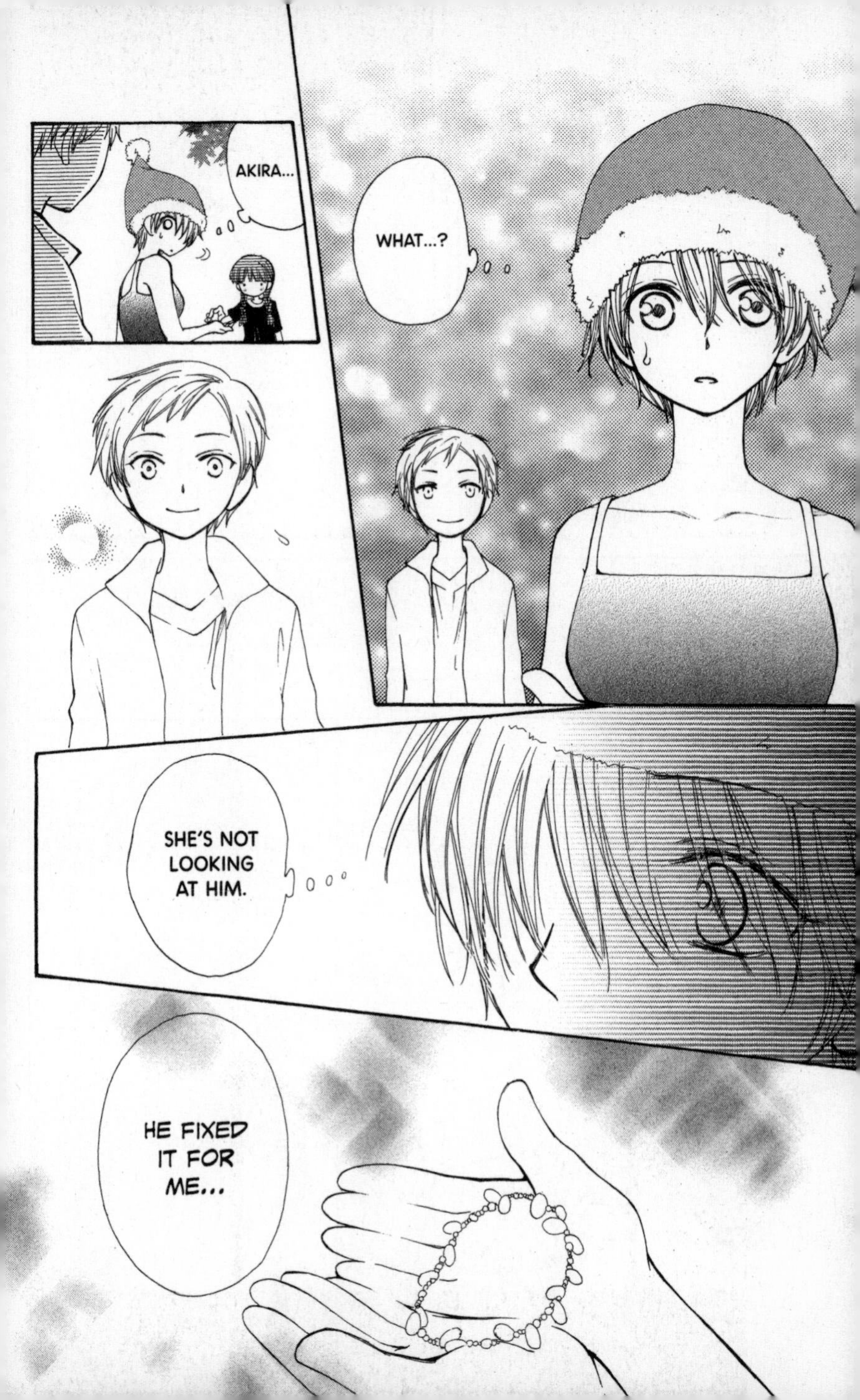
WHAT...?
AKIRA...
SHE'S NOT LOOKING AT HIM.
HE FIXED IT FOR ME...

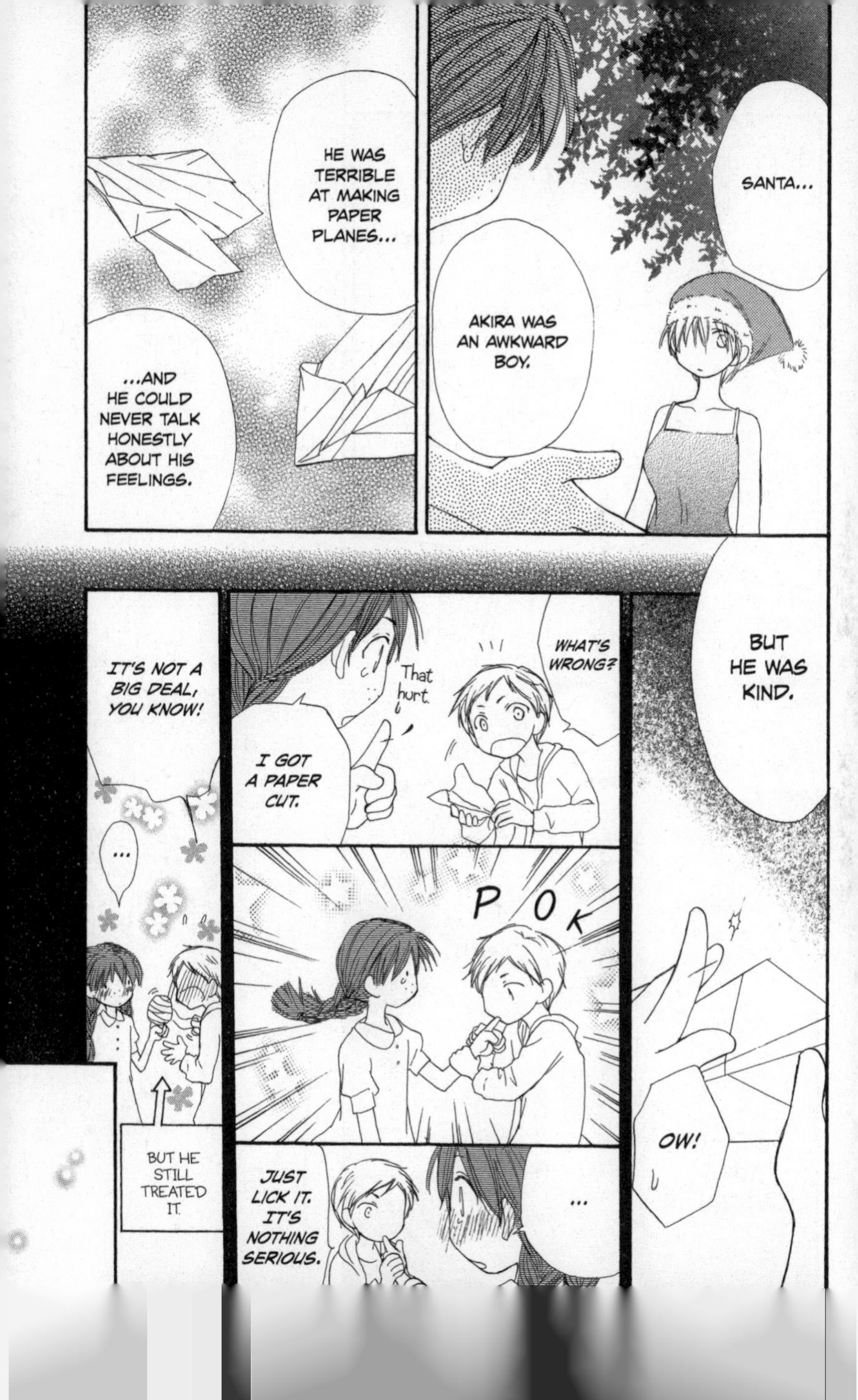

SANTA...
AKIRA WAS AN AWKWARD BOY.
HE WAS TERRIBLE AT MAKING PAPER PLANES...
...AND HE COULD NEVER TALK HONESTLY ABOUT HIS FEELINGS.
BUT HE WAS KIND.
OW!
WHAT'S WRONG?
That hurt.
I GOT A PAPER CUT.
POK
...
JUST LICK IT. IT'S NOTHING SERIOUS.
IT'S NOT A BIG DEAL, YOU KNOW!
...
BUT HE STILL TREATED IT.

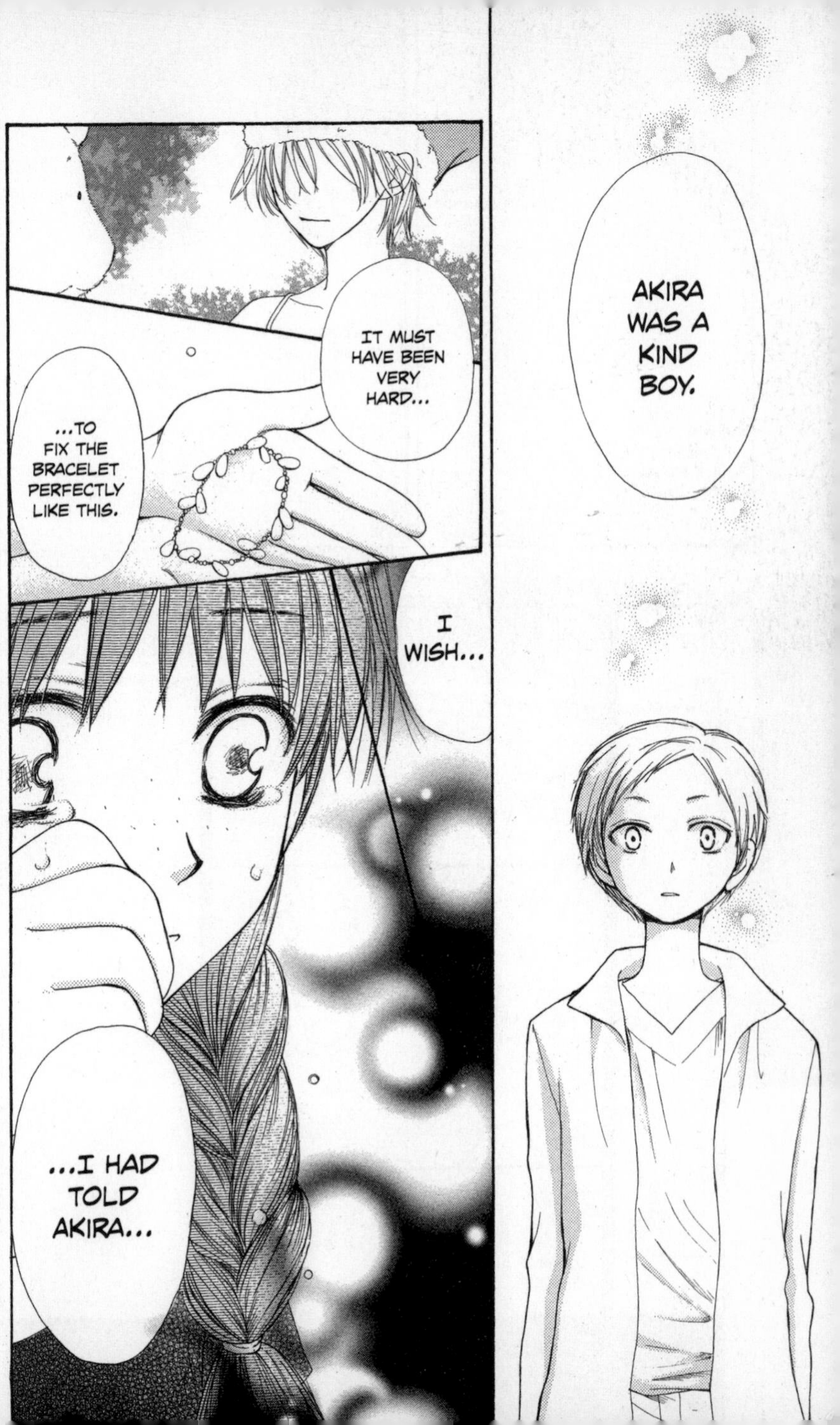
AKIRA WAS A KIND BOY.
IT MUST HAVE BEEN VERY HARD...
...TO FIX THE BRACELET PERFECTLY LIKE THIS.
I WISH...
...I HAD TOLD AKIRA...

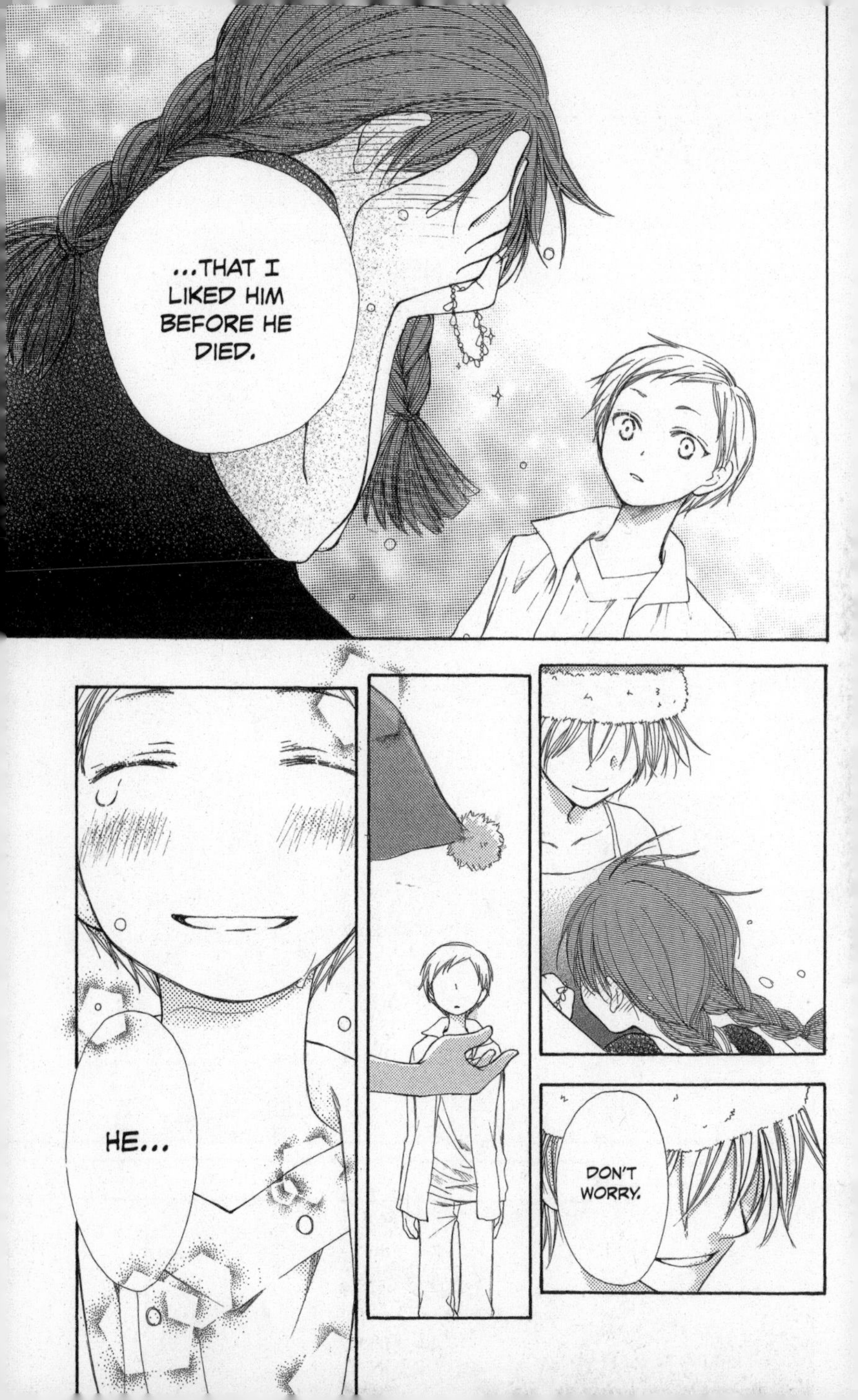
...THAT I LIKED HIM BEFORE HE DIED.
DON'T WORRY.
HE...

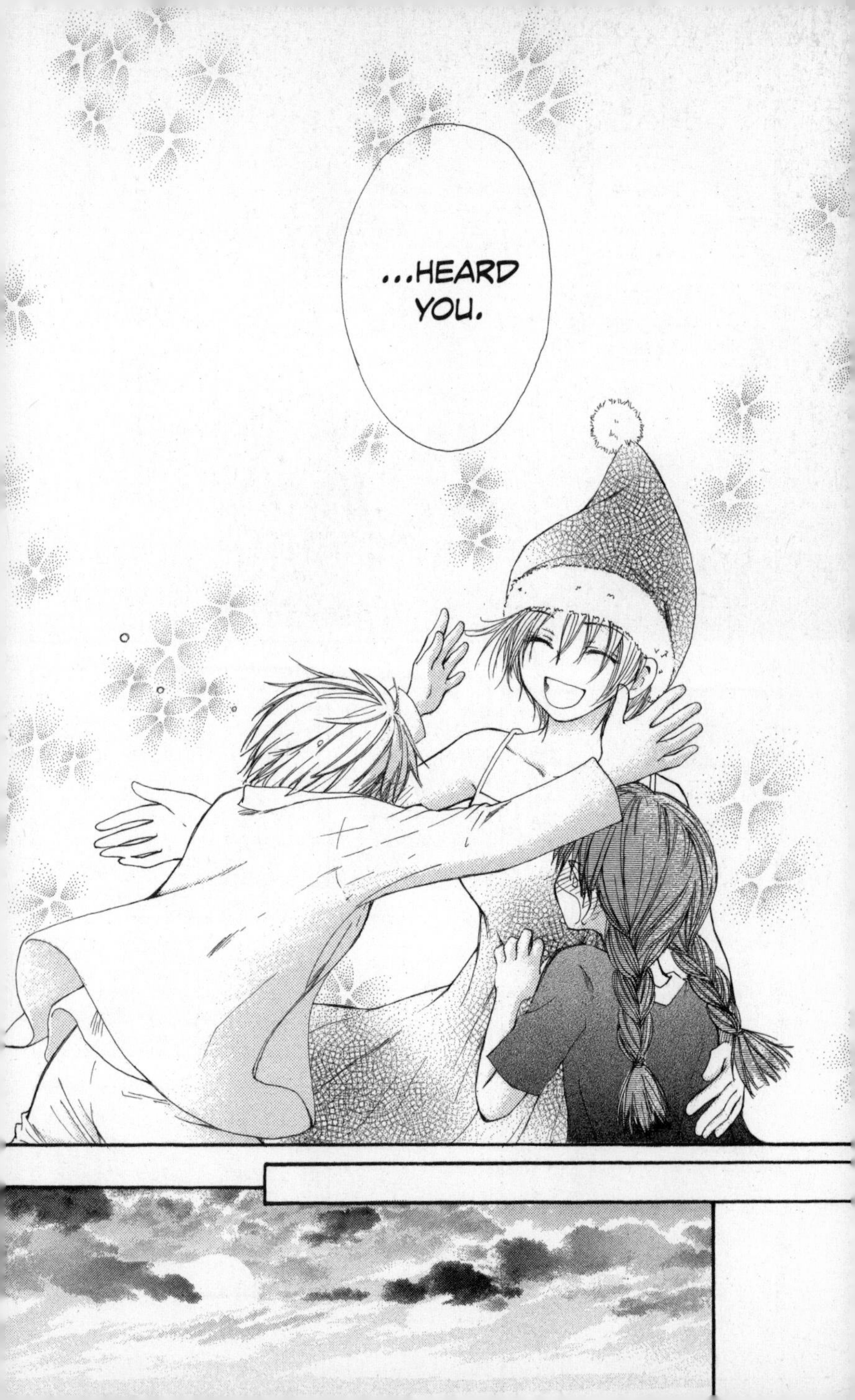
...HEARD YOU.

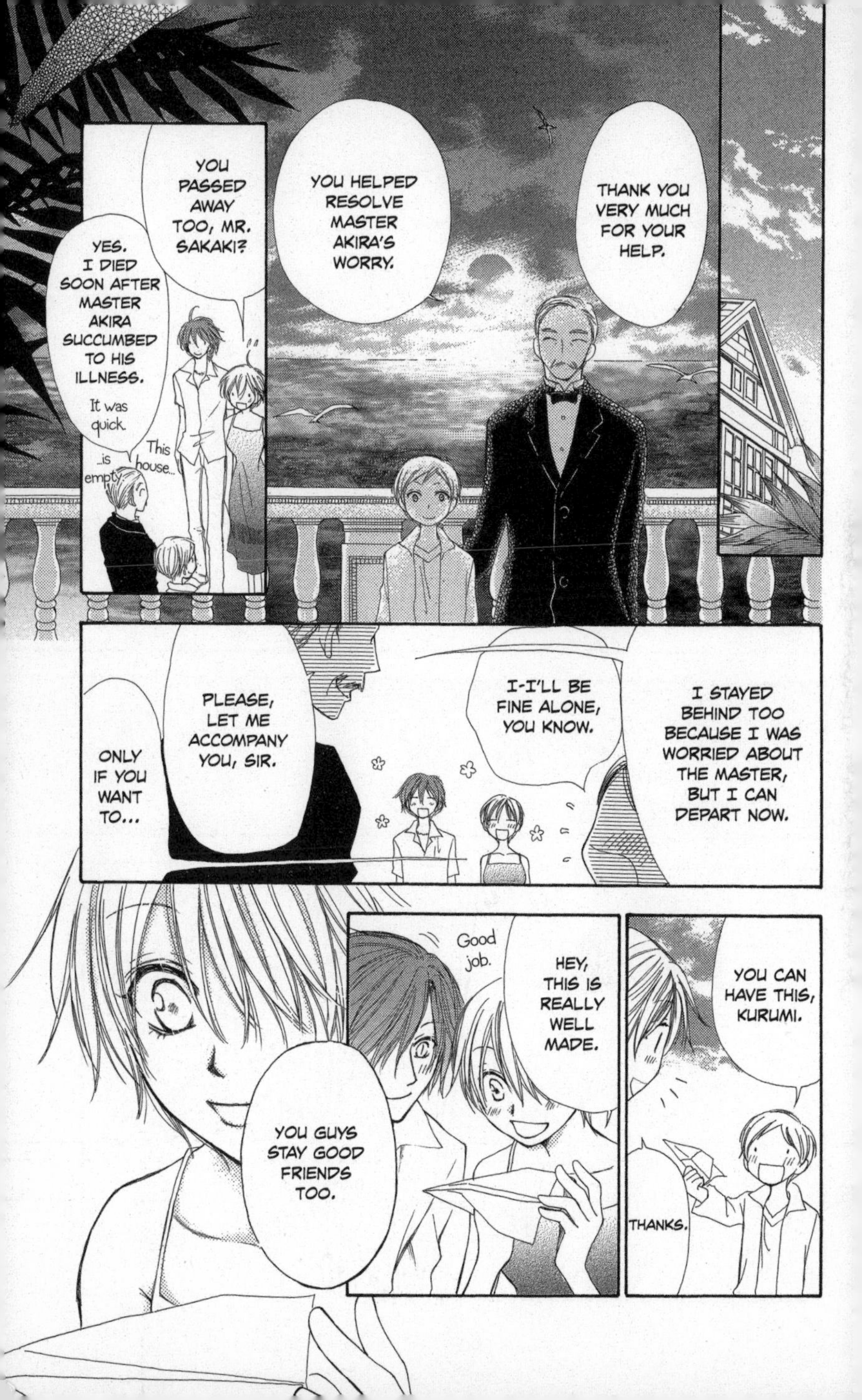
THANK YOU VERY MUCH FOR YOUR HELP.
YOU HELPED RESOLVE MASTER AKIRA'S WORRY.
YOU PASSED AWAY TOO, MR. SAKAKI?
YES. I DIED SOON AFTER MASTER AKIRA SUCCUMBED TO HIS ILLNESS.
It was quick.
This house...
...is empty.
I STAYED BEHIND TOO BECAUSE I WAS WORRIED ABOUT THE MASTER, BUT I CAN DEPART NOW.
I-I'LL BE FINE ALONE, YOU KNOW.
PLEASE, LET ME ACCOMPANY YOU, SIR.
ONLY IF YOU WANT TO...
YOU CAN HAVE THIS, KURUMI.
THANKS.
HEY, THIS IS REALLY WELL MADE.
Good job.
YOU GUYS STAY GOOD FRIENDS TOO.

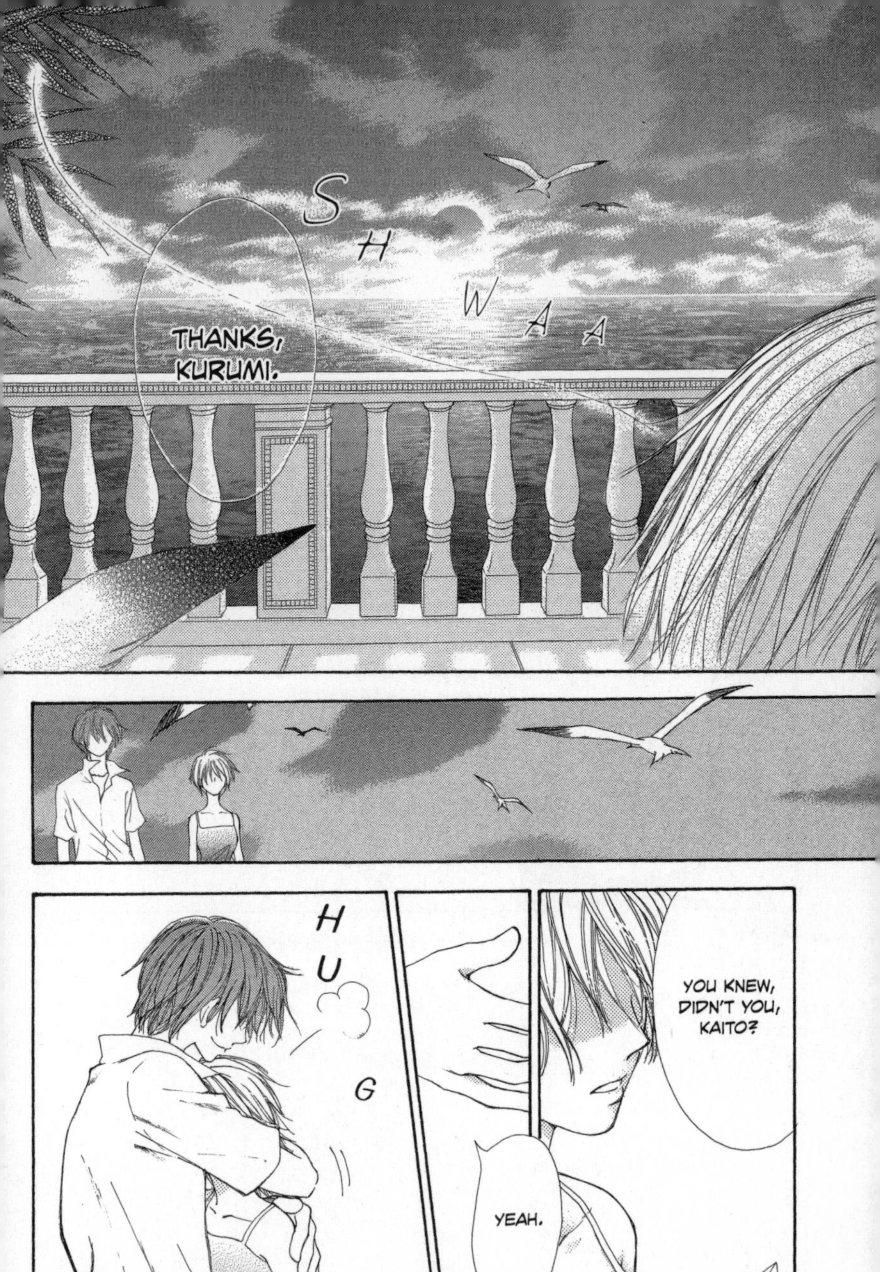
SHWAA
THANKS, KURUMI.
YOU KNEW, DIDN'T YOU, KAITO?
YEAH.
HUG

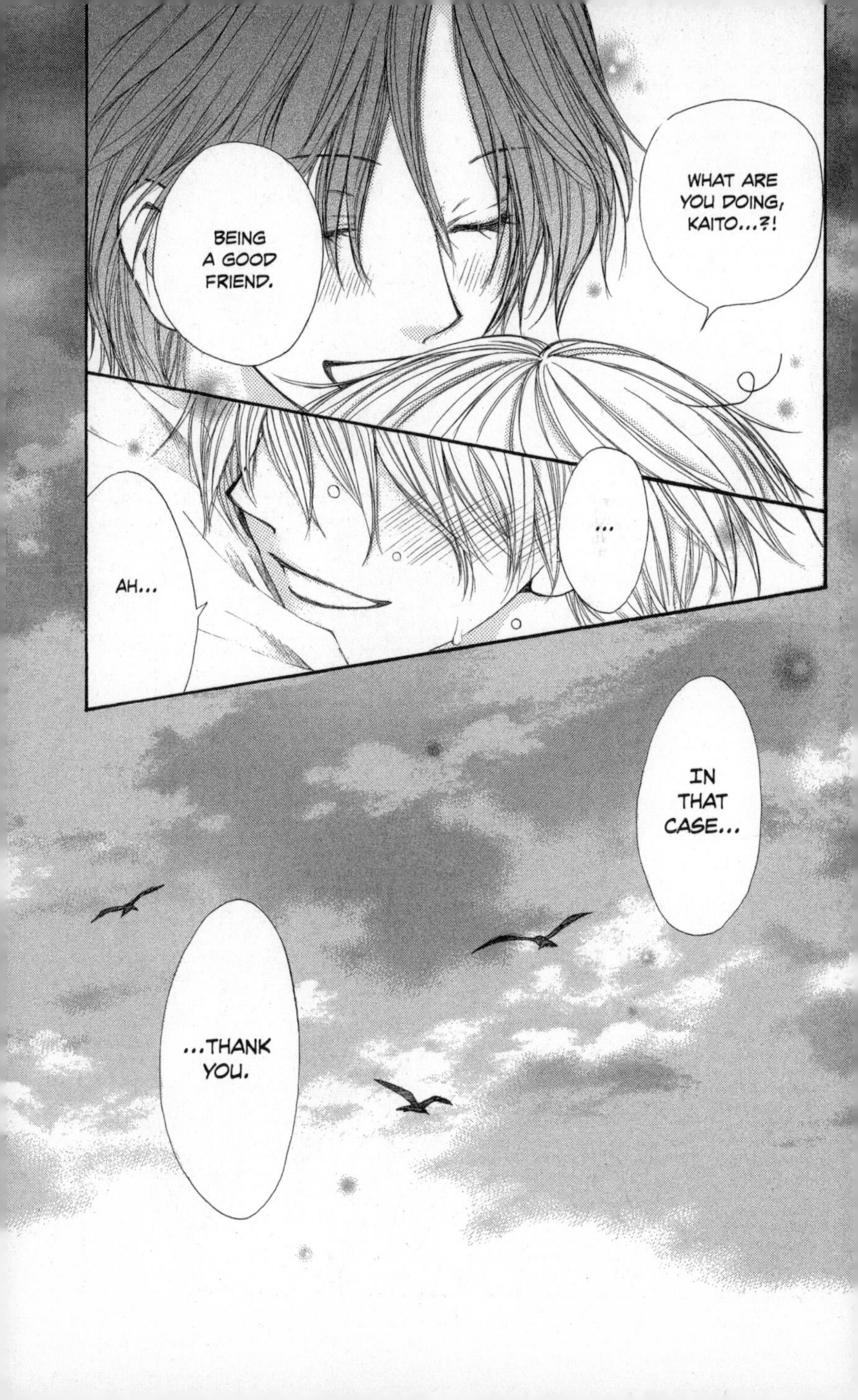
WHAT ARE YOU DOING, KAITO...?!
BEING A GOOD FRIEND.
...
AH...
IN THAT CASE...
...THANK YOU.

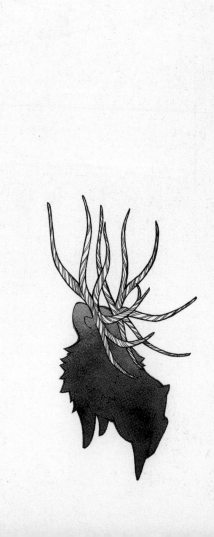

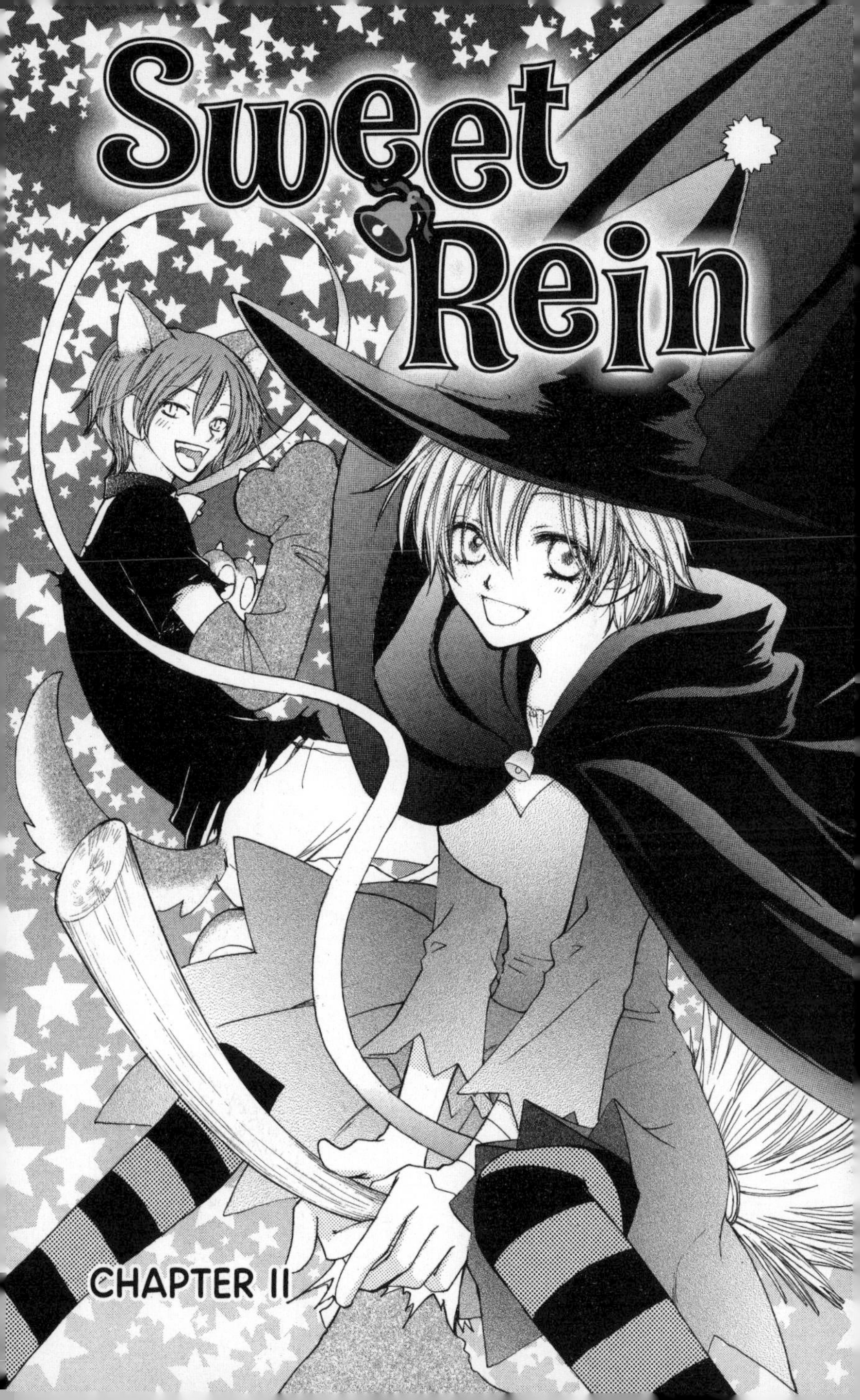
Sweet Rein
CHAPTER 11

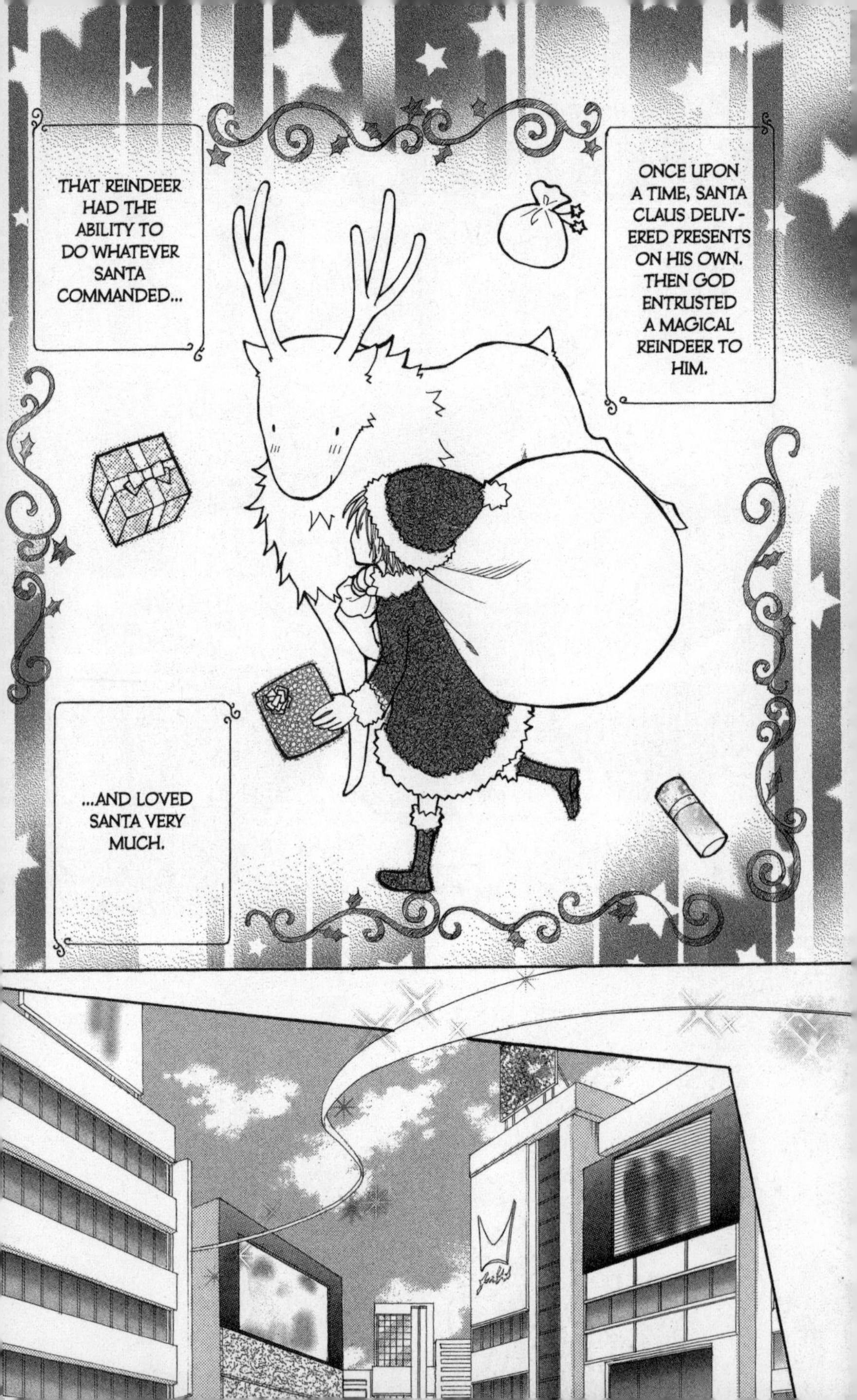
ONCE UPON A TIME, SANTA CLAUS DELIVERED PRESENTS ON HIS OWN. THEN GOD ENTRUSTED A MAGICAL REINDEER TO HIM.
THAT REINDEER HAD THE ABILITY TO DO WHATEVER SANTA COMMANDED...
...AND LOVED SANTA VERY MUCH.

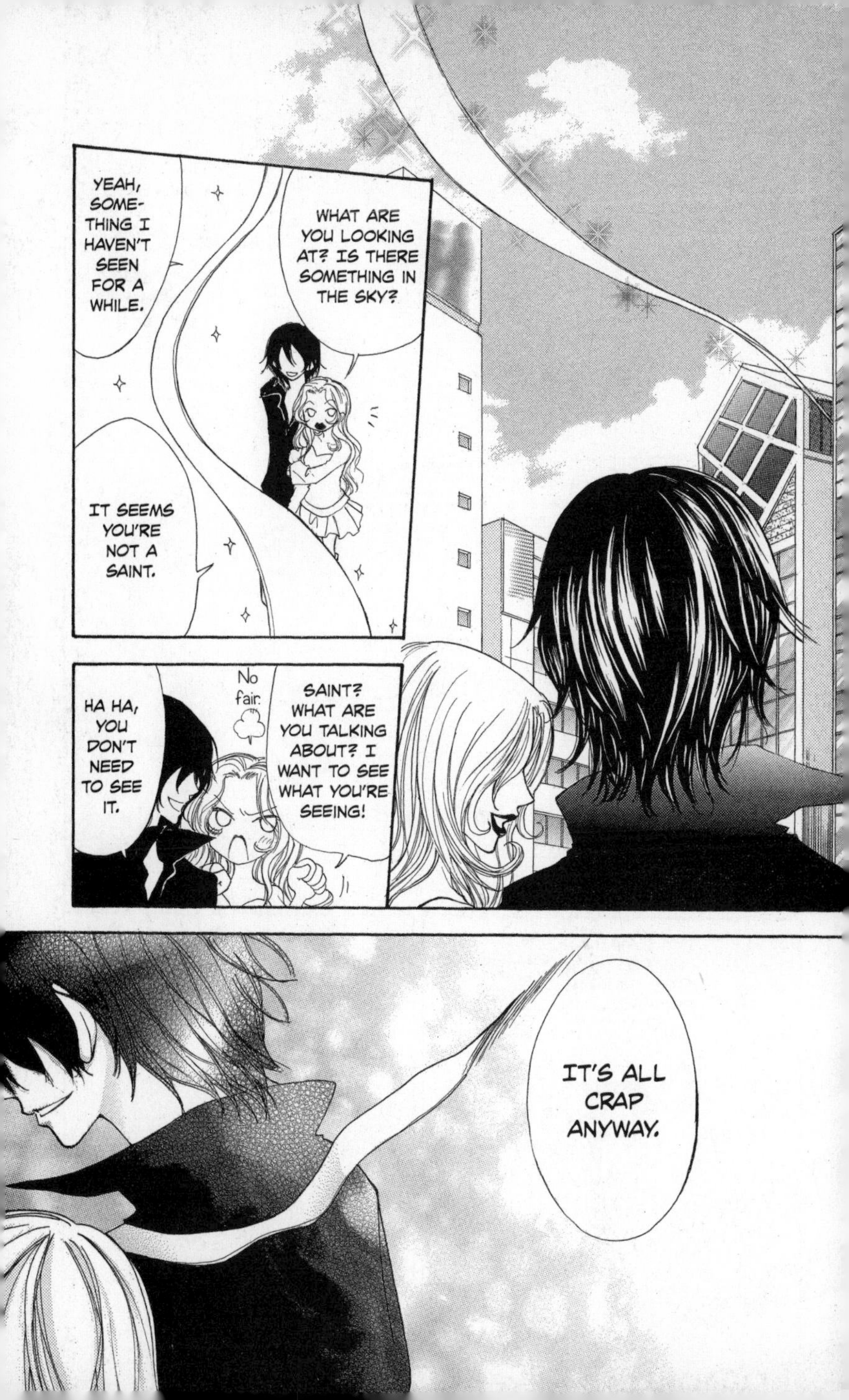
WHAT ARE YOU LOOKING AT? IS THERE SOMETHING IN THE SKY?
YEAH, SOME-THING I HAVEN'T SEEN FOR A WHILE.
IT SEEMS YOU'RE NOT A SAINT.
SAINT? WHAT ARE YOU TALKING ABOUT? I WANT TO SEE WHAT YOU'RE SEEING!
No fair.
HA HA, YOU DON'T NEED TO SEE IT.
IT'S ALL CRAP ANYWAY.

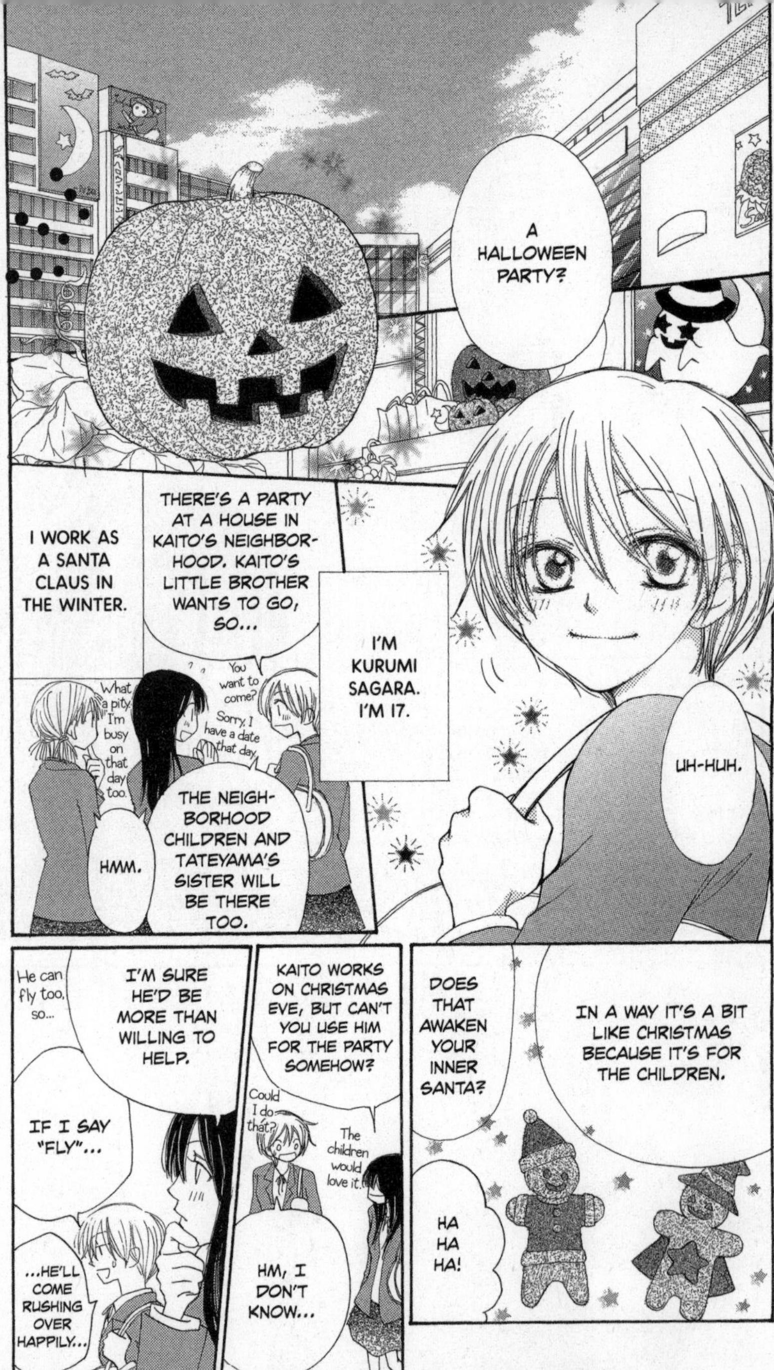
A HALLOWEEN PARTY?
UH-HUH.
I'M KURUMI SAGARA. I'M 17.
THERE'S A PARTY AT A HOUSE IN KAITO'S NEIGHBORHOOD. KAITO'S LITTLE BROTHER WANTS TO GO, SO...
I WORK AS A SANTA CLAUS IN THE WINTER.
You want to come?
Sorry, I have a date that day.
What a pity. I'm busy on that day too.
THE NEIGHBORHOOD CHILDREN AND TATEYAMA'S SISTER WILL BE THERE TOO.
HMM.
IN A WAY IT'S A BIT LIKE CHRISTMAS BECAUSE IT'S FOR THE CHILDREN.
DOES THAT AWAKEN YOUR INNER SANTA?
HA HA HA!
KAITO WORKS ON CHRISTMAS EVE, BUT CAN'T YOU USE HIM FOR THE PARTY SOMEHOW?
Could I do that?
The children would love it.
HM, I DON'T KNOW...
I'M SURE HE'D BE MORE THAN WILLING TO HELP.
He can fly too, so...
IF I SAY "FLY"...
...HE'LL COME RUSHING OVER HAPPILY...

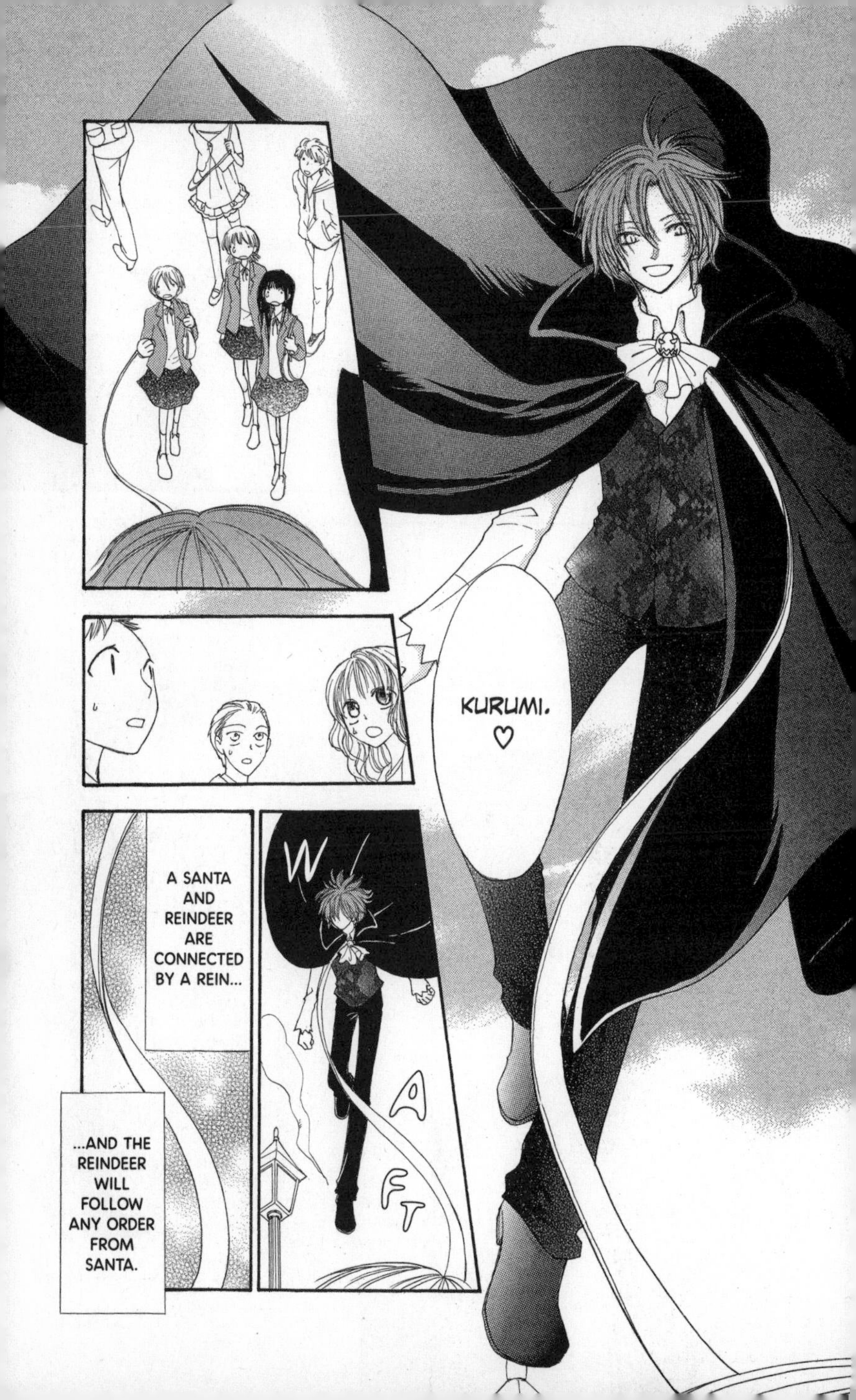
KURUMI. ♡
WAFT
A SANTA AND REINDEER ARE CONNECTED BY A REIN...
...AND THE REINDEER WILL FOLLOW ANY ORDER FROM SANTA.

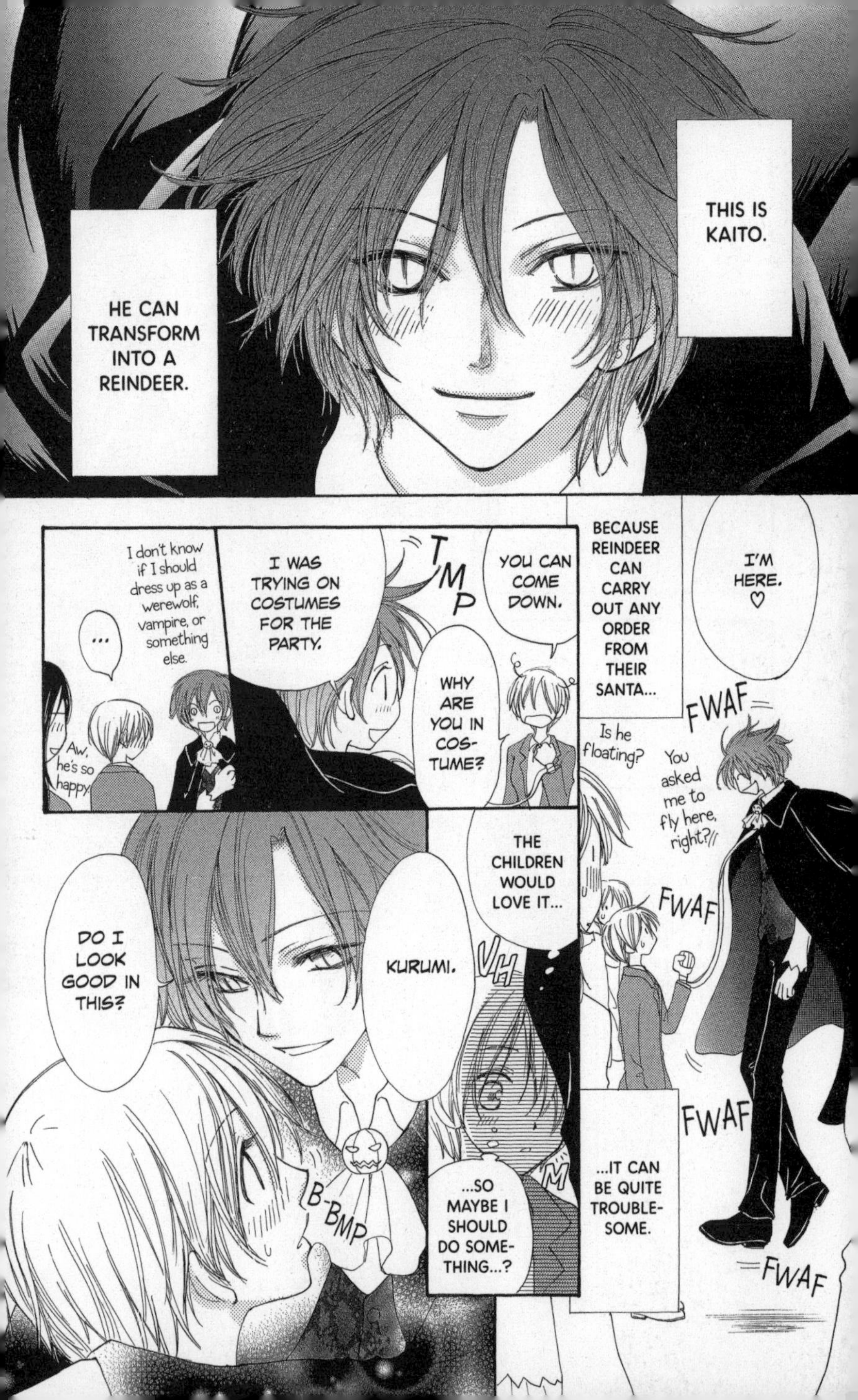
THIS IS KAITO.
HE CAN TRANSFORM INTO A REINDEER.
I'M HERE. ♡
BECAUSE REINDEER CAN CARRY OUT ANY ORDER FROM THEIR SANTA...
FWAF
Is he floating?
You asked me to fly here, right?
FWAF
FWAF
...IT CAN BE QUITE TROUBLESOME.
FWAF
YOU CAN COME DOWN.
TMP
WHY ARE YOU IN COS-TUME?
I WAS TRYING ON COSTUMES FOR THE PARTY.
I don't know if I should dress up as a werewolf, vampire, or something else.
...
Aw, he's so happy
THE CHILDREN WOULD LOVE IT...
VH
...SO MAYBE I SHOULD DO SOME-THING...?
M
KURUMI.
DO I LOOK GOOD IN THIS?
B-BMP

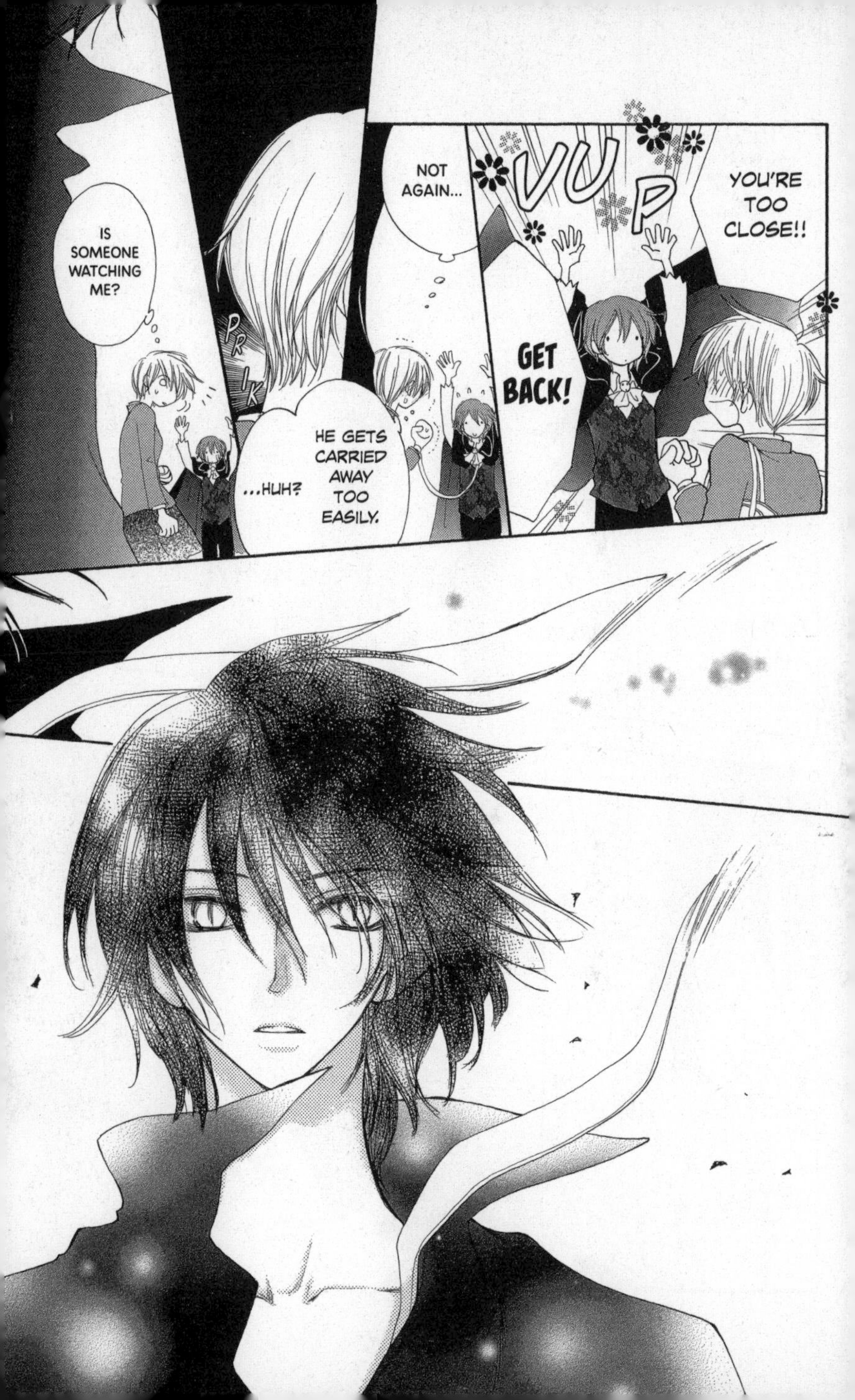
VUP
YOU'RE TOO CLOSE!!
GET BACK!
NOT AGAIN...
HE GETS CARRIED AWAY TOO EASILY.
PRIK
...HUH?
IS SOMEONE WATCHING ME?

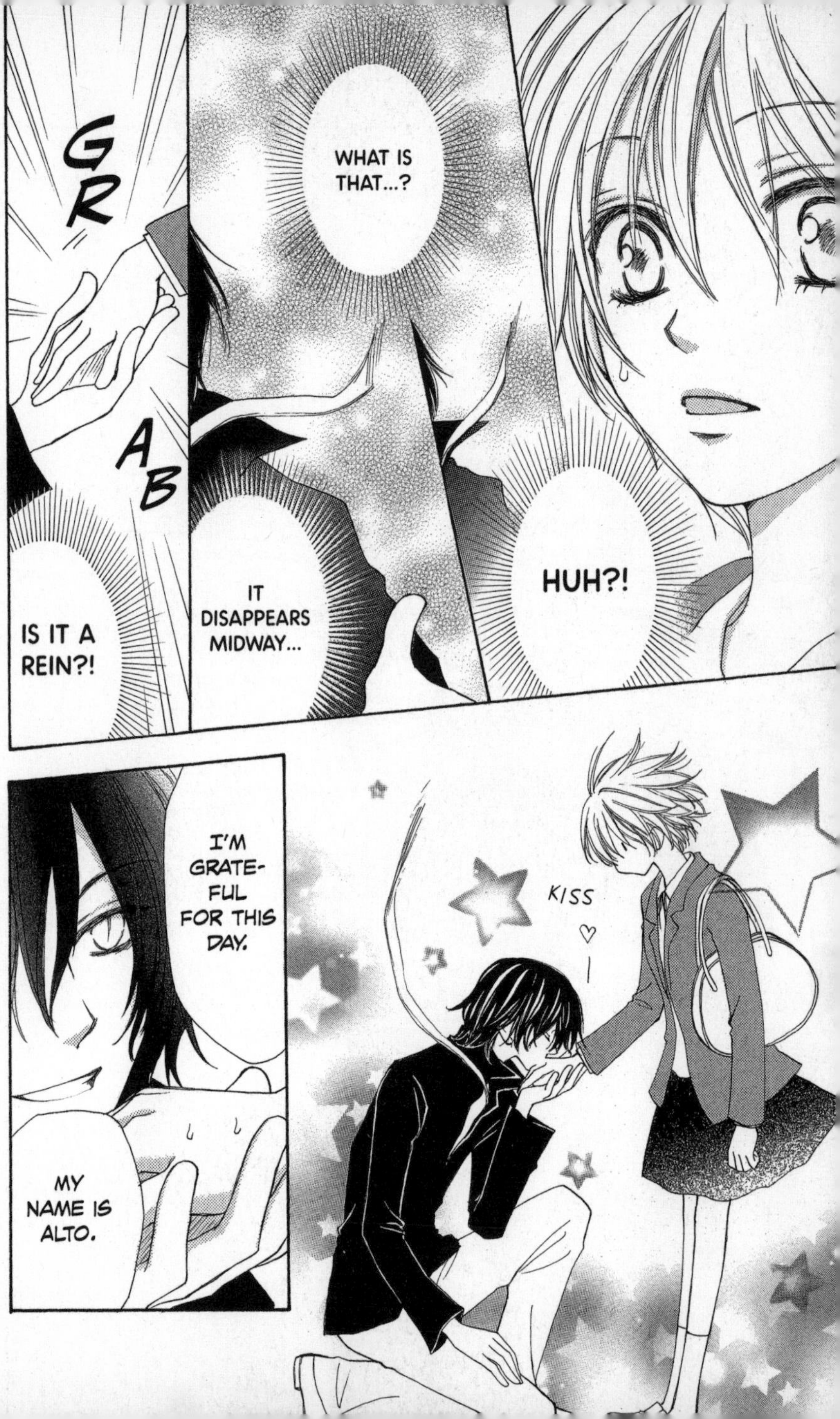
HUH?!
WHAT IS THAT...?
IT DISAPPEARS MIDWAY...
GRAB
IS IT A REIN?!
KISS
I'M GRATEFUL FOR THIS DAY.
MY NAME IS ALTO.

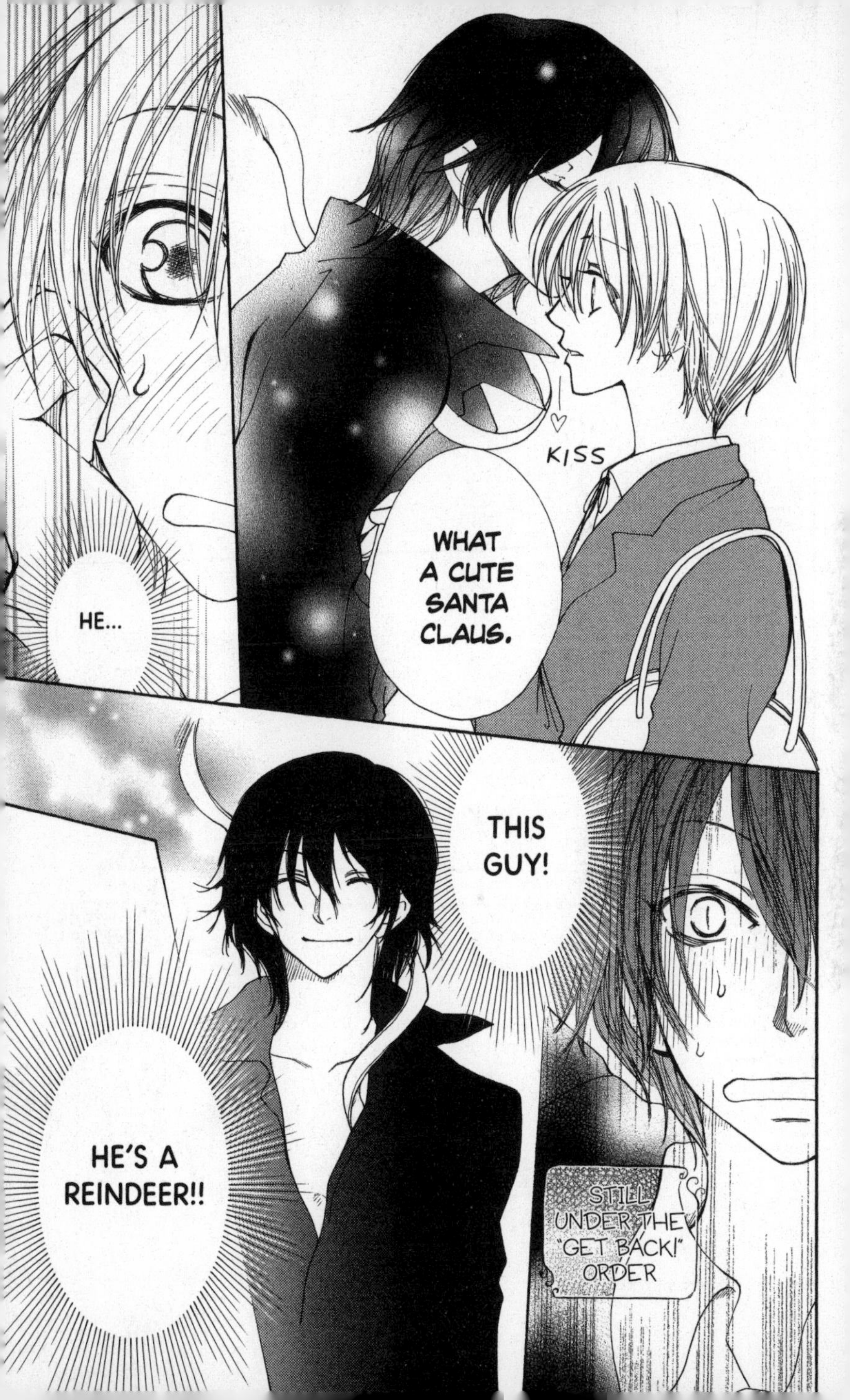
KISS
WHAT A CUTE SANTA CLAUS.
HE...
THIS GUY!
STILL UNDER THE "GET BACK!" ORDER
HE'S A REINDEER!!

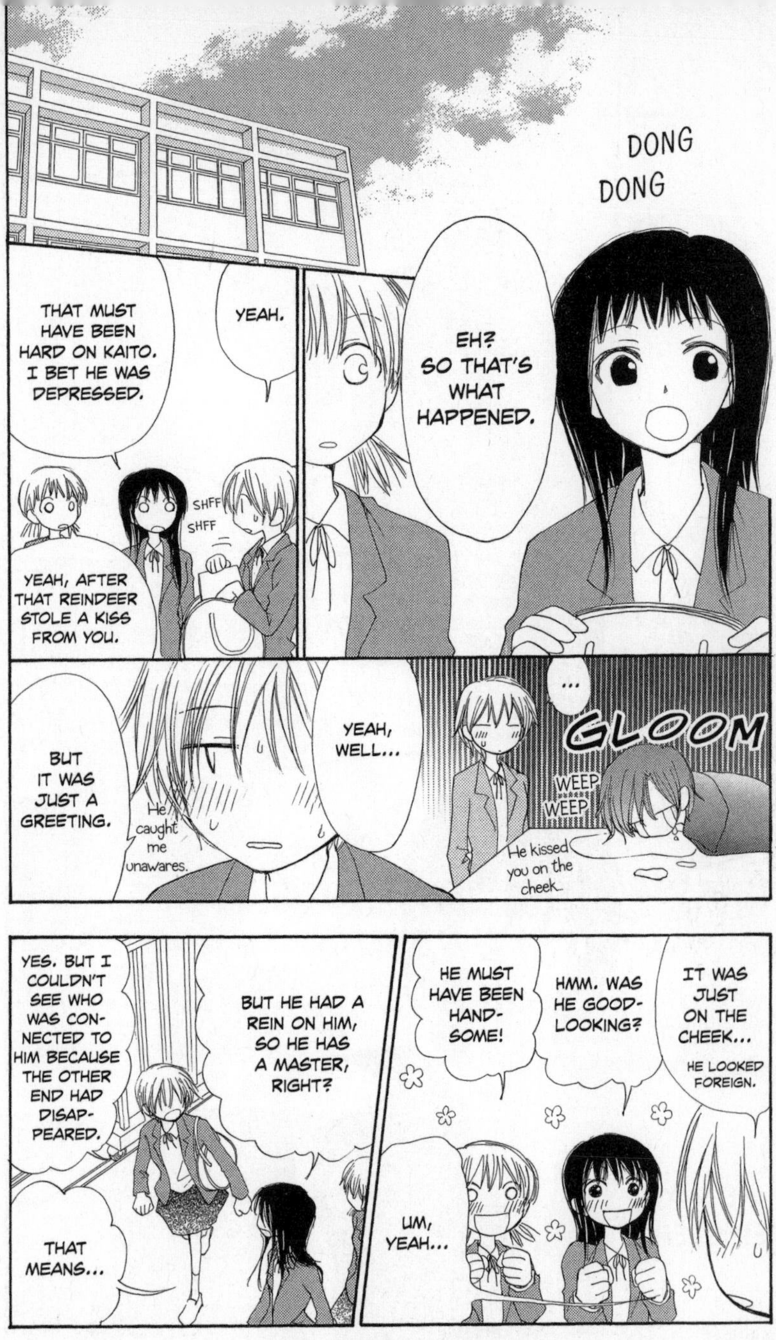
DONG DONG
EH? SO THAT'S WHAT HAPPENED.
YEAH.
THAT MUST HAVE BEEN HARD ON KAITO. I BET HE WAS DEPRESSED.
SHFF SHFF
YEAH, AFTER THAT REINDEER STOLE A KISS FROM YOU.
...
GLOOM
WEEP WEEP
He kissed you on the cheek...
YEAH, WELL...
BUT IT WAS JUST A GREETING.
He caught me unawares.
IT WAS JUST ON THE CHEEK...
HE LOOKED FOREIGN.
HMM. WAS HE GOOD-LOOKING?
HE MUST HAVE BEEN HAND-SOME!
UM, YEAH...
BUT HE HAD A REIN ON HIM, SO HE HAS A MASTER, RIGHT?
YES. BUT I COULDN'T SEE WHO WAS CON-NECTED TO HIM BECAUSE THE OTHER END HAD DISAP-PEARED.
THAT MEANS...

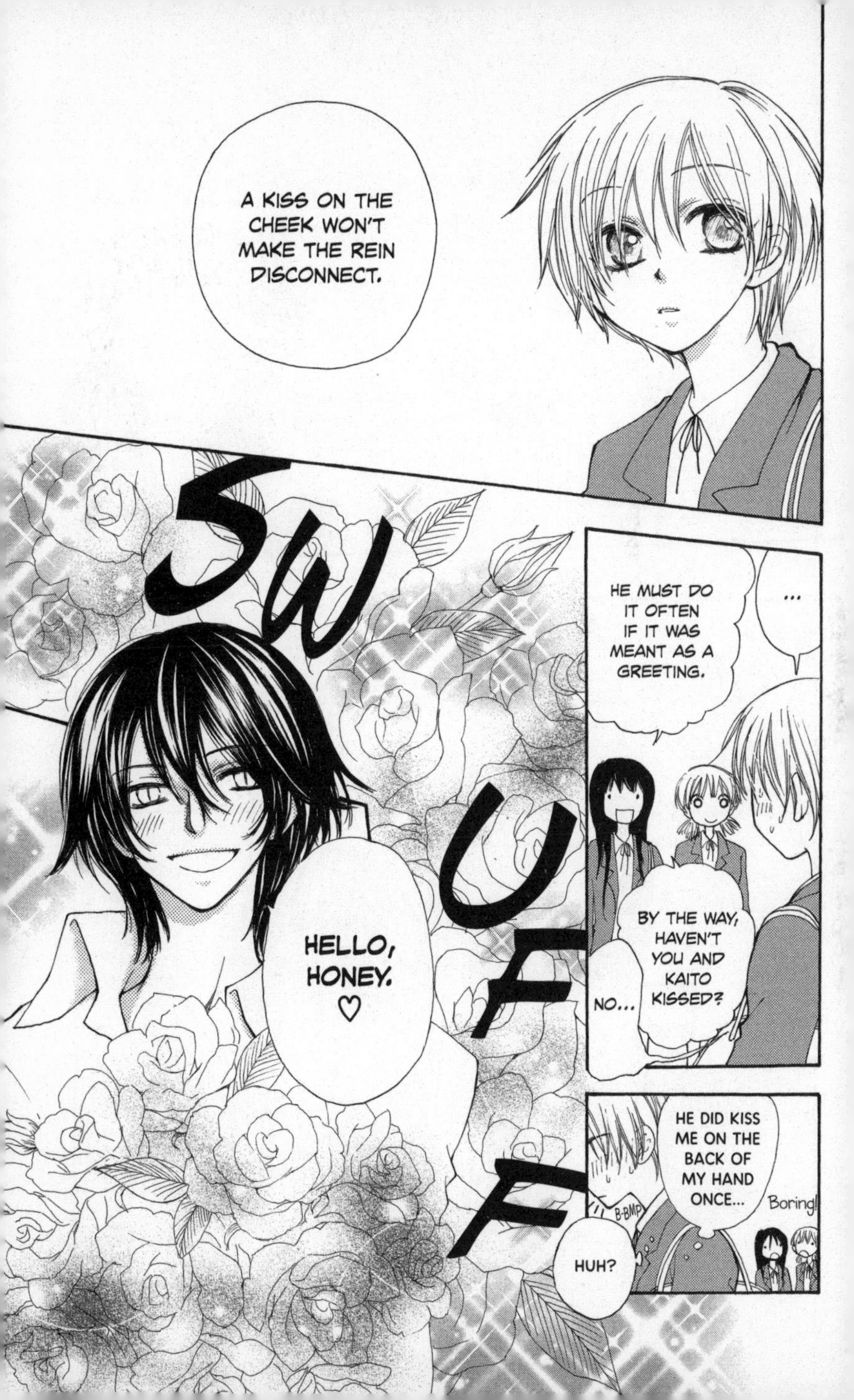
A KISS ON THE CHEEK WON'T MAKE THE REIN DISCONNECT.
...
HE MUST DO IT OFTEN IF IT WAS MEANT AS A GREETING.
BY THE WAY, HAVEN'T YOU AND KAITO KISSED?
NO...
HE DID KISS ME ON THE BACK OF MY HAND ONCE...
Boring!
B-BMP
HUH?
SWUFF
HELLO, HONEY. ♡

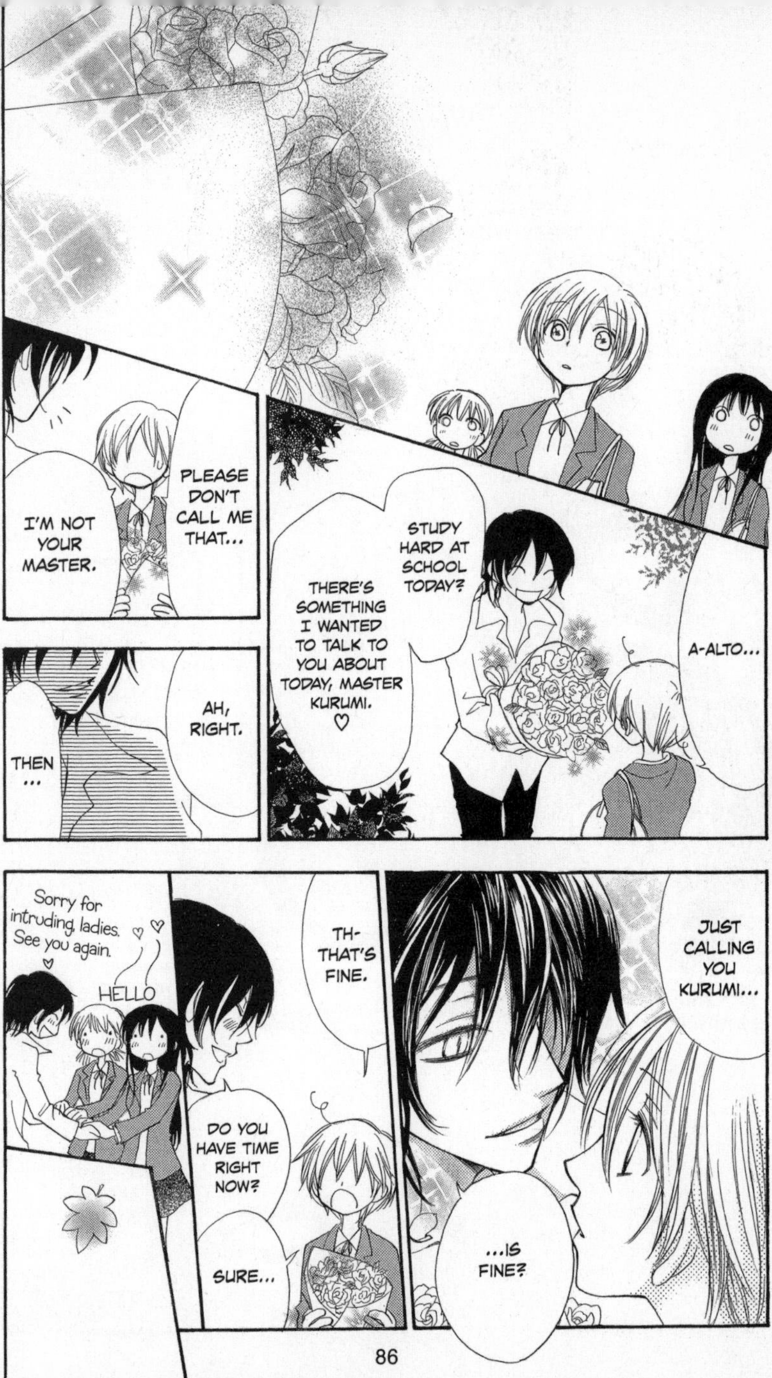
A-ALTO...
STUDY HARD AT SCHOOL TODAY?
THERE'S SOMETHING I WANTED TO TALK TO YOU ABOUT TODAY, MASTER KURUMI. ♡
PLEASE DON'T CALL ME THAT...
I'M NOT YOUR MASTER.
AH, RIGHT.
THEN...
JUST CALLING YOU KURUMI...
...IS FINE?
TH-THAT'S FINE.
DO YOU HAVE TIME RIGHT NOW?
SURE...
Sorry for intruding, ladies. See you again. ♡
HELLO

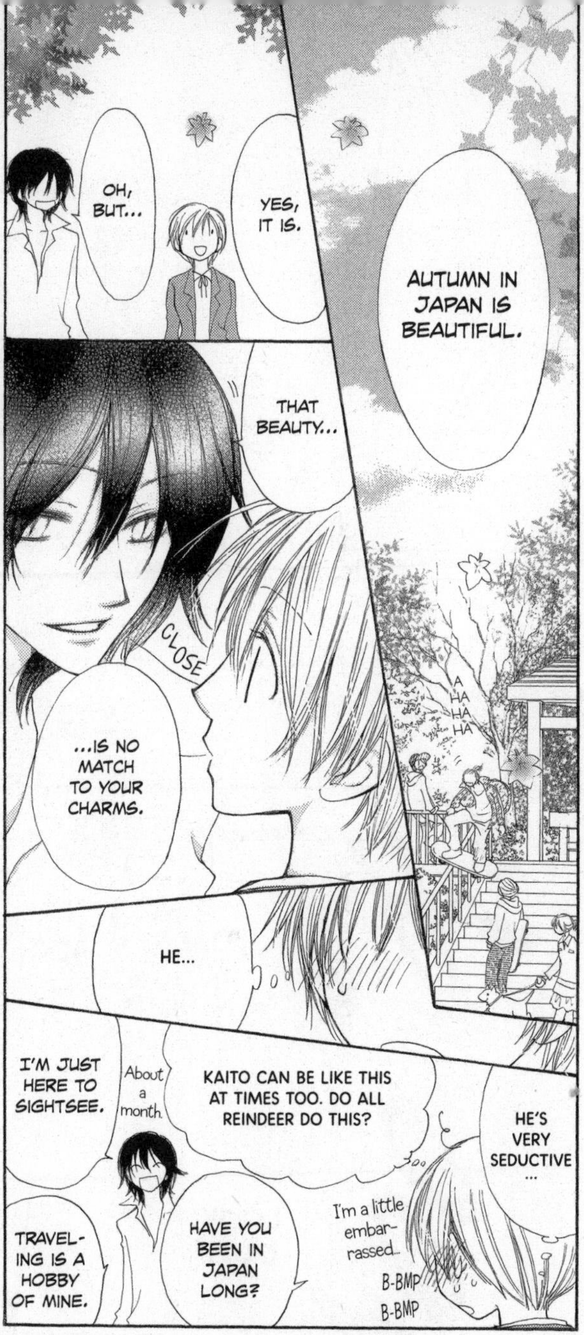
AUTUMN IN JAPAN IS BEAUTIFUL.
A HA HA HA
YES, IT IS.
OH, BUT...
THAT BEAUTY...
CLOSE
...IS NO MATCH TO YOUR CHARMS.
HE...
HE'S VERY SEDUCTIVE...
KAITO CAN BE LIKE THIS AT TIMES TOO. DO ALL REINDEER DO THIS?
I'm a little embarrassed...
B-BMP
B-BMP
HAVE YOU BEEN IN JAPAN LONG?
About a month.
I'M JUST HERE TO SIGHTSEE.
TRAVELING IS A HOBBY OF MINE.

1/4 Sakura Mail

Part 6

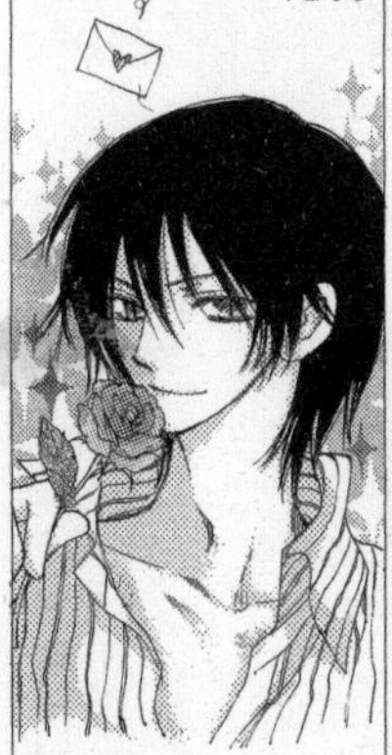

Autumn has arrived!! And when we talk about autumn, we must talk about autumn leaves! Halloween!! Costumes!!! Capes!!!! Hurray, capes!! Um... I love capes, you see! A fluttering cape excites me like a bull in a bullfight!! I like werewolves too, but I just had to go with the vampire costume here! Because of the cape!! Capes!

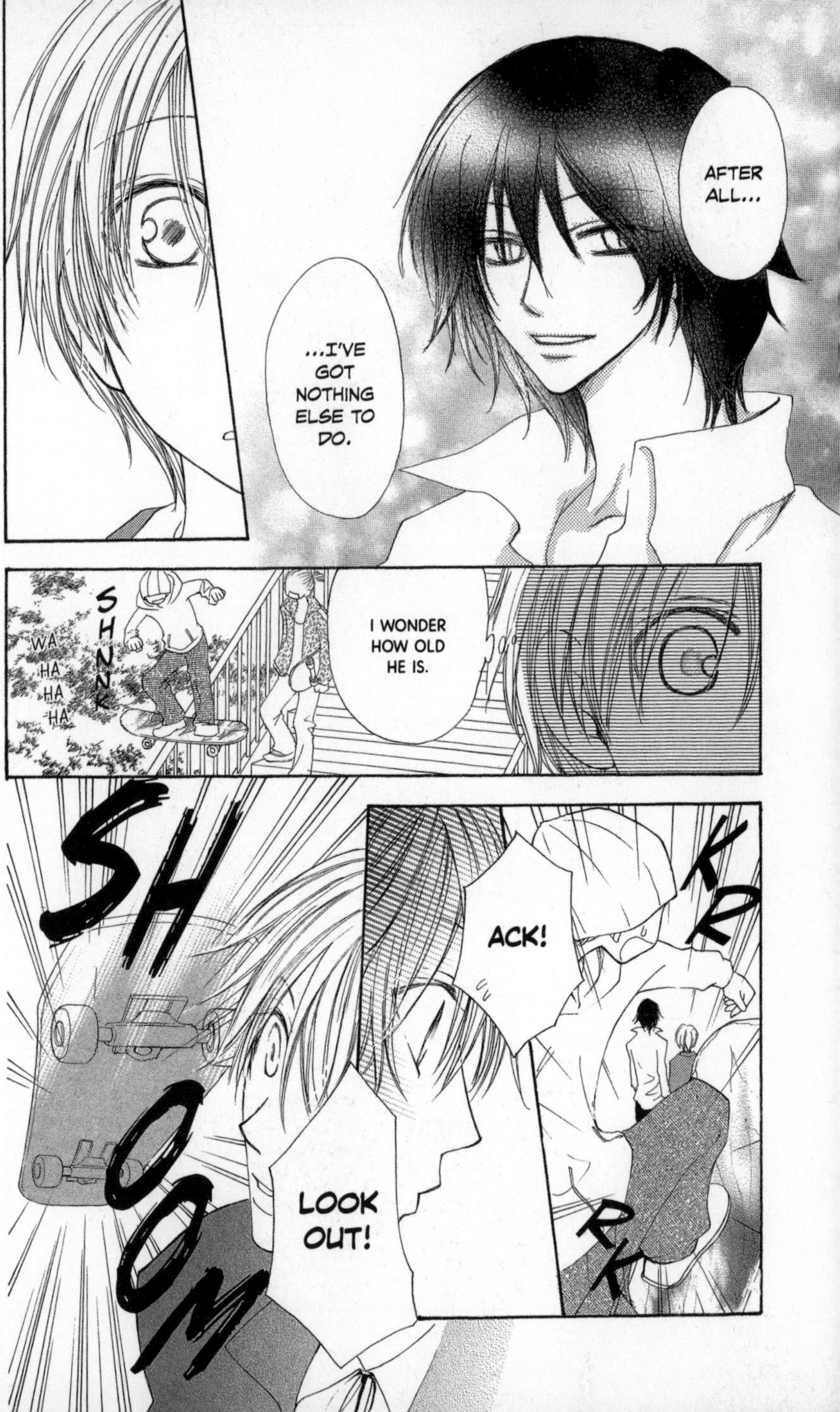
AFTER ALL...
...I'VE GOT NOTHING ELSE TO DO.
I WONDER HOW OLD HE IS.
SHNNK
WA HA HA HA
KRRK
ACK!
LOOK OUT!
SHOOM

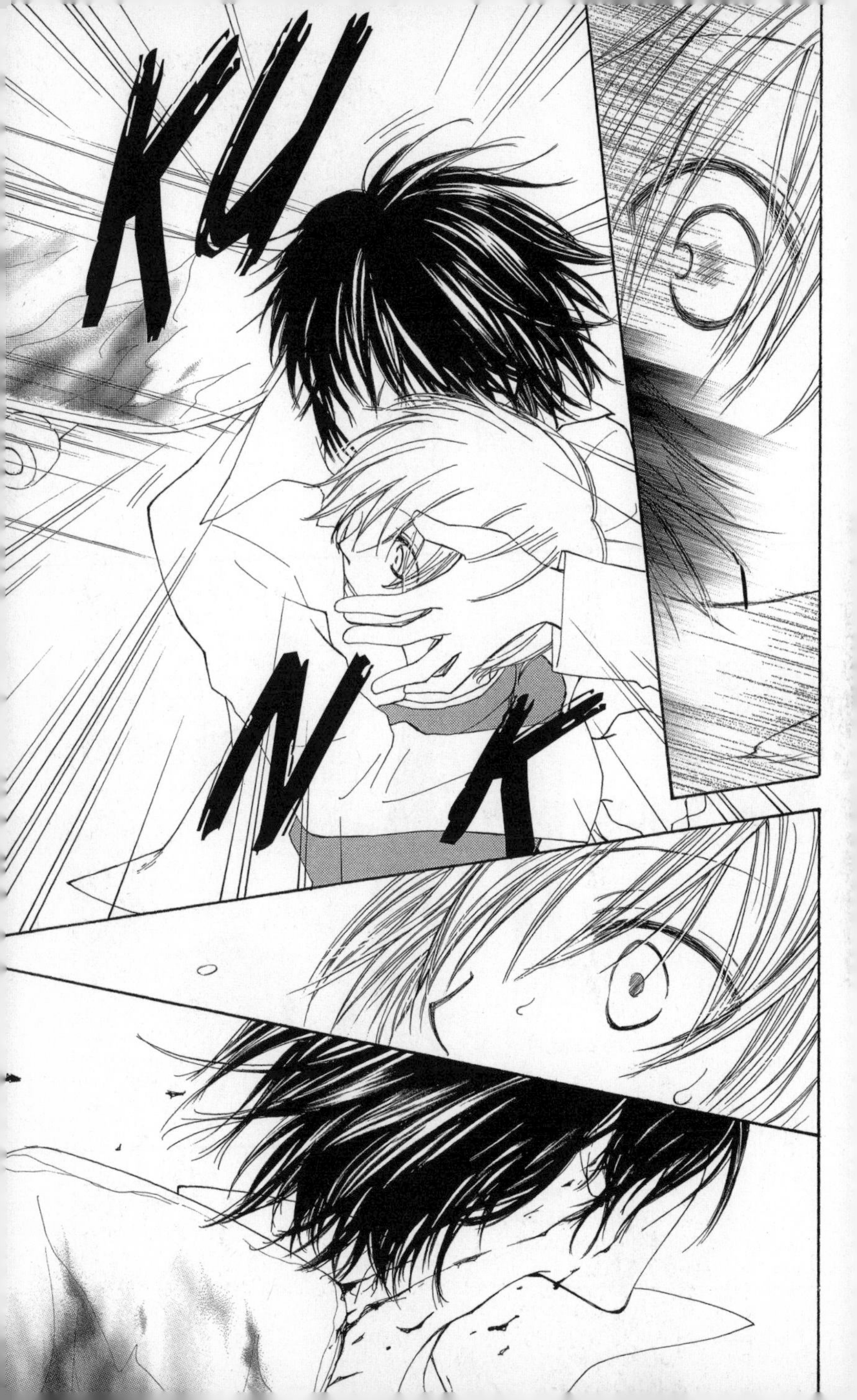
KUNK

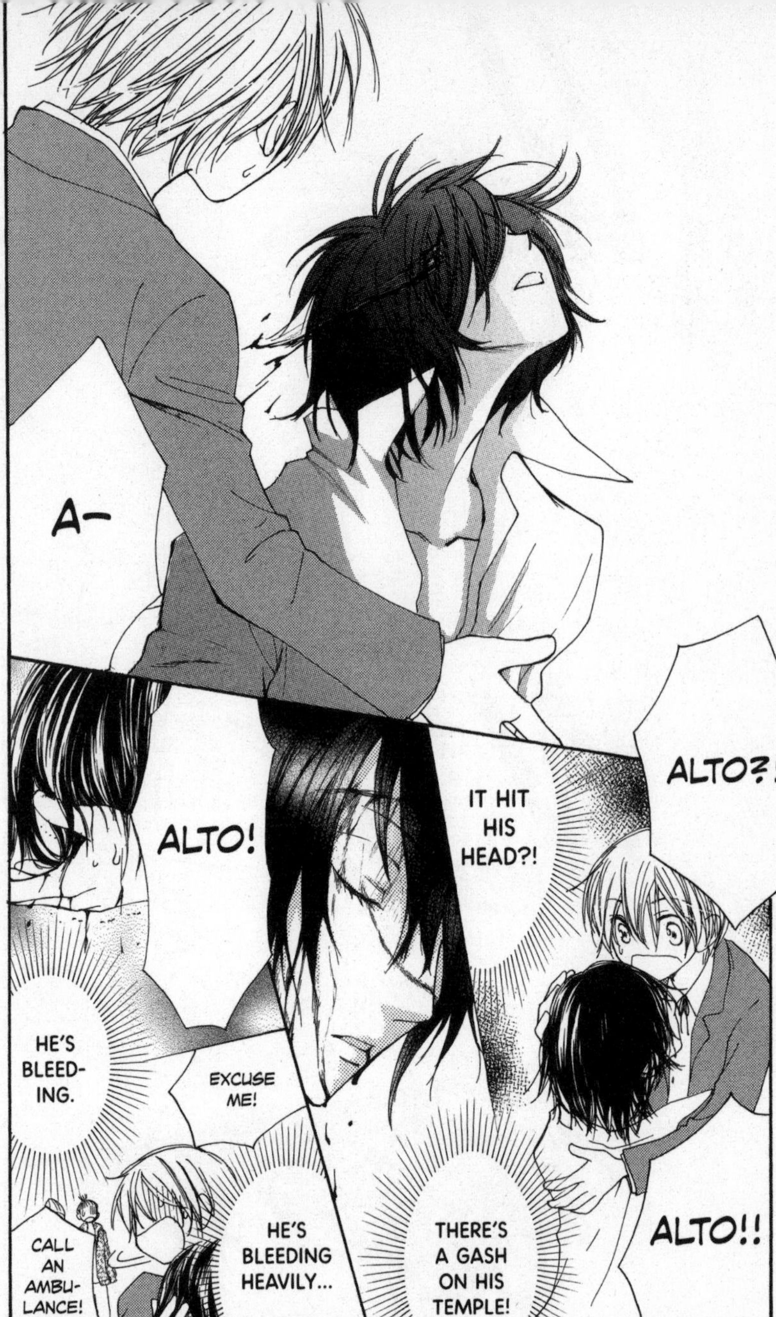
A-
ALTO?!
IT HIT HIS HEAD?!
ALTO!
ALTO!!
THERE'S A GASH ON HIS TEMPLE!
HE'S BLEEDING HEAVILY...
EXCUSE ME!
HE'S BLEEDING.
CALL AN AMBULANCE!

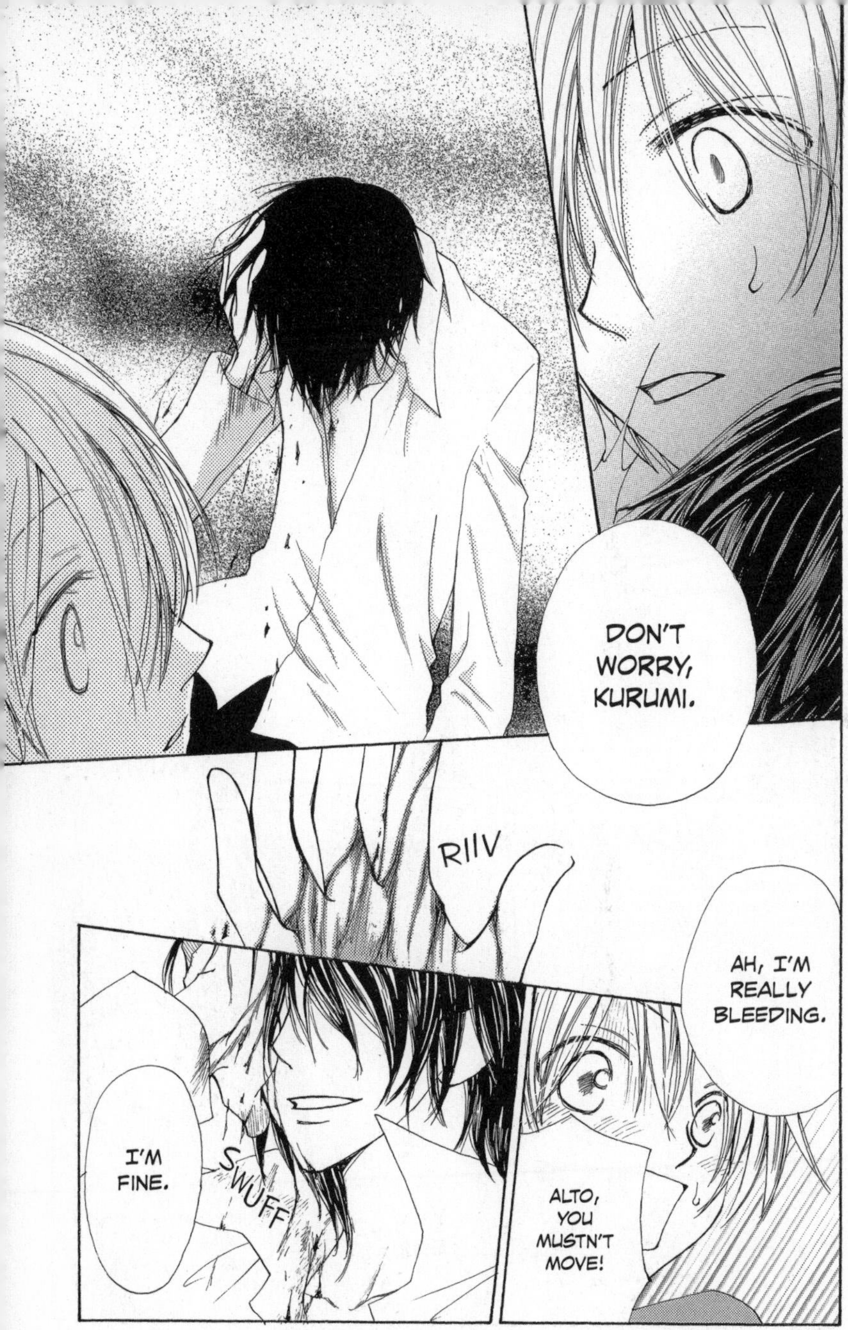
DON'T WORRY, KURUMI.
RIIV
AH, I'M REALLY BLEEDING.
ALTO, YOU MUSTN'T MOVE!
SWUFF
I'M FINE.

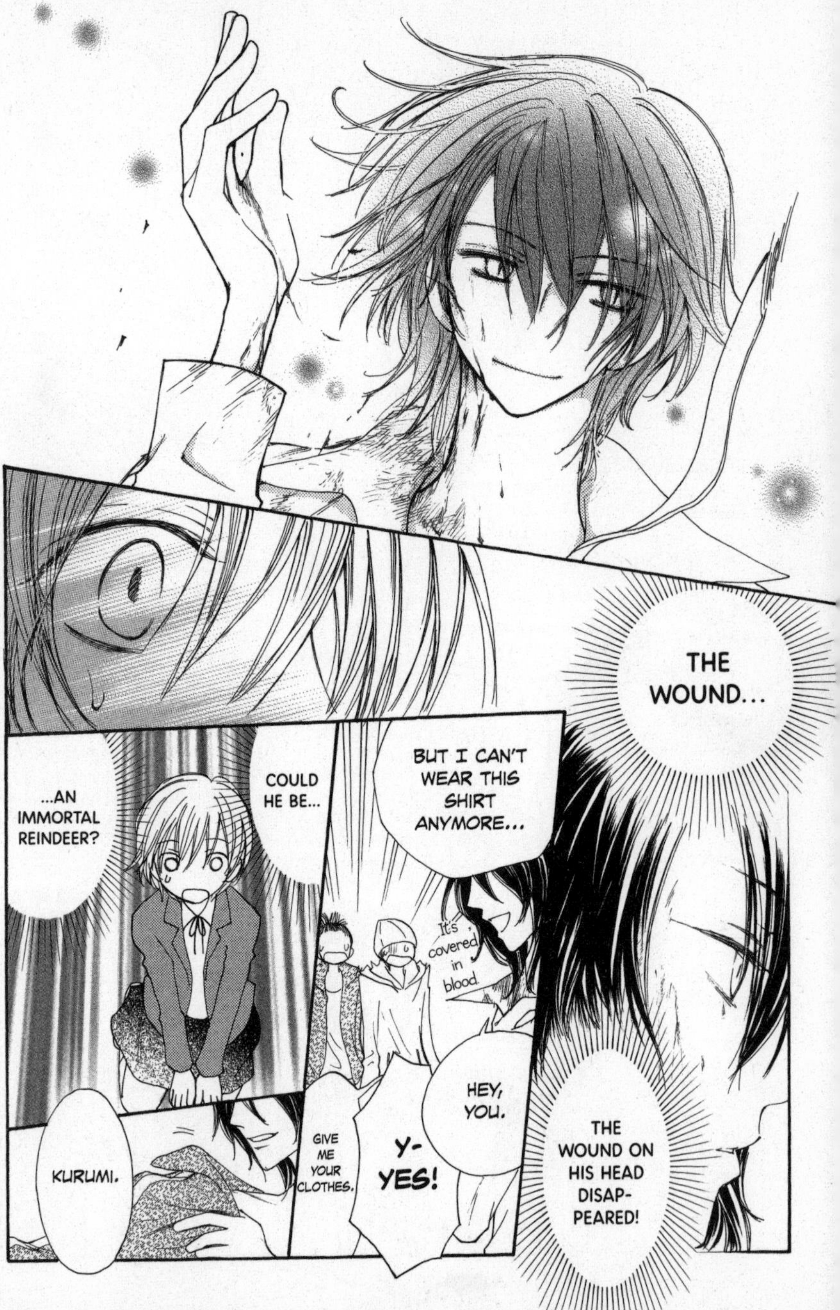
THE WOUND...
THE WOUND ON HIS HEAD DISAPPEARED!
BUT I CAN'T WEAR THIS SHIRT ANYMORE...
It's covered in blood.
HEY, YOU.
Y-YES!
GIVE ME YOUR CLOTHES.
COULD HE BE...
...AN IMMORTAL REINDEER?
KURUMI.

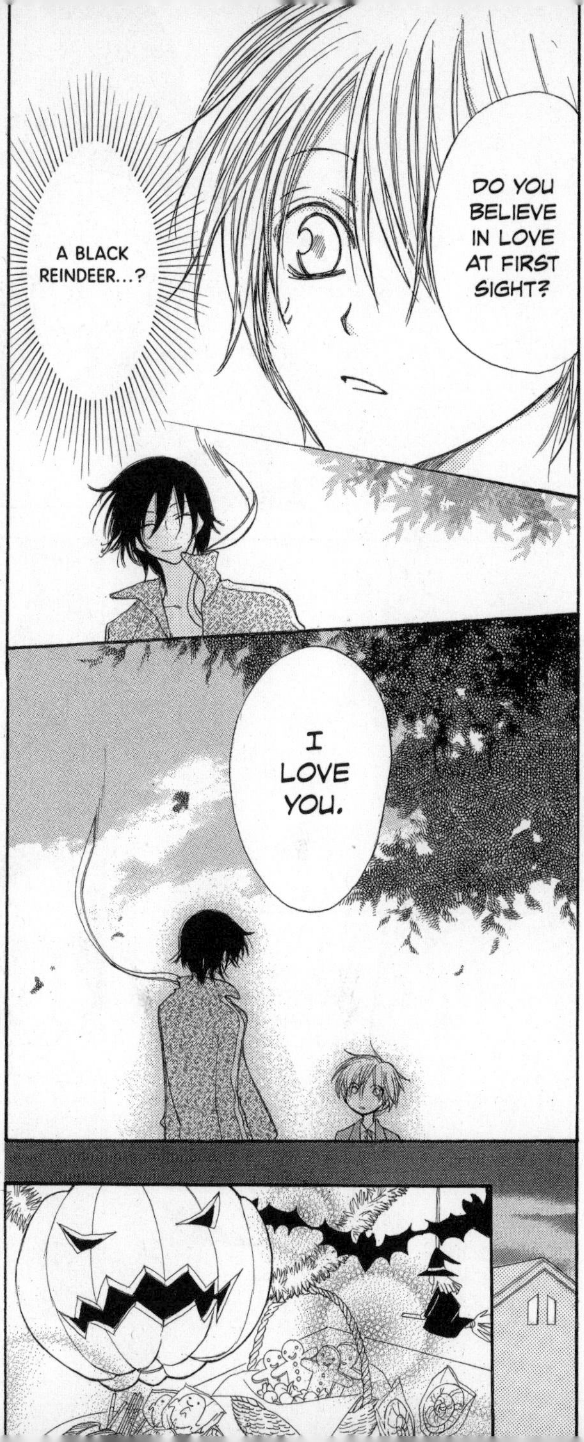
DO YOU BELIEVE IN LOVE AT FIRST SIGHT?
A BLACK REINDEER...?
I LOVE YOU.

1/4 Sakura Mail

Part 7

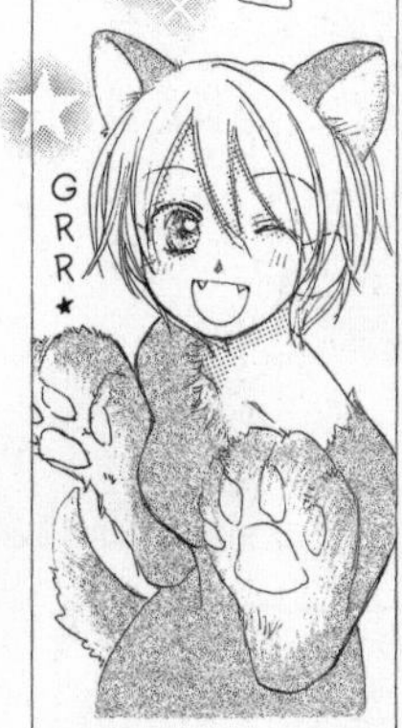
GRR★

Halloween costumes are so adorable!! ♡ Pumpkin orange is a nice warm color. It's probably not right to have a Christmas reindeer fly around on Halloween?...but we should be laid back about these kinds of things. I love festivals!

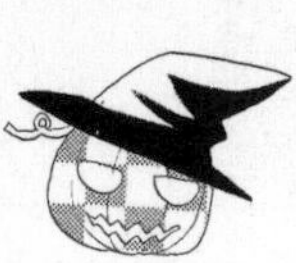

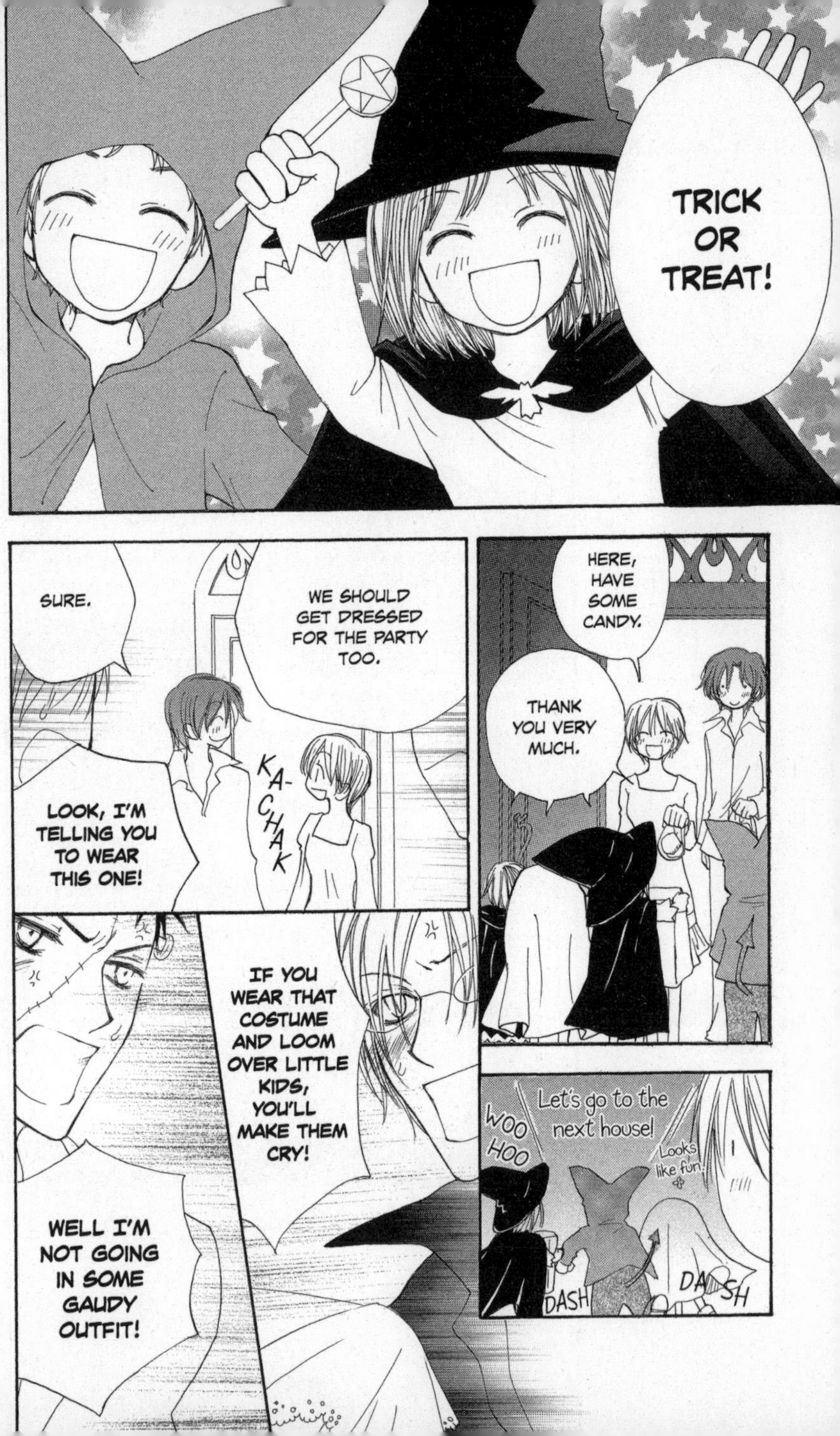
TRICK OR TREAT!
HERE, HAVE SOME CANDY.
THANK YOU VERY MUCH.
WOO HOO
Let's go to the next house!
Looks like fun.
DASH
DASH
WE SHOULD GET DRESSED FOR THE PARTY TOO.
SURE.
KA-CHAK
LOOK, I'M TELLING YOU TO WEAR THIS ONE!
IF YOU WEAR THAT COSTUME AND LOOM OVER LITTLE KIDS, YOU'LL MAKE THEM CRY!
WELL I'M NOT GOING IN SOME GAUDY OUTFIT!

1/4 Sakura Mail

Part 8

I love capes, but I also love furry creatures, so I just had to include animal ears. Nene is wearing the animal ears. The Dark Santa doesn't look interested in Halloween at all, but I bet he was jumping for joy inside.♥ As for the others, Tateyama is dressed up as Frankenstein, and Rihito was trying to get out of wearing a costume in the first place. But the situation changed drastically after the Dark Santa appeared... Heh heh... The story always unfolds easily once the Dark Santa and Nene appear because they can do the explanations for me. They're very useful characters to have around.

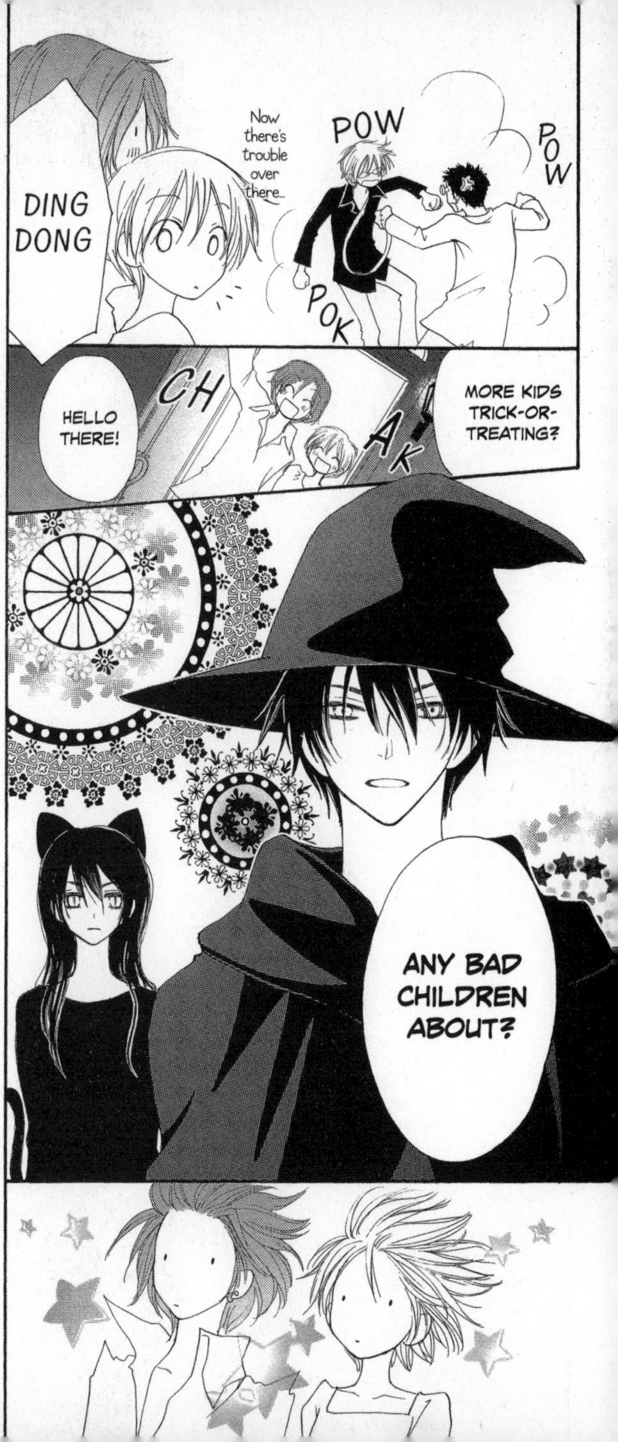
POW
POW
Now there's trouble over there...
POK
DING DONG
MORE KIDS TRICK-OR-TREATING?
CHAK
HELLO THERE!
ANY BAD CHILDREN ABOUT?

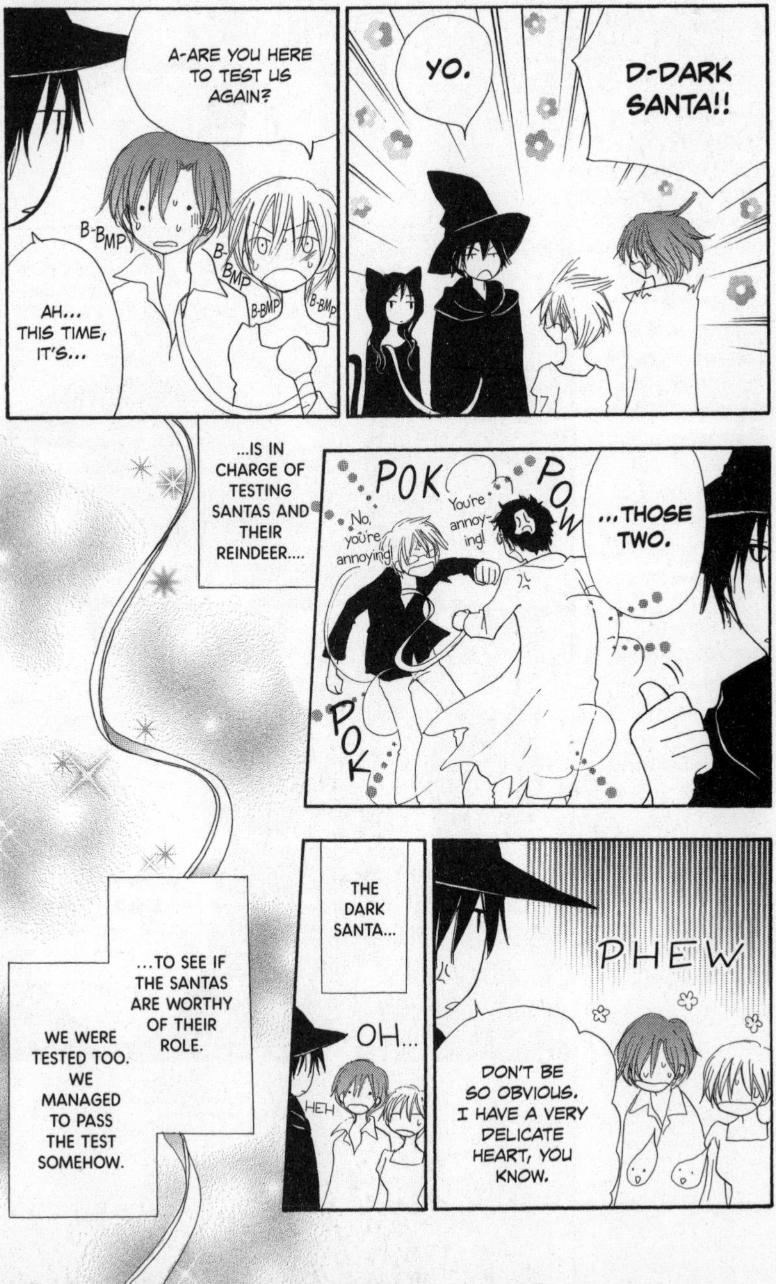
D-DARK SANTA!!
YO.
A-ARE YOU HERE TO TEST US AGAIN?
B-BMP
B-BMP
B-BMP
B-BMP
AH... THIS TIME, IT'S...
...THOSE TWO.
POW
You're annoying!
POK
No, you're annoying!
POK
...IS IN CHARGE OF TESTING SANTAS AND THEIR REINDEER....
PHEW
DON'T BE SO OBVIOUS. I HAVE A VERY DELICATE HEART, YOU KNOW.
THE DARK SANTA...
OH...
HEH
...TO SEE IF THE SANTAS ARE WORTHY OF THEIR ROLE.
WE WERE TESTED TOO. WE MANAGED TO PASS THE TEST SOMEHOW.

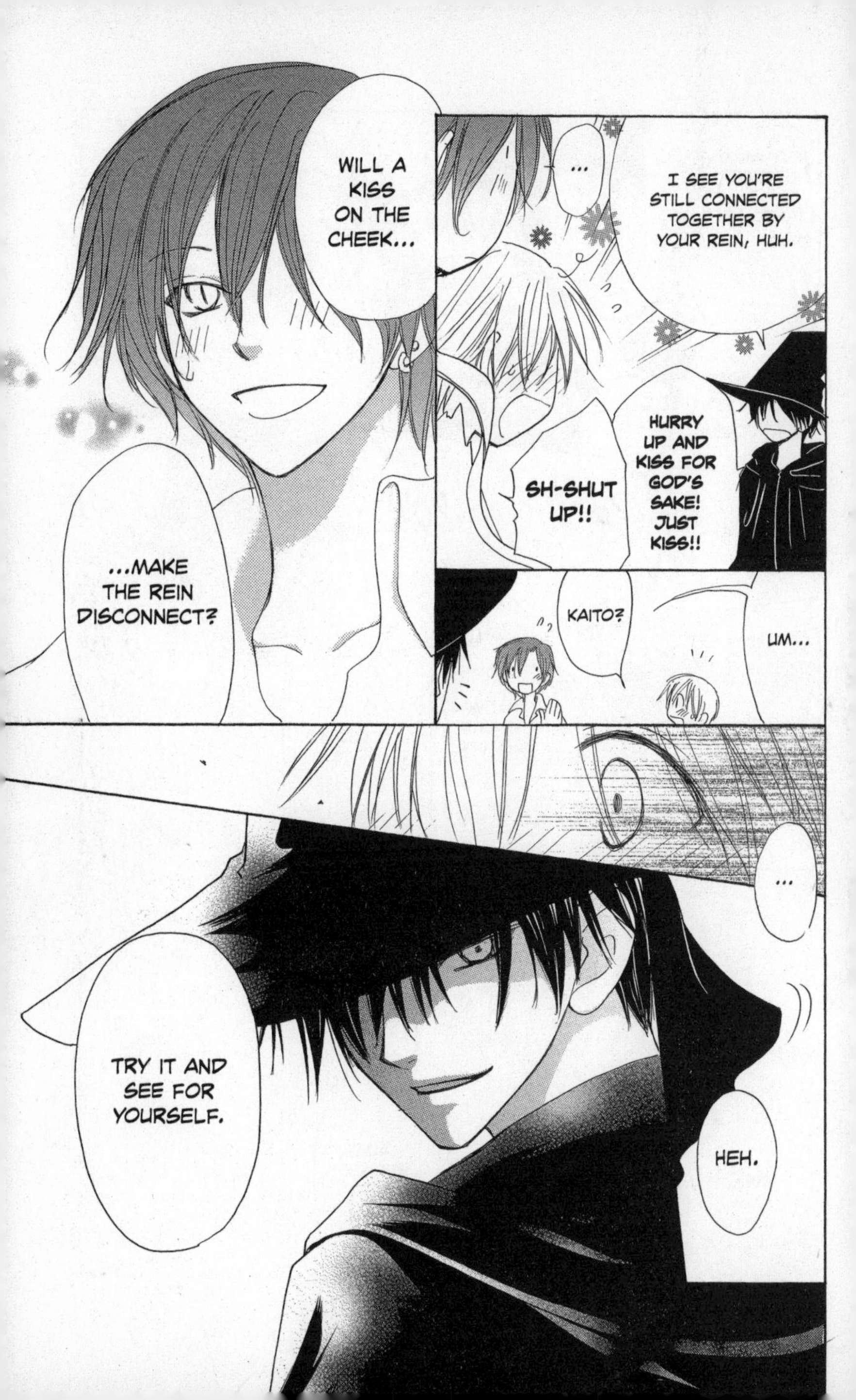

I SEE YOU'RE STILL CONNECTED TOGETHER BY YOUR REIN, HUH.
...
HURRY UP AND KISS FOR GOD'S SAKE! JUST KISS!!
SH-SHUT UP!!
UM...
KAITO?
WILL A KISS ON THE CHEEK...
...MAKE THE REIN DISCONNECT?
...
HEH.
TRY IT AND SEE FOR YOURSELF.

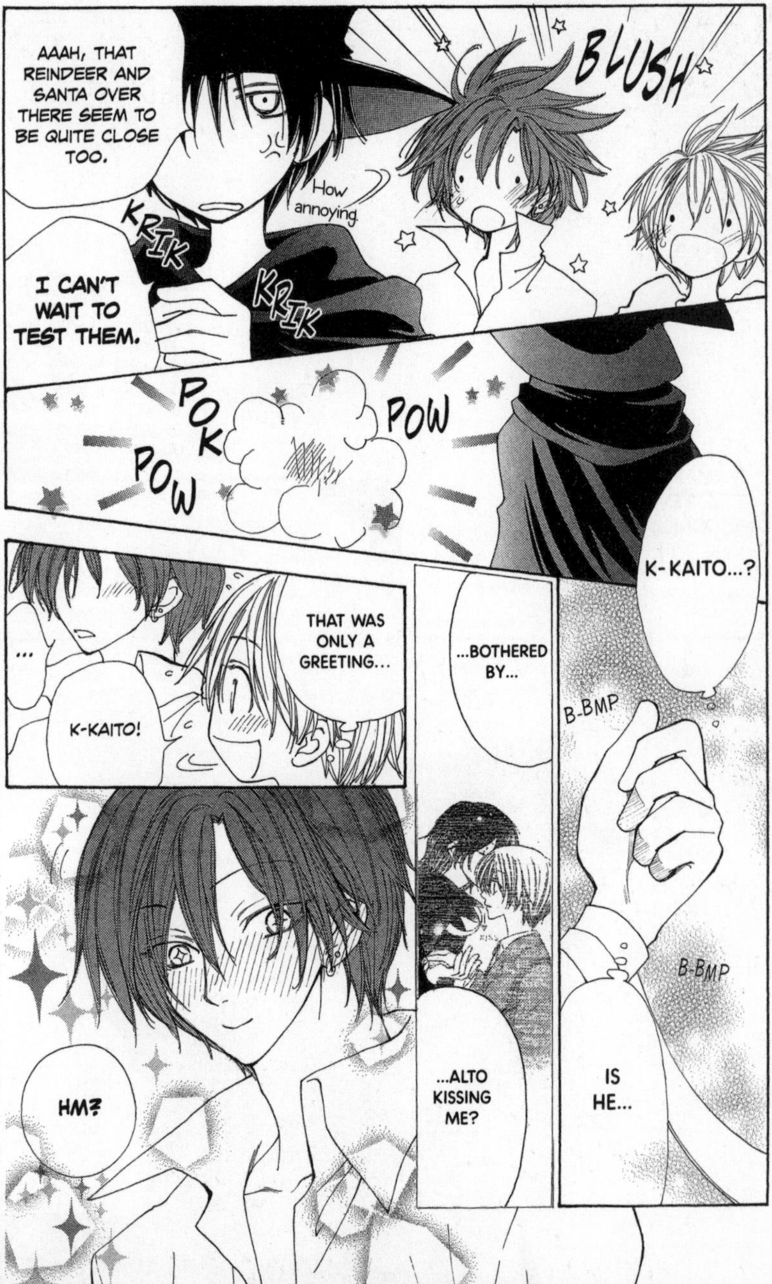
BLUSH
How annoying.
AAAH, THAT REINDEER AND SANTA OVER THERE SEEM TO BE QUITE CLOSE TOO.
KRIK
KRIK
I CAN'T WAIT TO TEST THEM.
POW
POK
POW
K-KAITO...?
B-BMP
B-BMP
IS HE...
...BOTHERED BY...
...ALTO KISSING ME?
THAT WAS ONLY A GREETING...
...
K-KAITO!
HM?

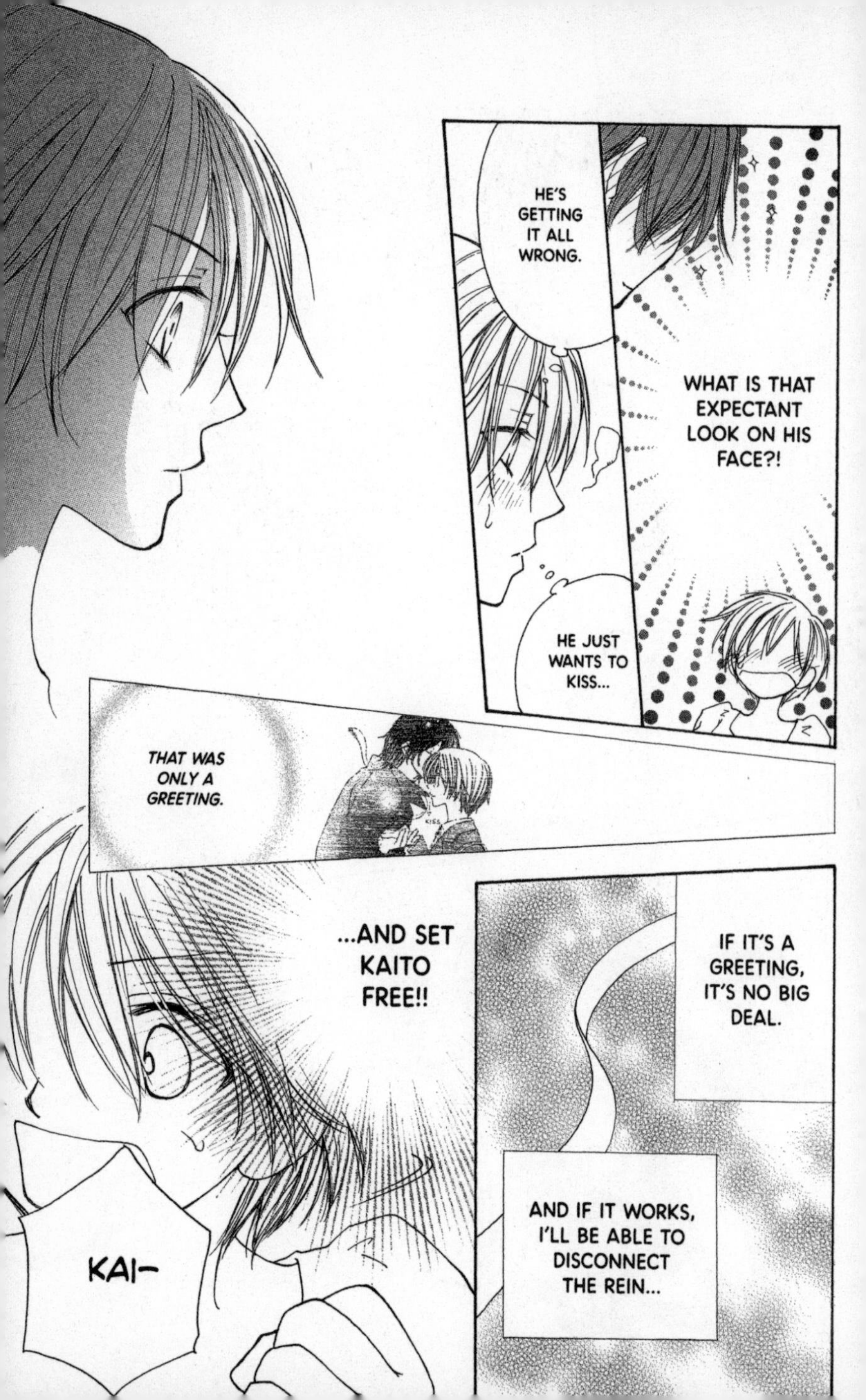
WHAT IS THAT EXPECTANT LOOK ON HIS FACE?!
HE'S GETTING IT ALL WRONG.
HE JUST WANTS TO KISS...
THAT WAS ONLY A GREETING.
KISS
IF IT'S A GREETING, IT'S NO BIG DEAL.
AND IF IT WORKS, I'LL BE ABLE TO DISCONNECT THE REIN...
...AND SET KAITO FREE!!
KAI-

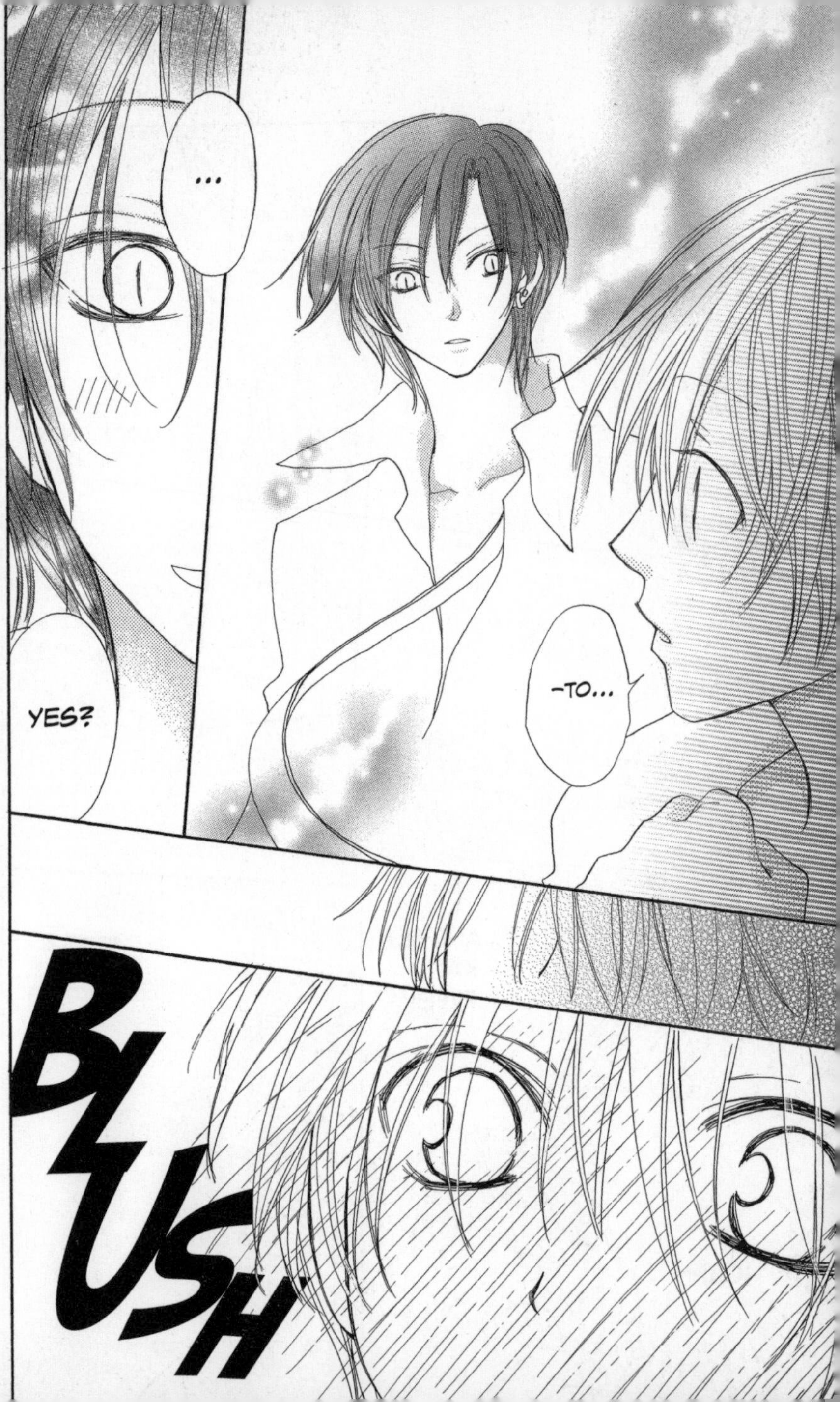
-TO...
...
YES?
BLUSH

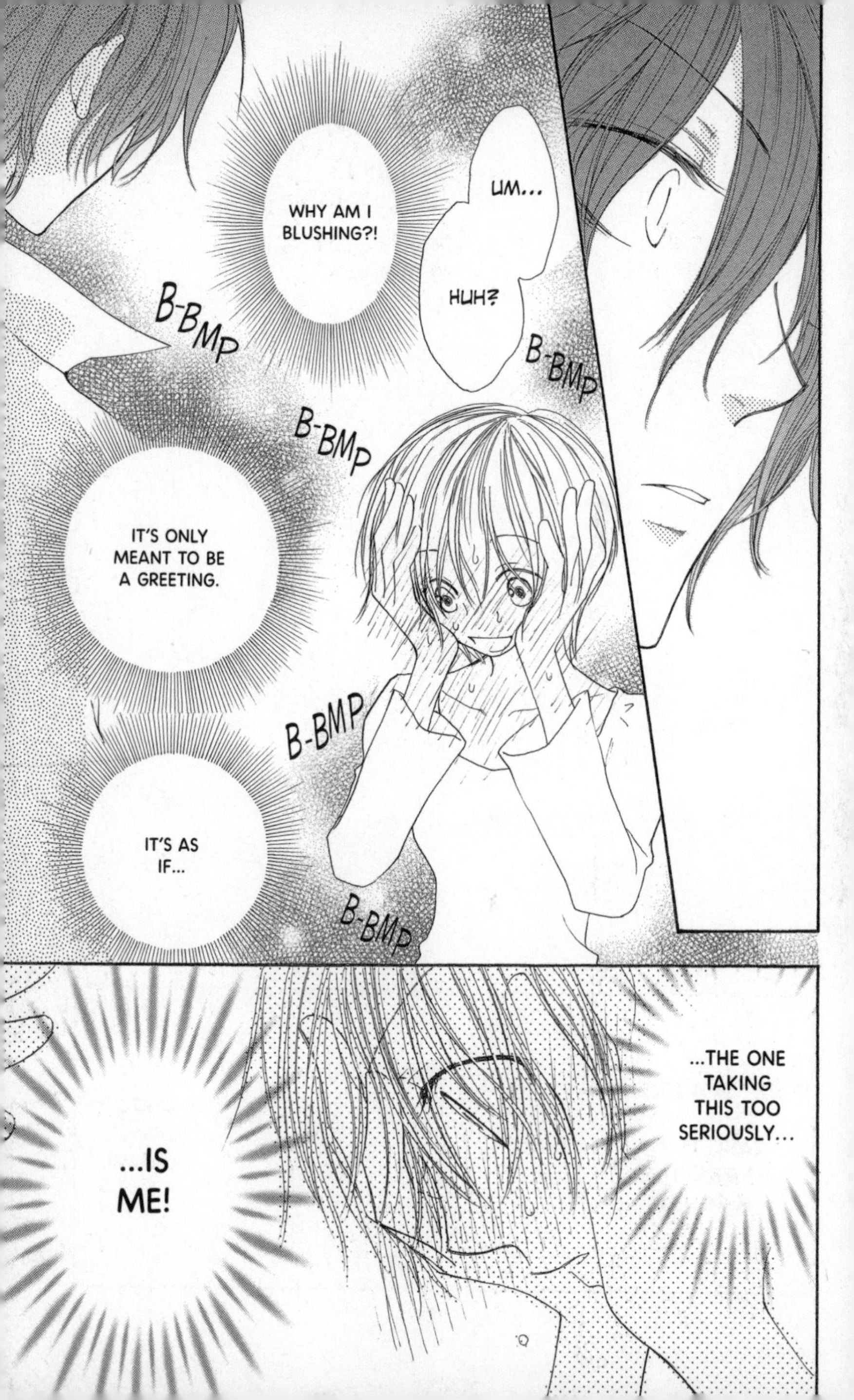
UM...
HUH?
WHY AM I BLUSHING?!
B-BMP
B-BMP
B-BMP
IT'S ONLY MEANT TO BE A GREETING.
B-BMP
IT'S AS IF...
B-BMP
...THE ONE TAKING THIS TOO SERIOUSLY...
...IS ME!

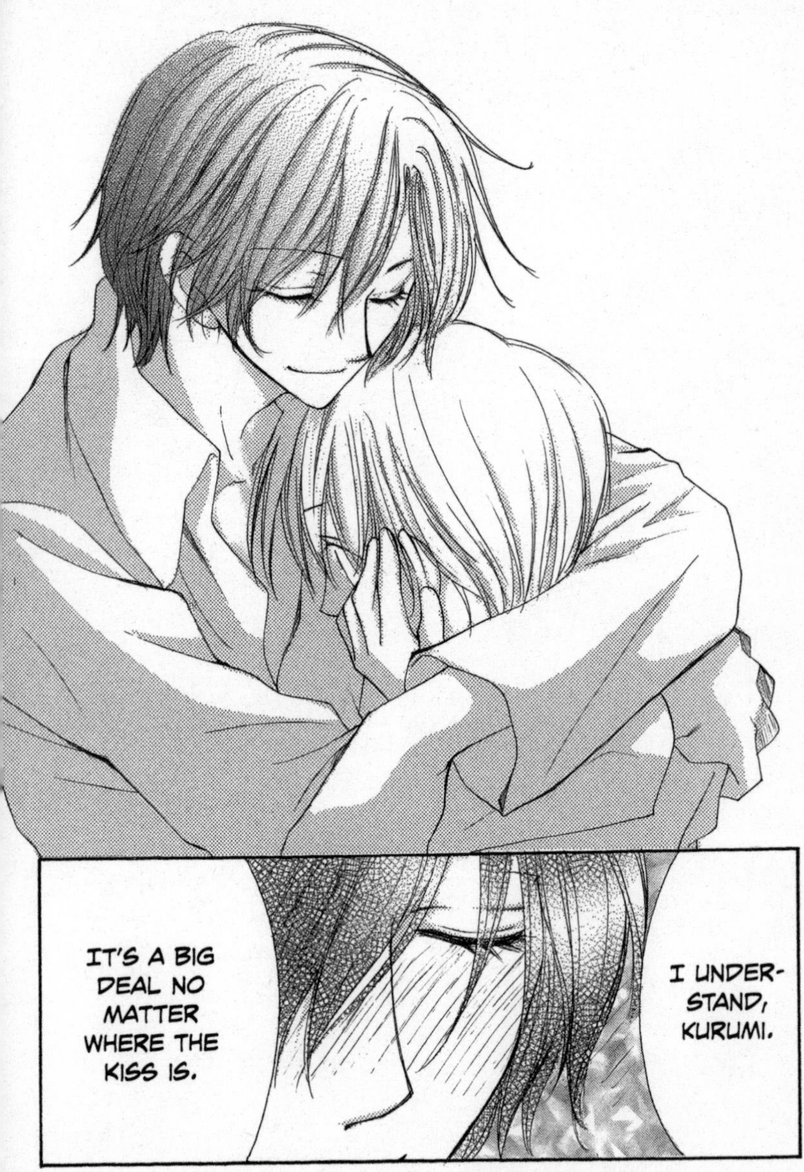
I UNDER-
STAND,
KURUMI.
IT'S A BIG
DEAL NO
MATTER
WHERE THE
KISS IS.

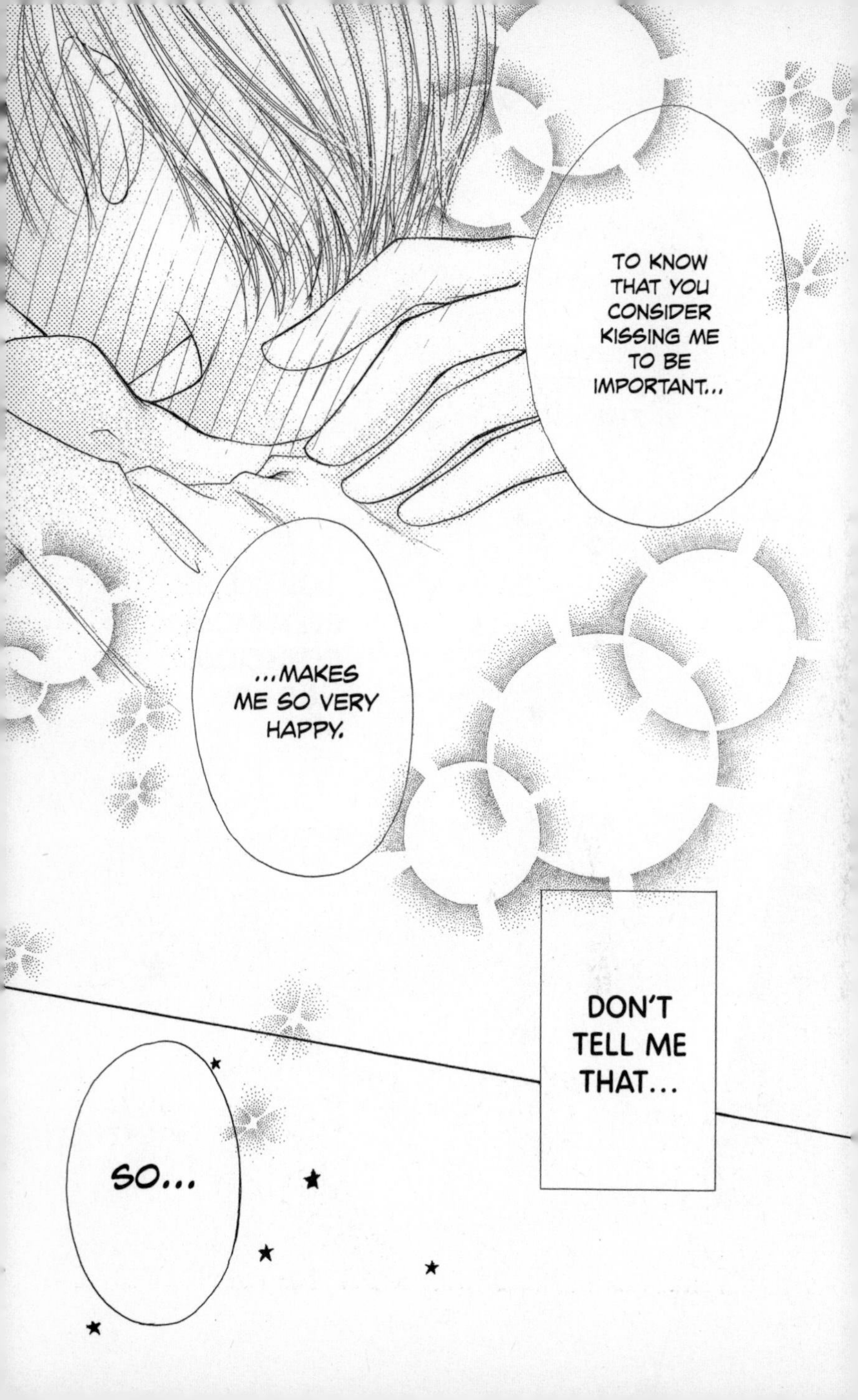
TO KNOW THAT YOU CONSIDER KISSING ME TO BE IMPORTANT...
...MAKES ME SO VERY HAPPY.
DON'T TELL ME THAT...
SO...

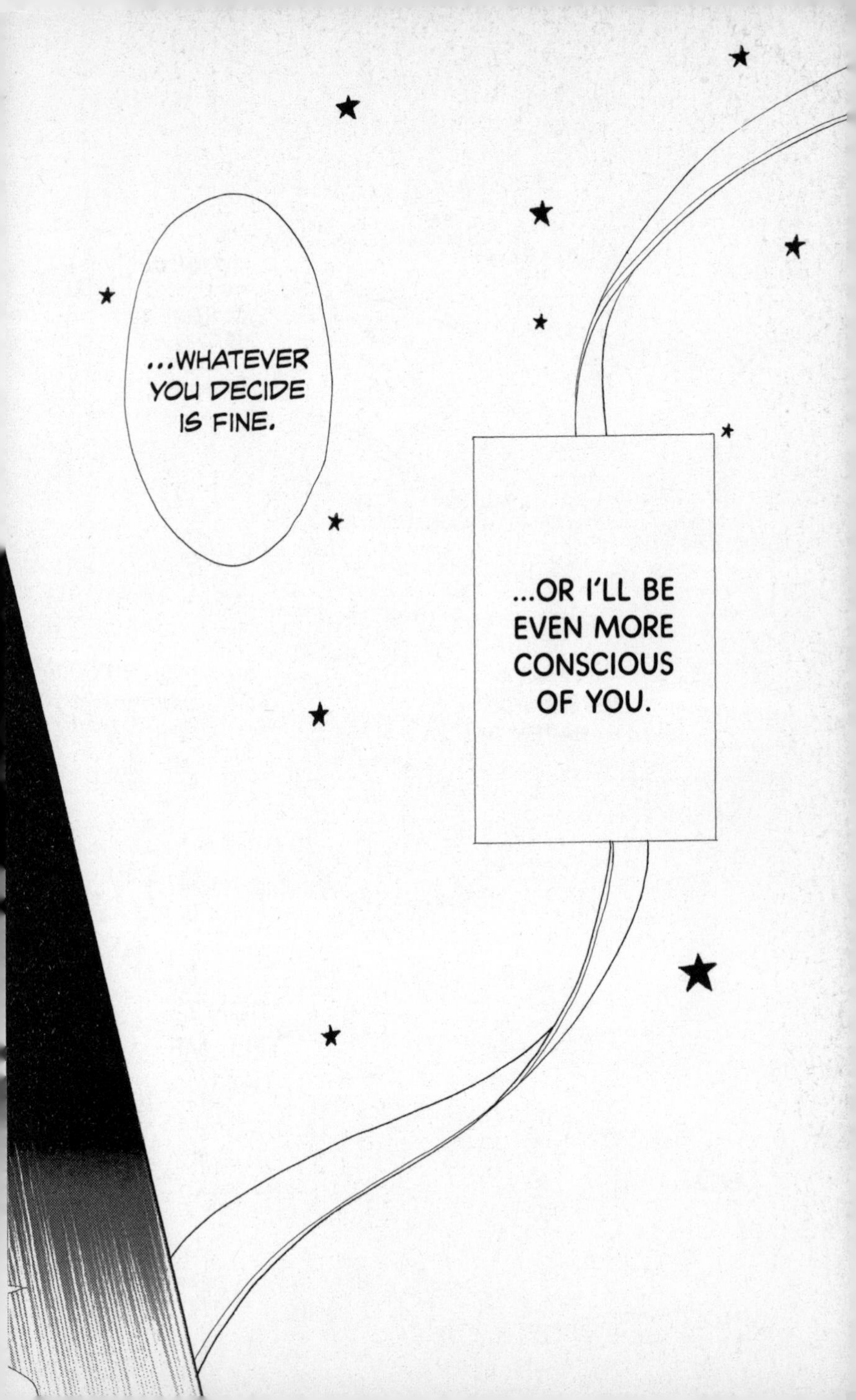
...OR I'LL BE EVEN MORE CONSCIOUS OF YOU.
...WHATEVER YOU DECIDE IS FINE.

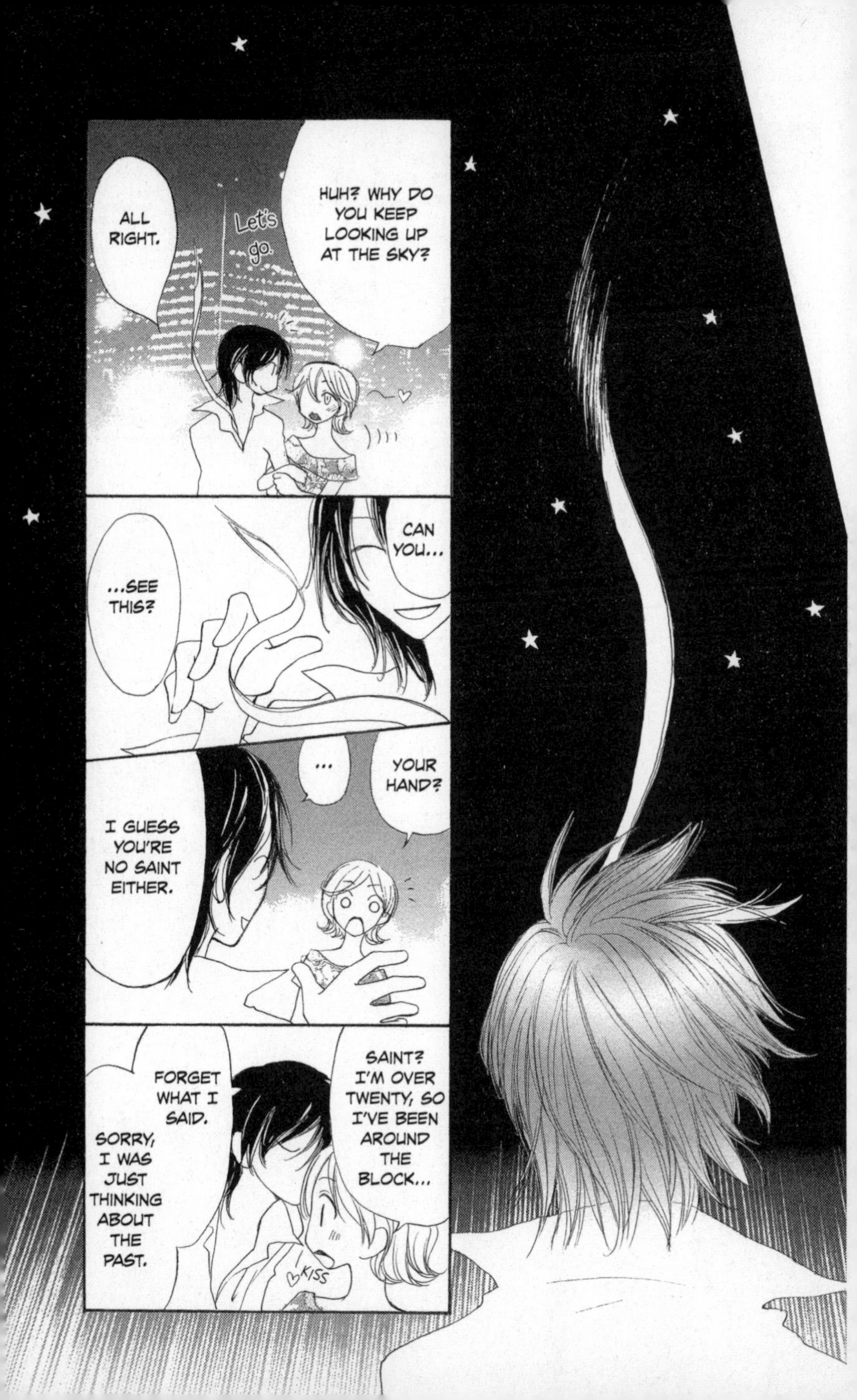
HUH? WHY DO YOU KEEP LOOKING UP AT THE SKY?
Let's go.
ALL RIGHT.
CAN YOU...
...SEE THIS?
YOUR HAND?
...
I GUESS YOU'RE NO SAINT EITHER.
SAINT? I'M OVER TWENTY, SO I'VE BEEN AROUND THE BLOCK...
FORGET WHAT I SAID.
SORRY, I WAS JUST THINKING ABOUT THE PAST.
KISS

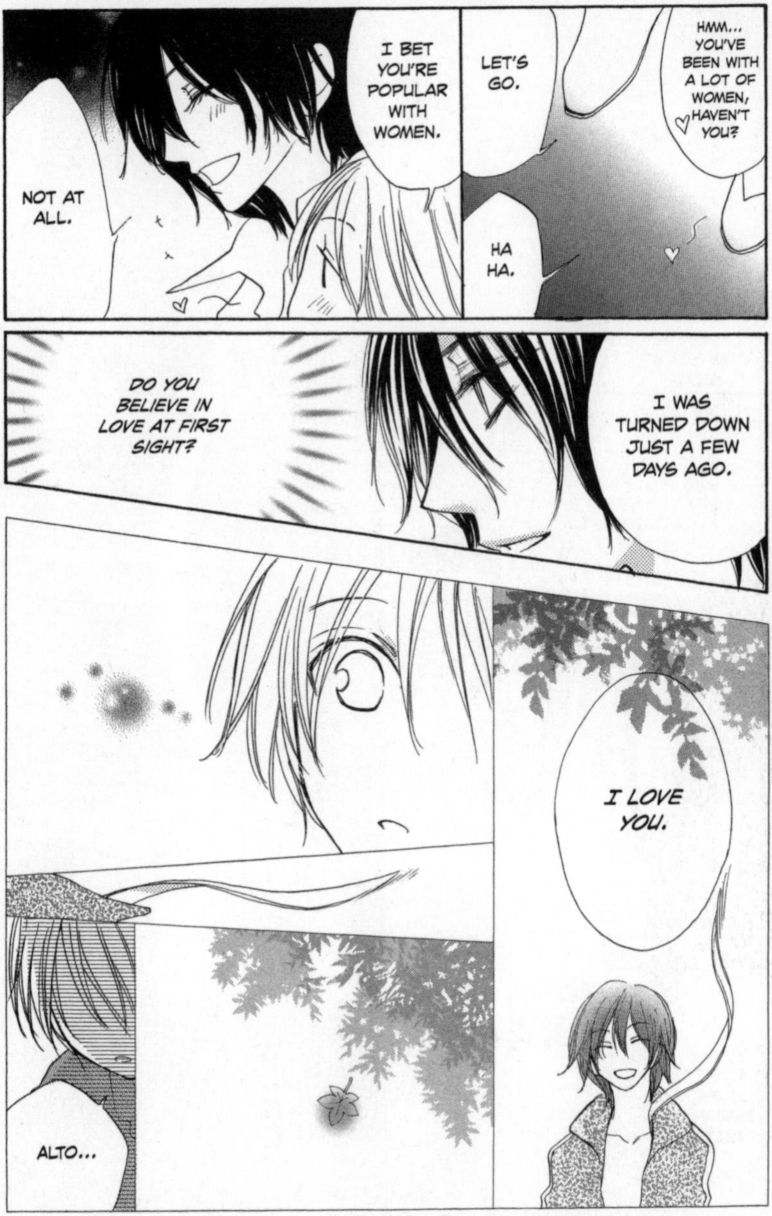
HMM... YOU'VE BEEN WITH A LOT OF WOMEN, HAVEN'T YOU?
LET'S GO.
HA HA.
I BET YOU'RE POPULAR WITH WOMEN.
NOT AT ALL.
I WAS TURNED DOWN JUST A FEW DAYS AGO.
DO YOU BELIEVE IN LOVE AT FIRST SIGHT?
I LOVE YOU.
ALTO...

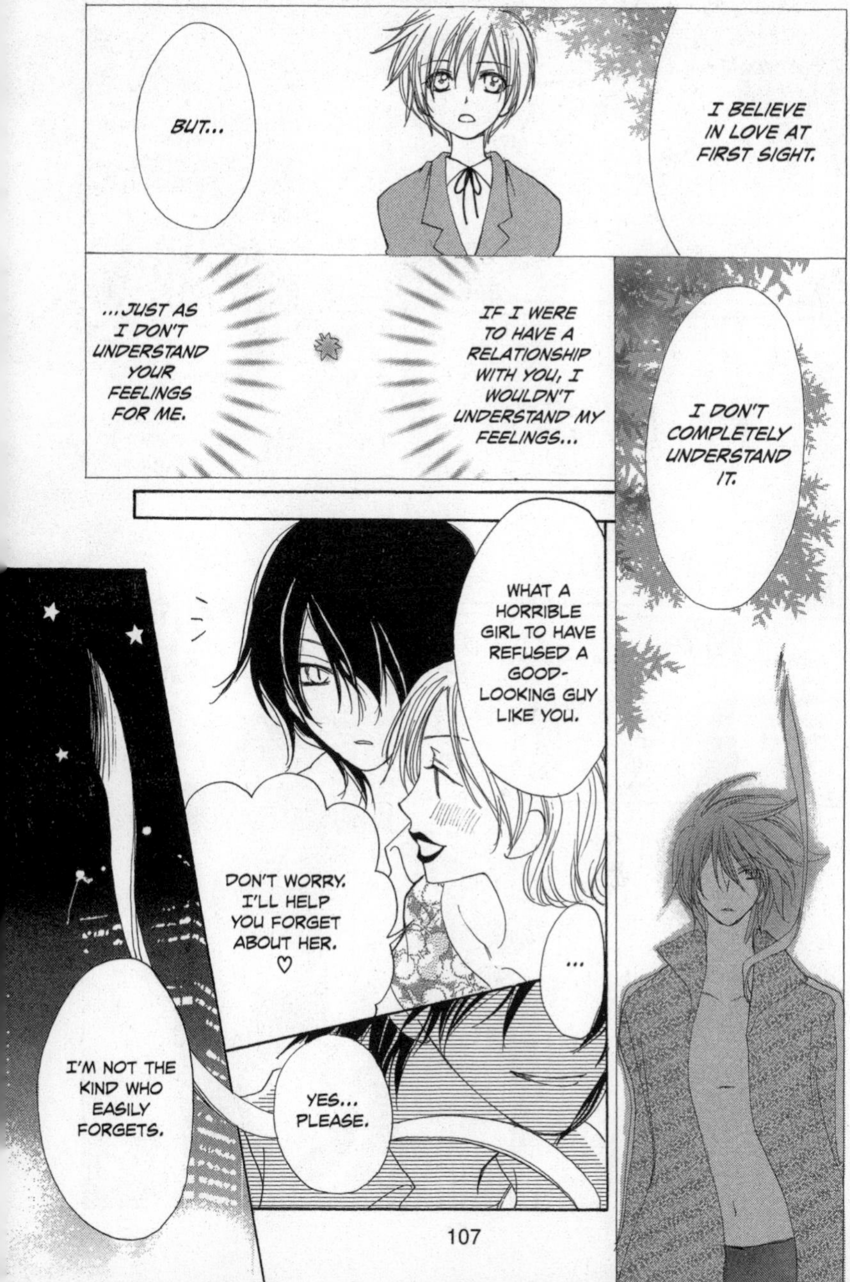
I BELIEVE IN LOVE AT FIRST SIGHT.
BUT...
I DON'T COMPLETELY UNDERSTAND IT.
IF I WERE TO HAVE A RELATIONSHIP WITH YOU, I WOULDN'T UNDERSTAND MY FEELINGS...
...JUST AS I DON'T UNDERSTAND YOUR FEELINGS FOR ME.
WHAT A HORRIBLE GIRL TO HAVE REFUSED A GOOD-LOOKING GUY LIKE YOU.
DON'T WORRY. I'LL HELP YOU FORGET ABOUT HER. ♡
...
YES... PLEASE.
I'M NOT THE KIND WHO EASILY FORGETS.

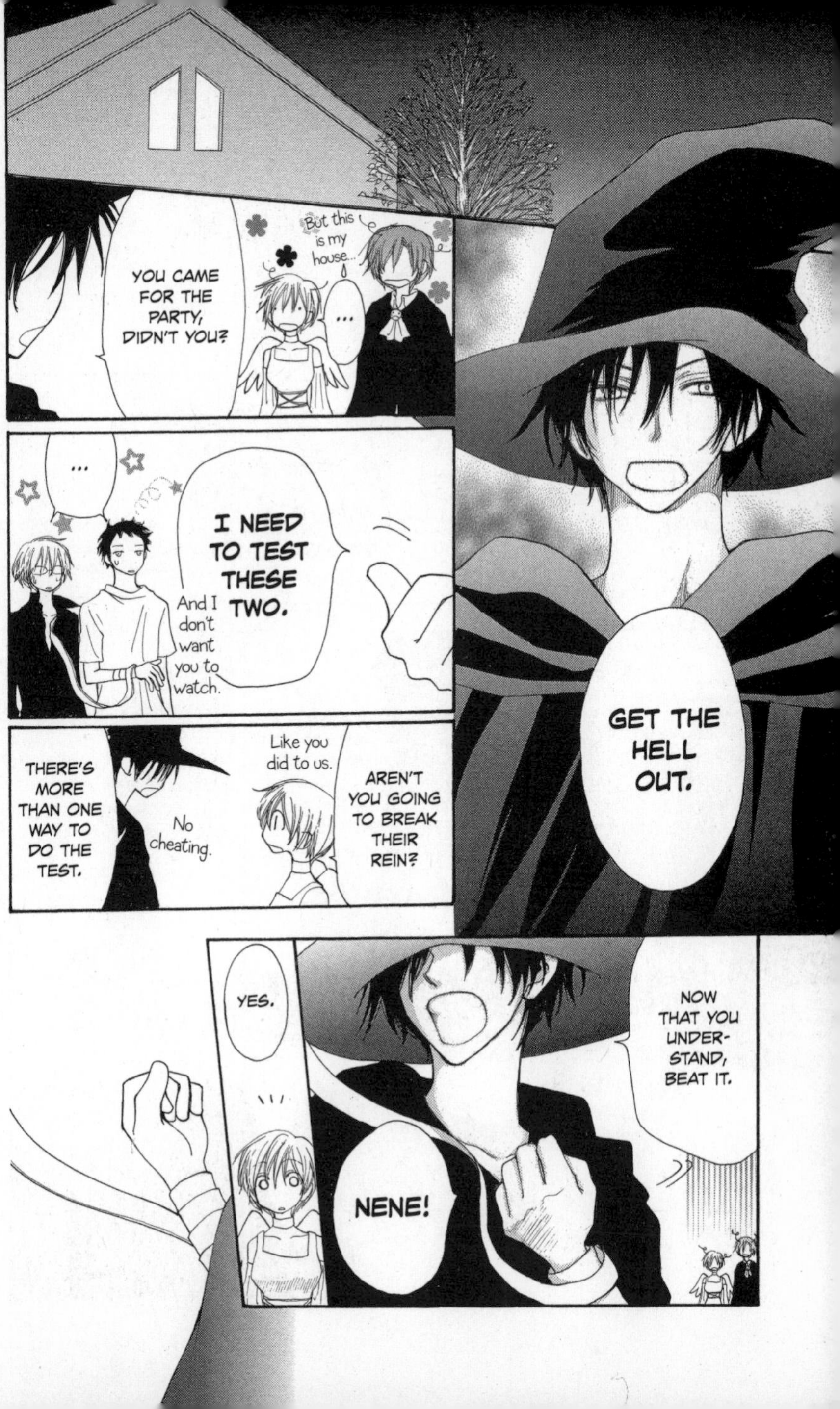
GET THE HELL OUT.
But this is my house...
...
YOU CAME FOR THE PARTY, DIDN'T YOU?
I NEED TO TEST THESE TWO.
And I don't want you to watch.
...
AREN'T YOU GOING TO BREAK THEIR REIN?
Like you did to us.
No cheating.
THERE'S MORE THAN ONE WAY TO DO THE TEST.
NOW THAT YOU UNDER-STAND, BEAT IT.
NENE!
YES.

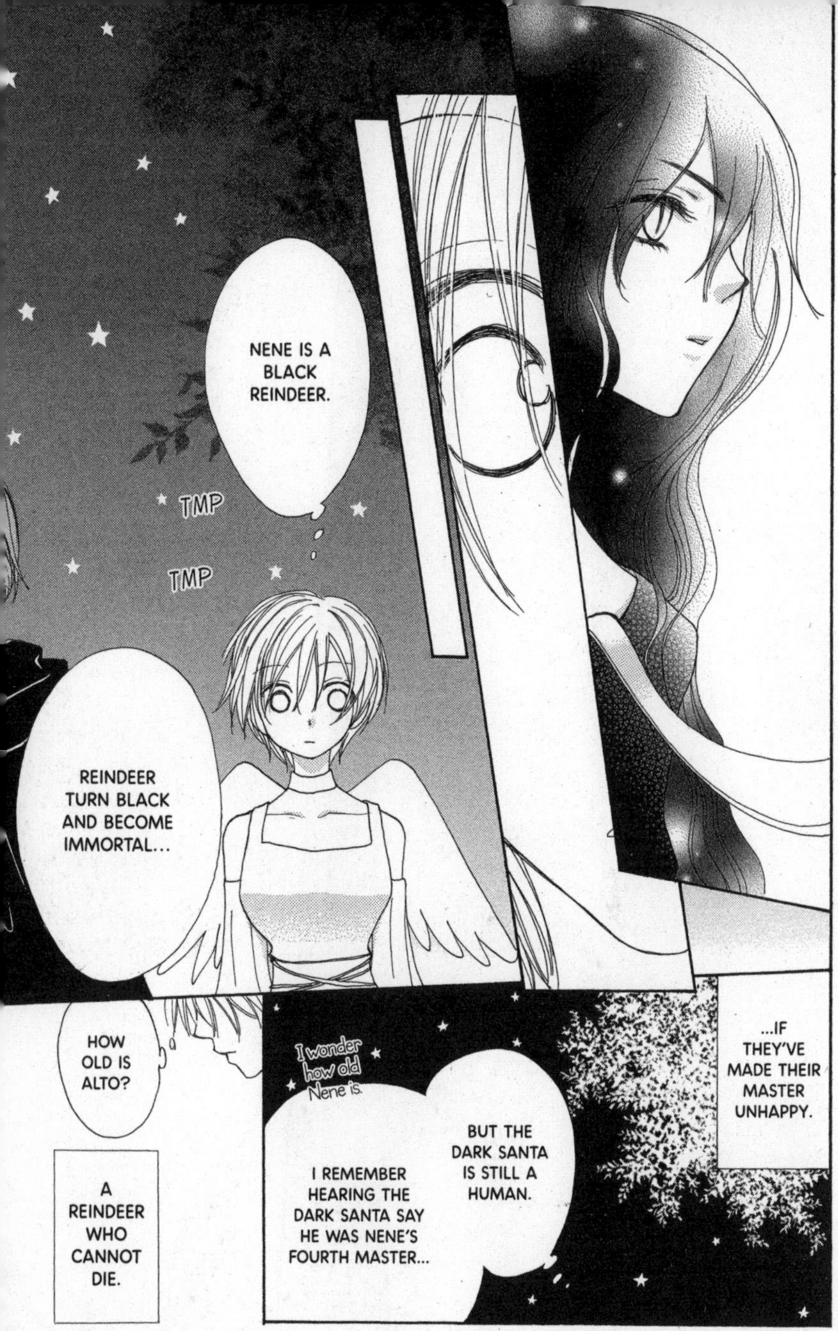
NENE IS A BLACK REINDEER.
TMP
TMP
REINDEER TURN BLACK AND BECOME IMMORTAL...
...IF THEY'VE MADE THEIR MASTER UNHAPPY.
BUT THE DARK SANTA IS STILL A HUMAN.
I REMEMBER HEARING THE DARK SANTA SAY HE WAS NENE'S FOURTH MASTER...
I wonder how old Nene is.
HOW OLD IS ALTO?
A REINDEER WHO CANNOT DIE.

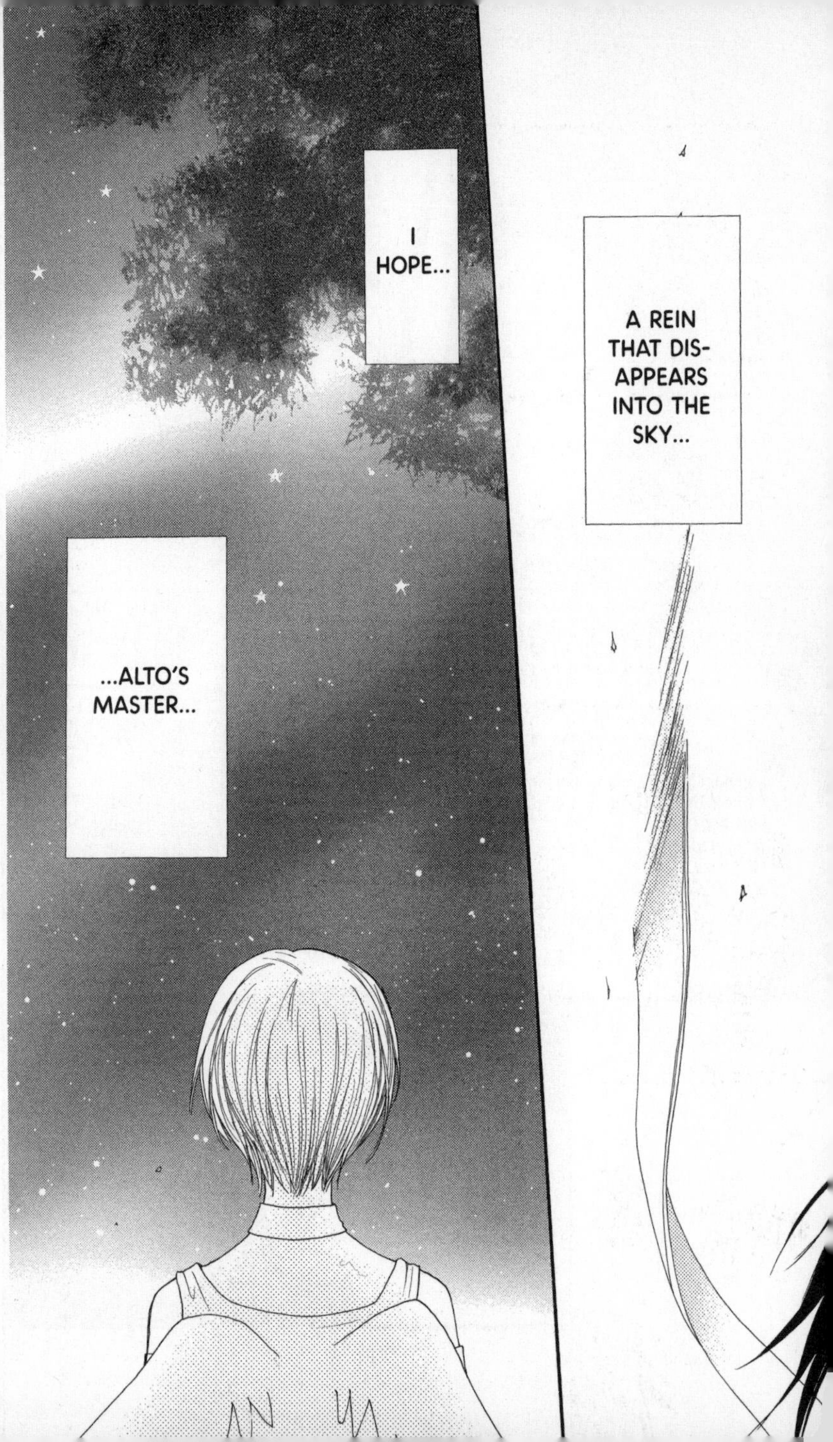
A REIN THAT DIS-APPEARS INTO THE SKY...
I HOPE...
...ALTO'S MASTER...

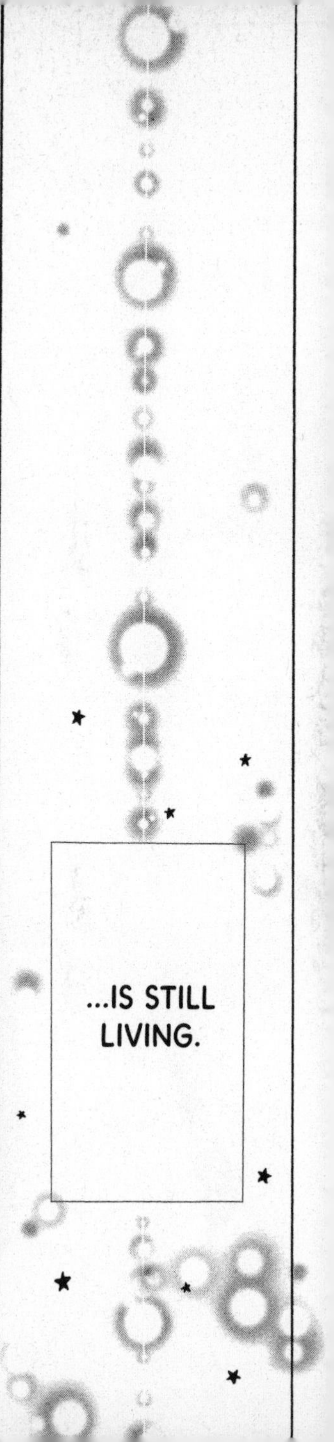
...IS STILL LIVING.

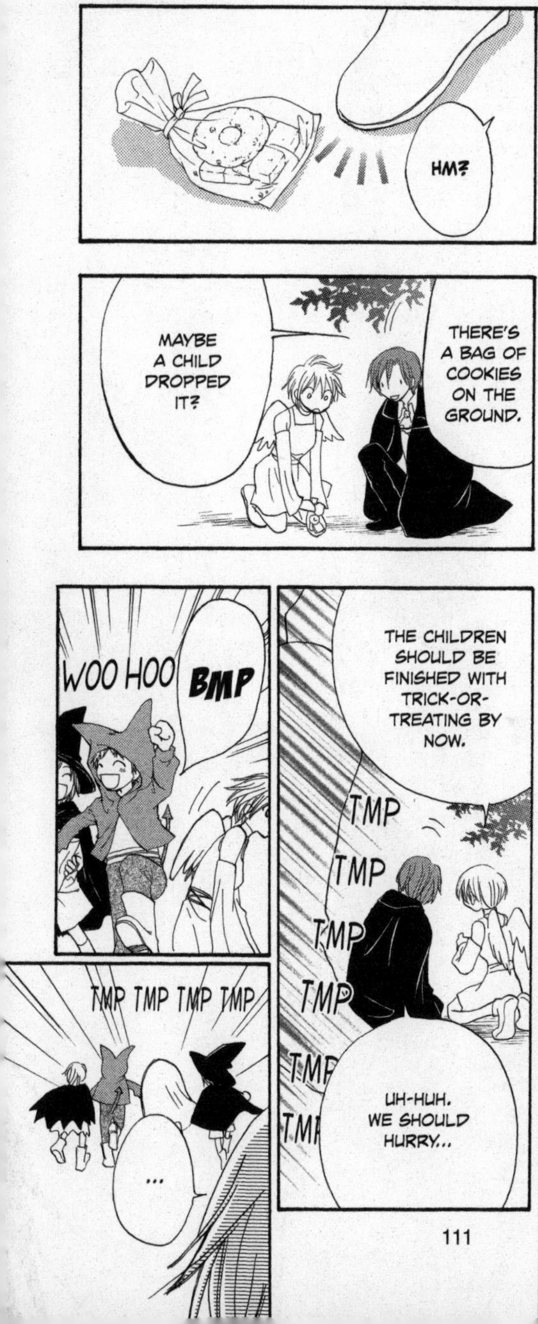
HM?
THERE'S A BAG OF COOKIES ON THE GROUND.
MAYBE A CHILD DROPPED IT?
THE CHILDREN SHOULD BE FINISHED WITH TRICK-OR-TREATING BY NOW.
TMP
TMP
TMP
TMP
TMP
TMP
UH-HUH. WE SHOULD HURRY...
BMP
WOO HOO
TMP TMP TMP TMP
...

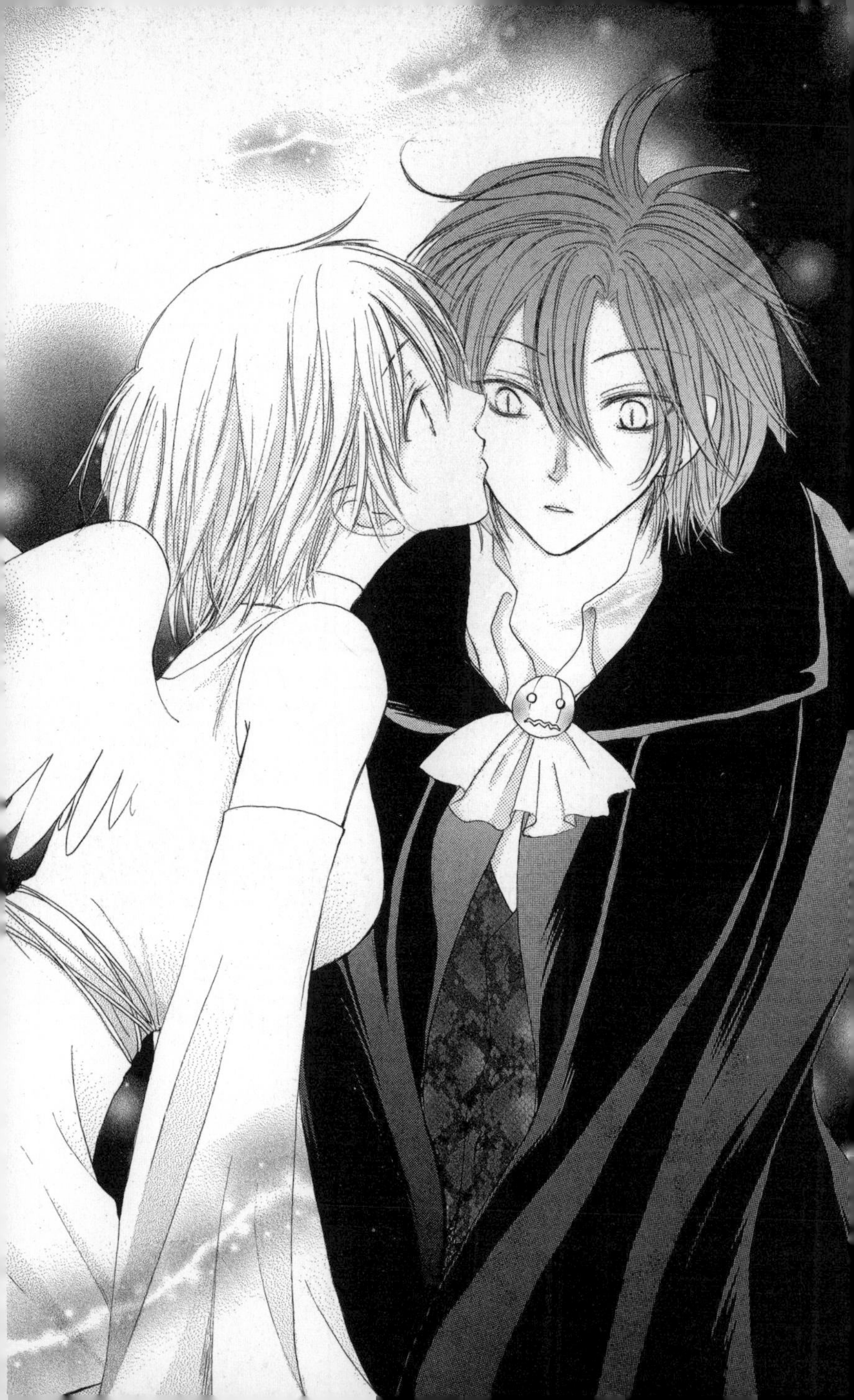

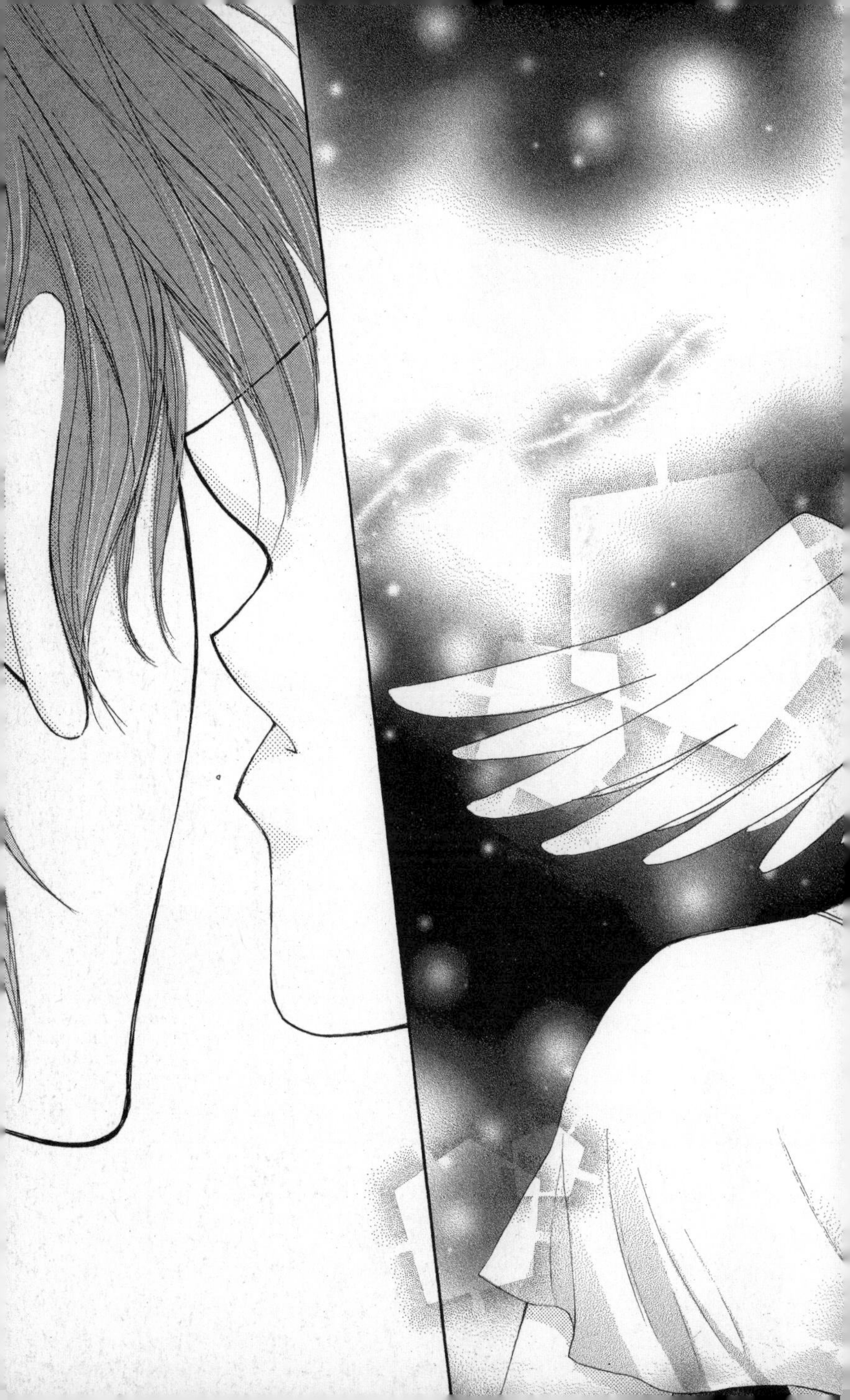

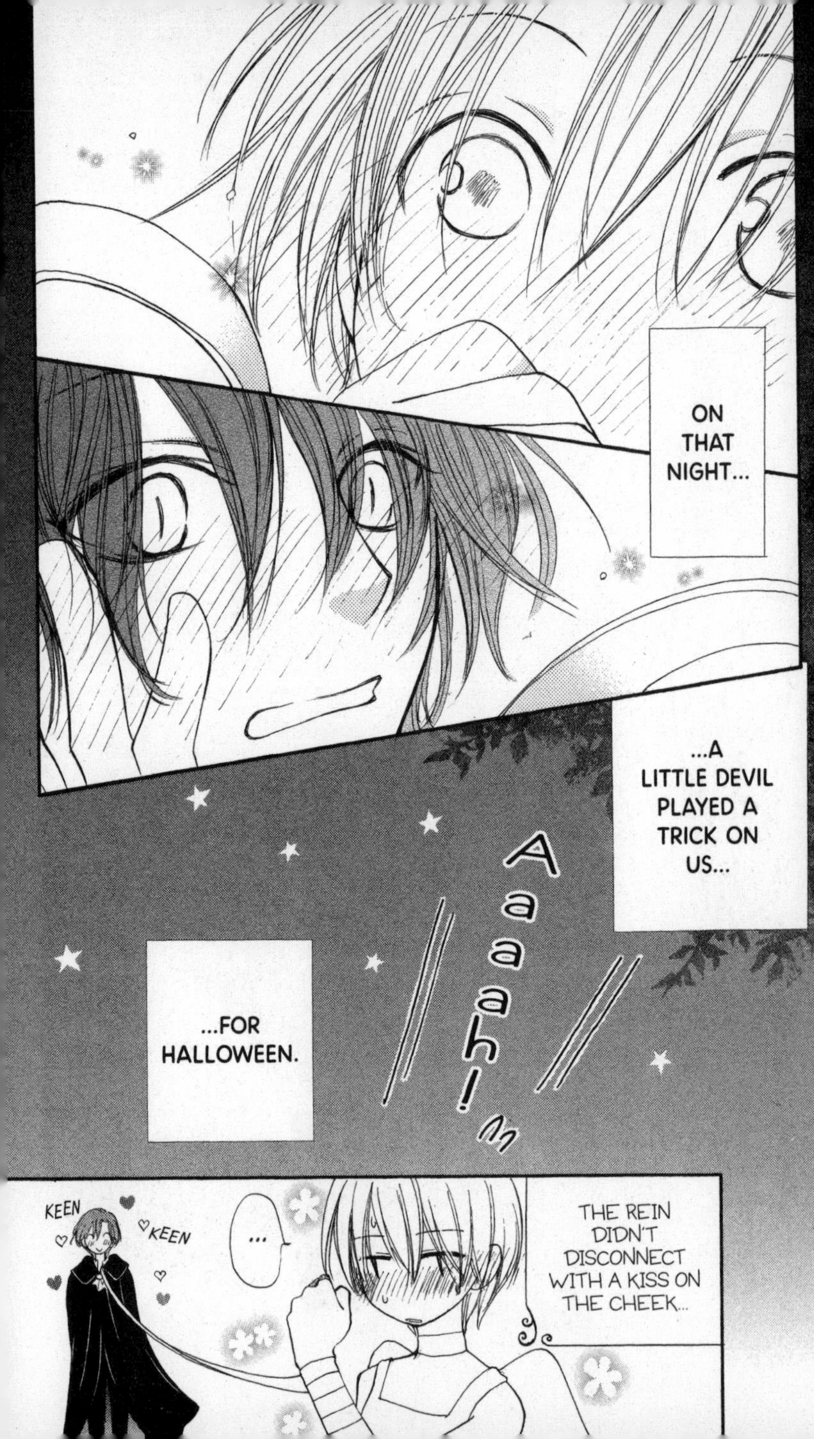
ON THAT NIGHT...
...A LITTLE DEVIL PLAYED A TRICK ON US...
...FOR HALLOWEEN.
Aaaah!
THE REIN DIDN'T DISCONNECT WITH A KISS ON THE CHEEK...
...
KEEN
KEEN

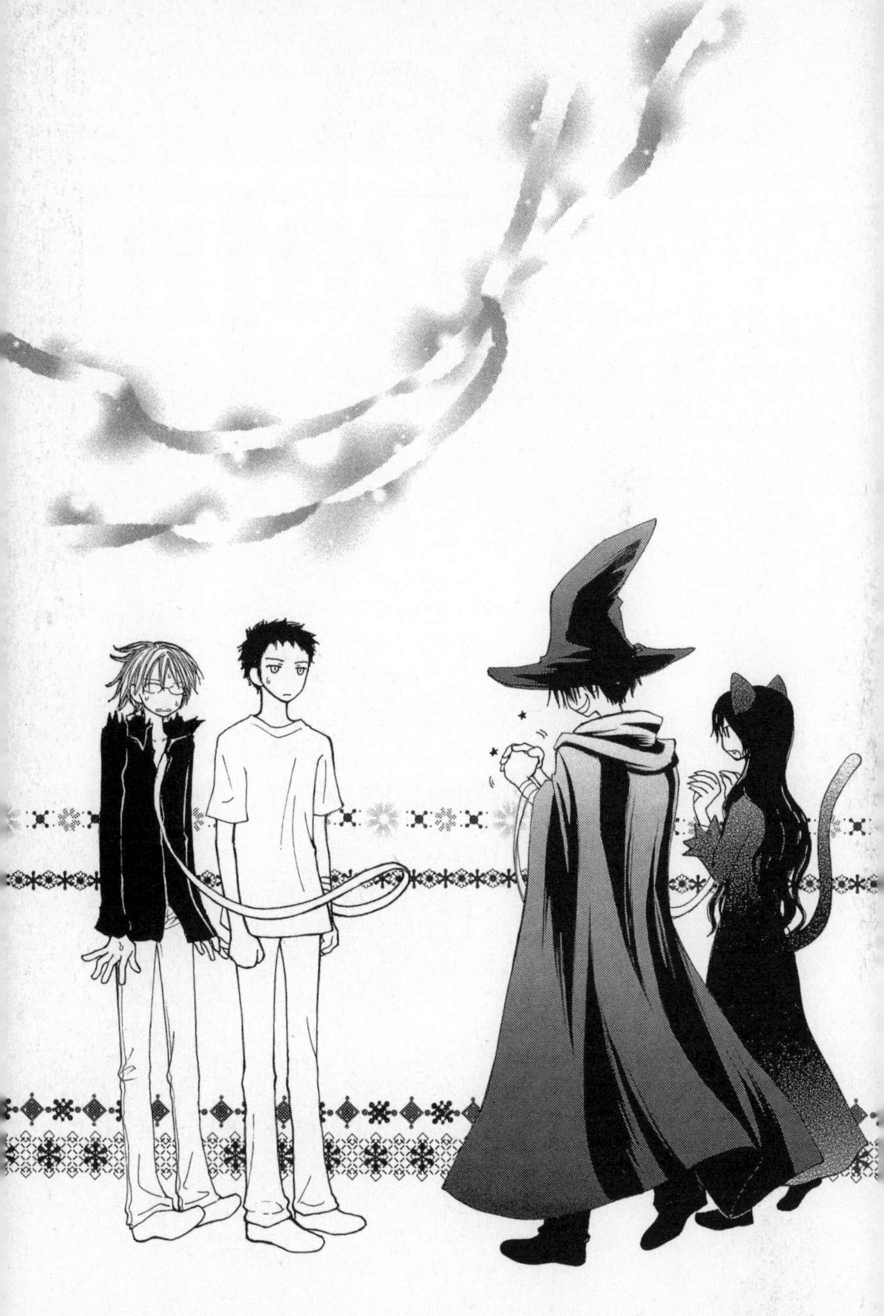

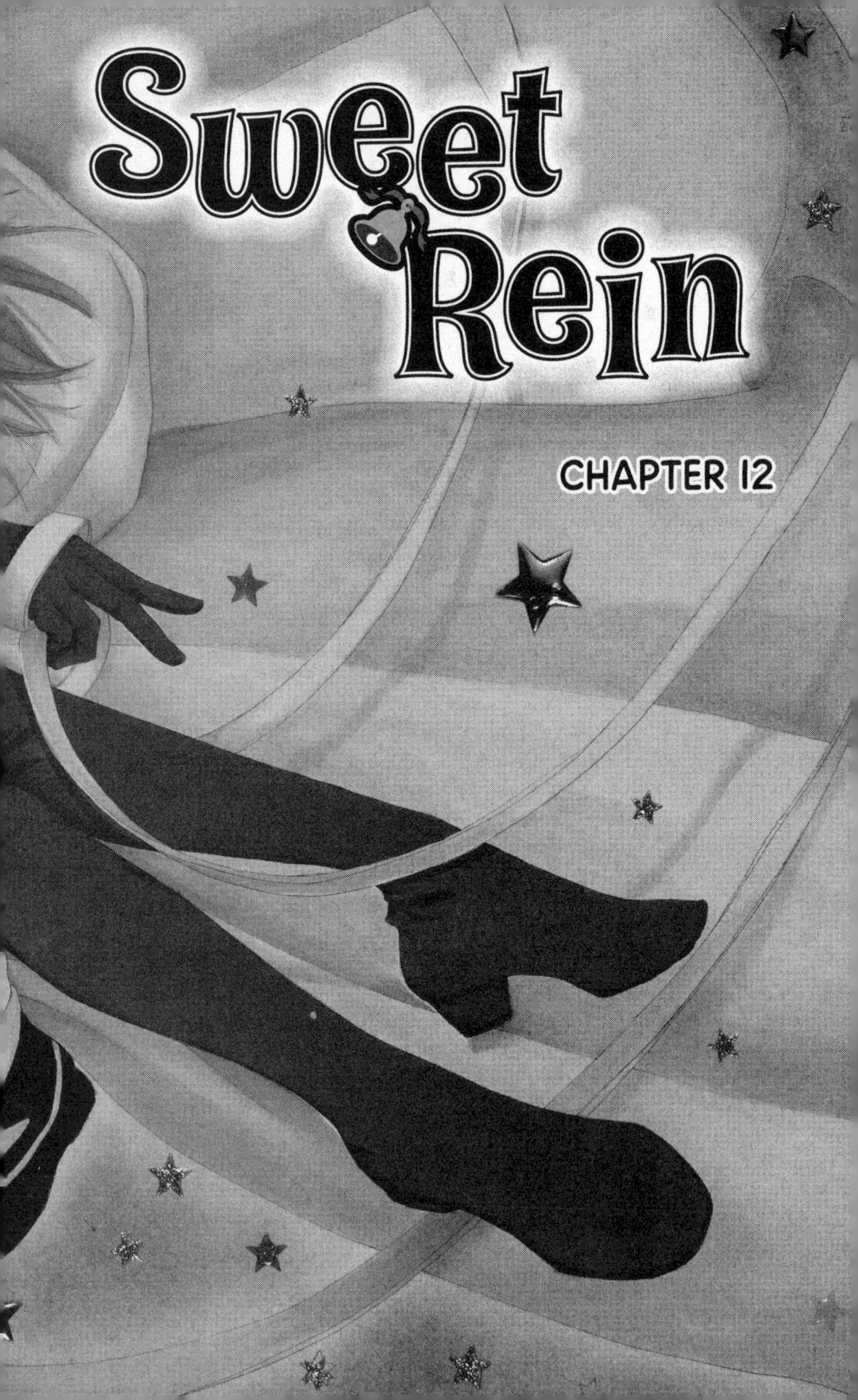
Sweet Rein
CHAPTER 12

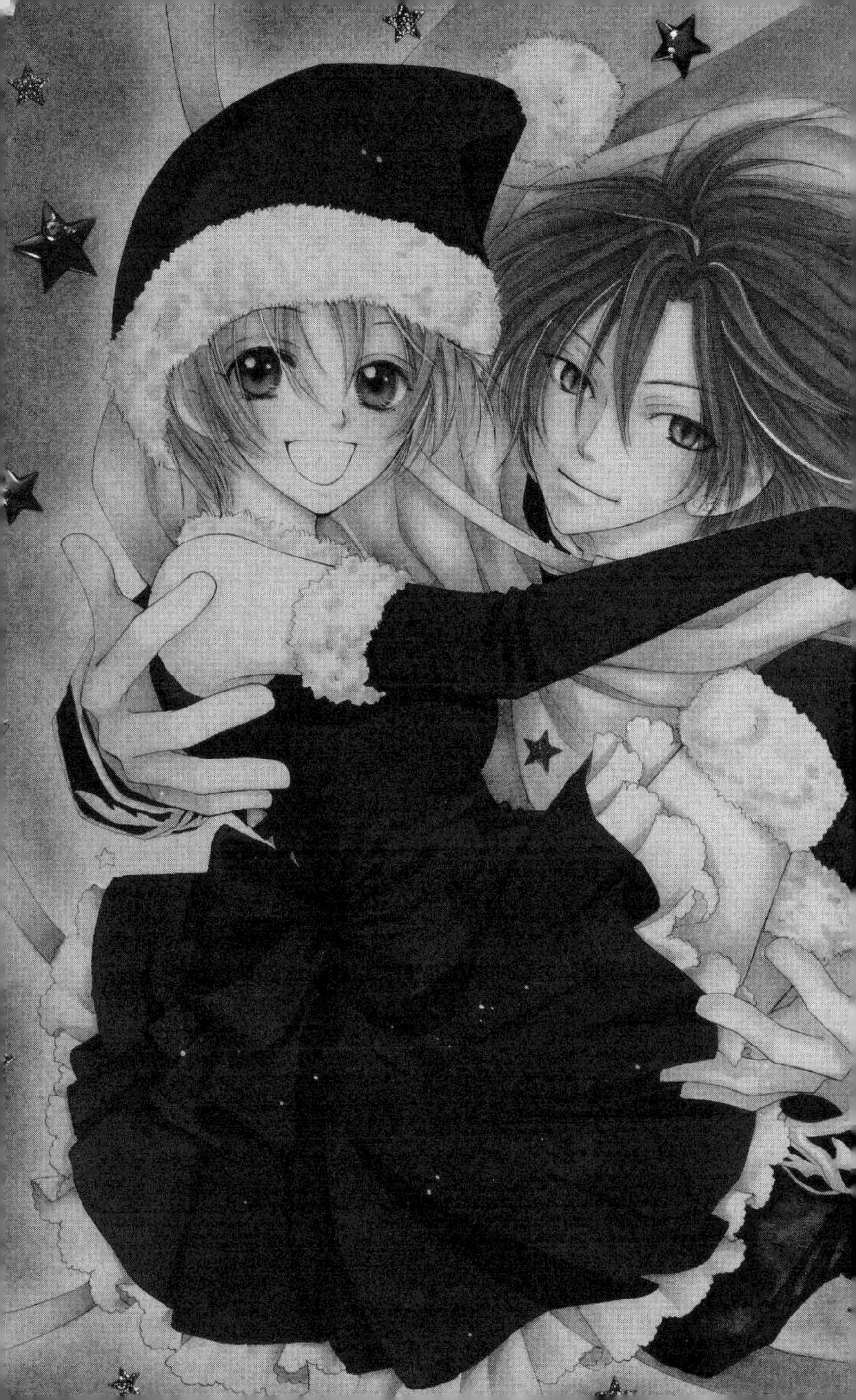

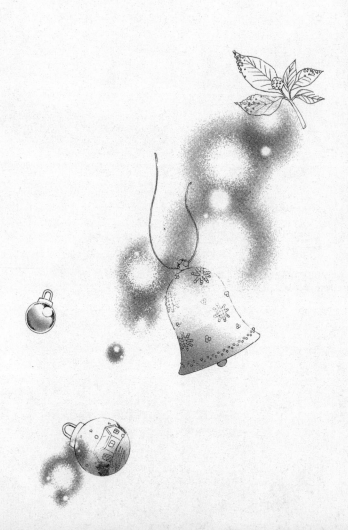

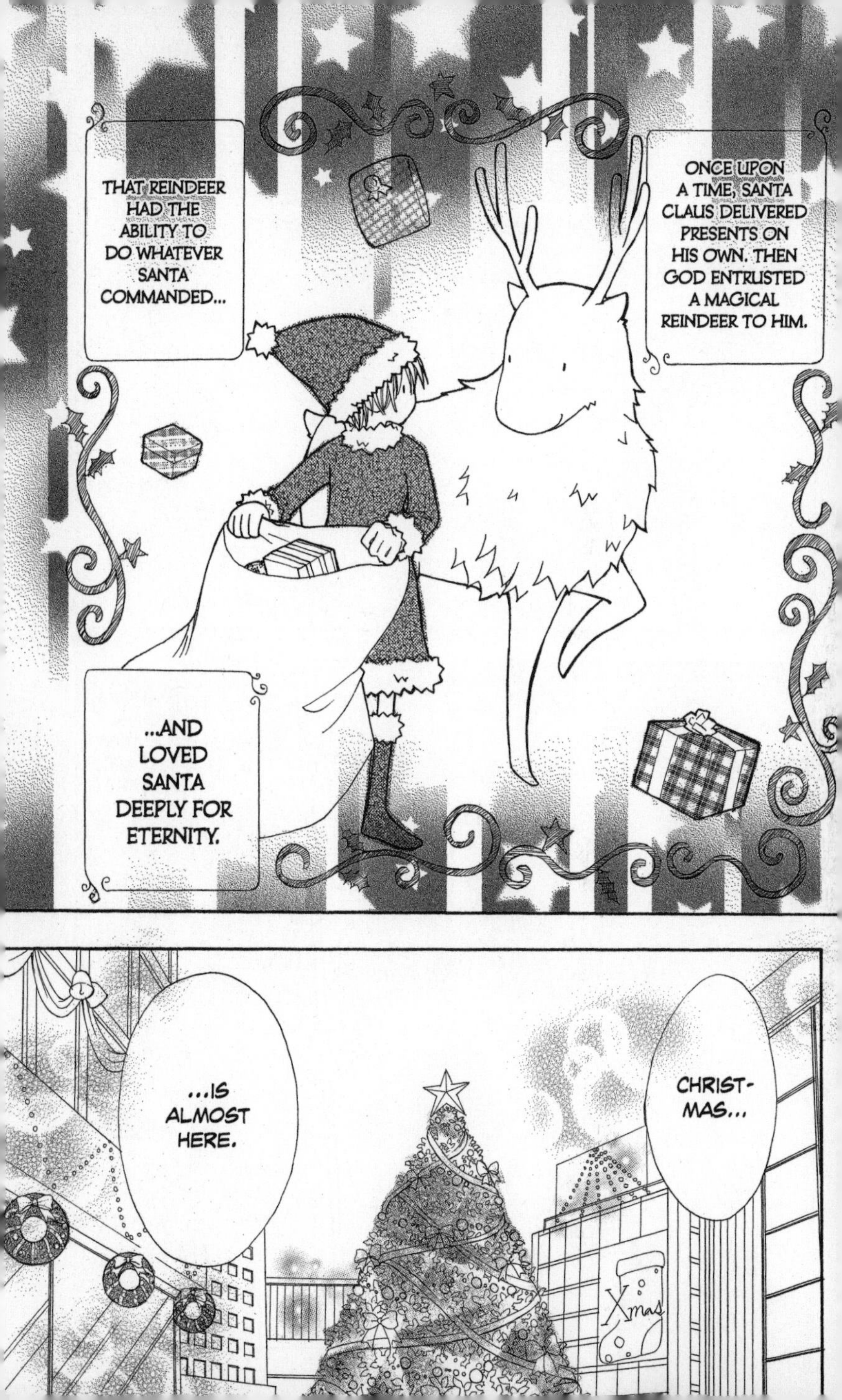
ONCE UPON A TIME, SANTA CLAUS DELIVERED PRESENTS ON HIS OWN. THEN GOD ENTRUSTED A MAGICAL REINDEER TO HIM.
THAT REINDEER HAD THE ABILITY TO DO WHATEVER SANTA COMMANDED...
...AND LOVED SANTA DEEPLY FOR ETERNITY.
CHRIST-MAS...
...IS ALMOST HERE.
Xmas

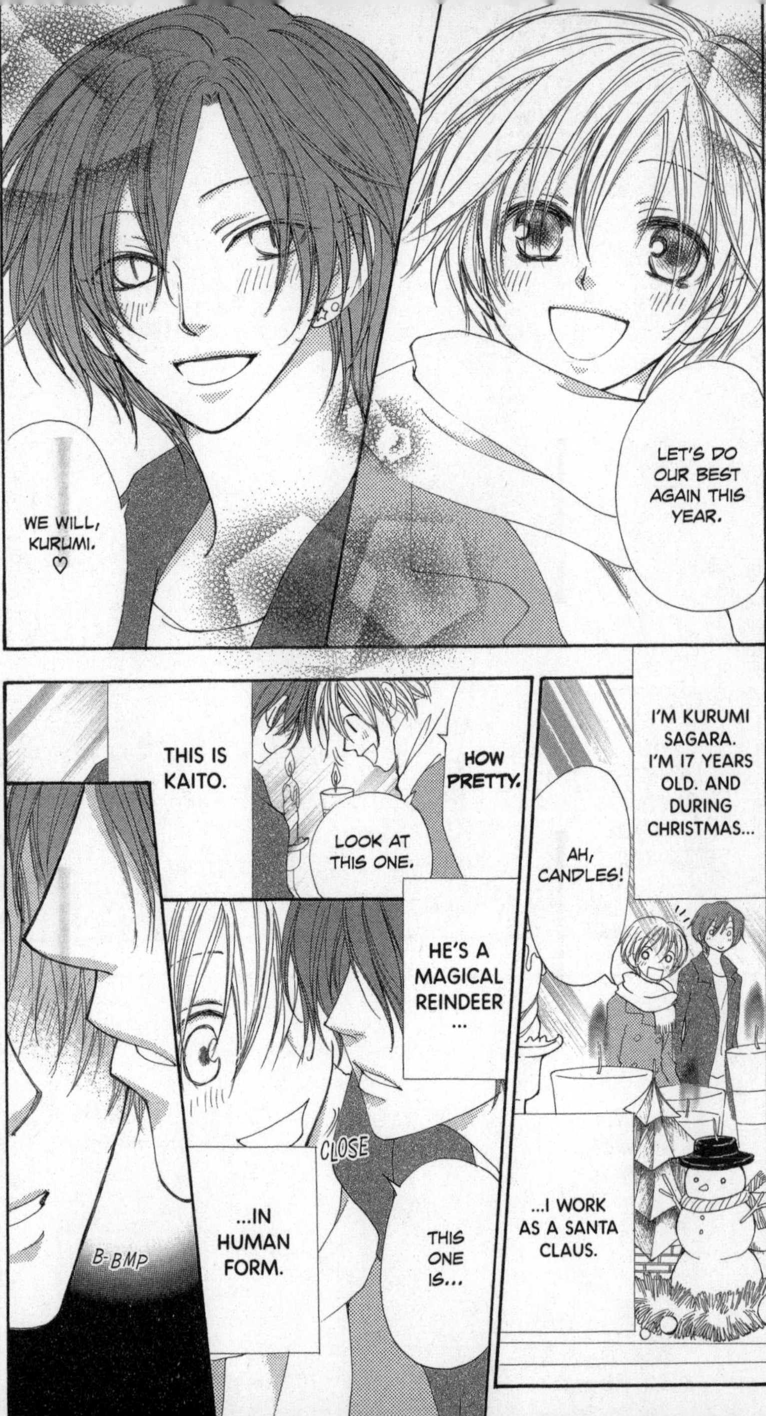
LET'S DO OUR BEST AGAIN THIS YEAR.
WE WILL, KURUMI. ♡
I'M KURUMI SAGARA. I'M 17 YEARS OLD. AND DURING CHRISTMAS...
AH, CANDLES!
...I WORK AS A SANTA CLAUS.
HOW PRETTY.
LOOK AT THIS ONE.
THIS IS KAITO.
HE'S A MAGICAL REINDEER ...
CLOSE
THIS ONE IS...
...IN HUMAN FORM.
B-BMP

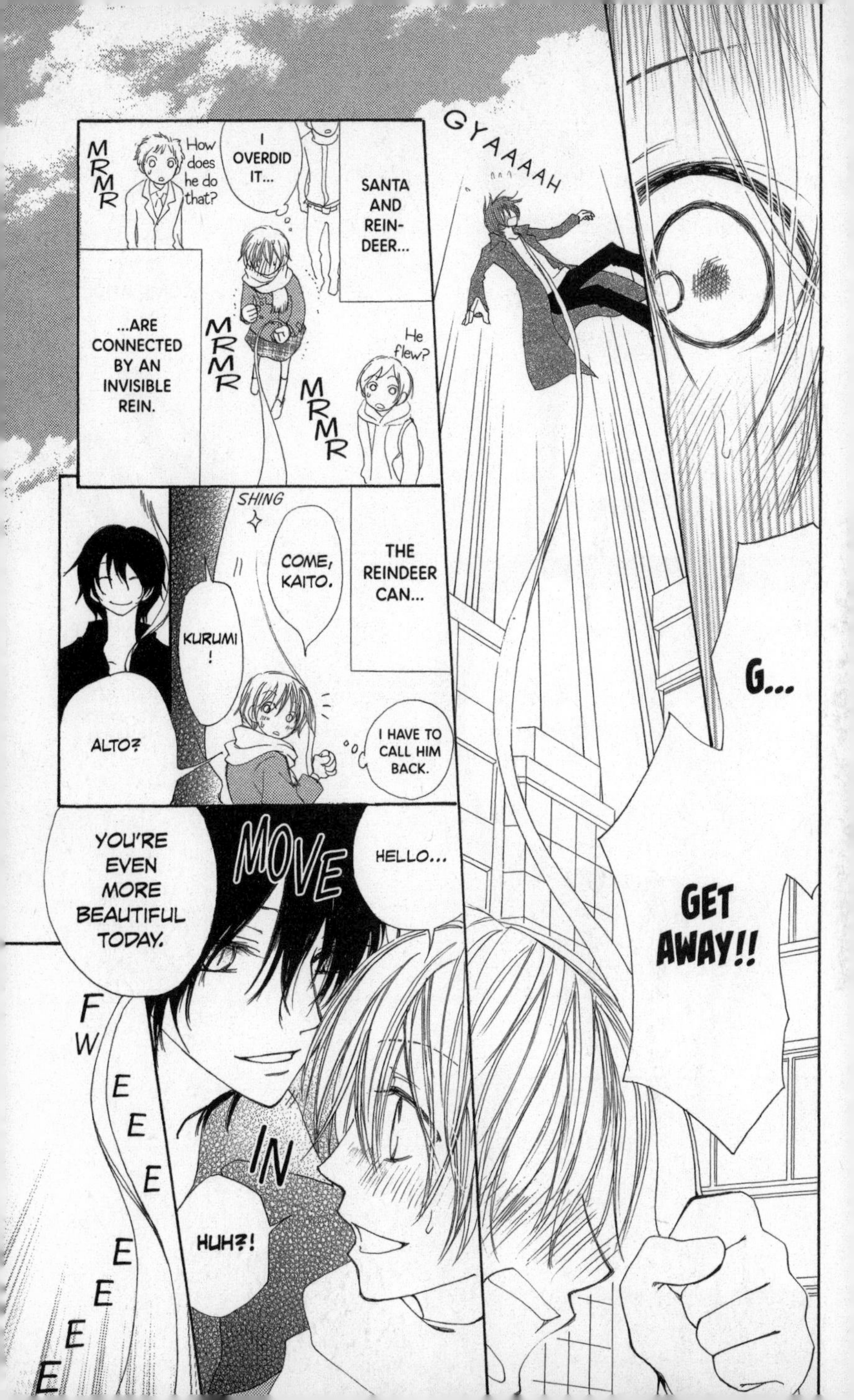
G...
GET AWAY!!
GYAAAAAH
SANTA AND REIN-DEER...
I OVERDID IT...
How does he do that?
MRMR
He flew?
MRMR
MRMR
...ARE CONNECTED BY AN INVISIBLE REIN.
THE REINDEER CAN...
SHING
COME, KAITO.
I HAVE TO CALL HIM BACK.
KURUMI!
ALTO?
HELLO...
MOVE
YOU'RE EVEN MORE BEAUTIFUL TODAY.
IN
HUH?!
FWEEEEEEEE

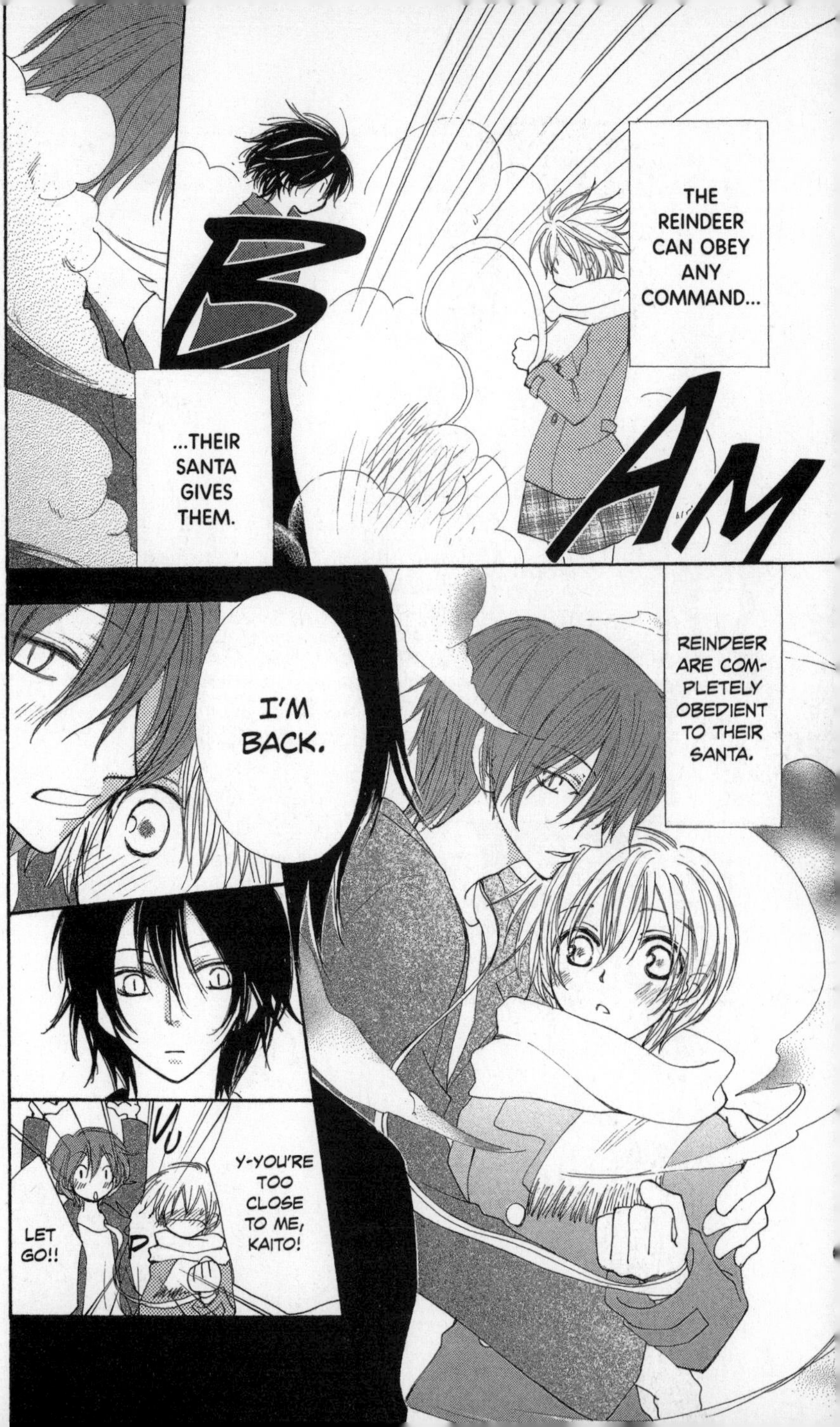
THE REINDEER CAN OBEY ANY COMMAND...
BAM
...THEIR SANTA GIVES THEM.
REINDEER ARE COM-PLETELY OBEDIENT TO THEIR SANTA.
I'M BACK.
Y-YOU'RE TOO CLOSE TO ME, KAITO!
LET GO!!

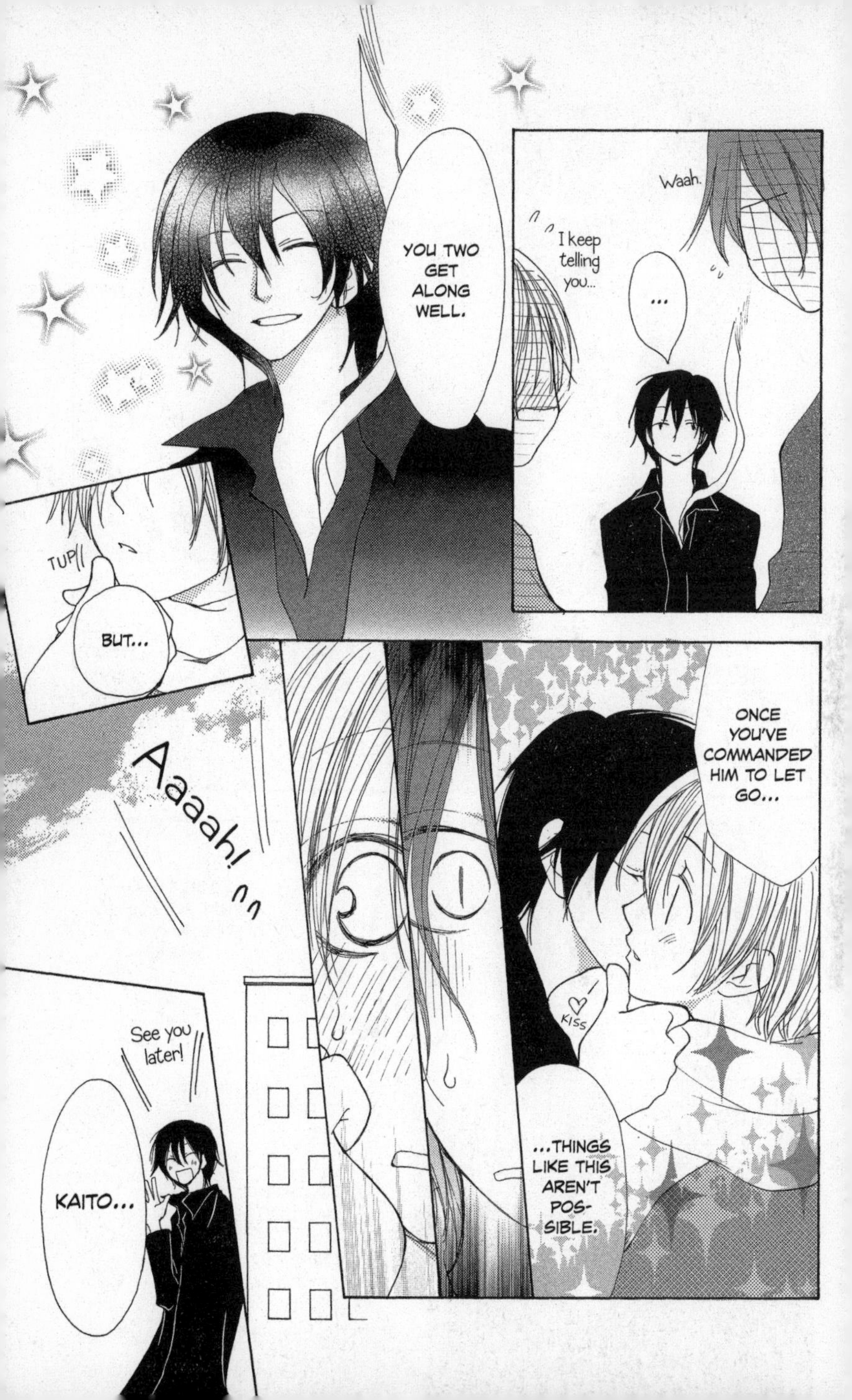
Waah.
I keep telling you...
...
YOU TWO GET ALONG WELL.
TUP
BUT...
ONCE YOU'VE COMMANDED HIM TO LET GO...
KISS
...THINGS LIKE THIS AREN'T POS-SIBLE.
Aaaah!
See you later!
KAITO...

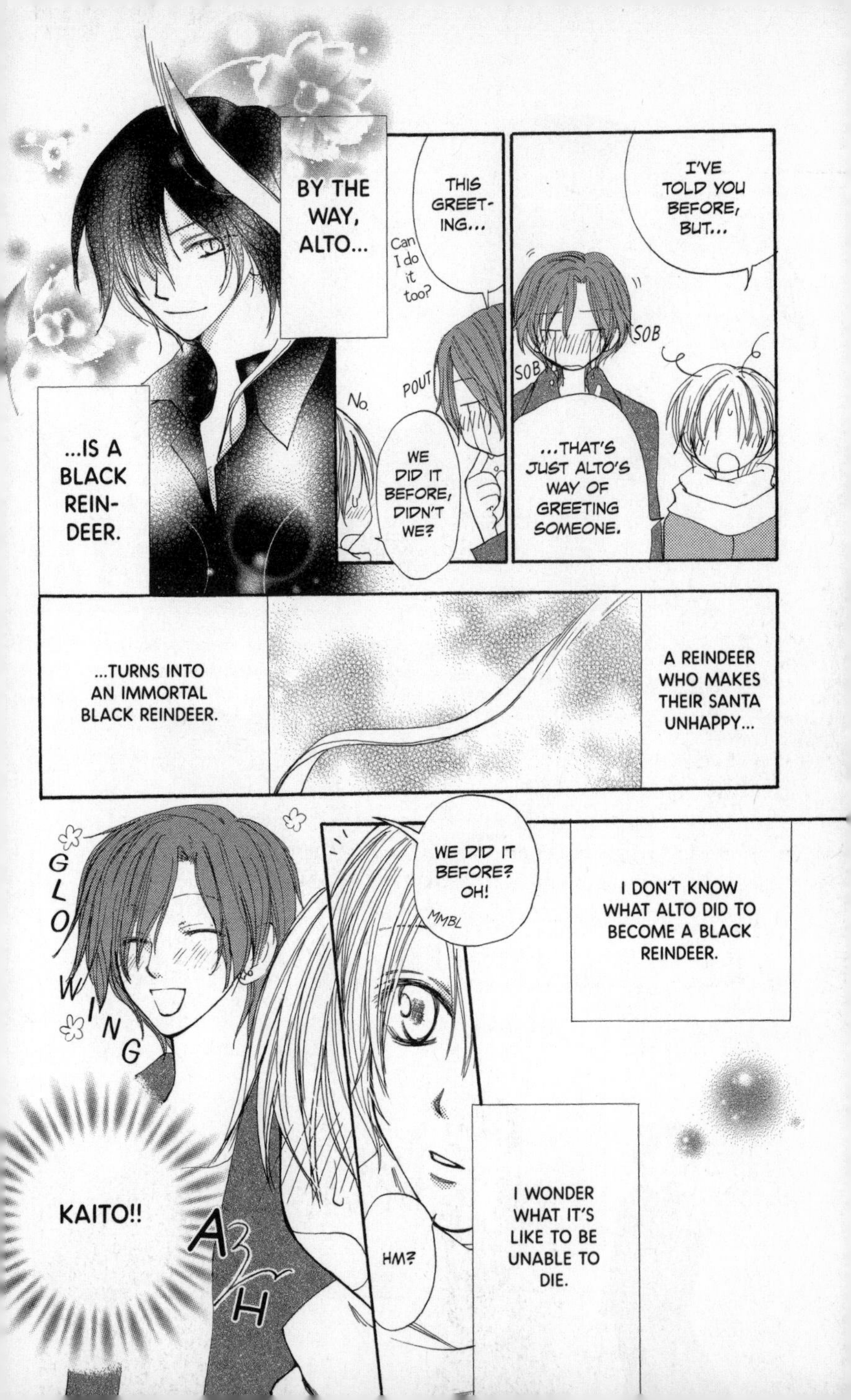
I'VE TOLD YOU BEFORE, BUT...
SOB
SOB
...THAT'S JUST ALTO'S WAY OF GREETING SOMEONE.
THIS GREETING...
Can I do it too?
POUT
No.
WE DID IT BEFORE, DIDN'T WE?
BY THE WAY, ALTO...
...IS A BLACK REINDEER.
A REINDEER WHO MAKES THEIR SANTA UNHAPPY...
...TURNS INTO AN IMMORTAL BLACK REINDEER.
I DON'T KNOW WHAT ALTO DID TO BECOME A BLACK REINDEER.
WE DID IT BEFORE? OH!
MMBL
I WONDER WHAT IT'S LIKE TO BE UNABLE TO DIE.
HM?
GLOWING
KAITO!!
AH

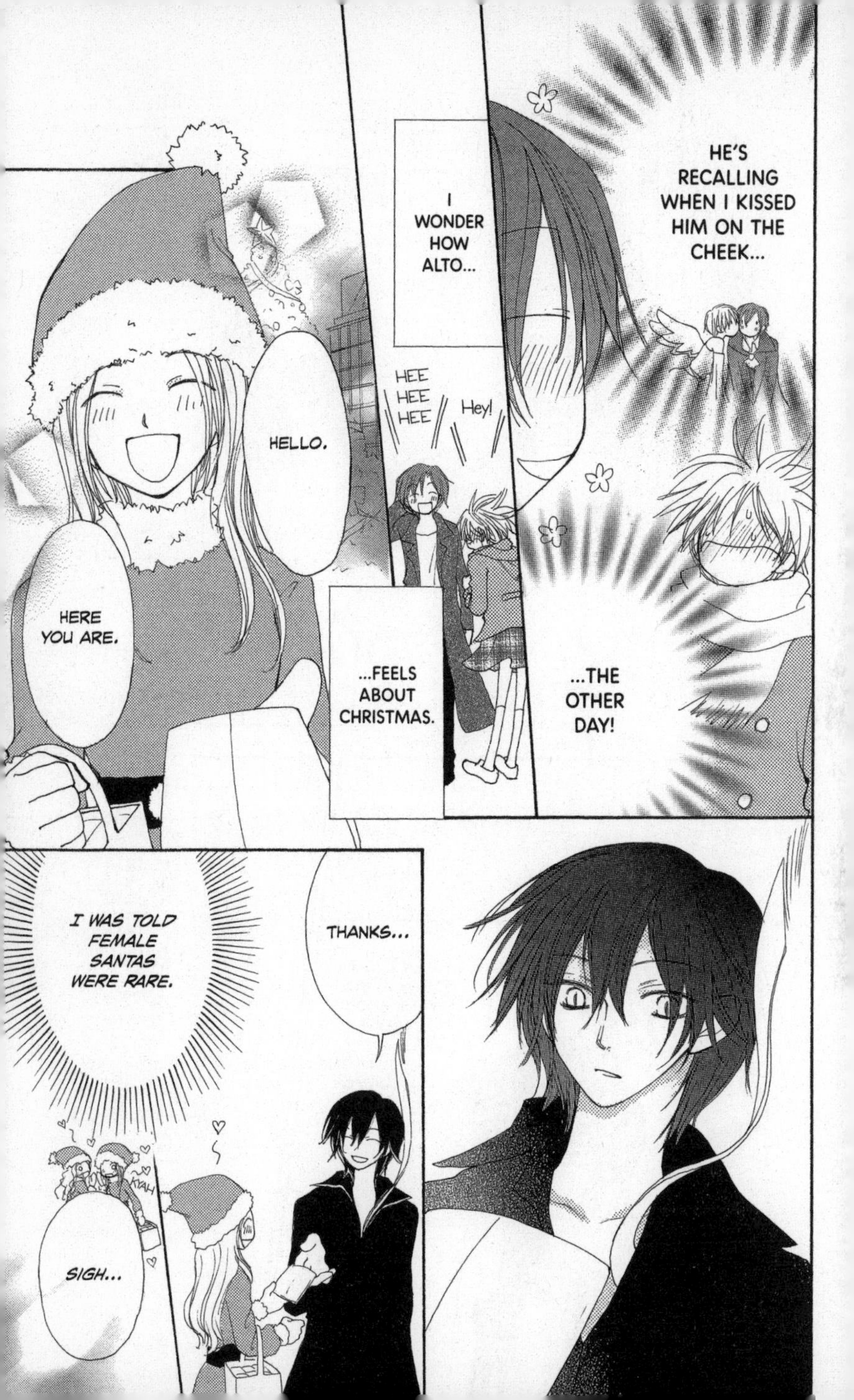
HE'S RECALLING WHEN I KISSED HIM ON THE CHEEK...
...THE OTHER DAY!
I WONDER HOW ALTO...
HEE HEE HEE
Hey!
...FEELS ABOUT CHRISTMAS.
HELLO.
HERE YOU ARE.
THANKS...
I WAS TOLD FEMALE SANTAS WERE RARE.
KYAH
SIGH...

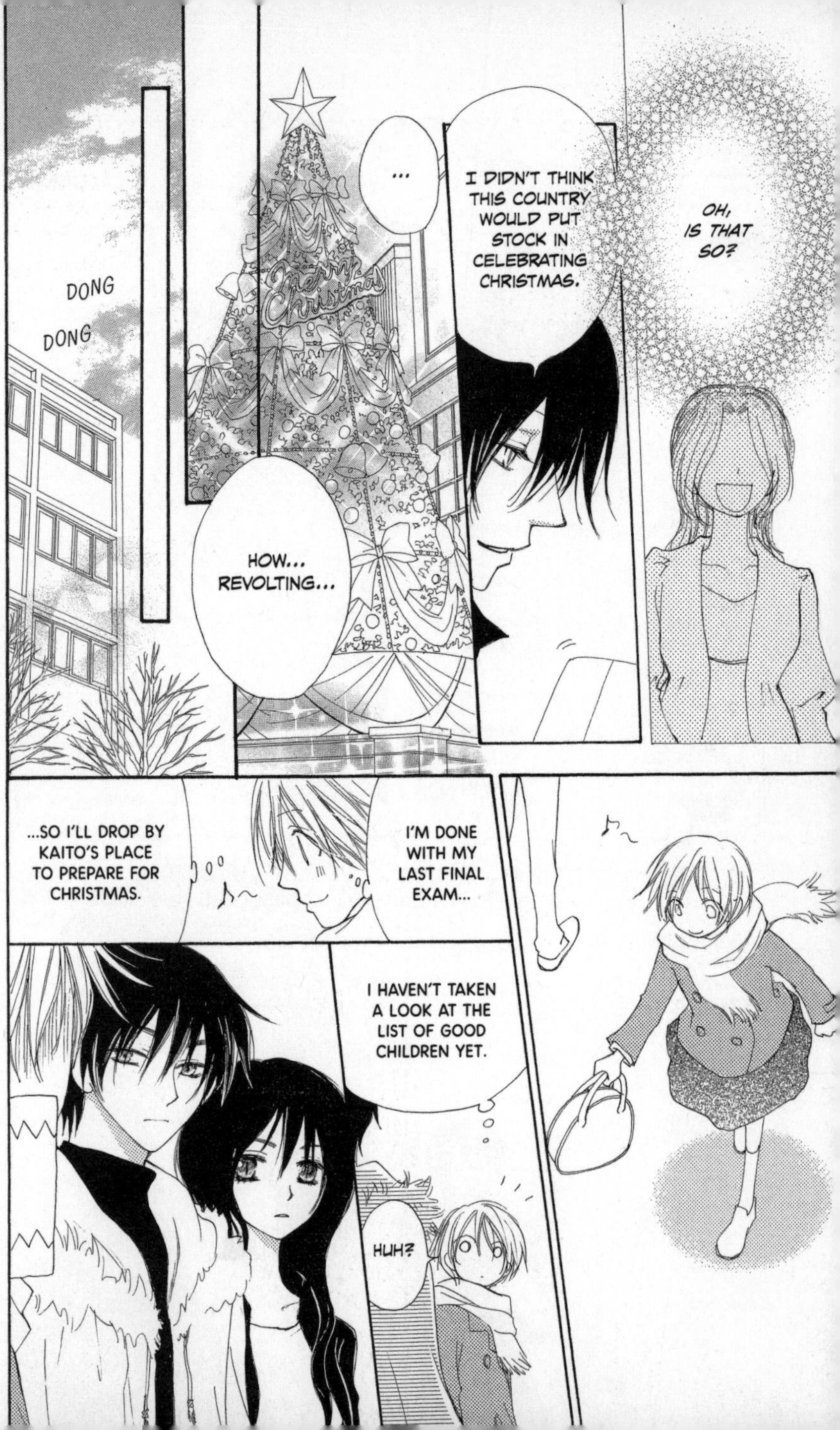

OH, IS THAT SO?
I DIDN'T THINK THIS COUNTRY WOULD PUT STOCK IN CELEBRATING CHRISTMAS.
...
HOW... REVOLTING...
Merry Christmas
DONG
DONG
I'M DONE WITH MY LAST FINAL EXAM...
...SO I'LL DROP BY KAITO'S PLACE TO PREPARE FOR CHRISTMAS.
I HAVEN'T TAKEN A LOOK AT THE LIST OF GOOD CHILDREN YET.
HUH?

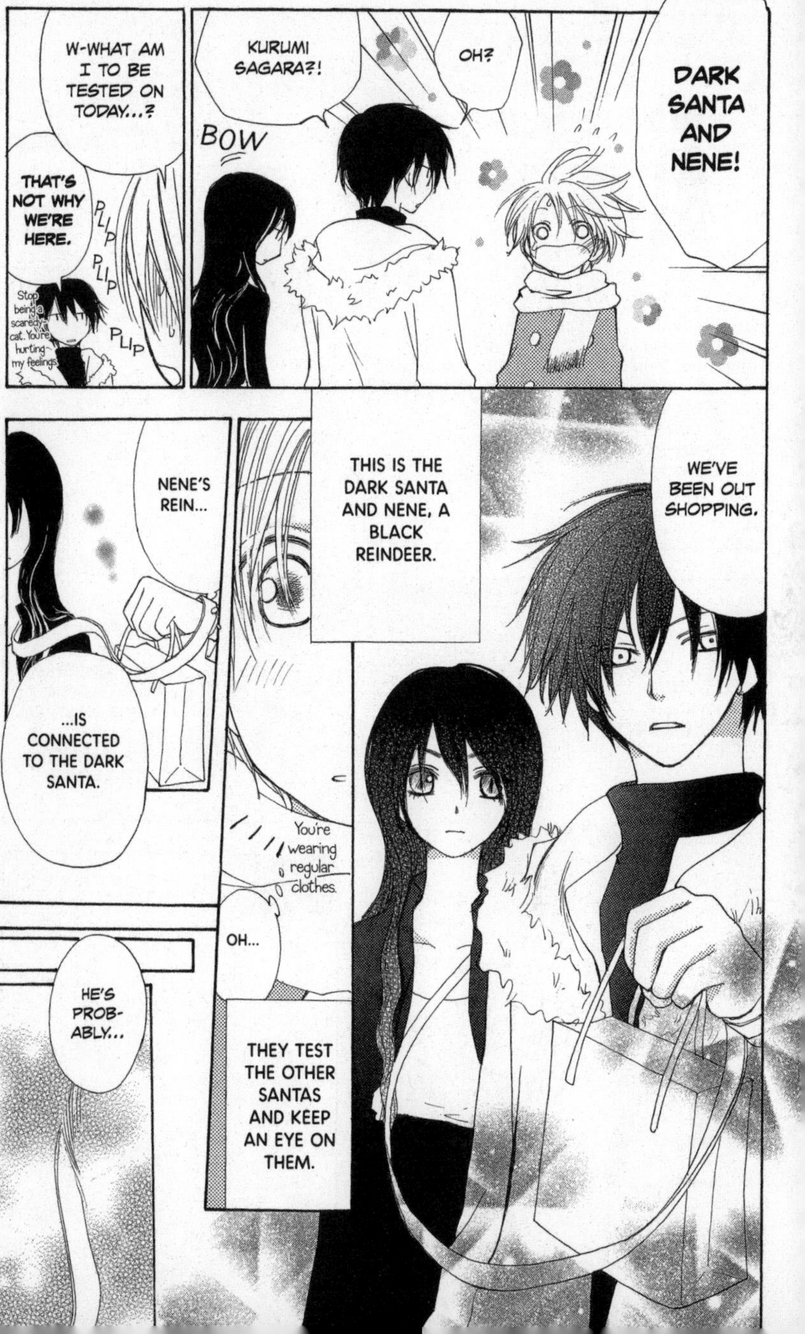
DARK SANTA AND NENE!
OH?
KURUMI SAGARA?!
BOW
W-WHAT AM I TO BE TESTED ON TODAY...?
THAT'S NOT WHY WE'RE HERE.
PLIP PLIP PLIP
Stop being a scaredy-cat. You're hurting my feelings.
WE'VE BEEN OUT SHOPPING.
THIS IS THE DARK SANTA AND NENE, A BLACK REINDEER.
THEY TEST THE OTHER SANTAS AND KEEP AN EYE ON THEM.
You're wearing regular clothes.
OH...
NENE'S REIN...
...IS CONNECTED TO THE DARK SANTA.
HE'S PROB-ABLY...

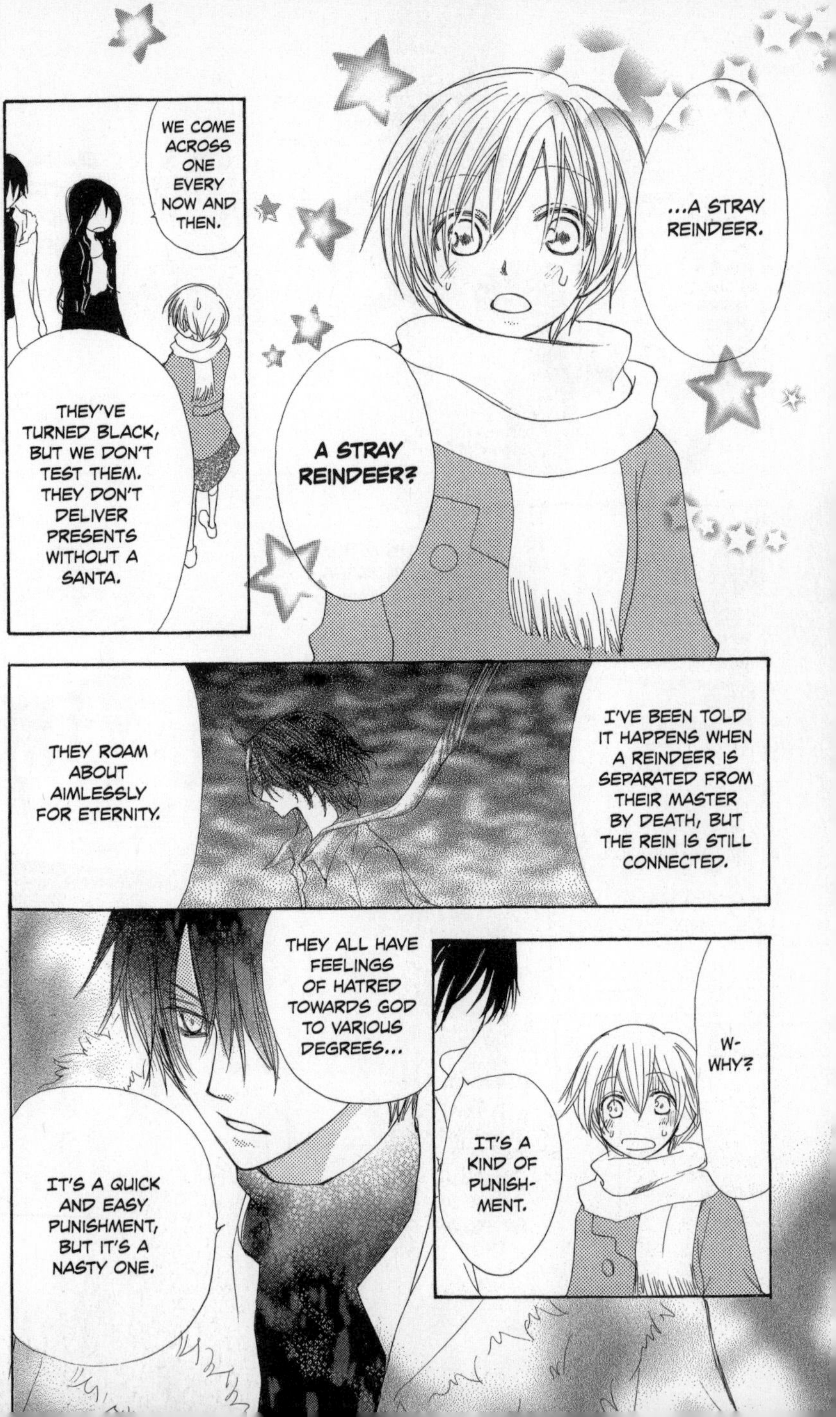
...A STRAY REINDEER.
A STRAY REINDEER?
WE COME ACROSS ONE EVERY NOW AND THEN.
THEY'VE TURNED BLACK, BUT WE DON'T TEST THEM. THEY DON'T DELIVER PRESENTS WITHOUT A SANTA.
I'VE BEEN TOLD IT HAPPENS WHEN A REINDEER IS SEPARATED FROM THEIR MASTER BY DEATH, BUT THE REIN IS STILL CONNECTED.
THEY ROAM ABOUT AIMLESSLY FOR ETERNITY.
W-WHY?
IT'S A KIND OF PUNISHMENT.
THEY ALL HAVE FEELINGS OF HATRED TOWARDS GOD TO VARIOUS DEGREES...
IT'S A QUICK AND EASY PUNISHMENT, BUT IT'S A NASTY ONE.

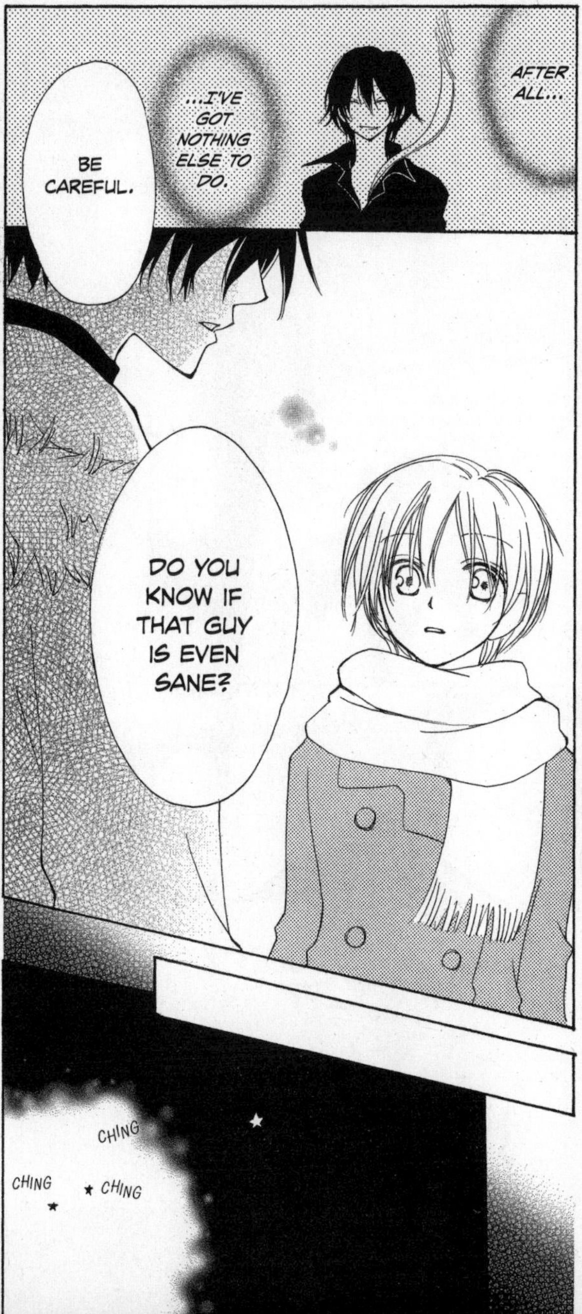
AFTER ALL...
...I'VE GOT NOTHING ELSE TO DO.
BE CAREFUL.
DO YOU KNOW IF THAT GUY IS EVEN SANE?
CHING
CHING
CHING

1/4 Sakura Mail

Part 9

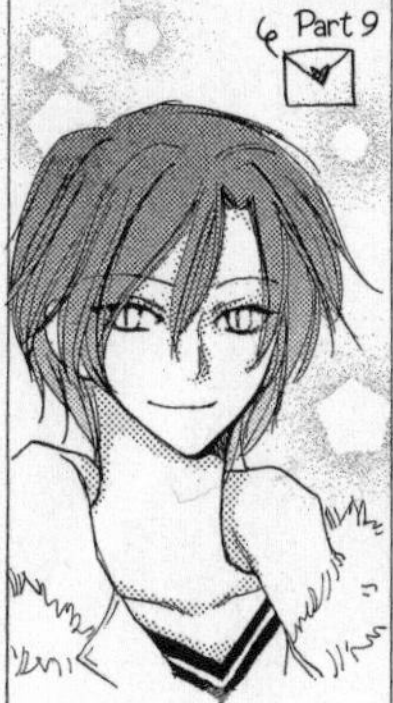

Christmas has come again! The key to this story is Alto, who first appeared in the previous chapter. Not all black reindeer are optimistic (?) like Nene. Many have become twisted. It must be hard for them: The stronger their love, the more twisted they become.

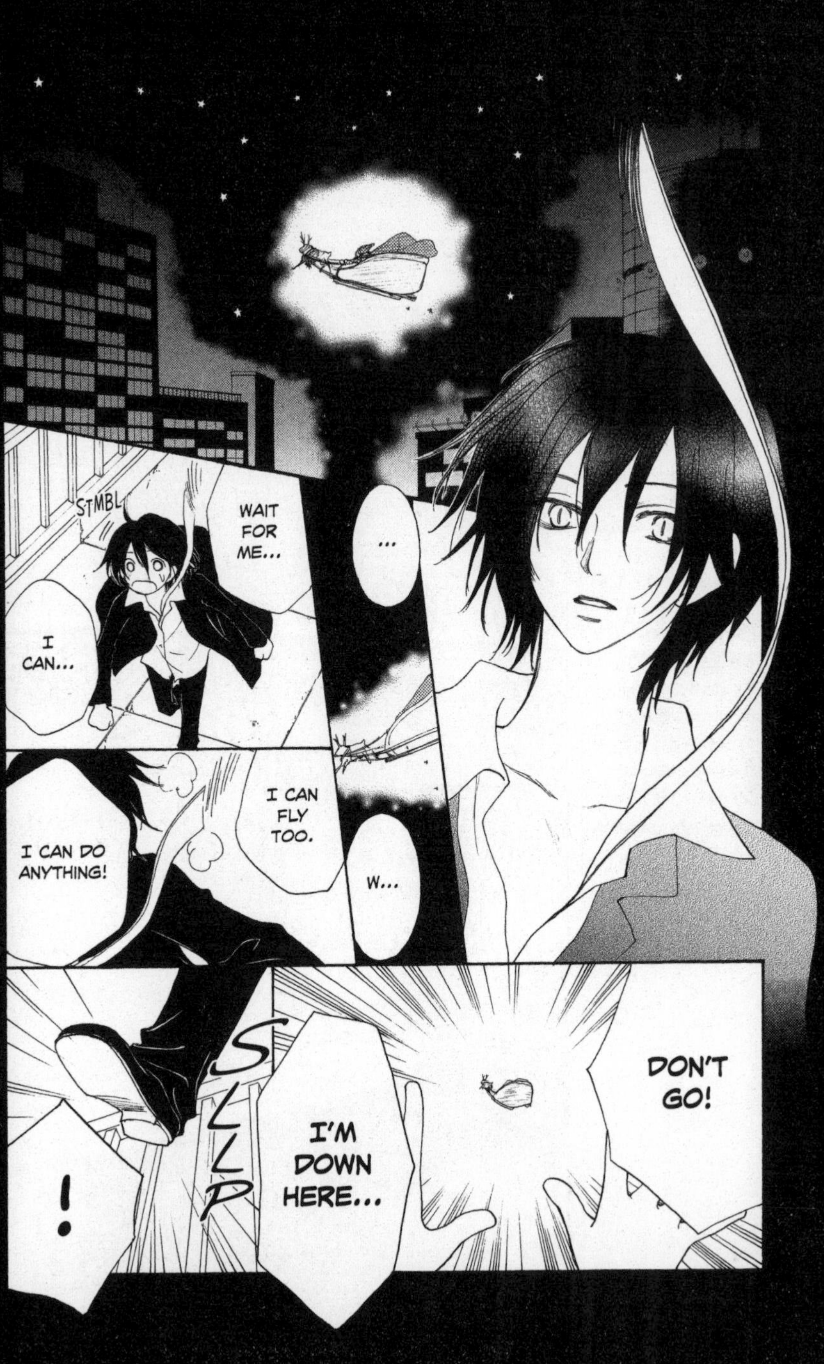
...
W...
WAIT FOR ME...
I CAN...
STMBL
I CAN FLY TOO.
I CAN DO ANYTHING!
DON'T GO!
I'M DOWN HERE...
SLLP
!

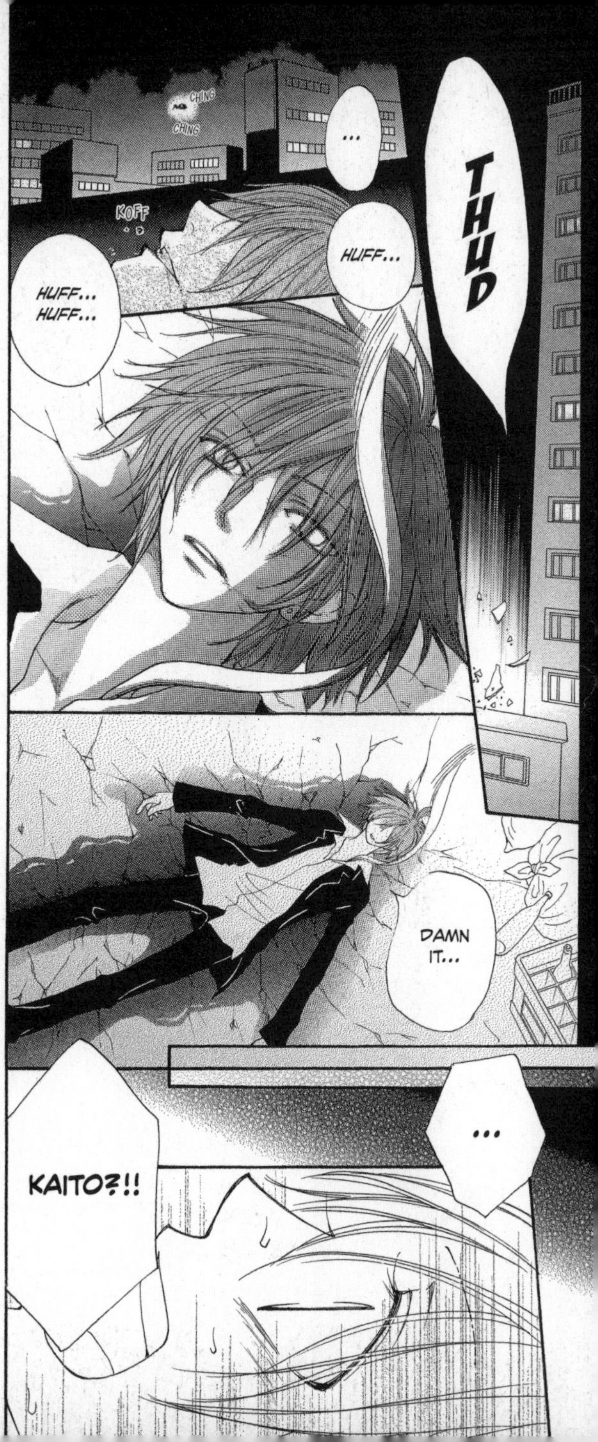
THUD
...
CHING CHING
HUFF...
KOFF
HUFF... HUFF...
DAMN IT...
...
KAITO?!!

1/4 Sakura Mail

Part 10

I drew Alto so that he'd look very similar to Kaito. In the beginning, I imagined him to be a darker version of Kaito. As I continued to draw him, I began to feel they were very different. As a matter of fact, Kaito seems to be the more dangerous one at times. I wrote that a reindeer will turn black if they make their Santa unhappy, but there are various meanings to that... A Santa may become unhappy, or a reindeer may turn black just by feeling responsible for making their Santa unhappy.

(continues)

BUTTOCKS

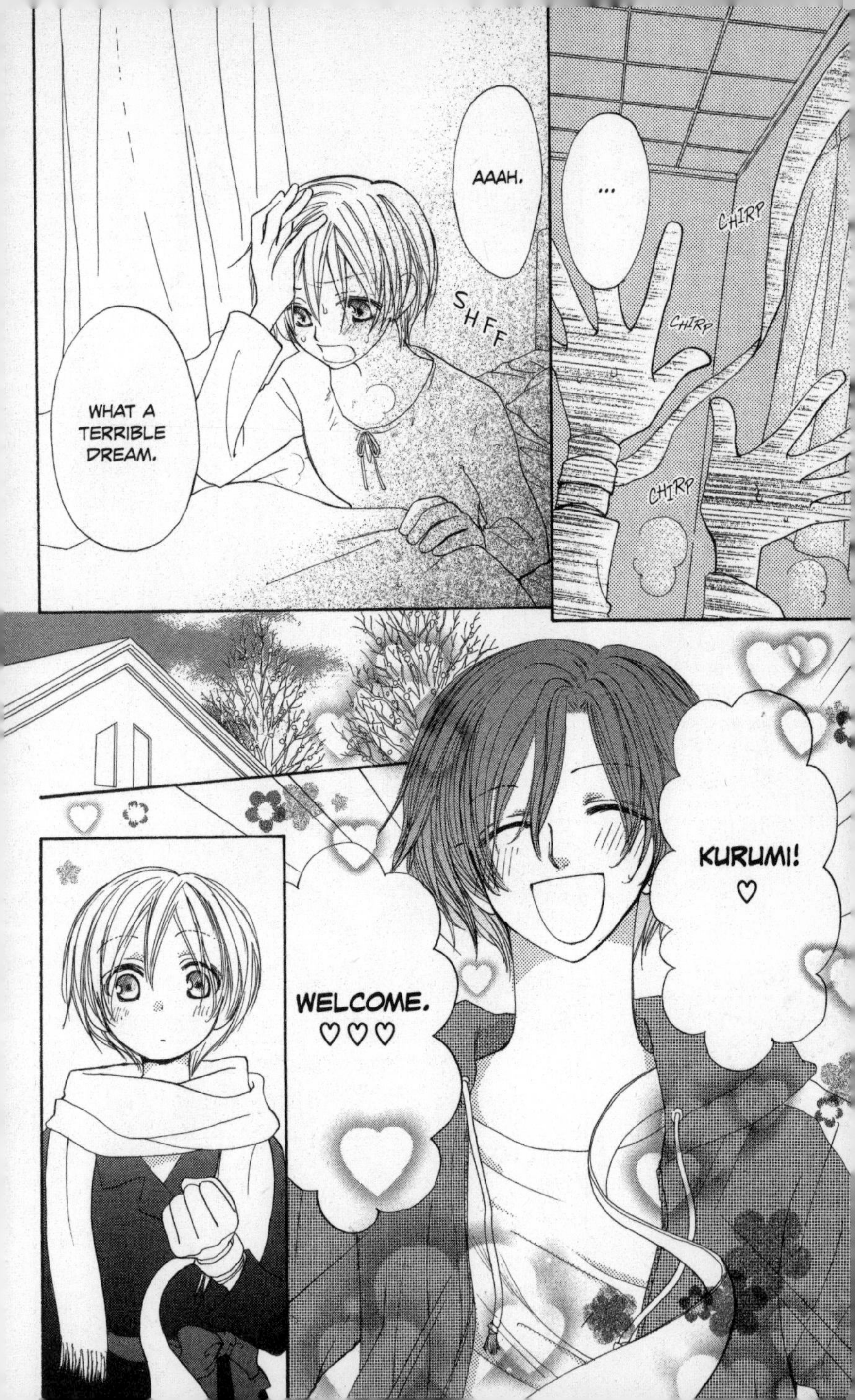
...
CHIRP
CHIRP
CHIRP
AAAH.
SHFF
WHAT A TERRIBLE DREAM.
KURUMI! ♡
WELCOME. ♡♡♡

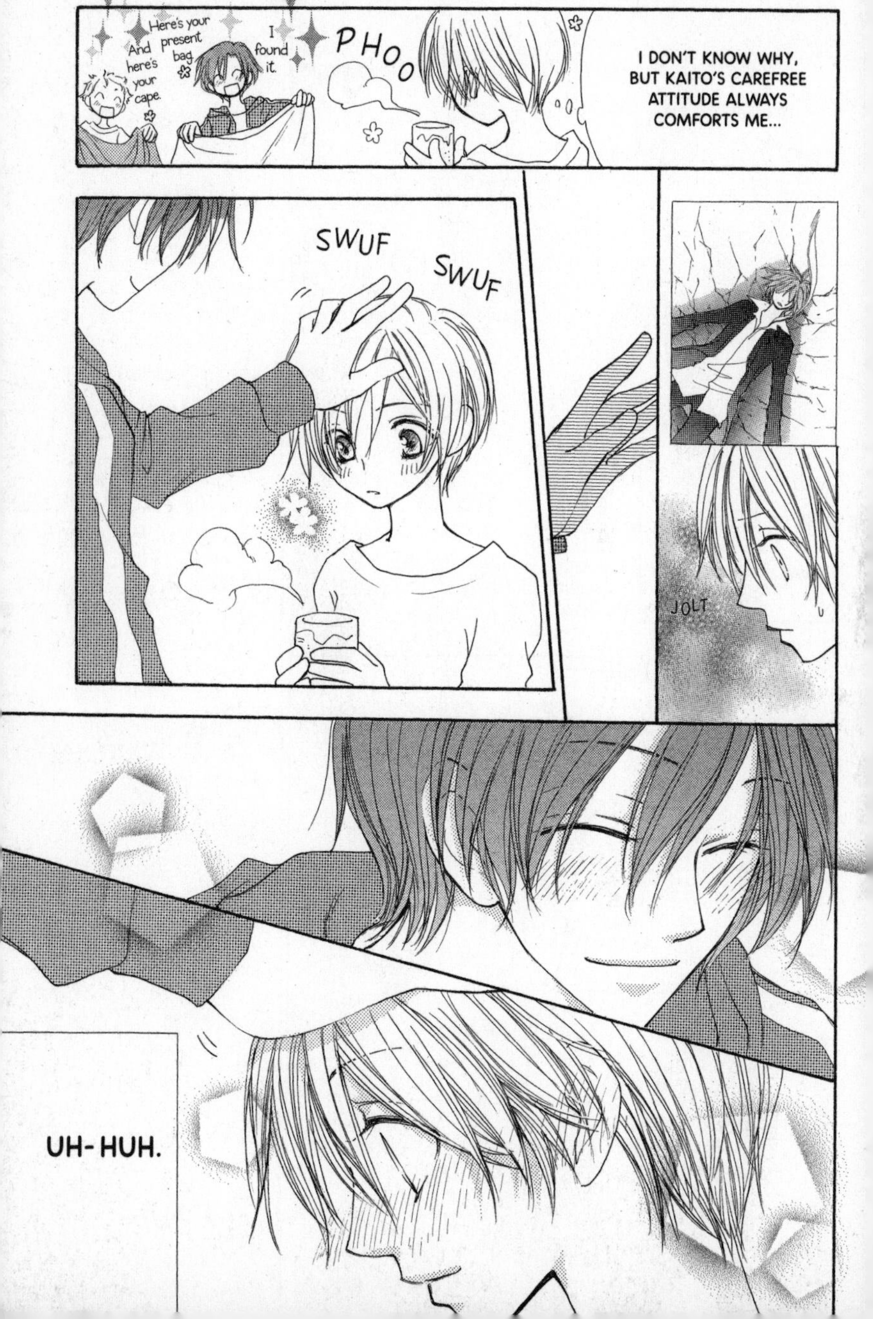

I DON'T KNOW WHY, BUT KAITO'S CAREFREE ATTITUDE ALWAYS COMFORTS ME...
PHOO
I found it.
Here's your present bag.
And here's your cape.
JOLT
SWUF
SWUF
UH-HUH.

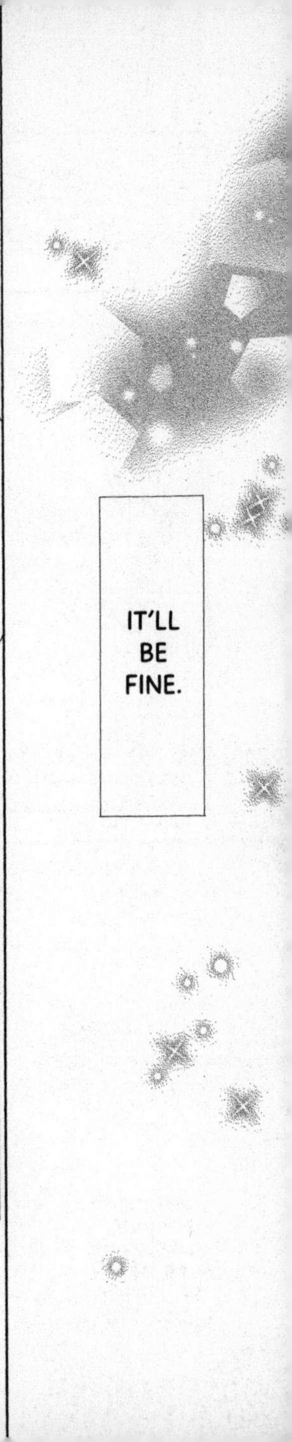
IT'LL BE FINE.
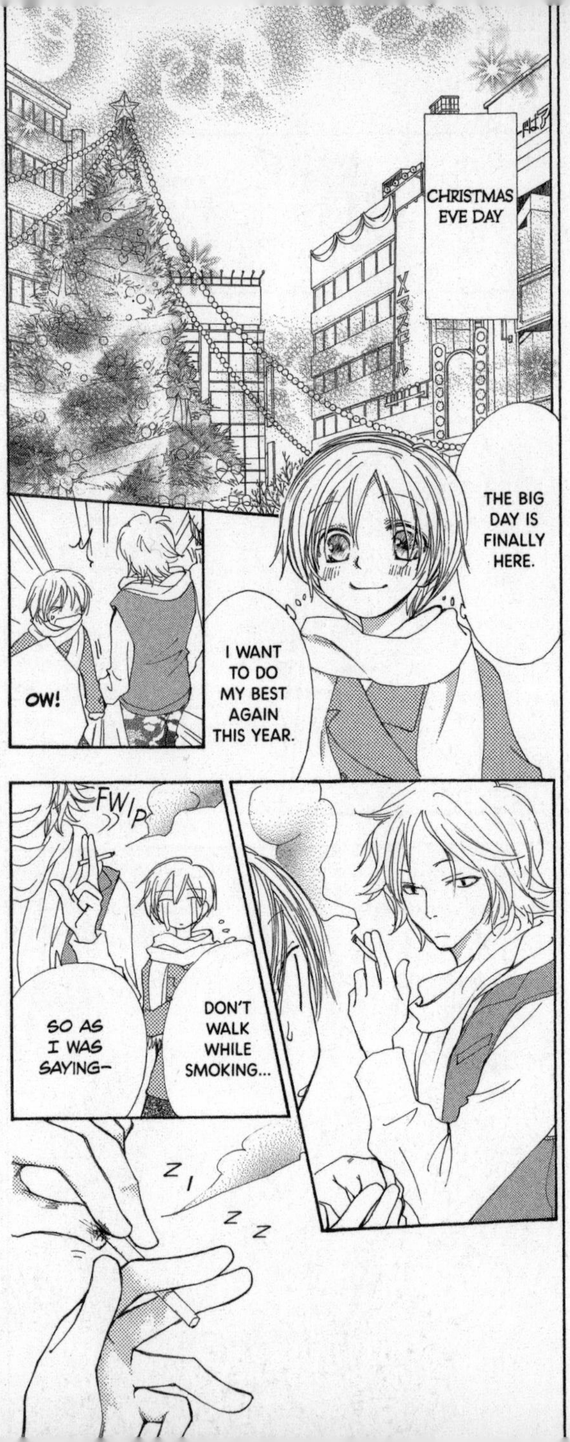
CHRISTMAS EVE DAY
THE BIG DAY IS FINALLY HERE.
I WANT TO DO MY BEST AGAIN THIS YEAR.
OW!
FWIP
DON'T WALK WHILE SMOKING...
SO AS I WAS SAYING–

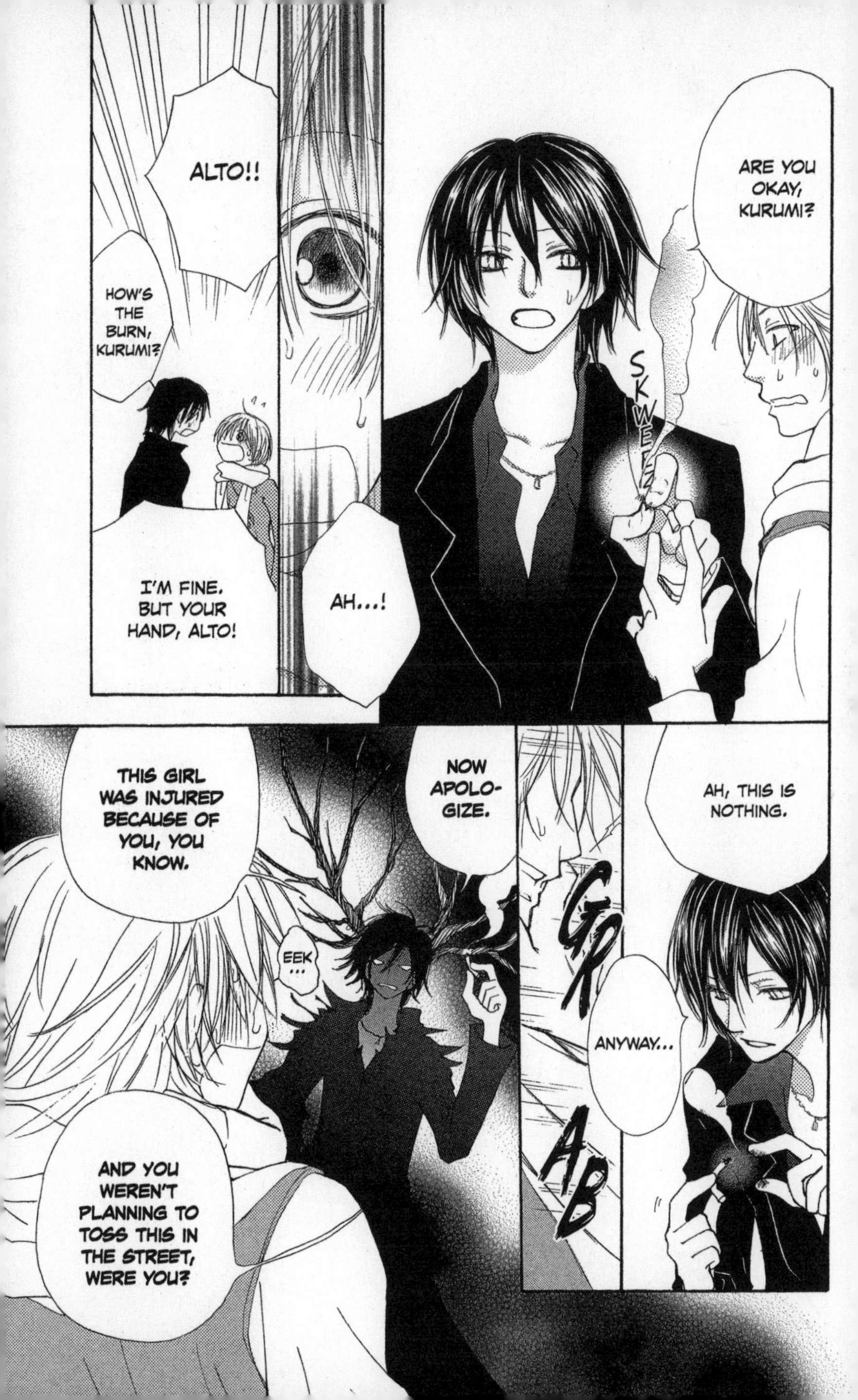

ARE YOU OKAY, KURUMI?
SKWEEZ
AH...!
ALTO!!
HOW'S THE BURN, KURUMI?
I'M FINE. BUT YOUR HAND, ALTO!
AH, THIS IS NOTHING.
ANYWAY...
GRAB
NOW APOLO-GIZE.
THIS GIRL WAS INJURED BECAUSE OF YOU, YOU KNOW.
EEK...
AND YOU WEREN'T PLANNING TO TOSS THIS IN THE STREET, WERE YOU?

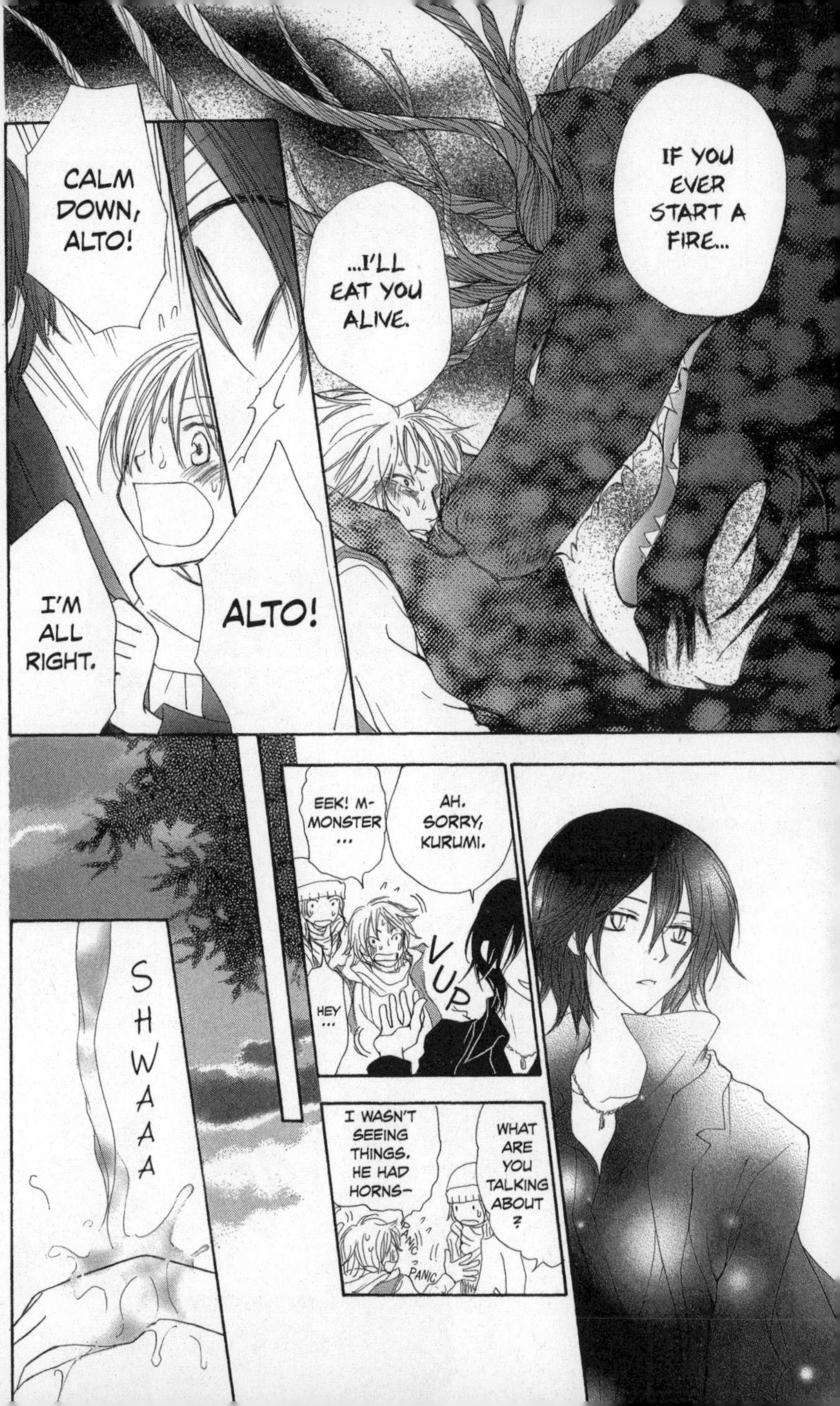
IF YOU EVER START A FIRE...
...I'LL EAT YOU ALIVE.
ALTO!
CALM DOWN, ALTO!
I'M ALL RIGHT.
AH. SORRY, KURUMI.
EEK! M-MONSTER ...
VUP
HEY ...
WHAT ARE YOU TALKING ABOUT?
I WASN'T SEEING THINGS. HE HAD HORNS-
PANIC
PANIC
SHWAAA

1/4 Sakura Mail

Part 11

(continued)

Coming up with things like that is fun too. I can't help but create all sorts of ordeals for the characters in the story. The cuter that character is, the more you want to tease them. ♡ Sorry. Alto.

This is the Sakura Mail sidebar that is 1/4 of a page, but I also write short comments on certain topics in the opening of the magazine. The topic in the magazine for this chapter was "Silly Jokes Grand Prix." I wrote that silly pun, *futon ga futtonda* (the futon mattress was blown away), but a few days after I had turned in the final draft, my futon really was blown away by a strong gust of wind! It was nowhere to be found! Where did it go?!

It was the mattress part...

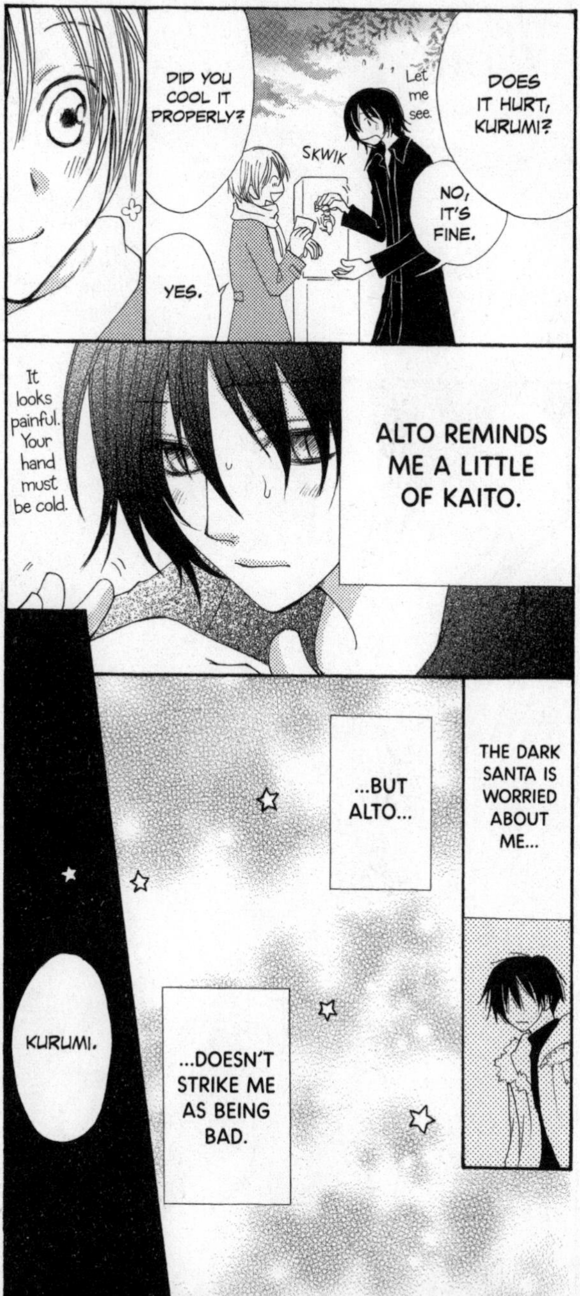
DOES IT HURT, KURUMI?
Let me see.
NO, IT'S FINE.
SKWIK
DID YOU COOL IT PROPERLY?
YES.
ALTO REMINDS ME A LITTLE OF KAITO.
It looks painful. Your hand must be cold.
THE DARK SANTA IS WORRIED ABOUT ME...
...BUT ALTO...
...DOESN'T STRIKE ME AS BEING BAD.
KURUMI.

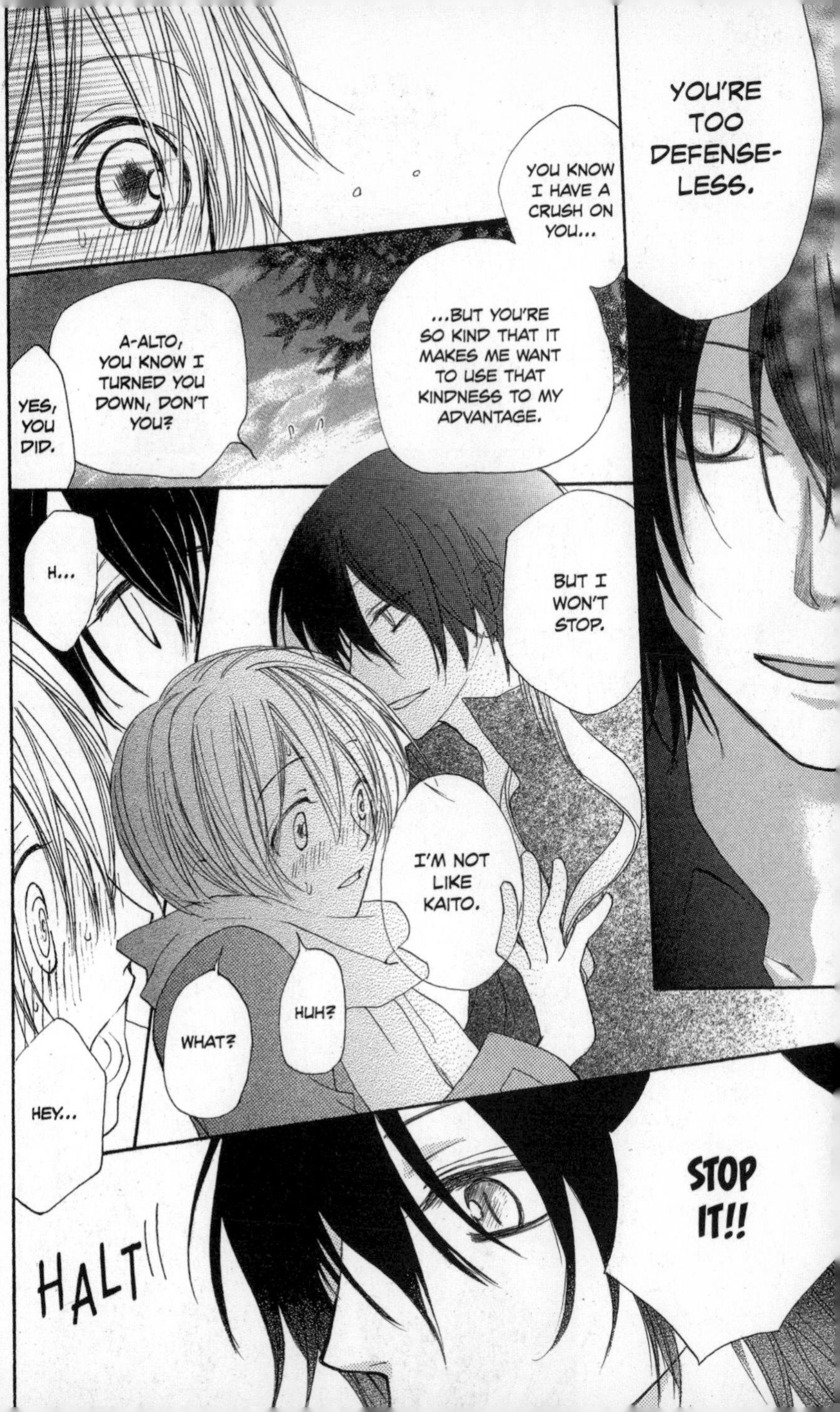
YOU'RE TOO DEFENSE-LESS.
YOU KNOW I HAVE A CRUSH ON YOU...
...BUT YOU'RE SO KIND THAT IT MAKES ME WANT TO USE THAT KINDNESS TO MY ADVANTAGE.
A-ALTO, YOU KNOW I TURNED YOU DOWN, DON'T YOU?
YES, YOU DID.
BUT I WON'T STOP.
I'M NOT LIKE KAITO.
H...
HUH?
WHAT?
HEY...
STOP IT!!
HALT

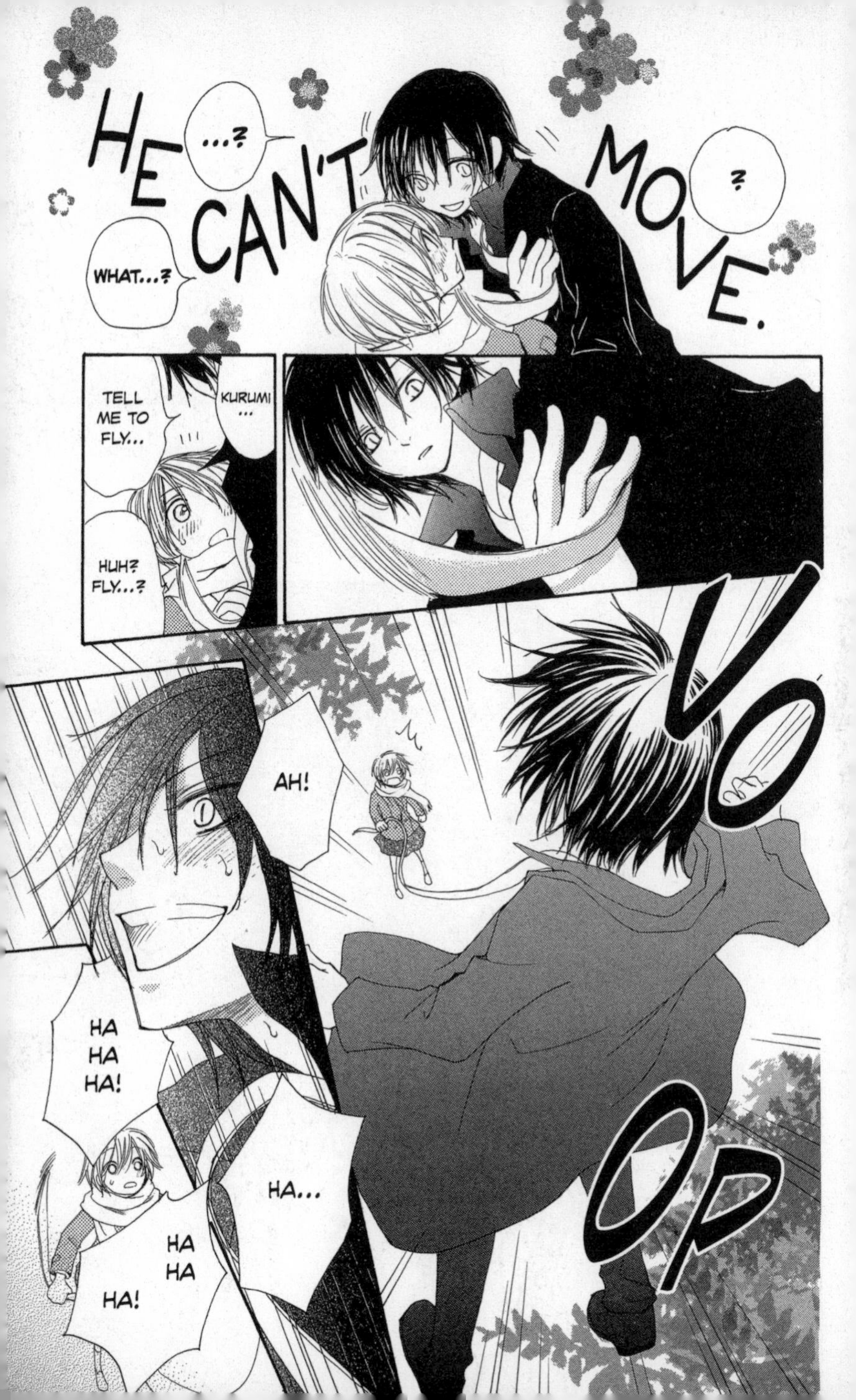
HE CAN'T MOVE.
?
...?
WHAT...?
KURUMI...
TELL ME TO FLY...
HUH? FLY...?
VO
OP
AH!
HA HA HA!
HA...
HA HA HA!

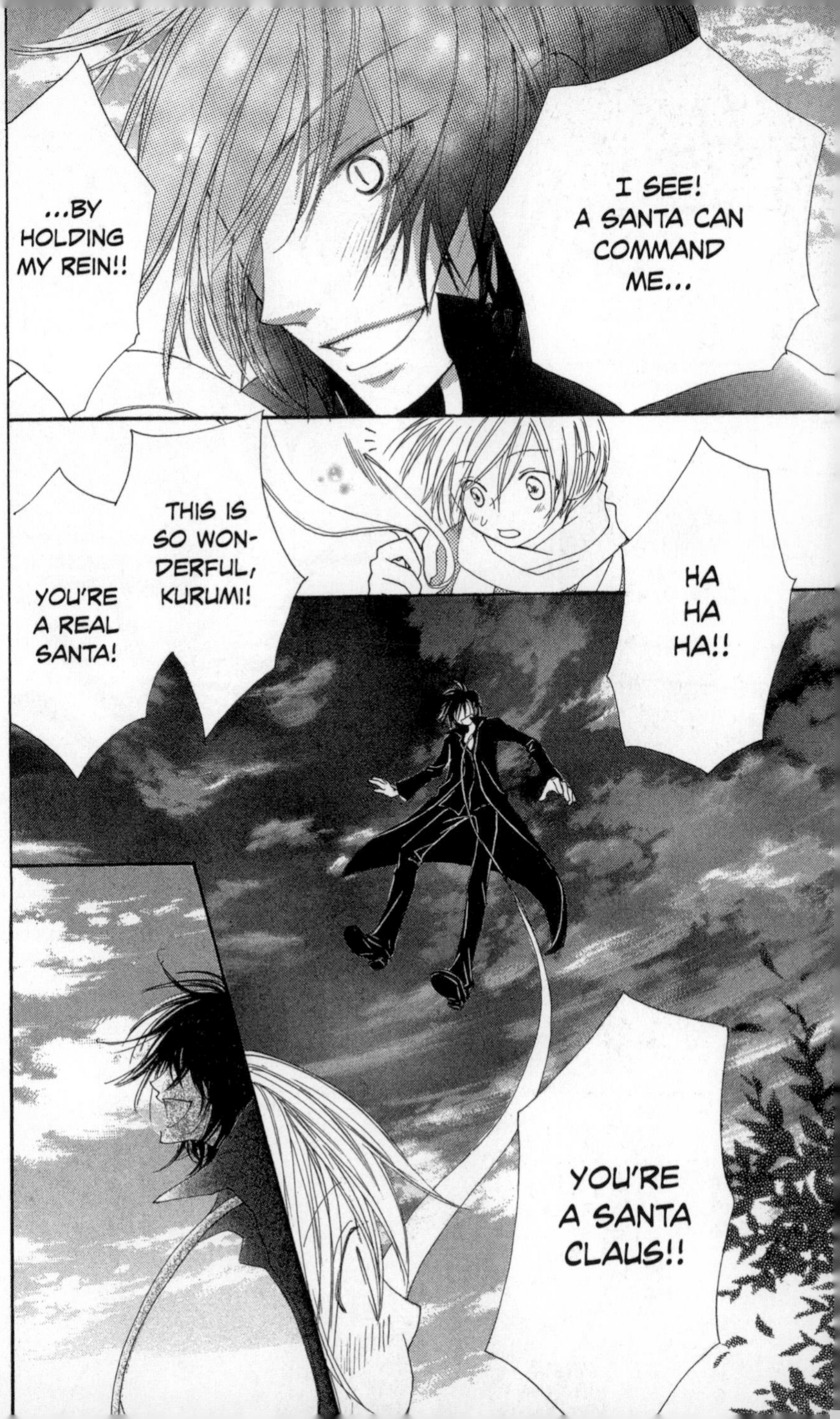
I SEE! A SANTA CAN COMMAND ME...
...BY HOLDING MY REIN!!
HA HA HA!!
THIS IS SO WON-DERFUL, KURUMI!
YOU'RE A REAL SANTA!
YOU'RE A SANTA CLAUS!!

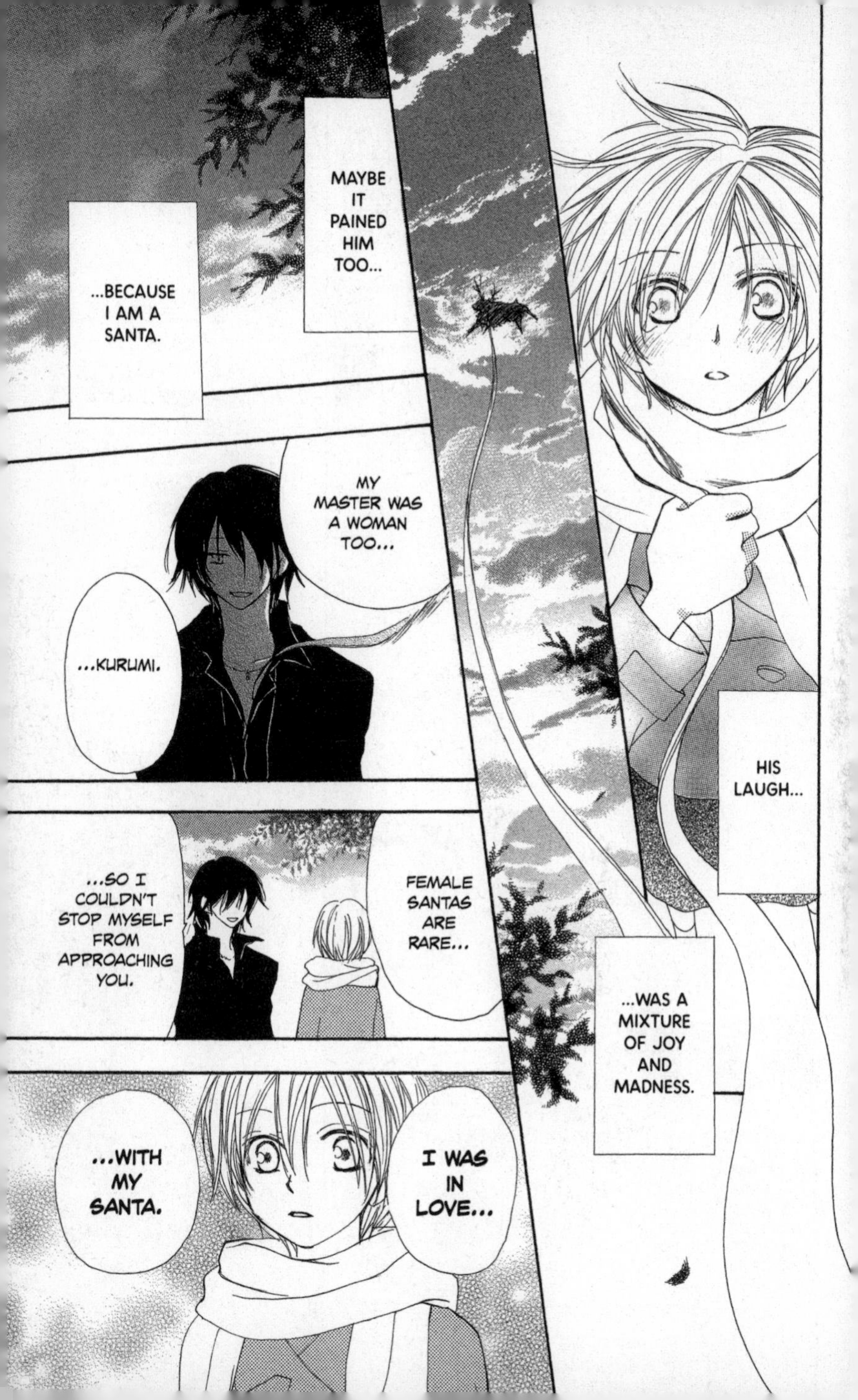
HIS LAUGH...
...WAS A MIXTURE OF JOY AND MADNESS.
MAYBE IT PAINED HIM TOO...
...BECAUSE I AM A SANTA.
MY MASTER WAS A WOMAN TOO...
...KURUMI.
FEMALE SANTAS ARE RARE...
...SO I COULDN'T STOP MYSELF FROM APPROACHING YOU.
I WAS IN LOVE...
...WITH MY SANTA.

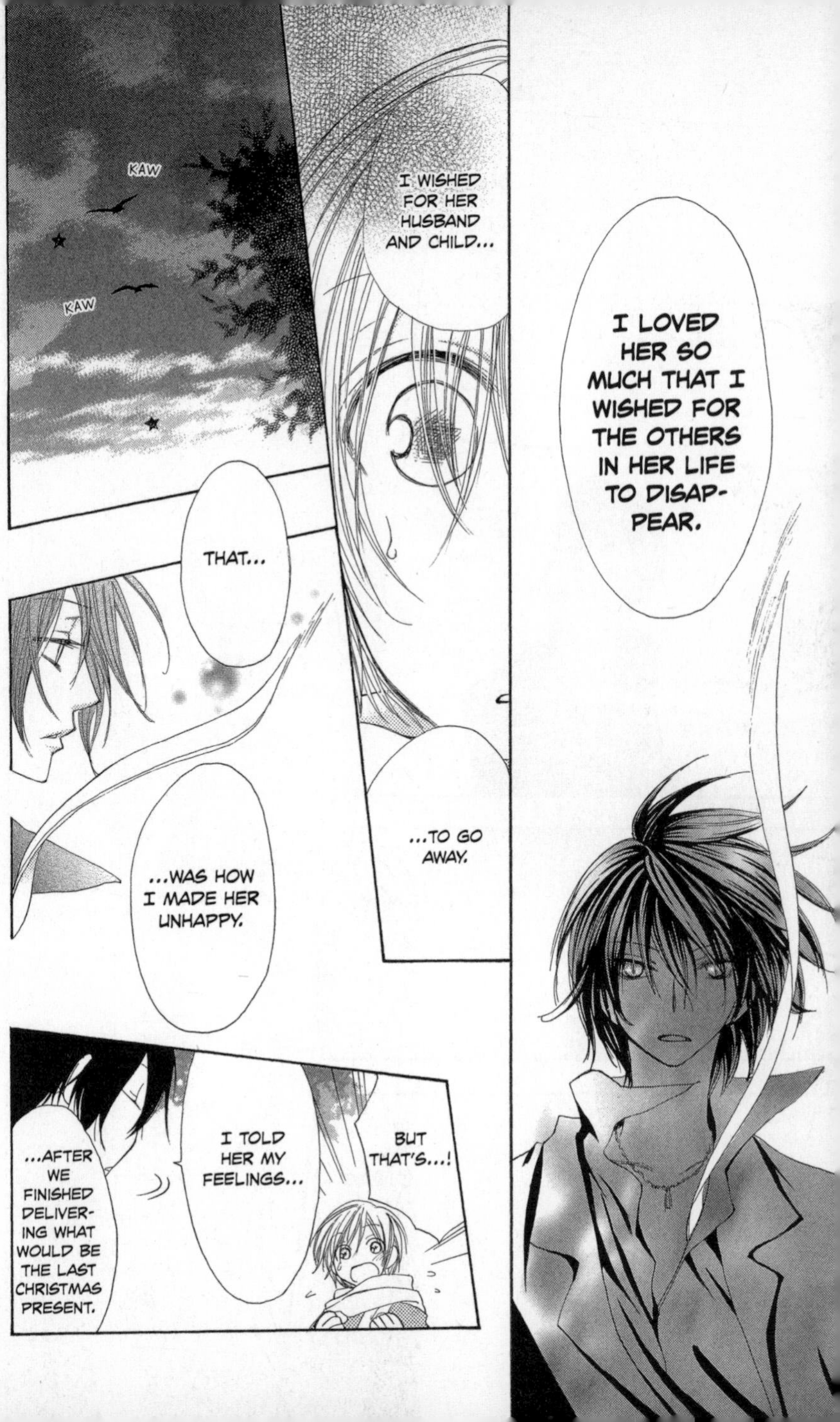
I LOVED HER SO MUCH THAT I WISHED FOR THE OTHERS IN HER LIFE TO DISAP-PEAR.
I WISHED FOR HER HUSBAND AND CHILD...
...TO GO AWAY.
KAW
KAW
THAT...
...WAS HOW I MADE HER UNHAPPY.
BUT THAT'S...!
I TOLD HER MY FEELINGS...
...AFTER WE FINISHED DELIVER-ING WHAT WOULD BE THE LAST CHRISTMAS PRESENT.

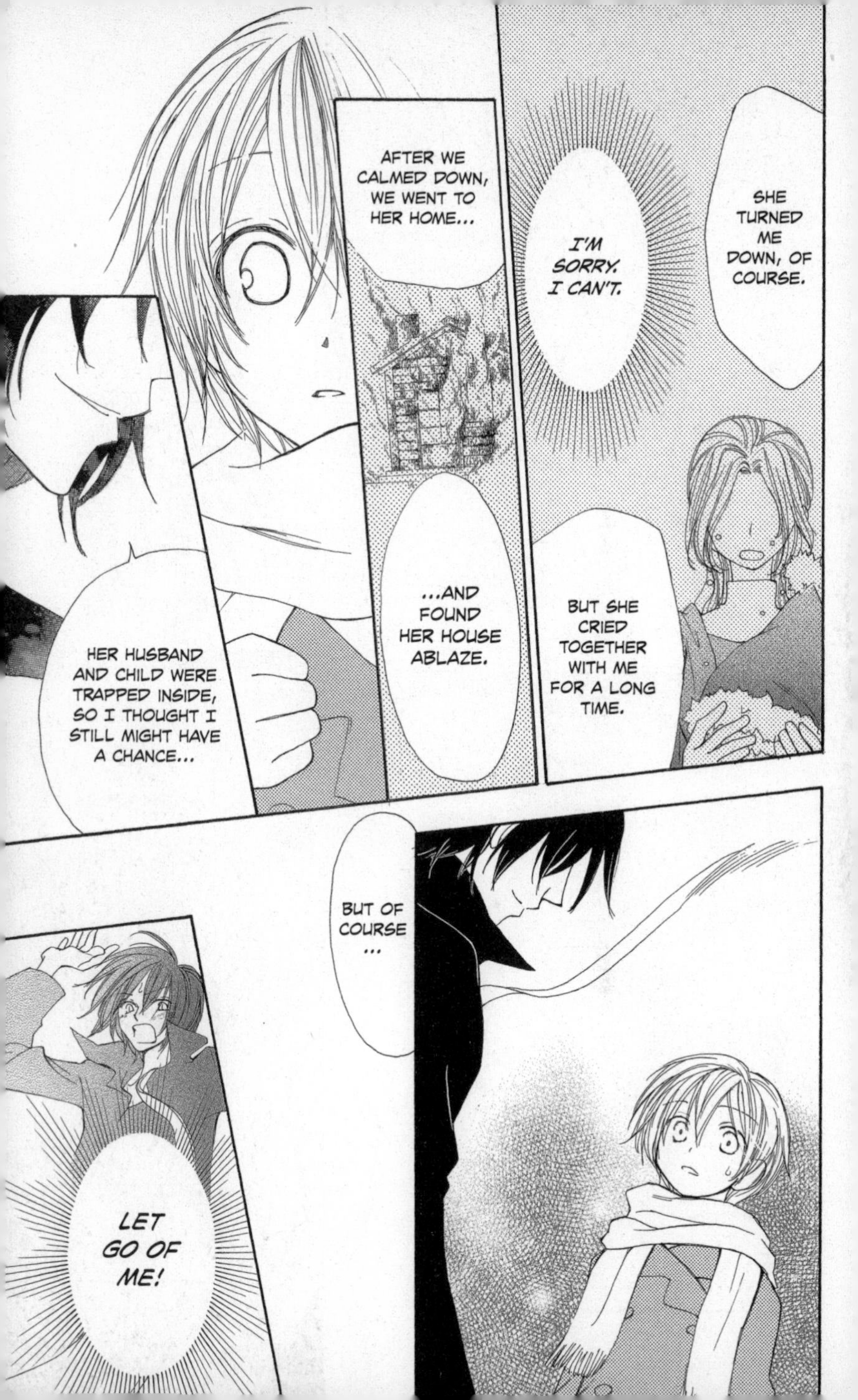
SHE TURNED ME DOWN, OF COURSE.
I'M SORRY. I CAN'T.
BUT SHE CRIED TOGETHER WITH ME FOR A LONG TIME.
AFTER WE CALMED DOWN, WE WENT TO HER HOME...
...AND FOUND HER HOUSE ABLAZE.
HER HUSBAND AND CHILD WERE TRAPPED INSIDE, SO I THOUGHT I STILL MIGHT HAVE A CHANCE...
BUT OF COURSE ...
LET GO OF ME!

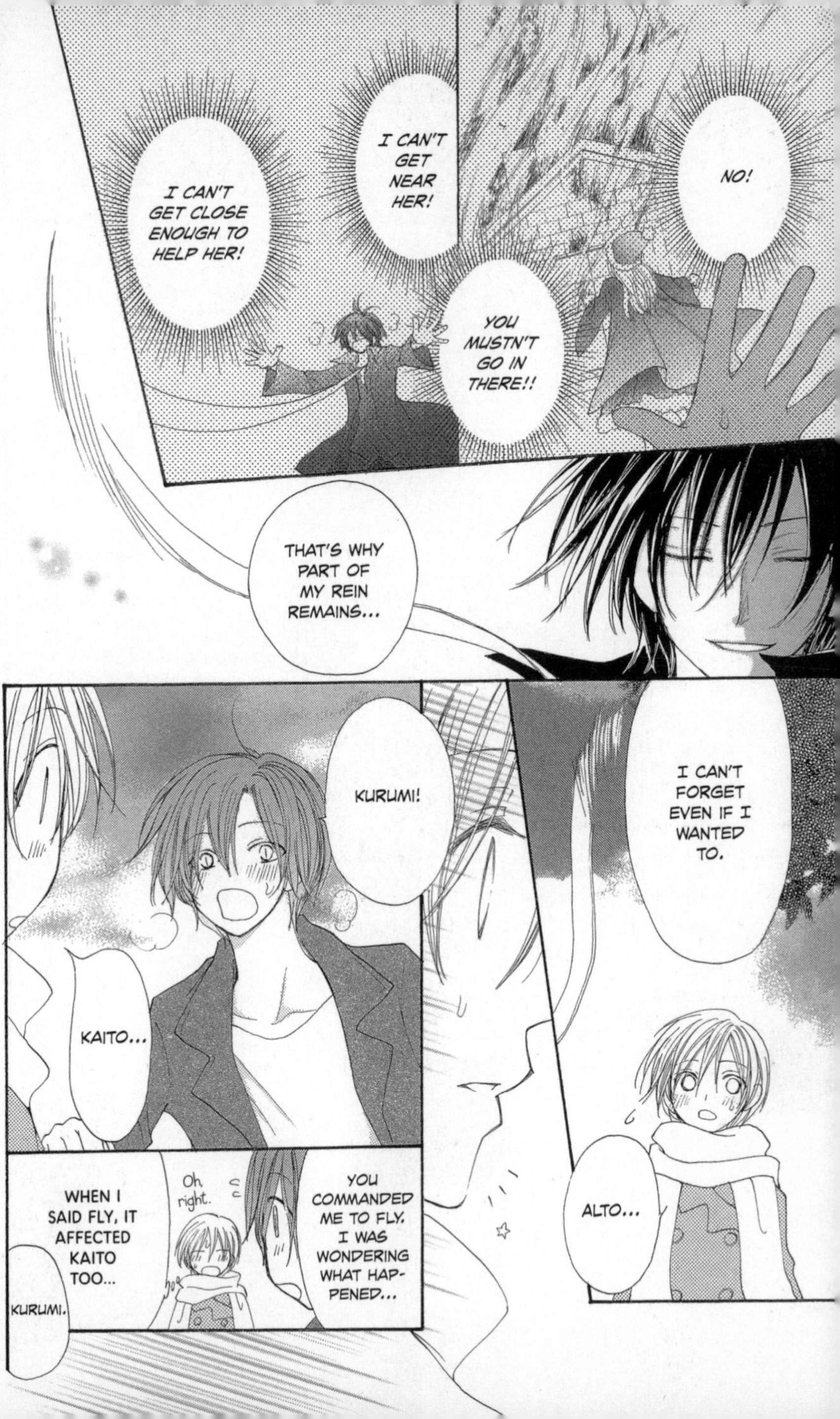
NO!
YOU MUSTN'T GO IN THERE!!
I CAN'T GET NEAR HER!
I CAN'T GET CLOSE ENOUGH TO HELP HER!
THAT'S WHY PART OF MY REIN REMAINS...
I CAN'T FORGET EVEN IF I WANTED TO.
ALTO...
KURUMI!
KAITO...
YOU COMMANDED ME TO FLY. I WAS WONDERING WHAT HAP-PENED...
Oh, right.
WHEN I SAID FLY, IT AFFECTED KAITO TOO...
KURUMI.

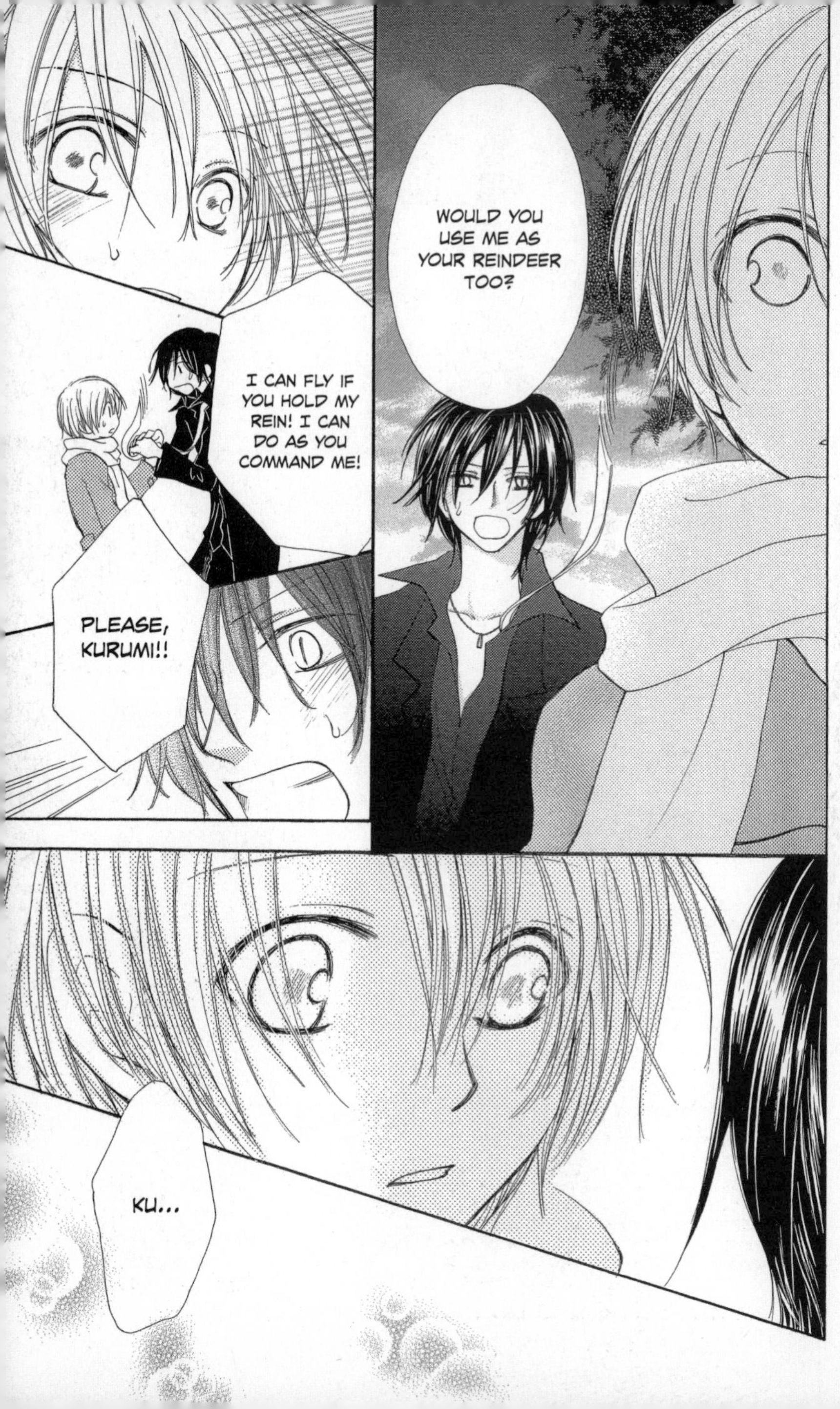
WOULD YOU USE ME AS YOUR REINDEER TOO?
I CAN FLY IF YOU HOLD MY REIN! I CAN DO AS YOU COMMAND ME!
PLEASE, KURUMI!!
KU...

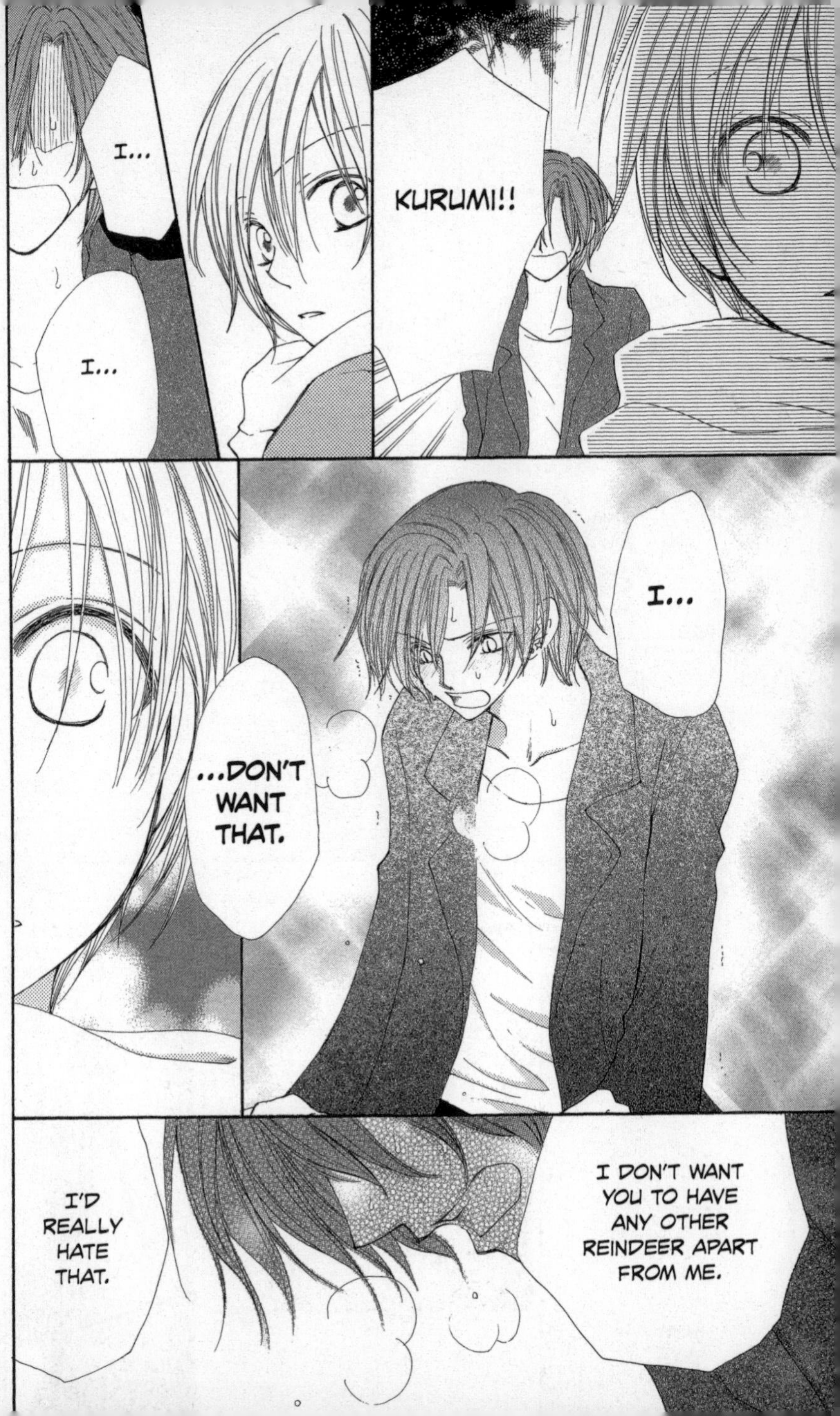
KURUMI!!
I...
I...
I...
...DON'T WANT THAT.
I DON'T WANT YOU TO HAVE ANY OTHER REINDEER APART FROM ME.
I'D REALLY HATE THAT.

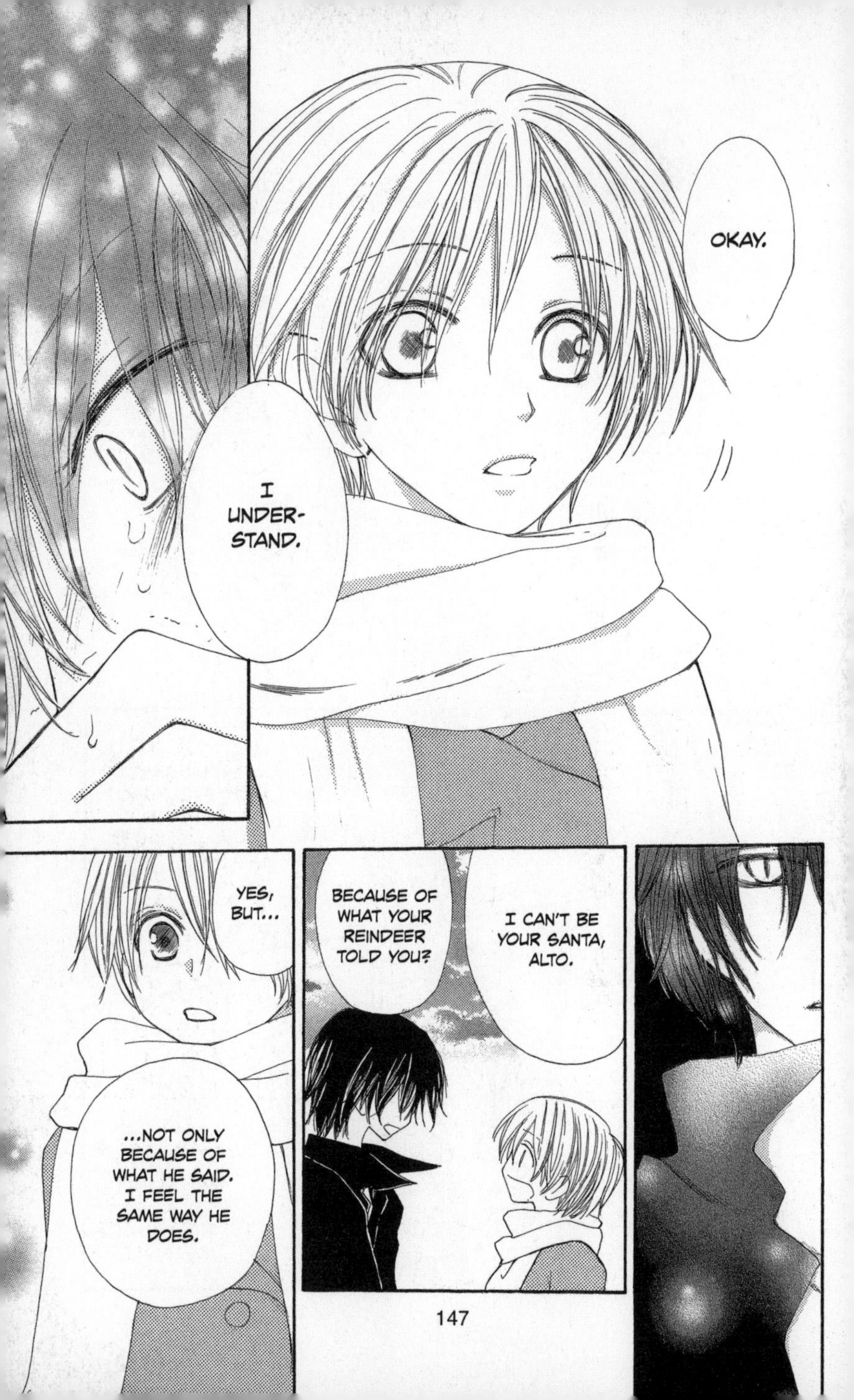
OKAY.
I UNDER-STAND.
I CAN'T BE YOUR SANTA, ALTO.
BECAUSE OF WHAT YOUR REINDEER TOLD YOU?
YES, BUT...
...NOT ONLY BECAUSE OF WHAT HE SAID. I FEEL THE SAME WAY HE DOES.

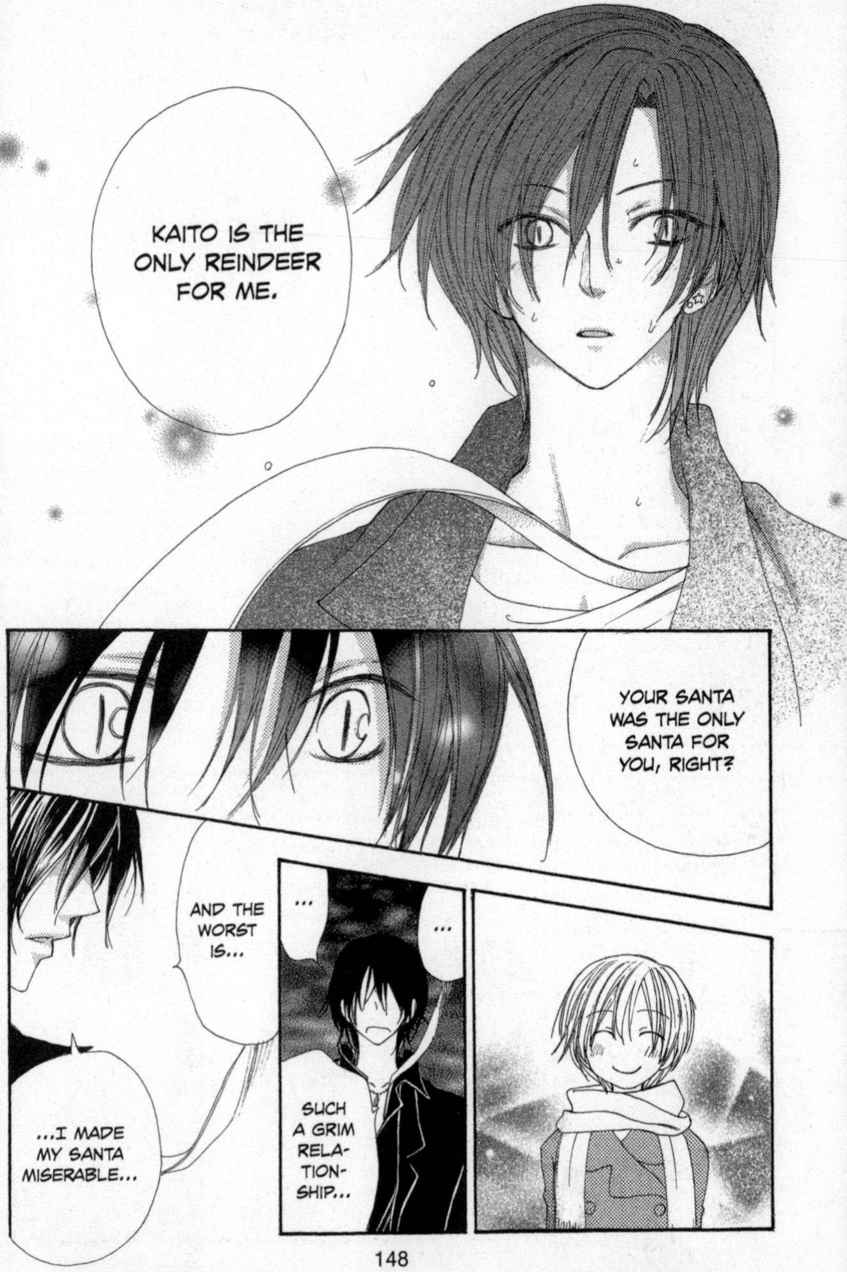
KAITO IS THE ONLY REINDEER FOR ME.
YOUR SANTA WAS THE ONLY SANTA FOR YOU, RIGHT?
...
...
SUCH A GRIM RELA-TION-SHIP...
AND THE WORST IS...
...I MADE MY SANTA MISERABLE...

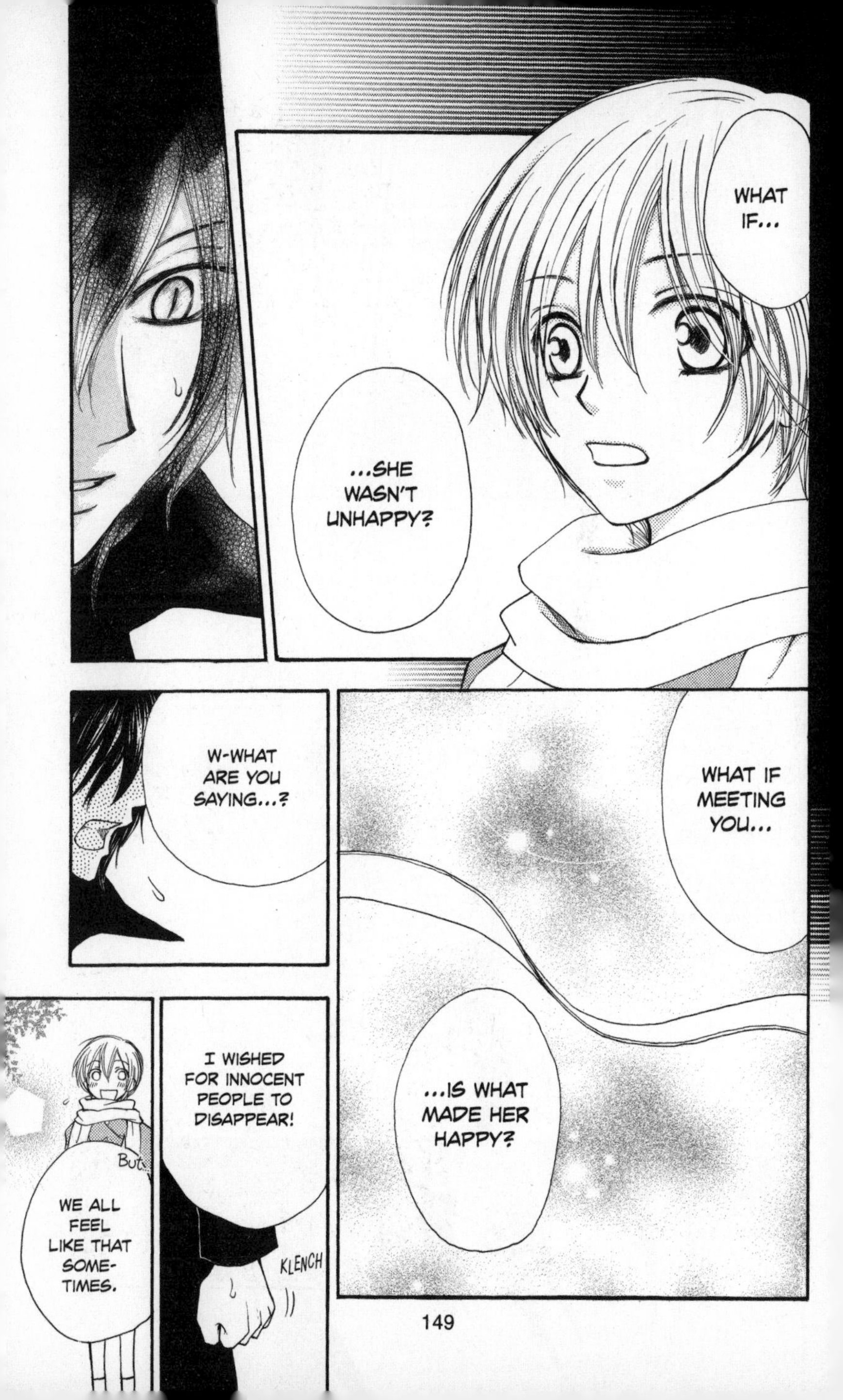
WHAT IF...
...SHE WASN'T UNHAPPY?
WHAT IF MEETING YOU...
...IS WHAT MADE HER HAPPY?
W-WHAT ARE YOU SAYING...?
I WISHED FOR INNOCENT PEOPLE TO DISAPPEAR!
KLENCH
But...
WE ALL FEEL LIKE THAT SOME-TIMES.

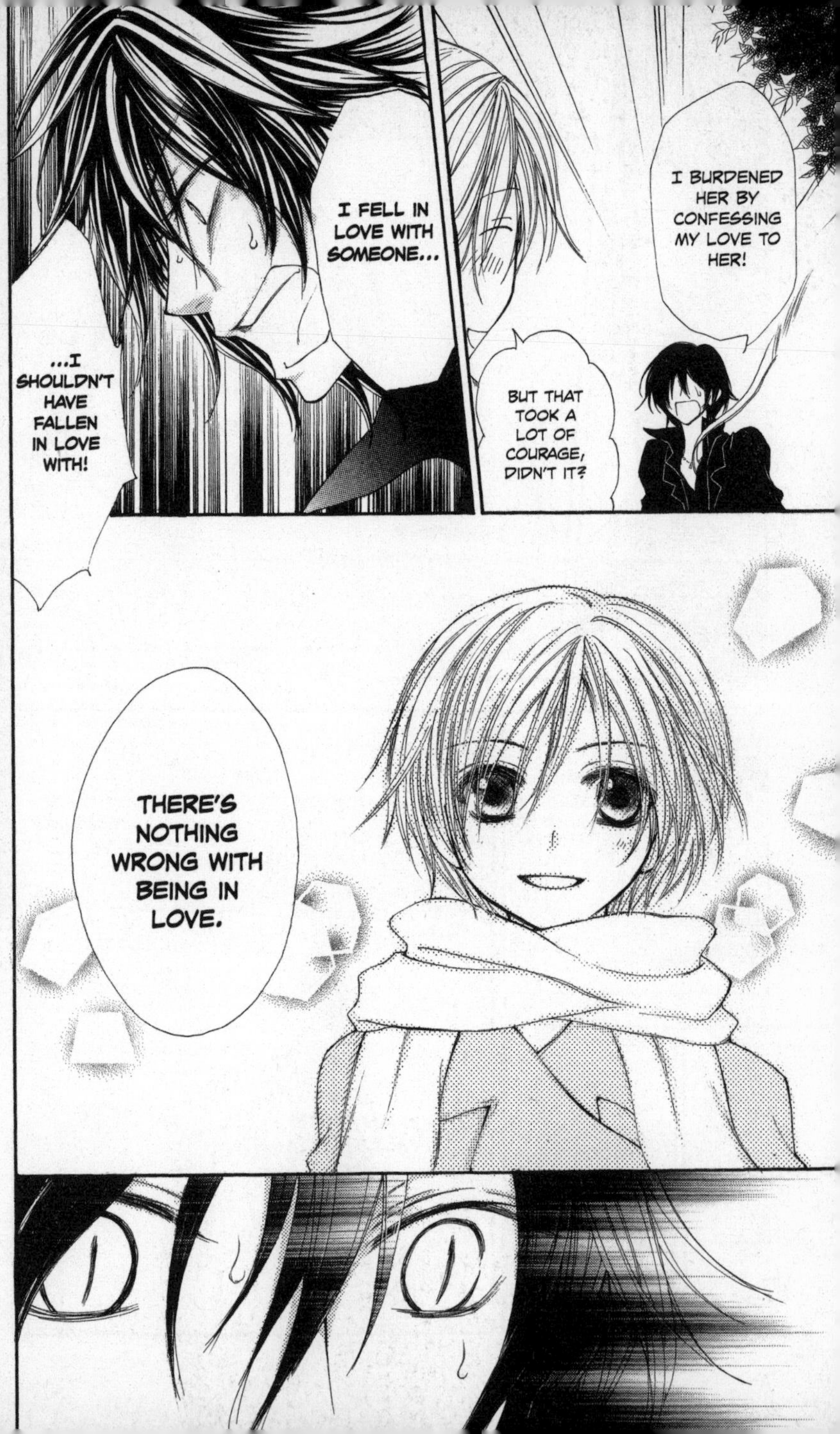
I BURDENED HER BY CONFESSING MY LOVE TO HER!
BUT THAT TOOK A LOT OF COURAGE, DIDN'T IT?
I FELL IN LOVE WITH SOMEONE...
...I SHOULDN'T HAVE FALLEN IN LOVE WITH!
THERE'S NOTHING WRONG WITH BEING IN LOVE.

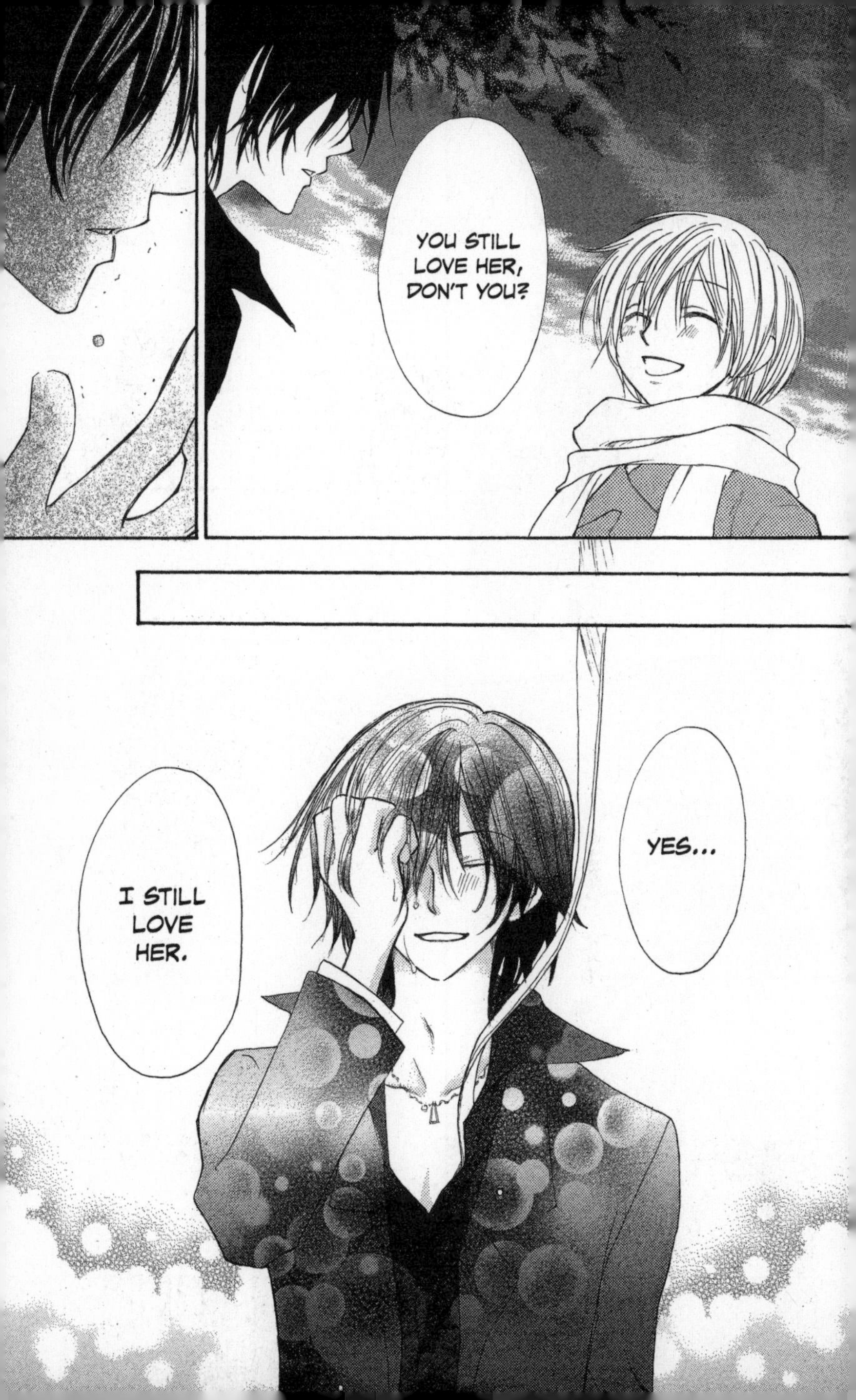
YOU STILL LOVE HER, DON'T YOU?
YES...
I STILL LOVE HER.

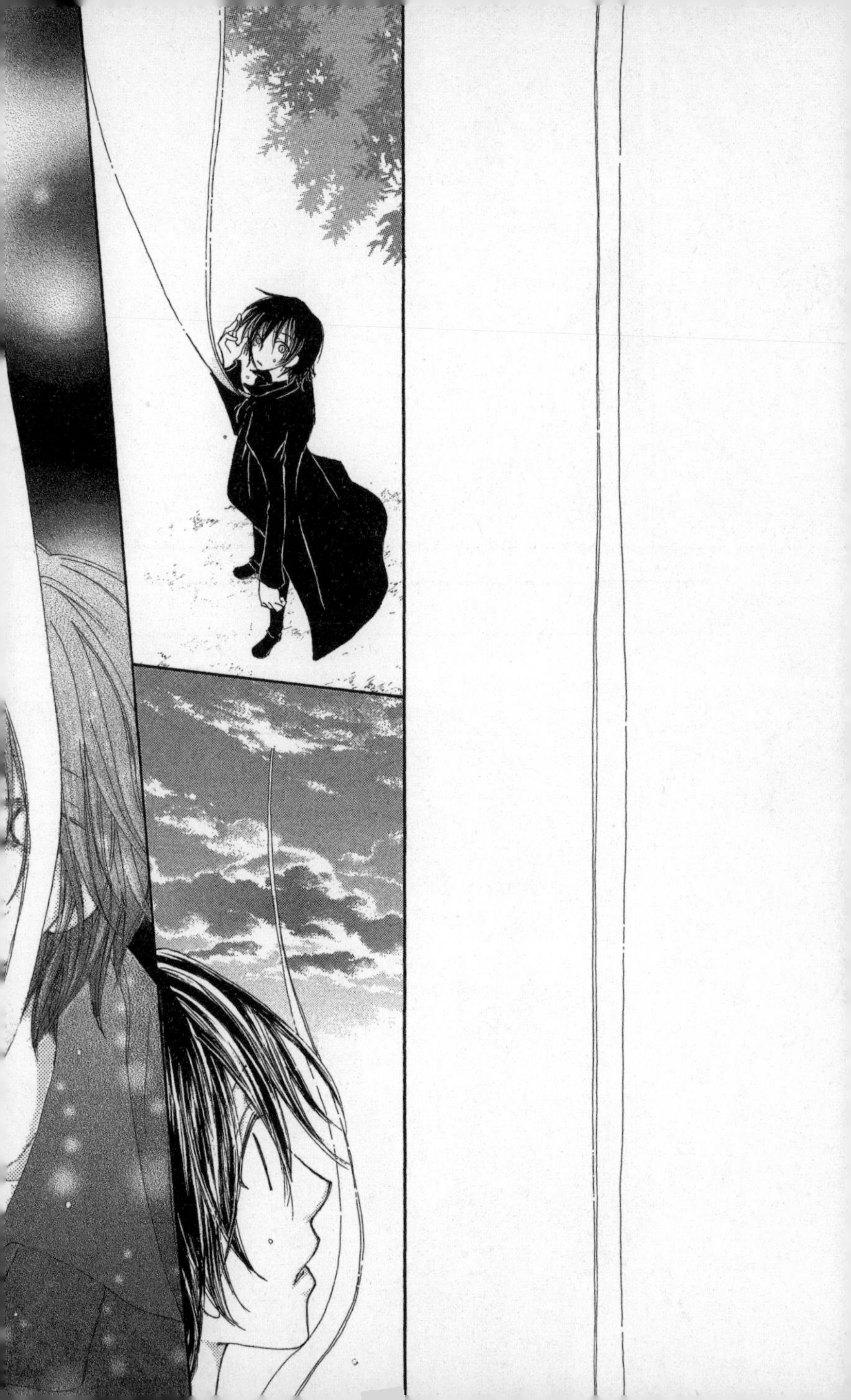

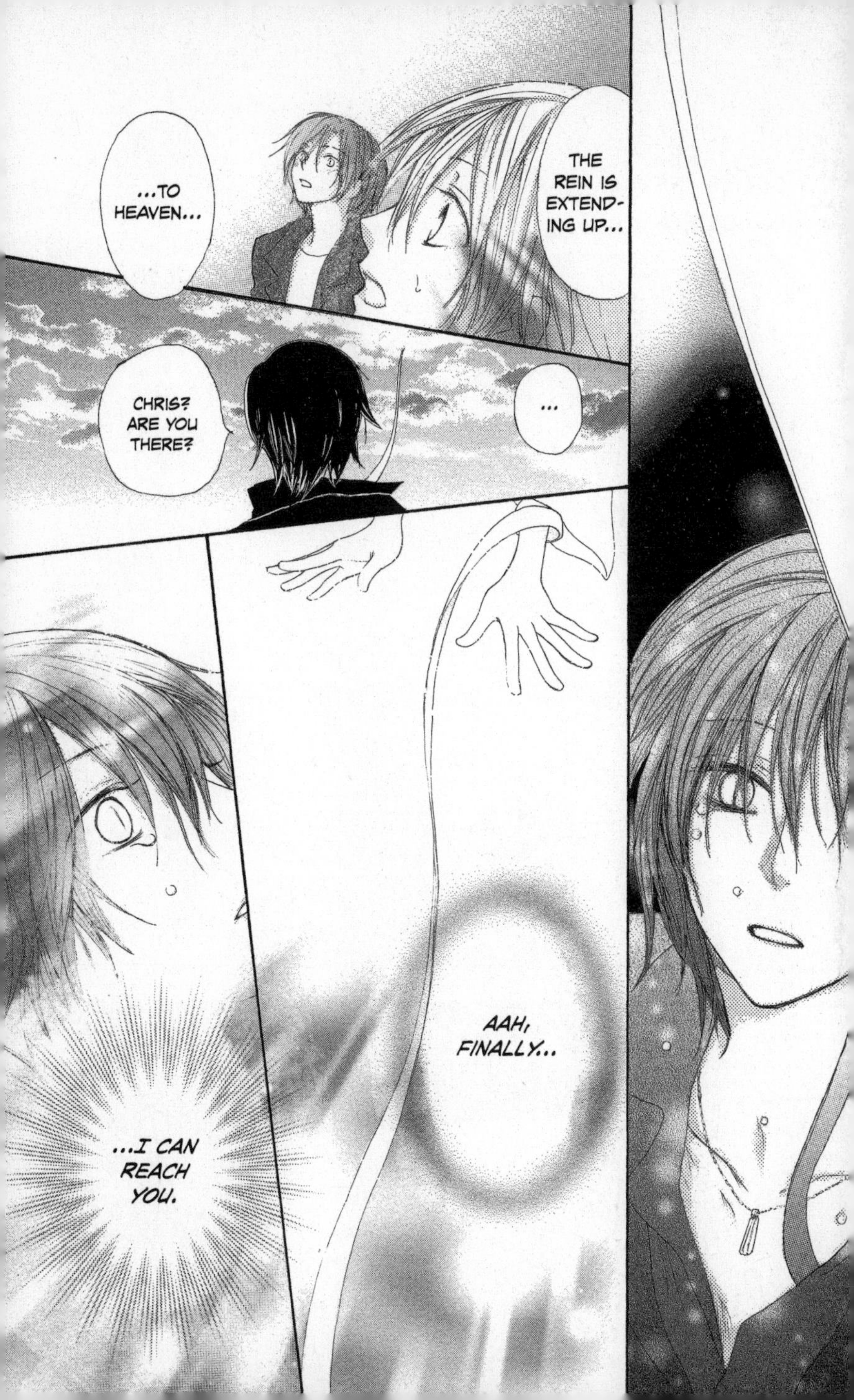
THE REIN IS EXTENDING UP...
...TO HEAVEN...
...
CHRIS? ARE YOU THERE?
AAH, FINALLY...
...I CAN REACH YOU.

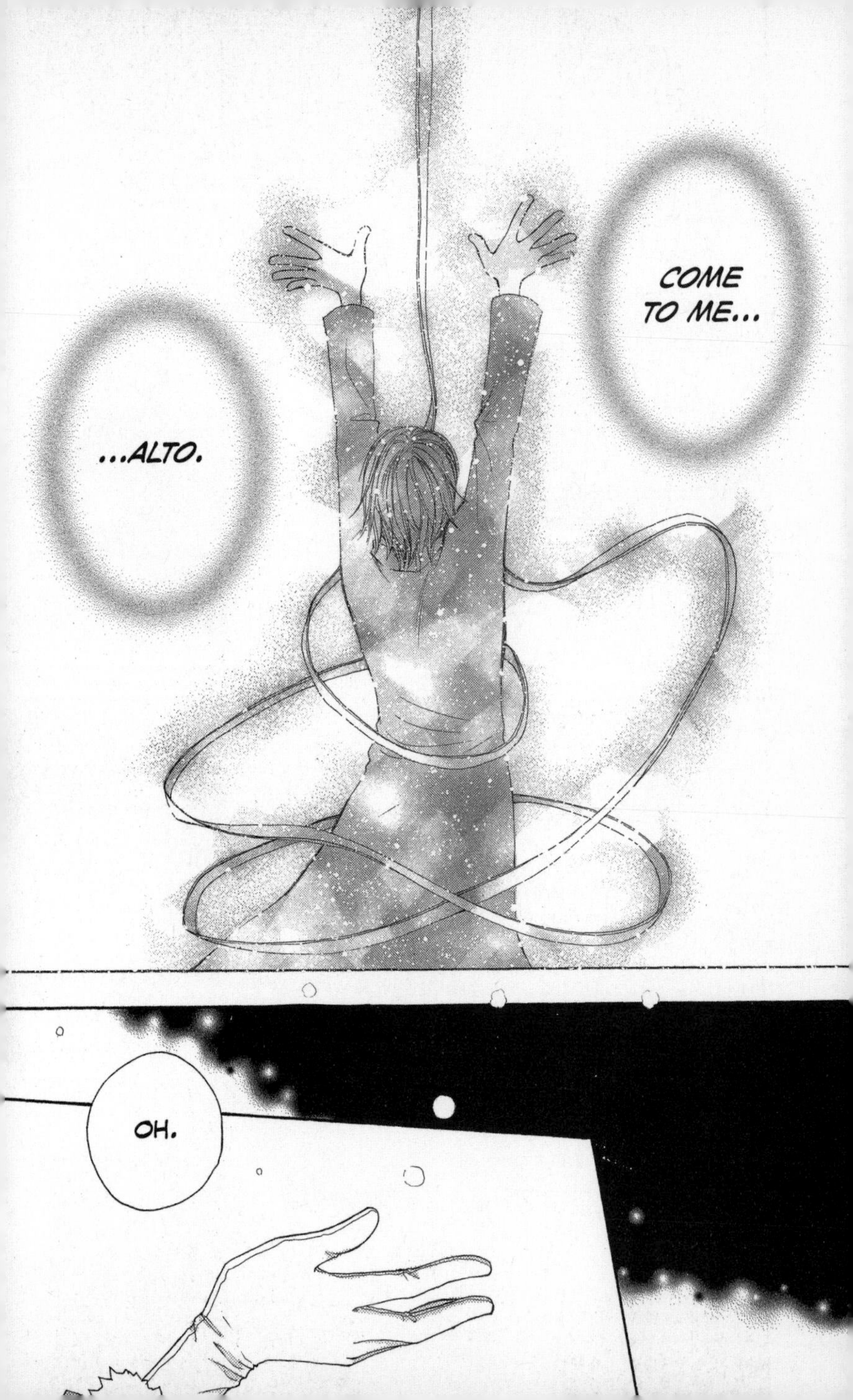
COME TO ME...
...ALTO.
OH.

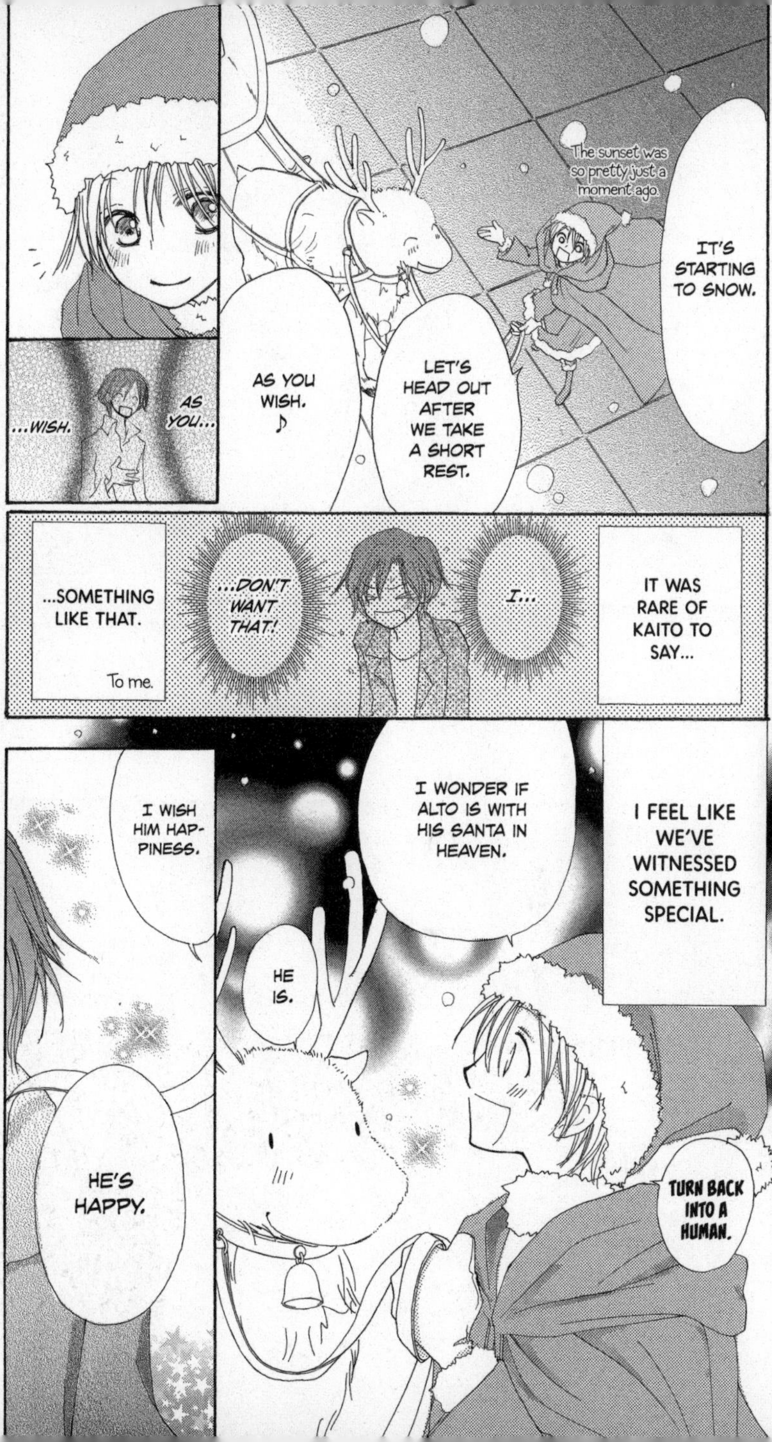
IT'S STARTING TO SNOW.
The sunset was so pretty just a moment ago.
LET'S HEAD OUT AFTER WE TAKE A SHORT REST.
AS YOU WISH. ♪
AS YOU...
...WISH.
IT WAS RARE OF KAITO TO SAY...
I...
...DON'T WANT THAT!
...SOMETHING LIKE THAT.
To me.
I FEEL LIKE WE'VE WITNESSED SOMETHING SPECIAL.
I WONDER IF ALTO IS WITH HIS SANTA IN HEAVEN.
HE IS.
TURN BACK INTO A HUMAN.
I WISH HIM HAPPINESS.
HE'S HAPPY.

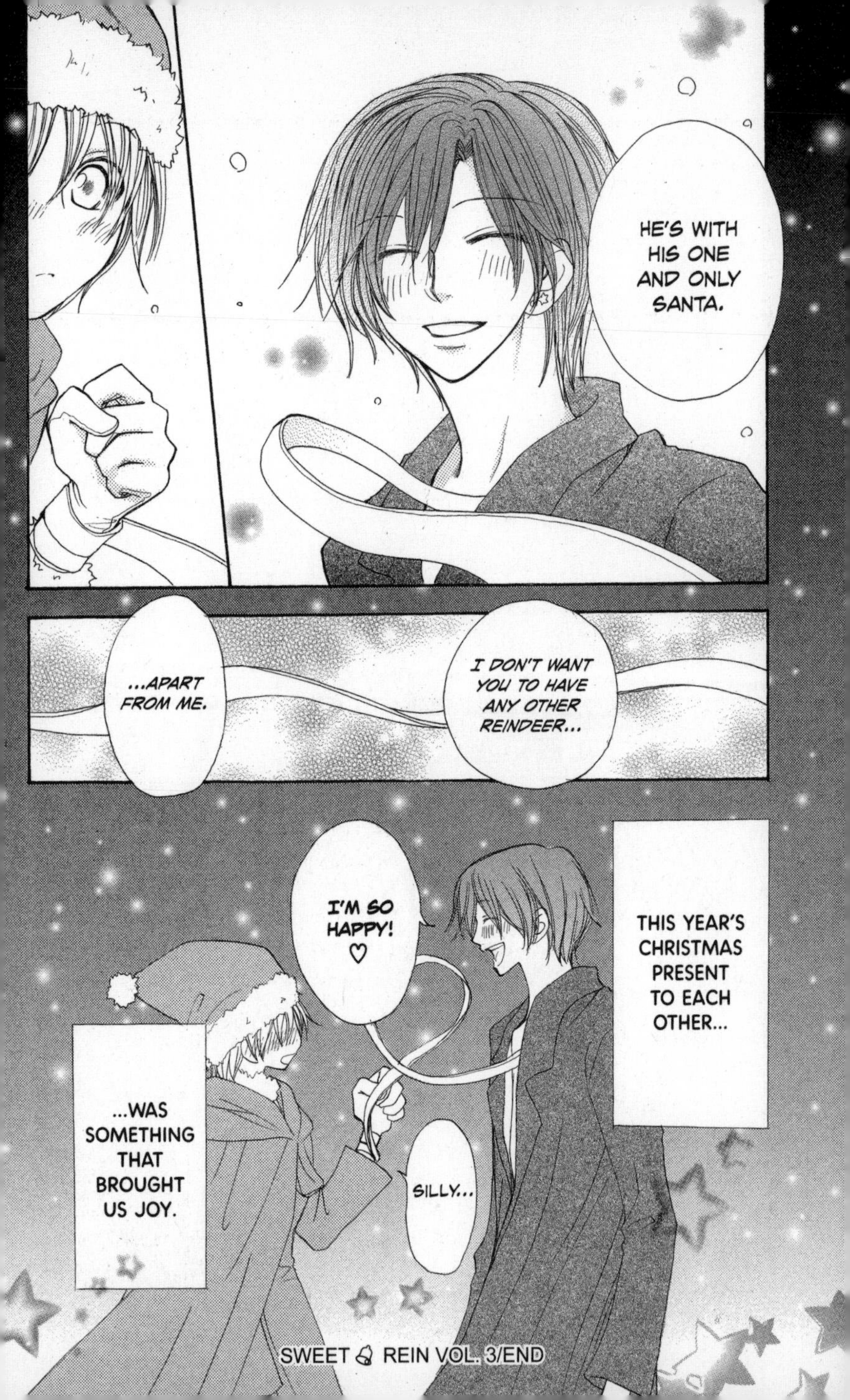
HE'S WITH HIS ONE AND ONLY SANTA.
I DON'T WANT YOU TO HAVE ANY OTHER REINDEER...
...APART FROM ME.
THIS YEAR'S CHRISTMAS PRESENT TO EACH OTHER...
I'M SO HAPPY! ♡
SILLY...
...WAS SOMETHING THAT BROUGHT US JOY.
SWEET REIN VOL. 3/END

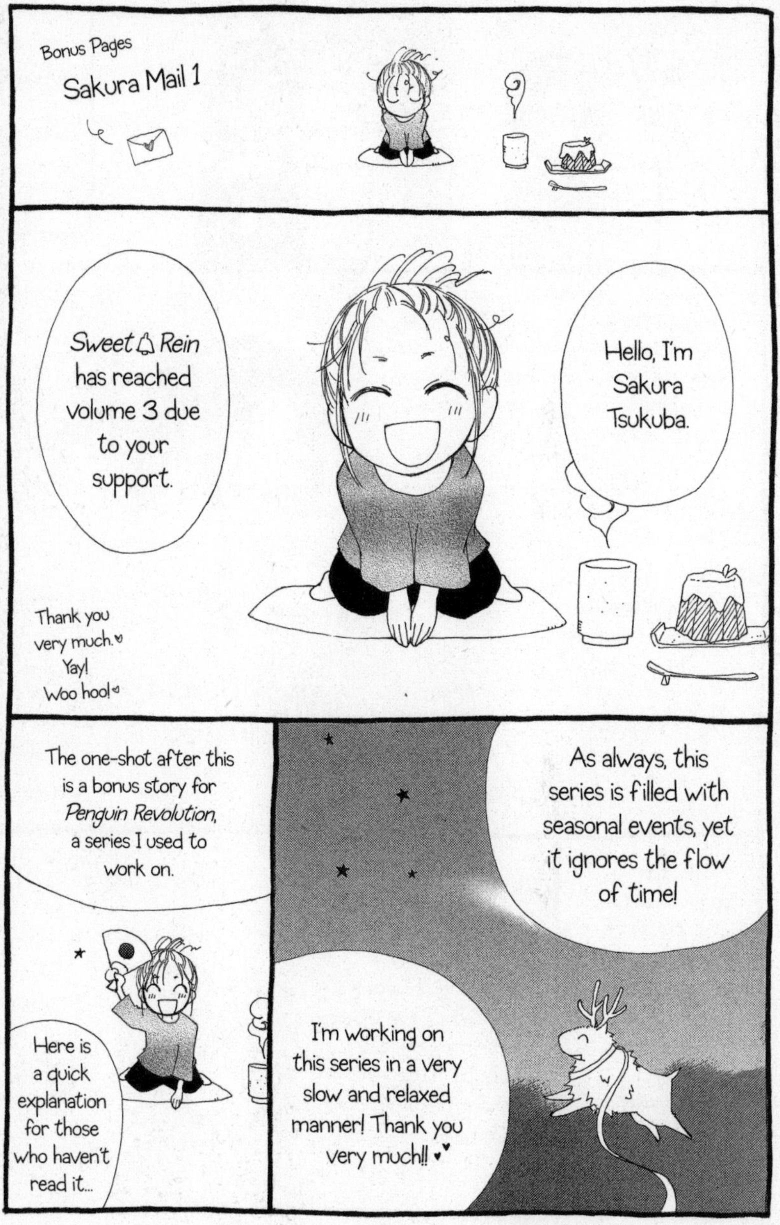

Bonus Pages
Sakura Mail 1
Hello, I'm Sakura Tsukuba.
Sweet Rein has reached volume 3 due to your support.
Thank you very much. Yay! Woo hoo!
As always, this series is filled with seasonal events, yet it ignores the flow of time!
I'm working on this series in a very slow and relaxed manner! Thank you very much!!
The one-shot after this is a bonus story for Penguin Revolution, a series I used to work on.
Here is a quick explanation for those who haven't read it...

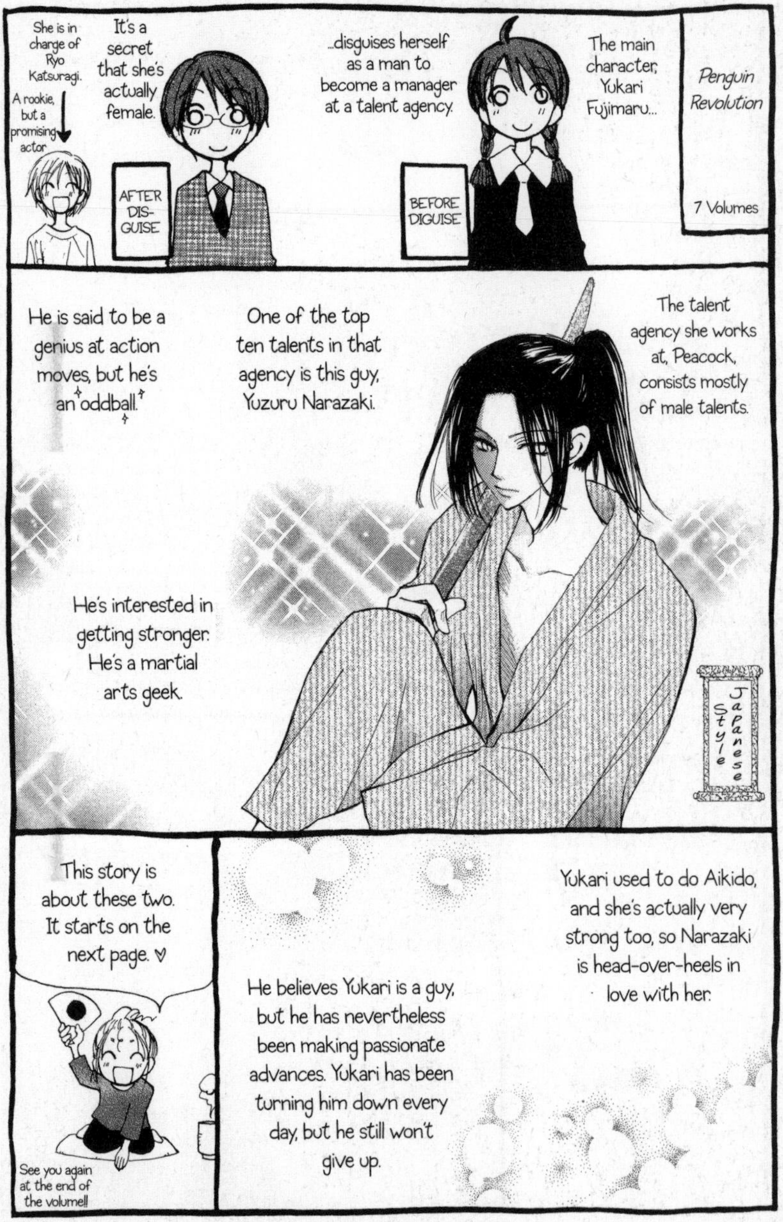
Penguin Revolution
7 Volumes
The main character, Yukari Fujimaru...
...disguises herself as a man to become a manager at a talent agency.
BEFORE DIGUISE
It's a secret that she's actually female.
AFTER DIS-GUISE
She is in charge of Ryo Katsuragi.
A rookie, but a promising actor
The talent agency she works at, Peacock, consists mostly of male talents.
One of the top ten talents in that agency is this guy, Yuzuru Narazaki.
He is said to be a genius at action moves, but he's an oddball.
Japanese Style
He's interested in getting stronger. He's a martial arts geek.
Yukari used to do Aikido, and she's actually very strong too, so Narazaki is head-over-heels in love with her.
He believes Yukari is a guy, but he has nevertheless been making passionate advances. Yukari has been turning him down every day, but he still won't give up.
This story is about these two. It starts on the next page. ♡
See you again at the end of the volume!!

SAKURA MAIL 1/END

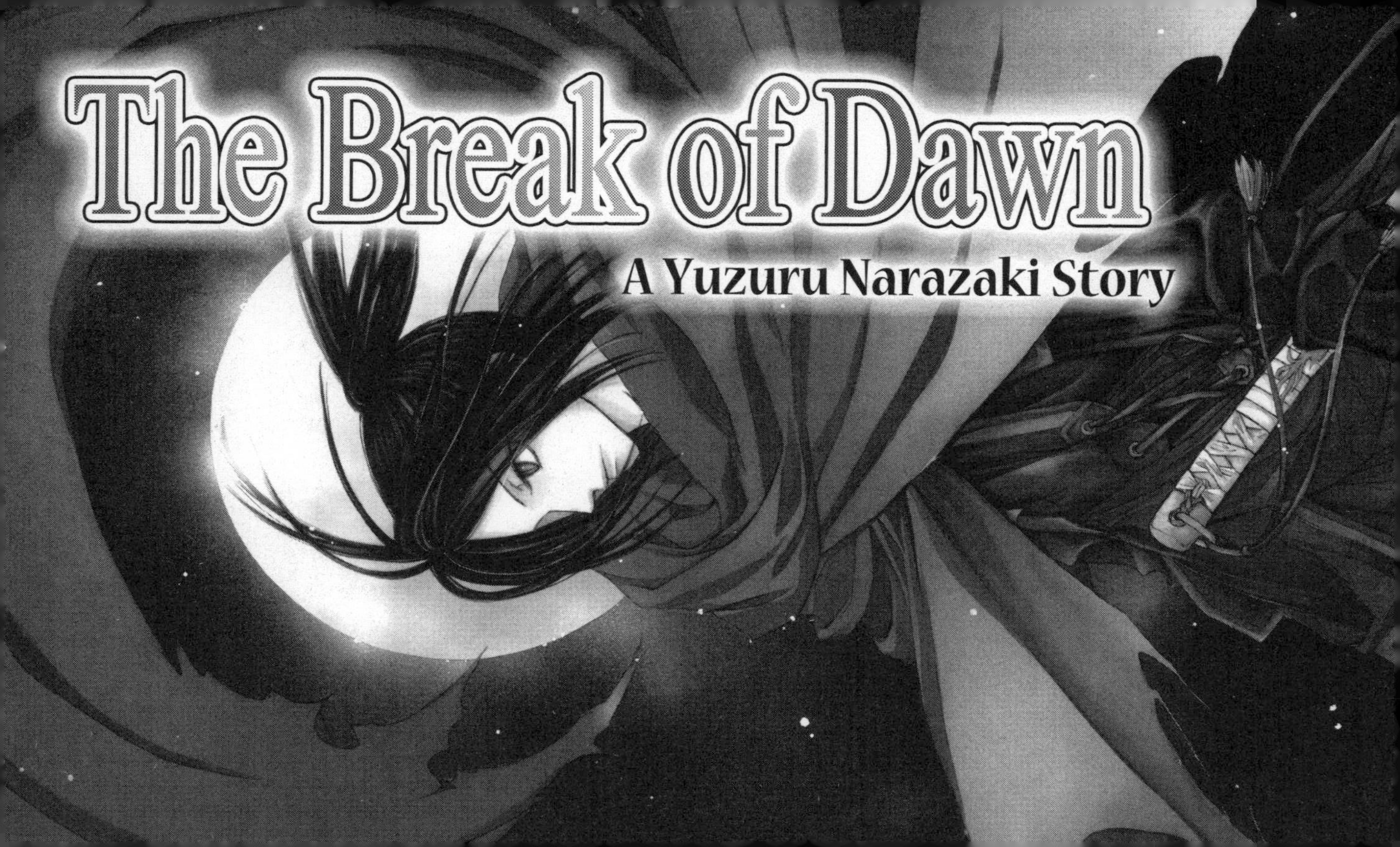
The Break of Dawn
A Yuzuru Narazaki Story

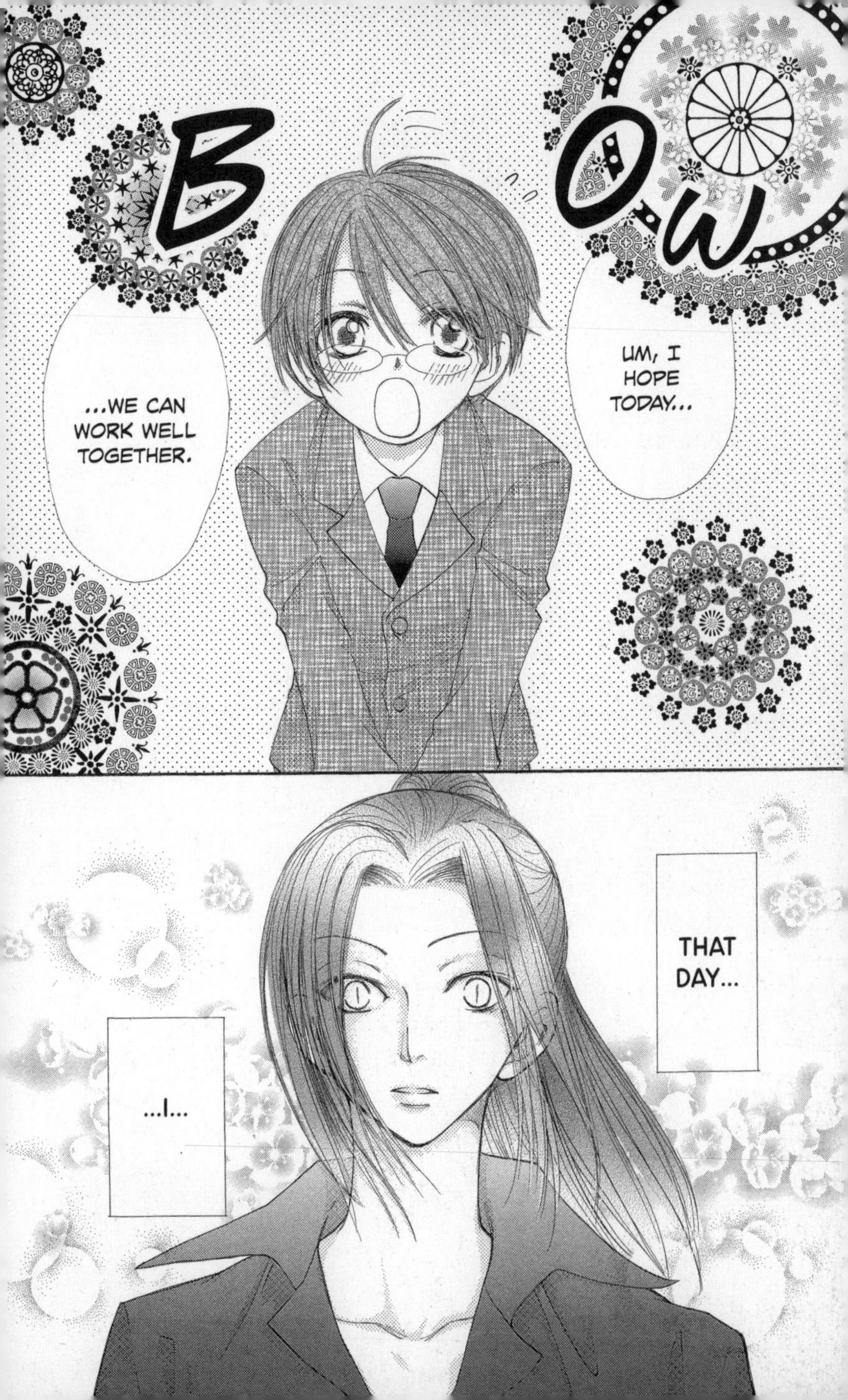
BOW
UM, I HOPE TODAY...
...WE CAN WORK WELL TOGETHER.
THAT DAY...
...I...

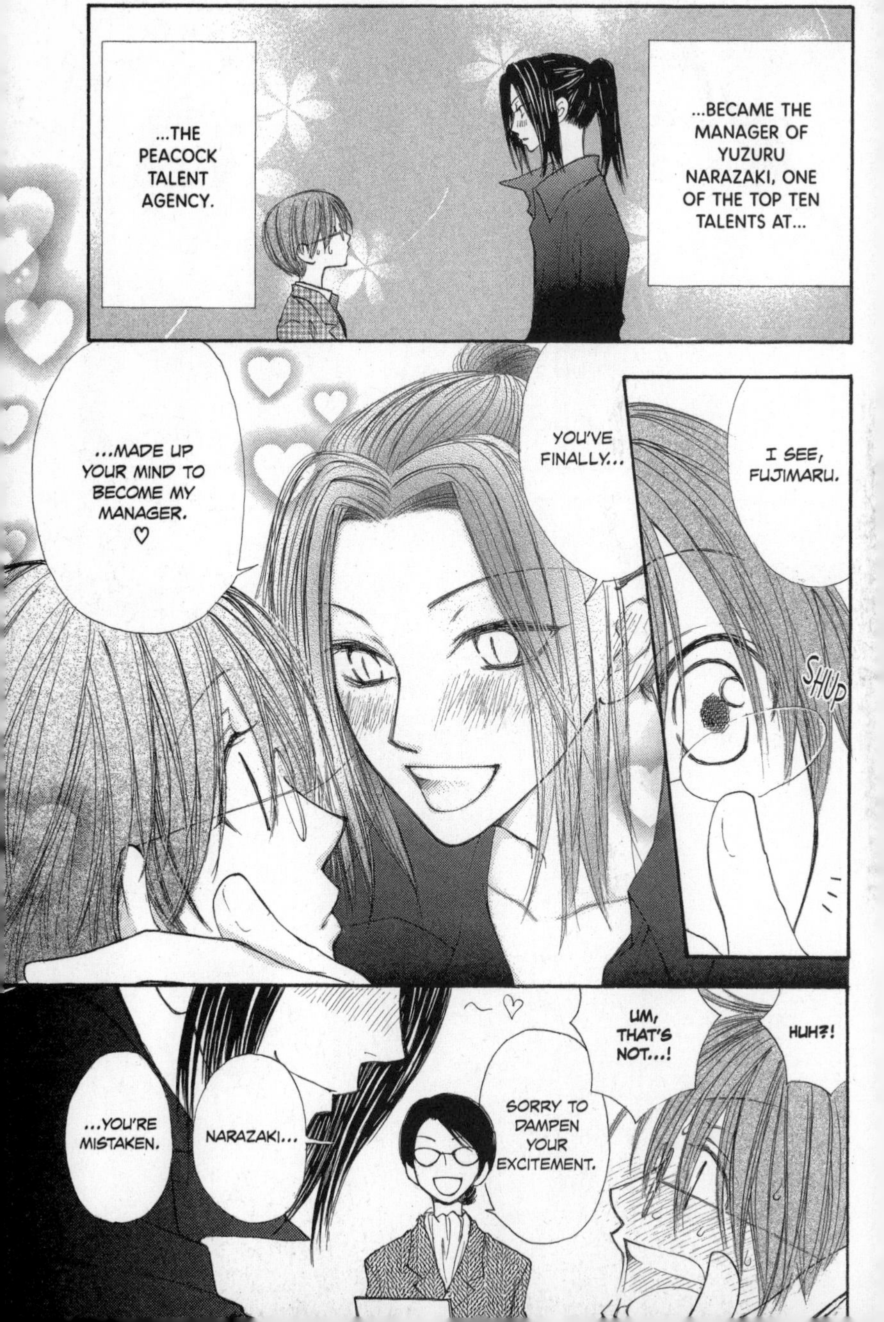
...BECAME THE MANAGER OF YUZURU NARAZAKI, ONE OF THE TOP TEN TALENTS AT...
...THE PEACOCK TALENT AGENCY.
I SEE, FUJIMARU.
SHUP
YOU'VE FINALLY...
...MADE UP YOUR MIND TO BECOME MY MANAGER. ♡
HUH?!
UM, THAT'S NOT...!
~♡
SORRY TO DAMPEN YOUR EXCITEMENT.
NARAZAKI...
...YOU'RE MISTAKEN.

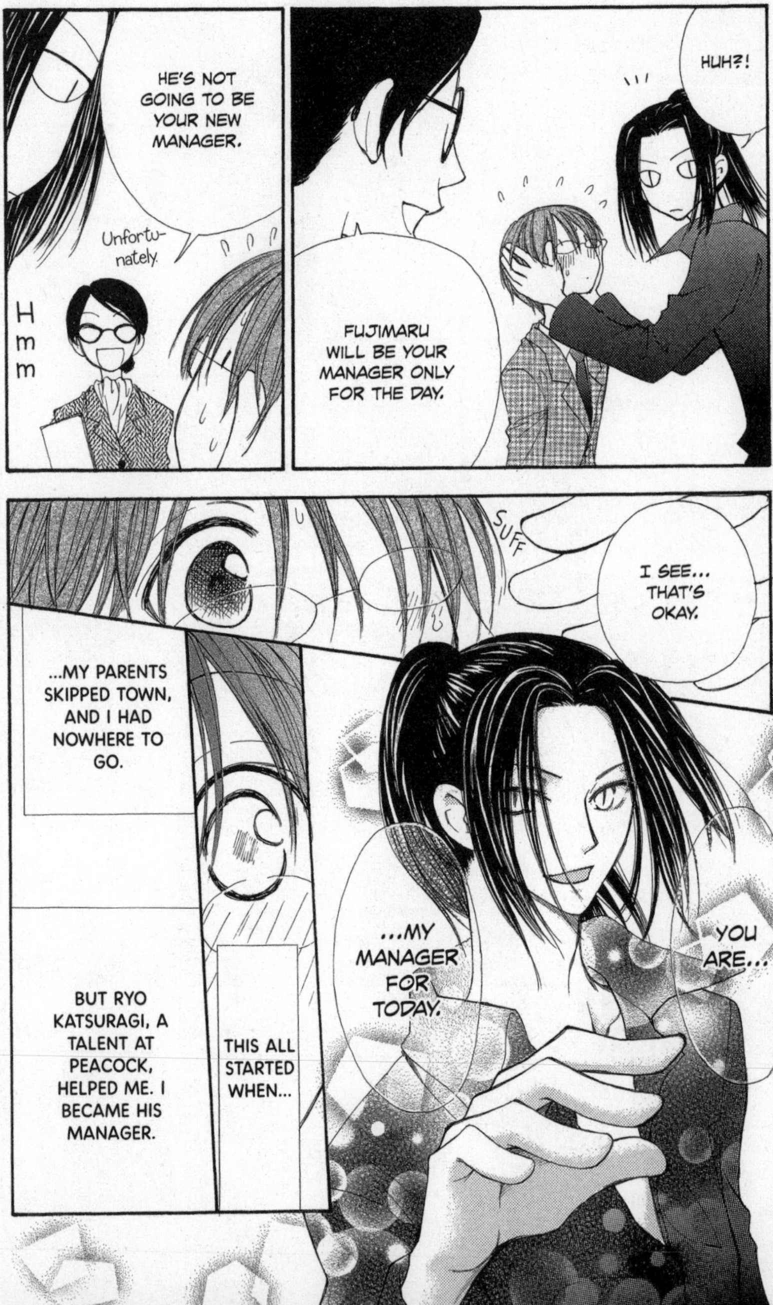
HUH?!
FUJIMARU WILL BE YOUR MANAGER ONLY FOR THE DAY.
HE'S NOT GOING TO BE YOUR NEW MANAGER.
Unfortunately.
Hmm
SUFF
I SEE... THAT'S OKAY.
YOU ARE...
...MY MANAGER FOR TODAY.
THIS ALL STARTED WHEN...
...MY PARENTS SKIPPED TOWN, AND I HAD NOWHERE TO GO.
BUT RYO KATSURAGI, A TALENT AT PEACOCK, HELPED ME. I BECAME HIS MANAGER.

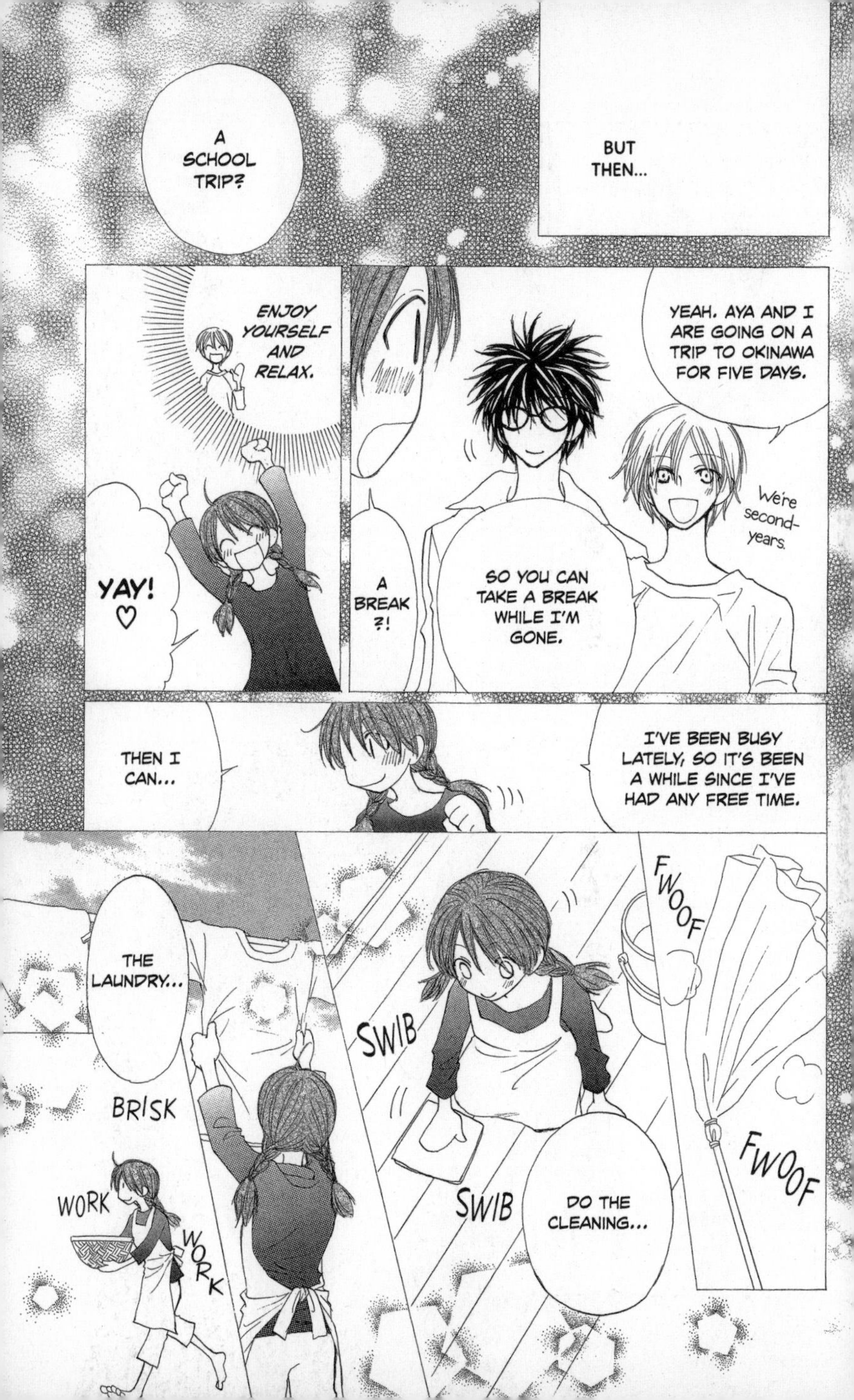
BUT THEN...
A SCHOOL TRIP?
YEAH. AYA AND I ARE GOING ON A TRIP TO OKINAWA FOR FIVE DAYS.
We're second-years.
SO YOU CAN TAKE A BREAK WHILE I'M GONE.
A BREAK?!
ENJOY YOURSELF AND RELAX.
YAY! ♡
I'VE BEEN BUSY LATELY, SO IT'S BEEN A WHILE SINCE I'VE HAD ANY FREE TIME.
THEN I CAN...
FWOOF
FWOOF
DO THE CLEANING...
SWIB
SWIB
THE LAUNDRY...
BRISK
WORK
WORK

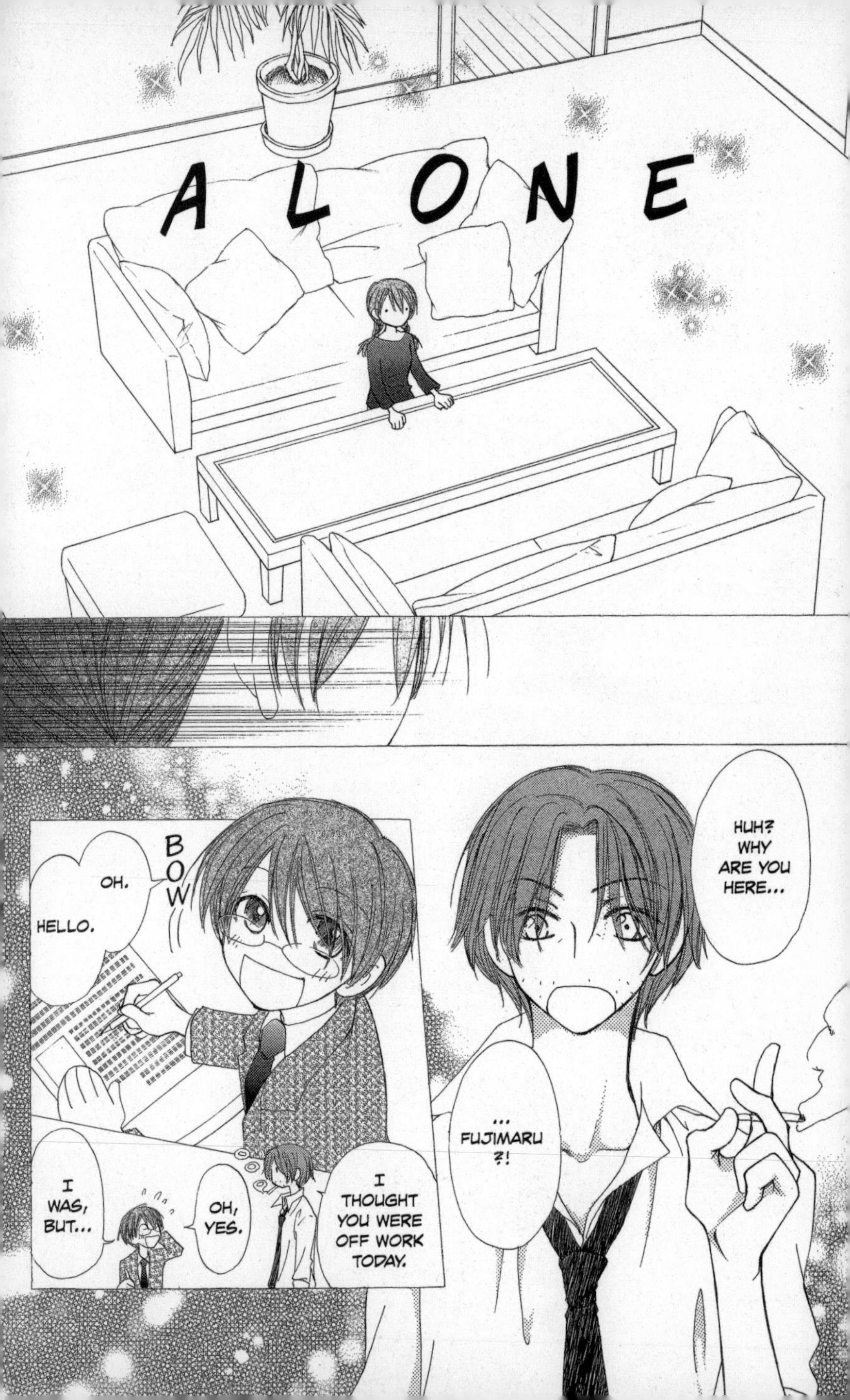
ALONE
HUH? WHY ARE YOU HERE...
...FUJIMARU ?!
OH.
HELLO.
BOW
I THOUGHT YOU WERE OFF WORK TODAY.
OH, YES.
I WAS, BUT...

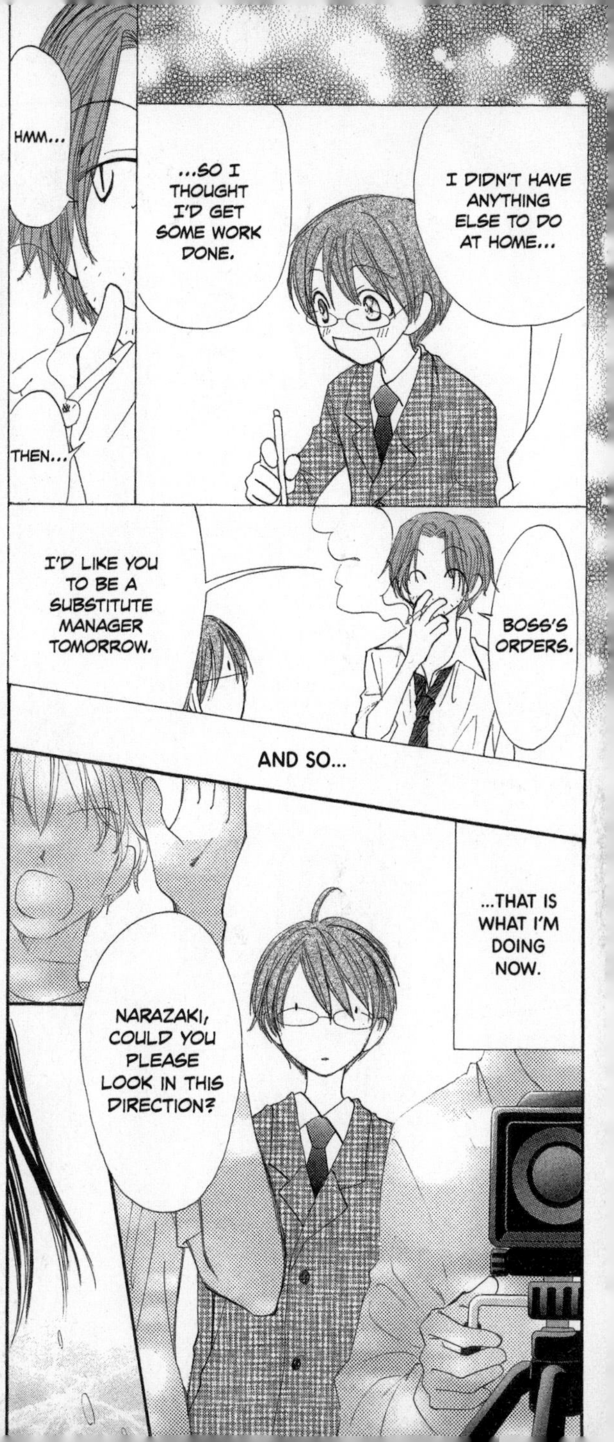
I DIDN'T HAVE ANYTHING ELSE TO DO AT HOME...
...SO I THOUGHT I'D GET SOME WORK DONE.
HMM...
THEN...
BOSS'S ORDERS.
I'D LIKE YOU TO BE A SUBSTITUTE MANAGER TOMORROW.
AND SO...
...THAT IS WHAT I'M DOING NOW.
NARAZAKI, COULD YOU PLEASE LOOK IN THIS DIRECTION?

1/4 Sakura Mail

Part 12

Narazaki has the same eyes as a reindeer.

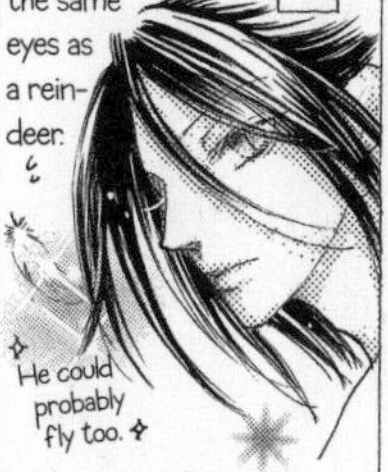
He could probably fly too.

This one-shot was created as a bonus story for *Penguin Revolution* to let Narazaki have a good time!! Yukari, or Yuka-chin, is the heroine of the series. She is pretty much bonded by fate to Ryo, the talent she is in charge of. She kind of had a vaguely romantic relationship with him too, so the odds were against Narazaki since he appeared later on in the series. But being an oddball, Narazaki keeps hitting on Yuka-chin without ever giving up. He's one tough guy. He was a wild guy who moved around as he pleased in the thoughts of his creator.

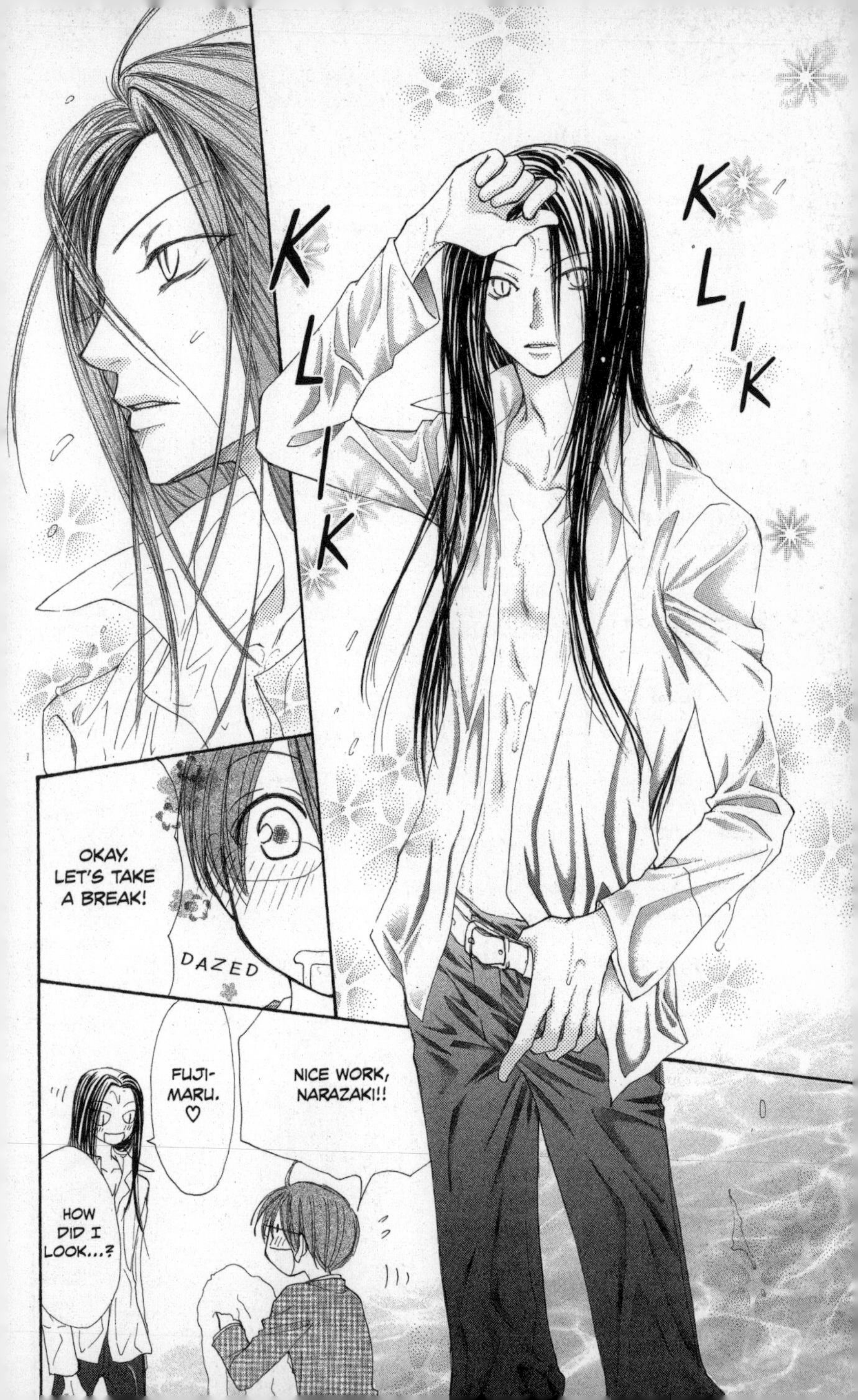
KLIK
KLIK
OKAY. LET'S TAKE A BREAK!
DAZED
NICE WORK, NARAZAKI!!
FUJI-MARU. ♡
HOW DID I LOOK...?

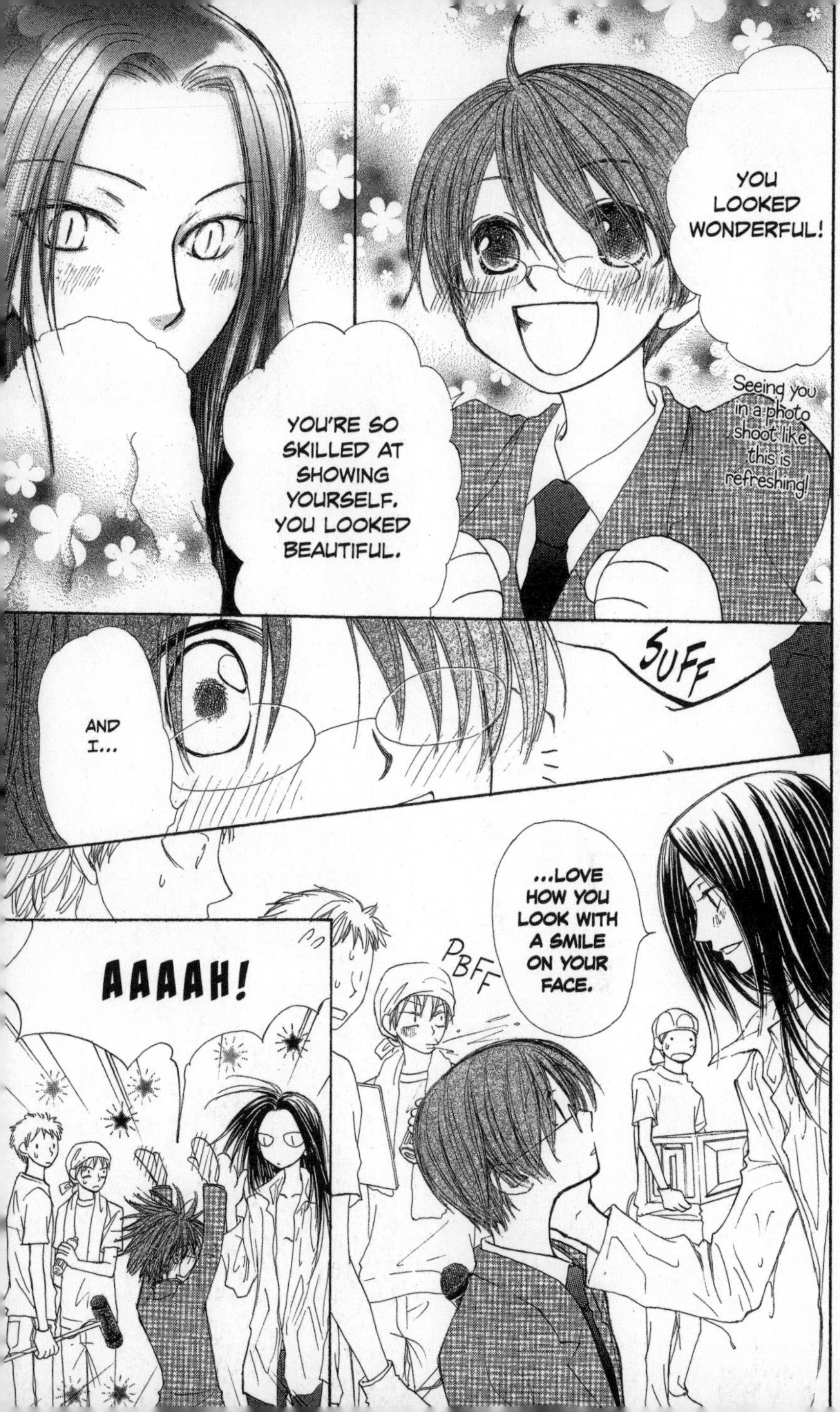
YOU LOOKED WONDERFUL!
Seeing you in a photo shoot like this is refreshing!
YOU'RE SO SKILLED AT SHOWING YOURSELF. YOU LOOKED BEAUTIFUL.
SUFF
AND I...
...LOVE HOW YOU LOOK WITH A SMILE ON YOUR FACE.
PBFF
AAAAH!

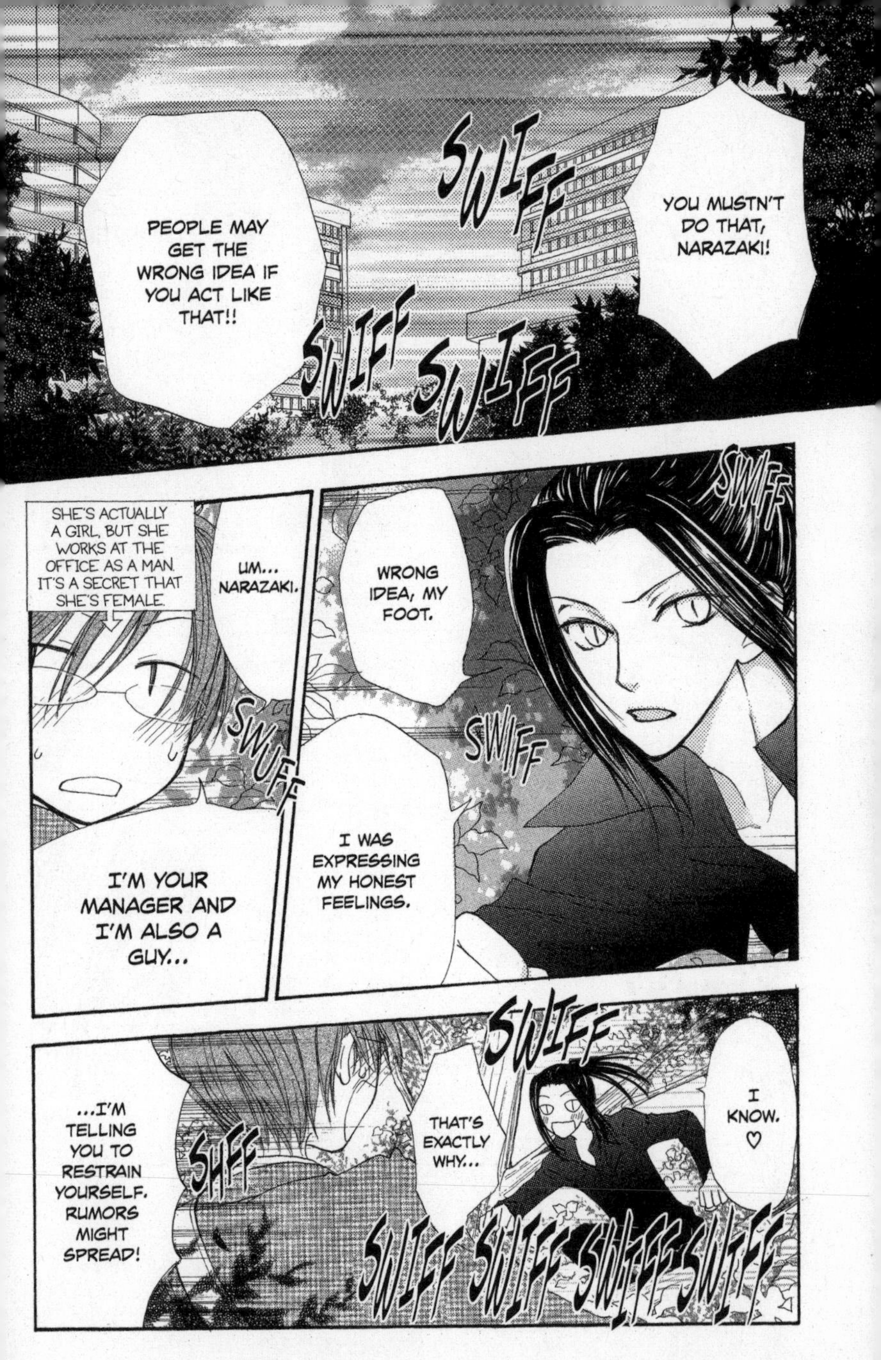
YOU MUSTN'T DO THAT, NARAZAKI!
SWIFF
PEOPLE MAY GET THE WRONG IDEA IF YOU ACT LIKE THAT!!
SWIFF
SWIFF
SWIFF
WRONG IDEA, MY FOOT.
SWIFF
I WAS EXPRESSING MY HONEST FEELINGS.
SHE'S ACTUALLY A GIRL, BUT SHE WORKS AT THE OFFICE AS A MAN. IT'S A SECRET THAT SHE'S FEMALE.
UM... NARAZAKI.
SWUFF
I'M YOUR MANAGER AND I'M ALSO A GUY...
I KNOW. ♡
SWIFF
THAT'S EXACTLY WHY...
SHFF
...I'M TELLING YOU TO RESTRAIN YOURSELF. RUMORS MIGHT SPREAD!
SWIFF SWIFF SWIFF SWIFF

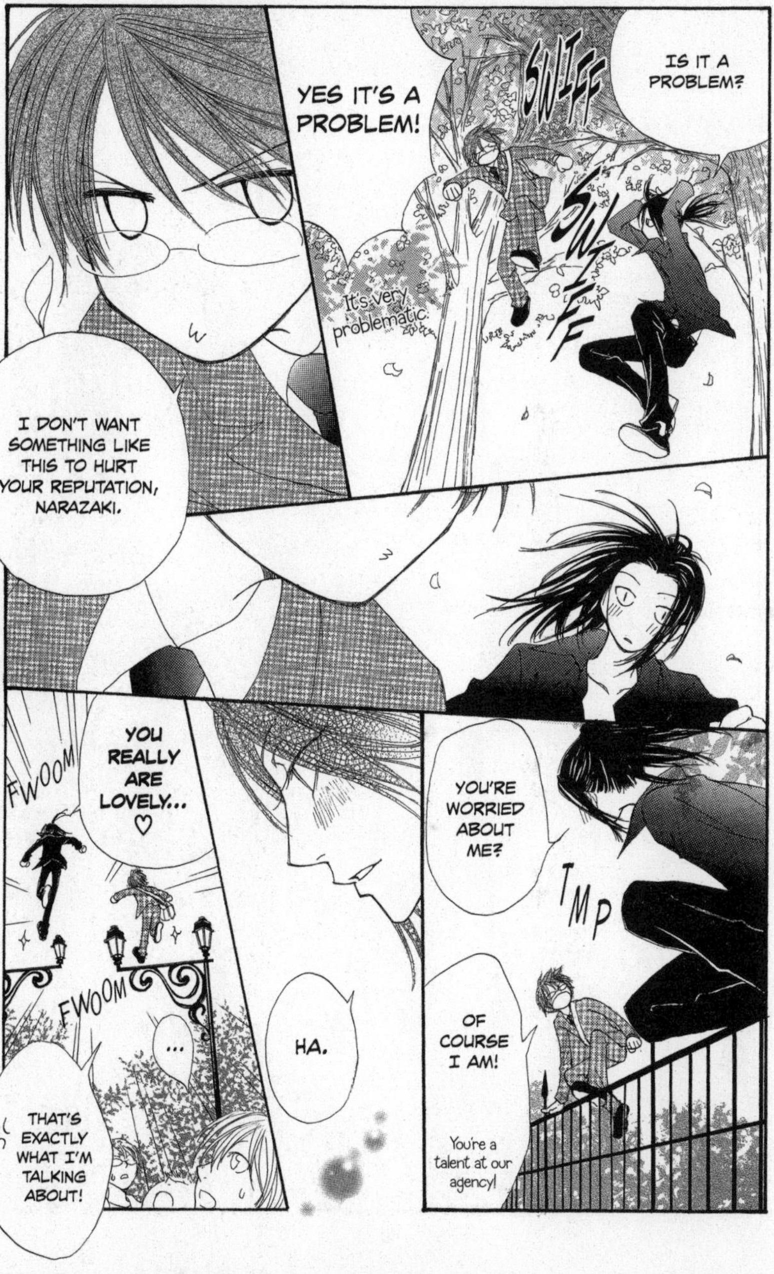
IS IT A PROBLEM?
SWIFF
SWIFF
YES IT'S A PROBLEM!
It's very problematic.
I DON'T WANT SOMETHING LIKE THIS TO HURT YOUR REPUTATION, NARAZAKI.
YOU'RE WORRIED ABOUT ME?
TMP
OF COURSE I AM!
You're a talent at our agency!
HA.
YOU REALLY ARE LOVELY... ♡
FWOOM
FWOOM
...
THAT'S EXACTLY WHAT I'M TALKING ABOUT!

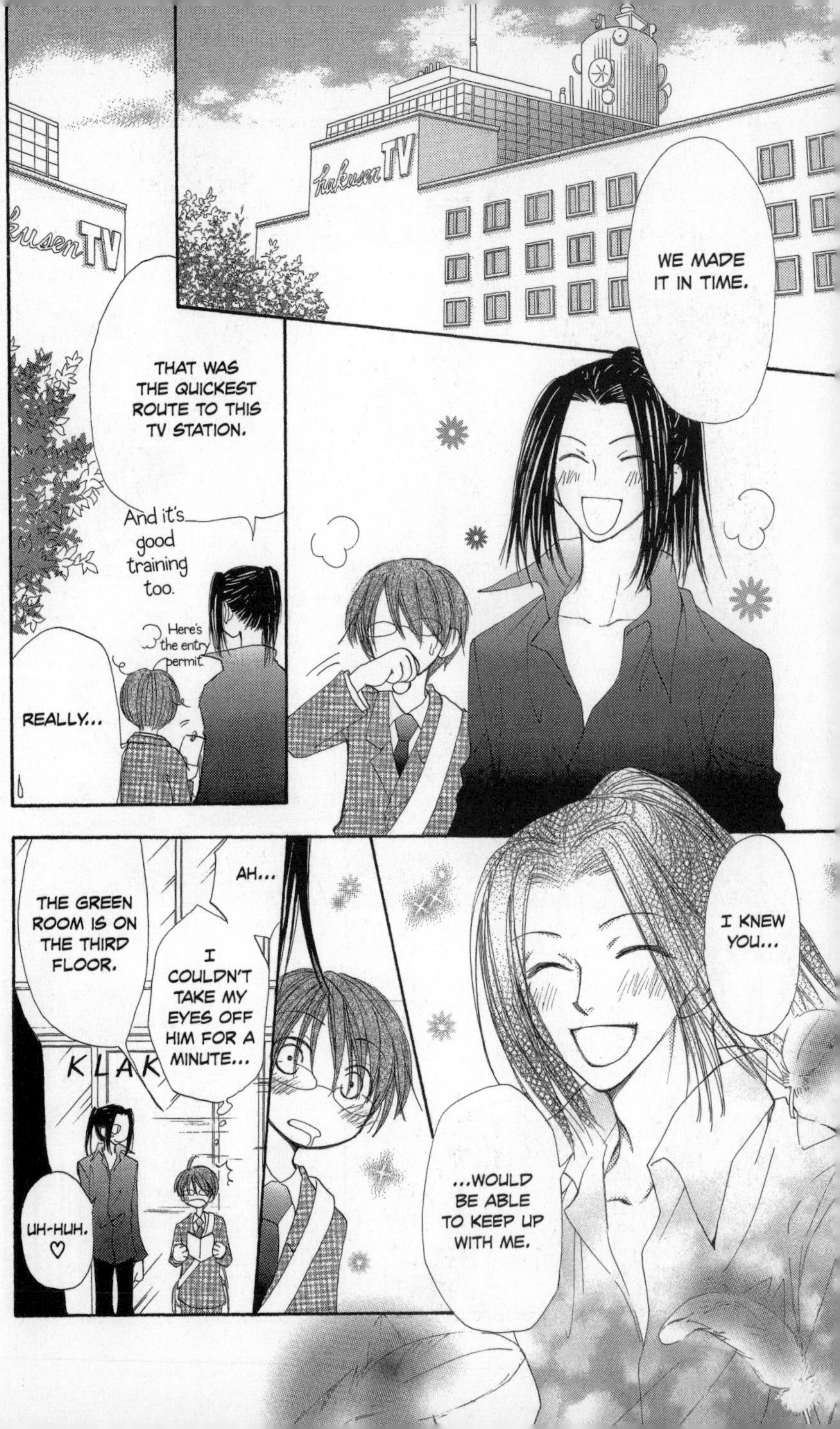
hakusen TV
kusen TV
WE MADE IT IN TIME.
THAT WAS THE QUICKEST ROUTE TO THIS TV STATION.
And it's good training too.
Here's the entry permit.
REALLY...
I KNEW YOU...
...WOULD BE ABLE TO KEEP UP WITH ME.
AH...
I COULDN'T TAKE MY EYES OFF HIM FOR A MINUTE...
THE GREEN ROOM IS ON THE THIRD FLOOR.
KLAK
UH-HUH. ♡

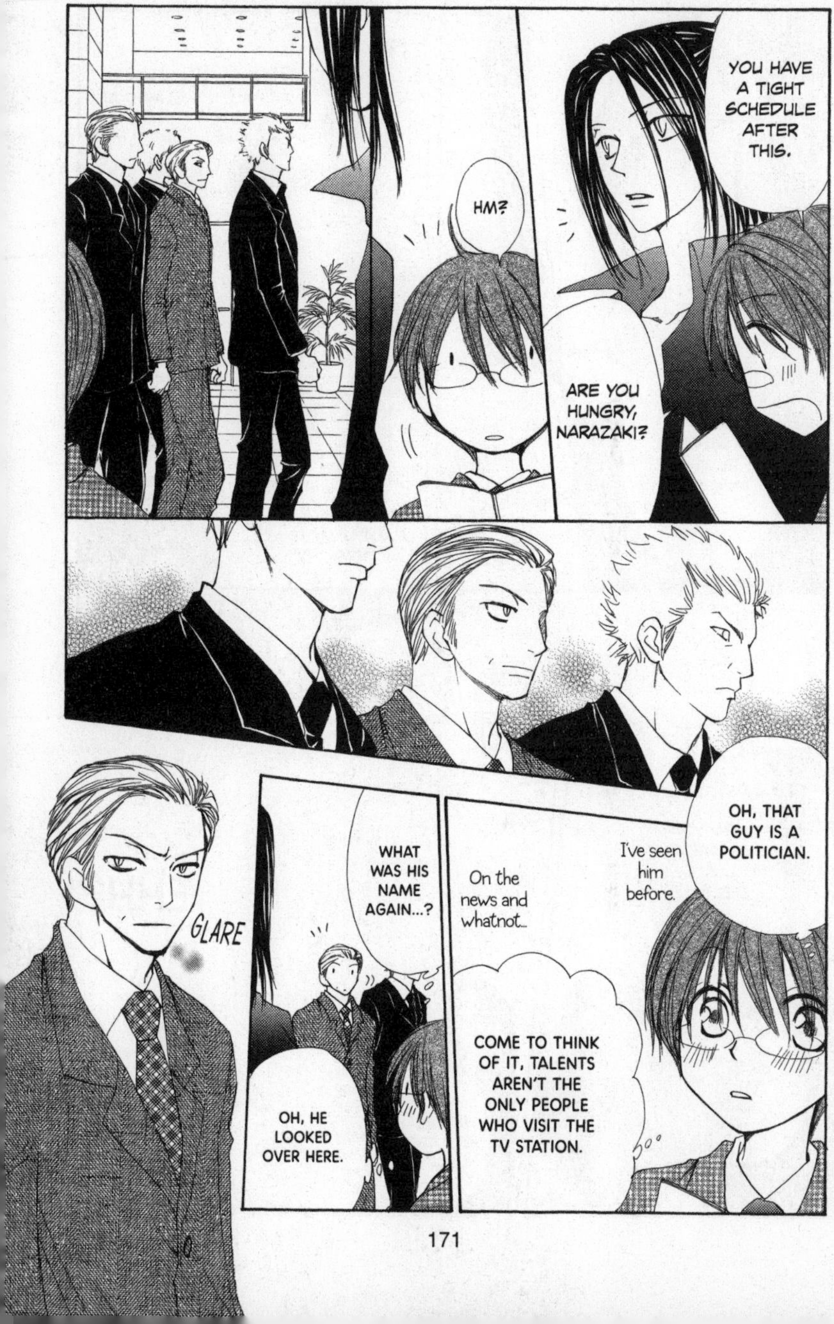
YOU HAVE A TIGHT SCHEDULE AFTER THIS.
ARE YOU HUNGRY, NARAZAKI?
HM?
OH, THAT GUY IS A POLITICIAN.
I've seen him before.
On the news and whatnot...
COME TO THINK OF IT, TALENTS AREN'T THE ONLY PEOPLE WHO VISIT THE TV STATION.
WHAT WAS HIS NAME AGAIN...?
OH, HE LOOKED OVER HERE.
GLARE

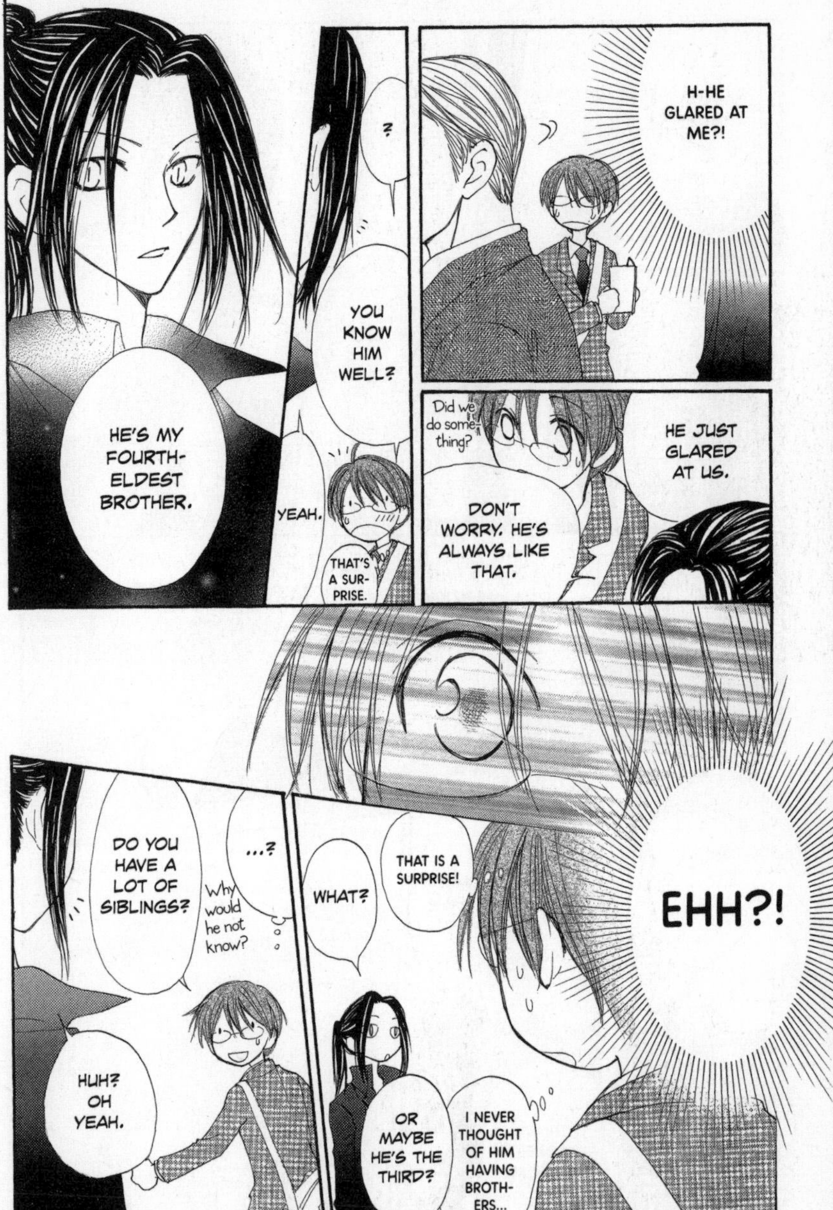

H-HE GLARED AT ME?!
HE JUST GLARED AT US.
Did we do something?
DON'T WORRY. HE'S ALWAYS LIKE THAT.
?
YOU KNOW HIM WELL?
YEAH.
THAT'S A SURPRISE.
HE'S MY FOURTH-ELDEST BROTHER.
EHH?!
THAT IS A SURPRISE!
WHAT?
I NEVER THOUGHT OF HIM HAVING BROTHERS...
OR MAYBE HE'S THE THIRD?
...?
Why would he not know?
DO YOU HAVE A LOT OF SIBLINGS?
HUH? OH YEAH.

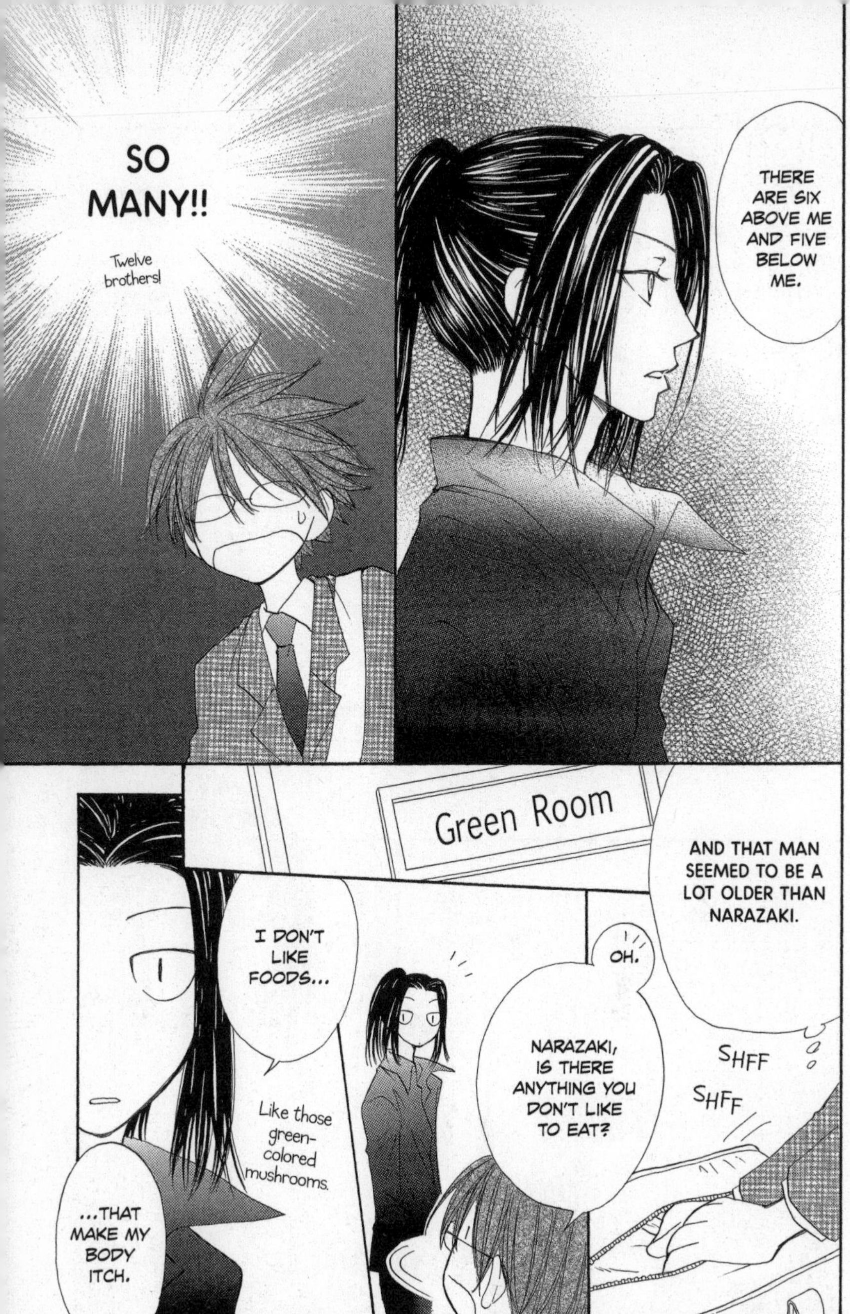
THERE ARE SIX ABOVE ME AND FIVE BELOW ME.
SO MANY!!
Twelve brothers!
Green Room
AND THAT MAN SEEMED TO BE A LOT OLDER THAN NARAZAKI.
OH.
NARAZAKI, IS THERE ANYTHING YOU DON'T LIKE TO EAT?
SHFF
SHFF
I DON'T LIKE FOODS...
Like those green-colored mushrooms.
...THAT MAKE MY BODY ITCH.

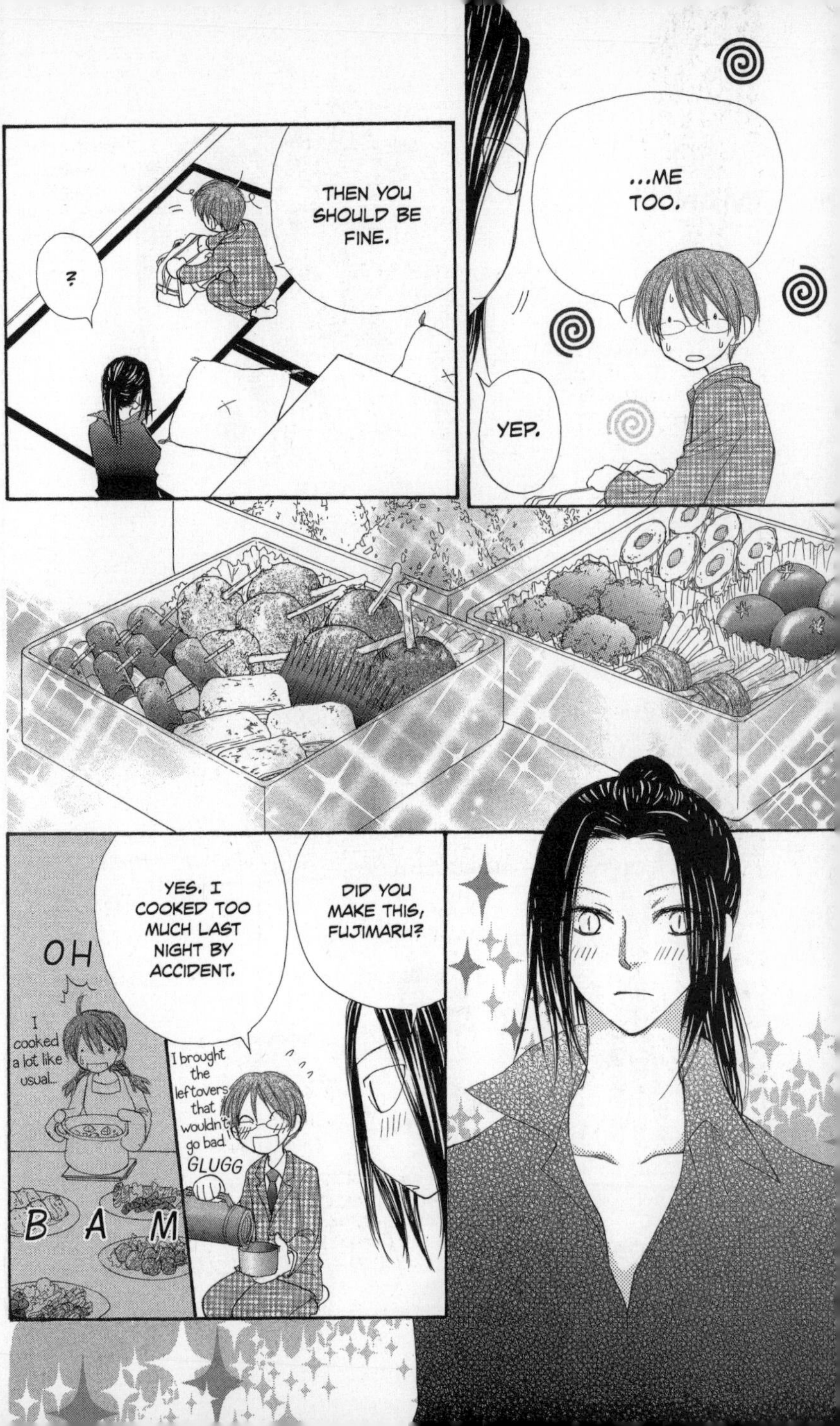

...ME TOO.
YEP.
THEN YOU SHOULD BE FINE.
?
DID YOU MAKE THIS, FUJIMARU?
YES. I COOKED TOO MUCH LAST NIGHT BY ACCIDENT.
OH
I cooked a lot like usual...
B A M
I brought the leftovers that wouldn't go bad.
GLUGG

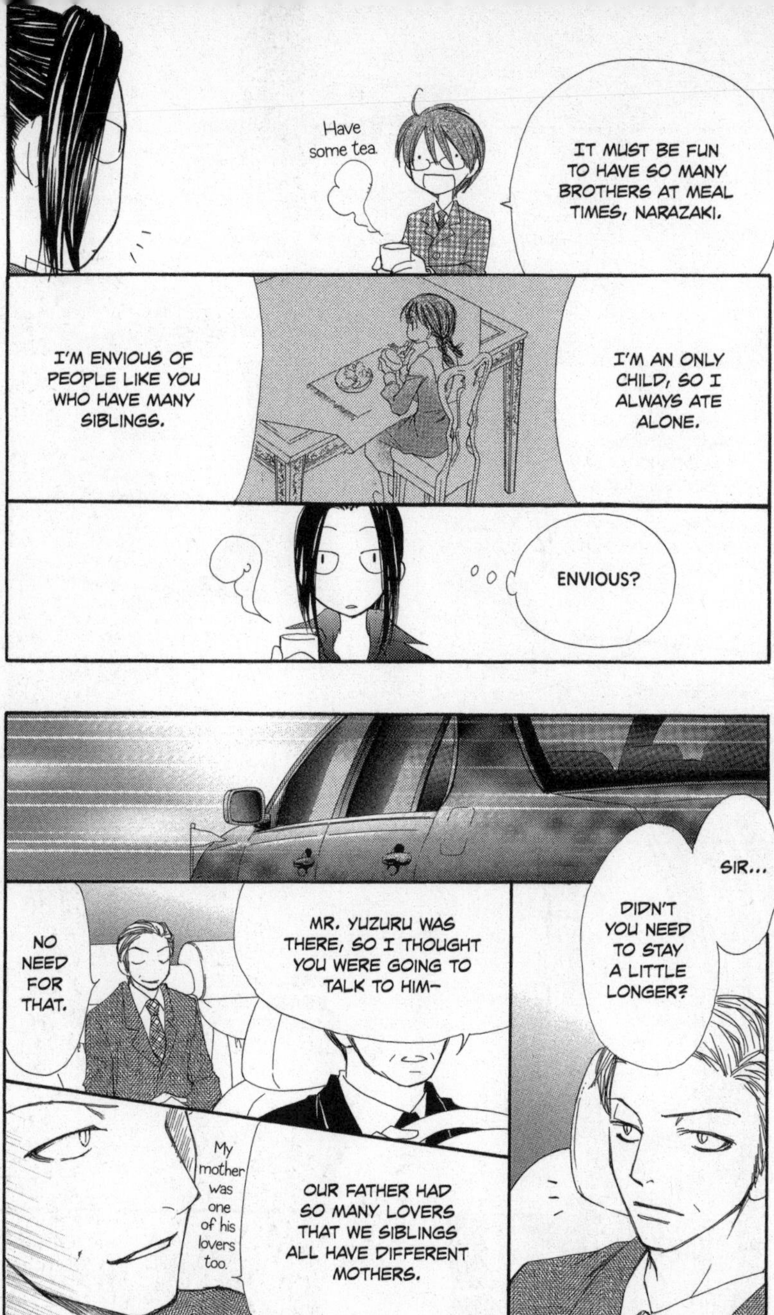
IT MUST BE FUN TO HAVE SO MANY BROTHERS AT MEAL TIMES, NARAZAKI.
Have some tea.
I'M AN ONLY CHILD, SO I ALWAYS ATE ALONE.
I'M ENVIOUS OF PEOPLE LIKE YOU WHO HAVE MANY SIBLINGS.
ENVIOUS?
SIR...
DIDN'T YOU NEED TO STAY A LITTLE LONGER?
MR. YUZURU WAS THERE, SO I THOUGHT YOU WERE GOING TO TALK TO HIM–
NO NEED FOR THAT.
OUR FATHER HAD SO MANY LOVERS THAT WE SIBLINGS ALL HAVE DIFFERENT MOTHERS.
My mother was one of his lovers too.

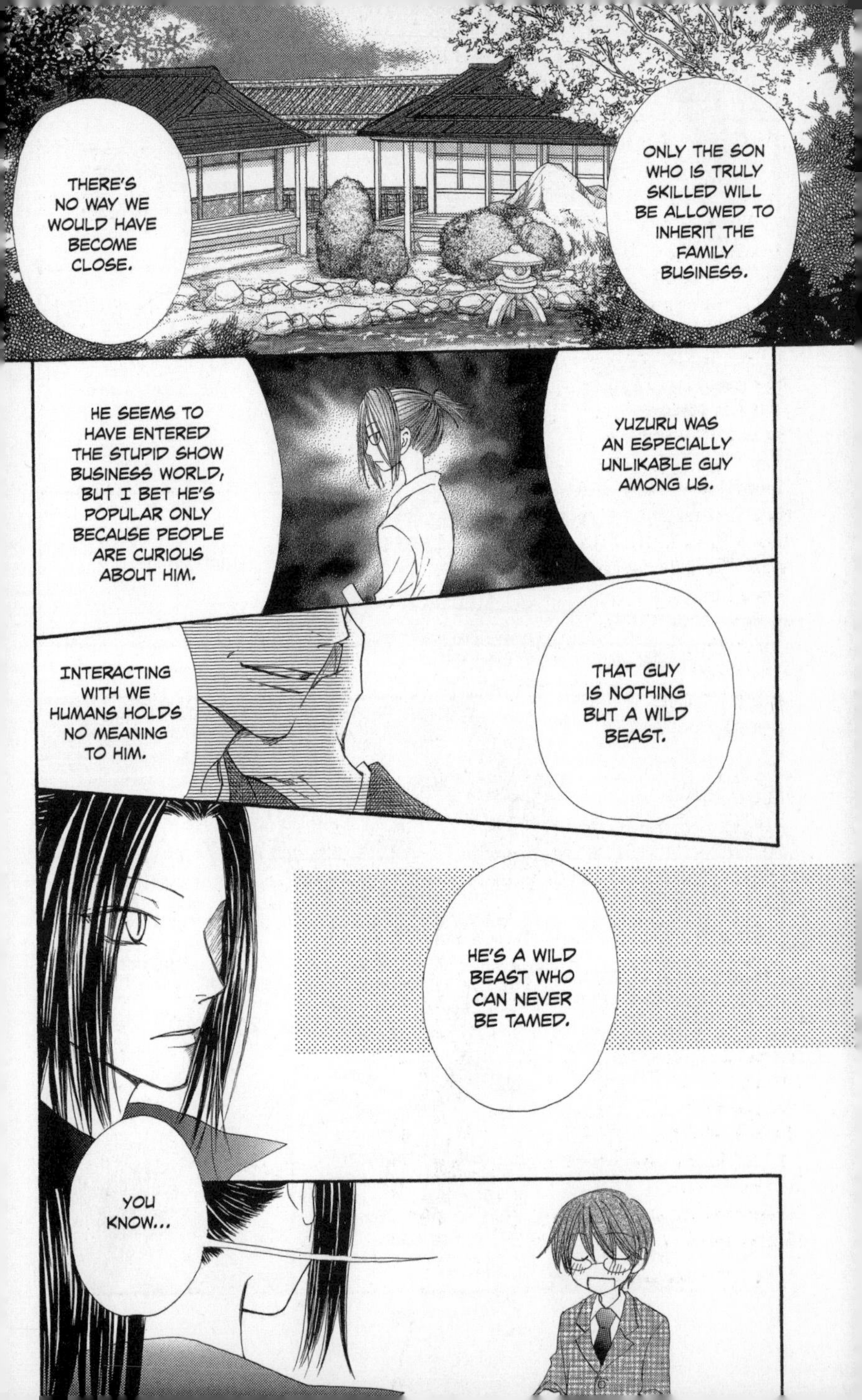
ONLY THE SON WHO IS TRULY SKILLED WILL BE ALLOWED TO INHERIT THE FAMILY BUSINESS.
THERE'S NO WAY WE WOULD HAVE BECOME CLOSE.
YUZURU WAS AN ESPECIALLY UNLIKABLE GUY AMONG US.
HE SEEMS TO HAVE ENTERED THE STUPID SHOW BUSINESS WORLD, BUT I BET HE'S POPULAR ONLY BECAUSE PEOPLE ARE CURIOUS ABOUT HIM.
THAT GUY IS NOTHING BUT A WILD BEAST.
INTERACTING WITH WE HUMANS HOLDS NO MEANING TO HIM.
HE'S A WILD BEAST WHO CAN NEVER BE TAMED.
YOU KNOW...

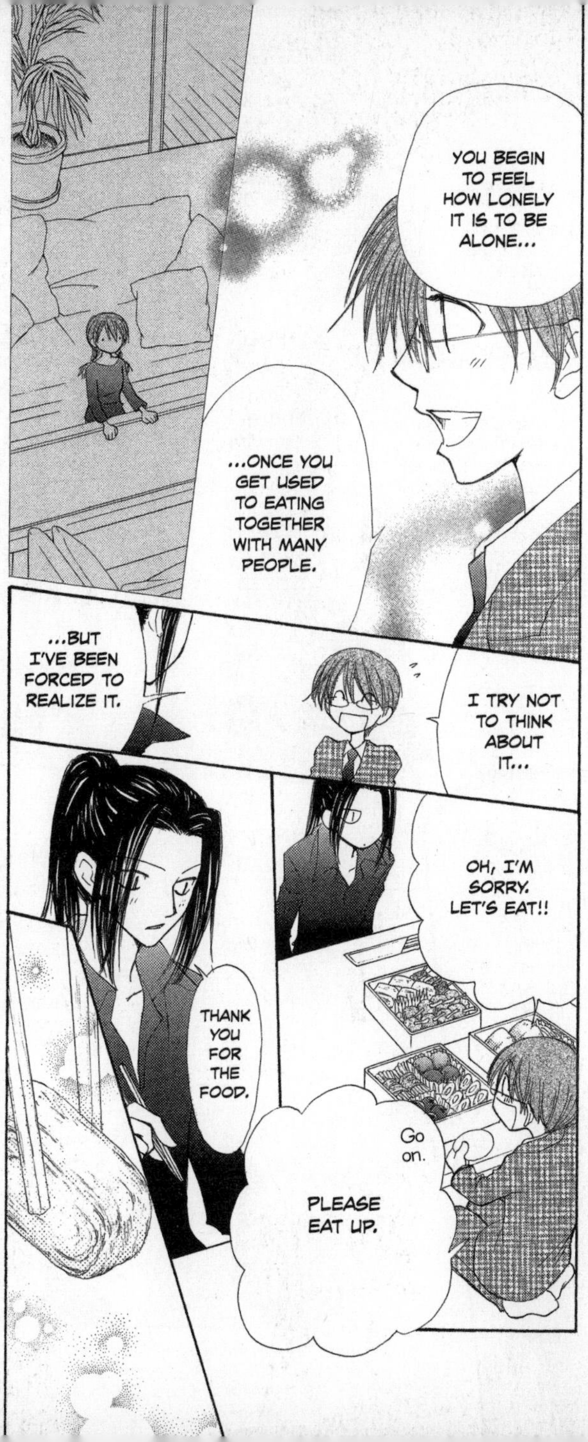
YOU BEGIN TO FEEL HOW LONELY IT IS TO BE ALONE...
...ONCE YOU GET USED TO EATING TOGETHER WITH MANY PEOPLE.
I TRY NOT TO THINK ABOUT IT...
...BUT I'VE BEEN FORCED TO REALIZE IT.
OH, I'M SORRY. LET'S EAT!!
Go on.
PLEASE EAT UP.
THANK YOU FOR THE FOOD.

1/4 Sakura Mail

Part 13

On the way back home after the meeting about this story, I was thinking up all sorts of ways to make Narazaki and Yuka-chin into an item just like he wanted. But no matter how many times I simulated the situation, Narazaki's feelings for Yuka-chin would never get through to her... I empathized with him so much that I couldn't stop crying at the thought of it. Inside the train!!

During rush hour too.

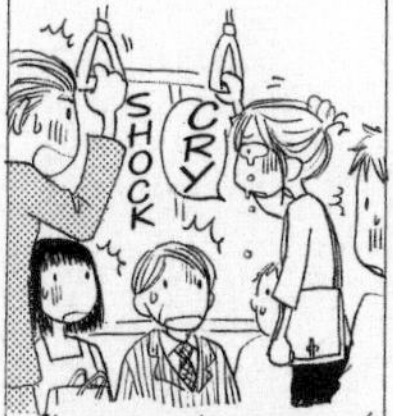
SHOCK
CRY

It was so embarrassing.

By the way, Tamika-chan who helped me with my final draft sympathized with Narazaki and cried too. But now that I've completed this, I feel that Narazaki will be fine. Why did I even cry for him? See you again!!

Sakura Tsukuba

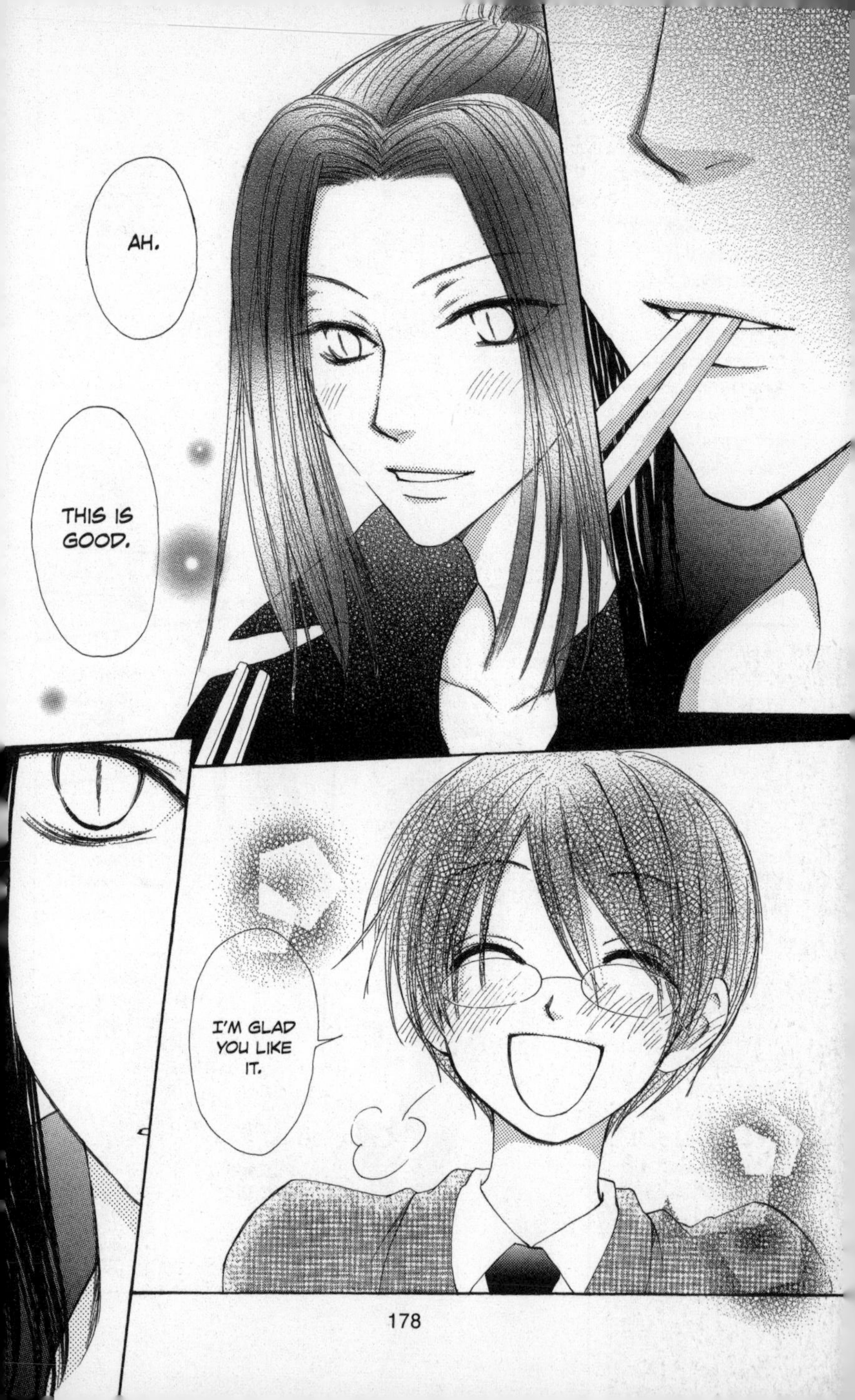
AH.
THIS IS GOOD.
I'M GLAD YOU LIKE IT.

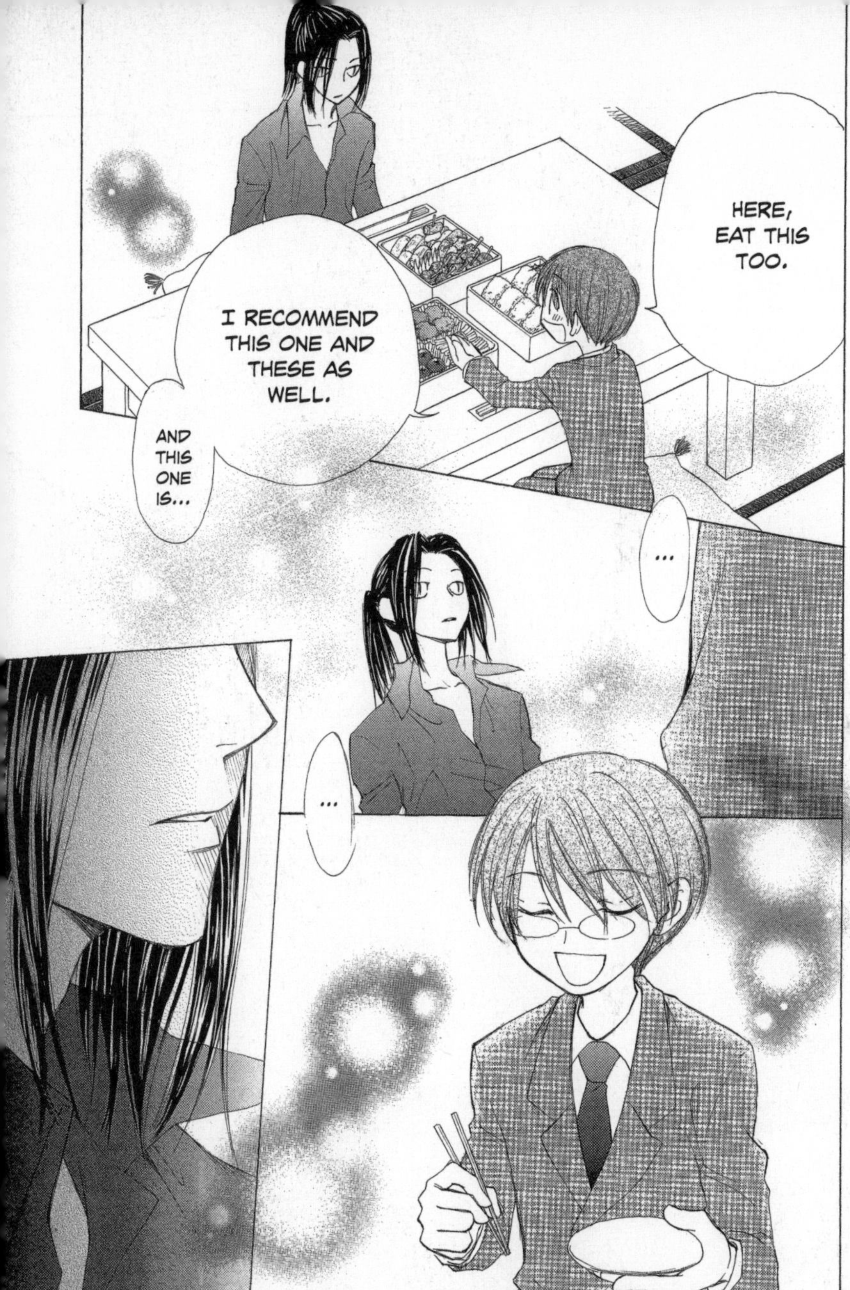
HERE, EAT THIS TOO.
I RECOMMEND THIS ONE AND THESE AS WELL.
AND THIS ONE IS...
...
...

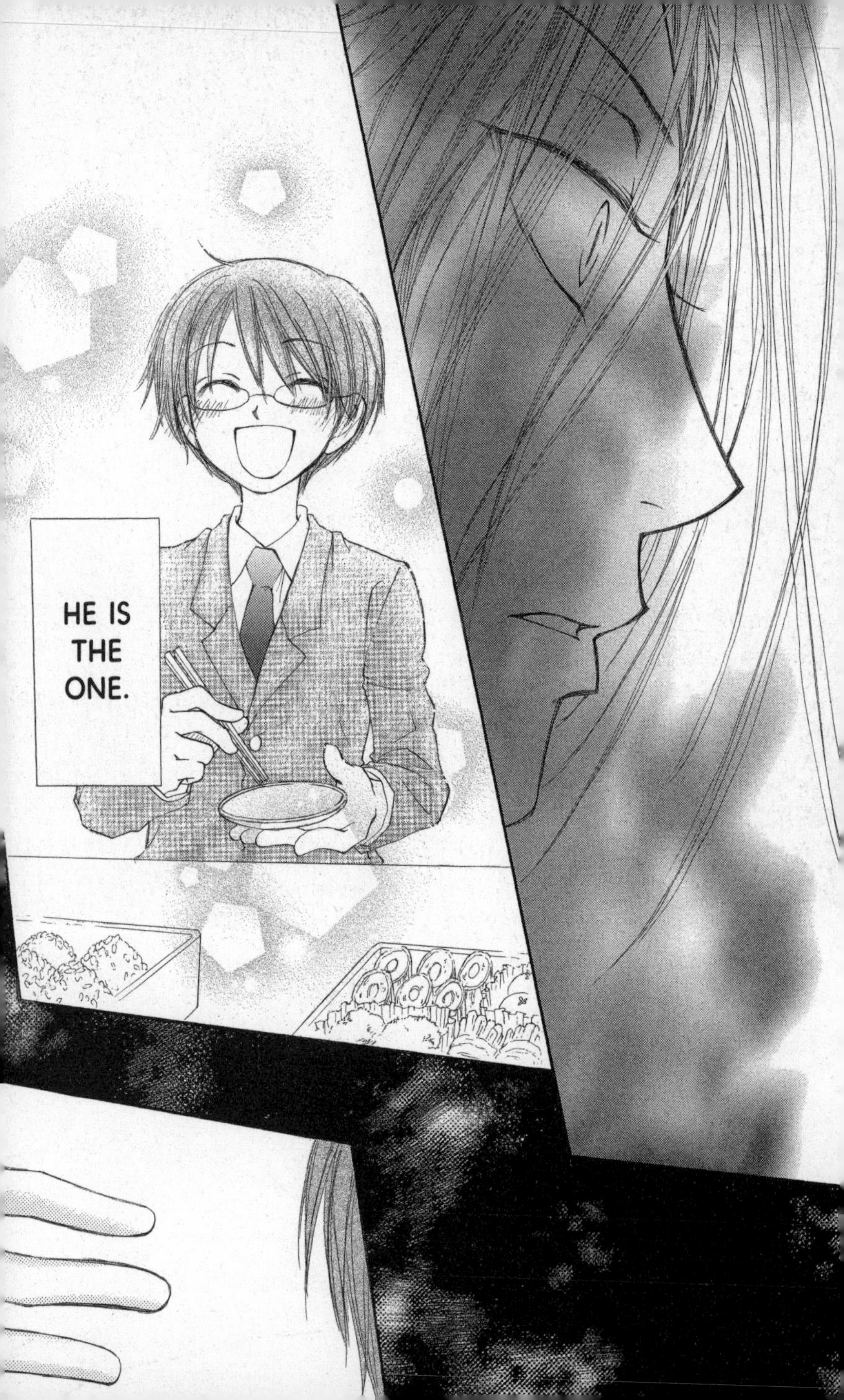
HE IS THE ONE.

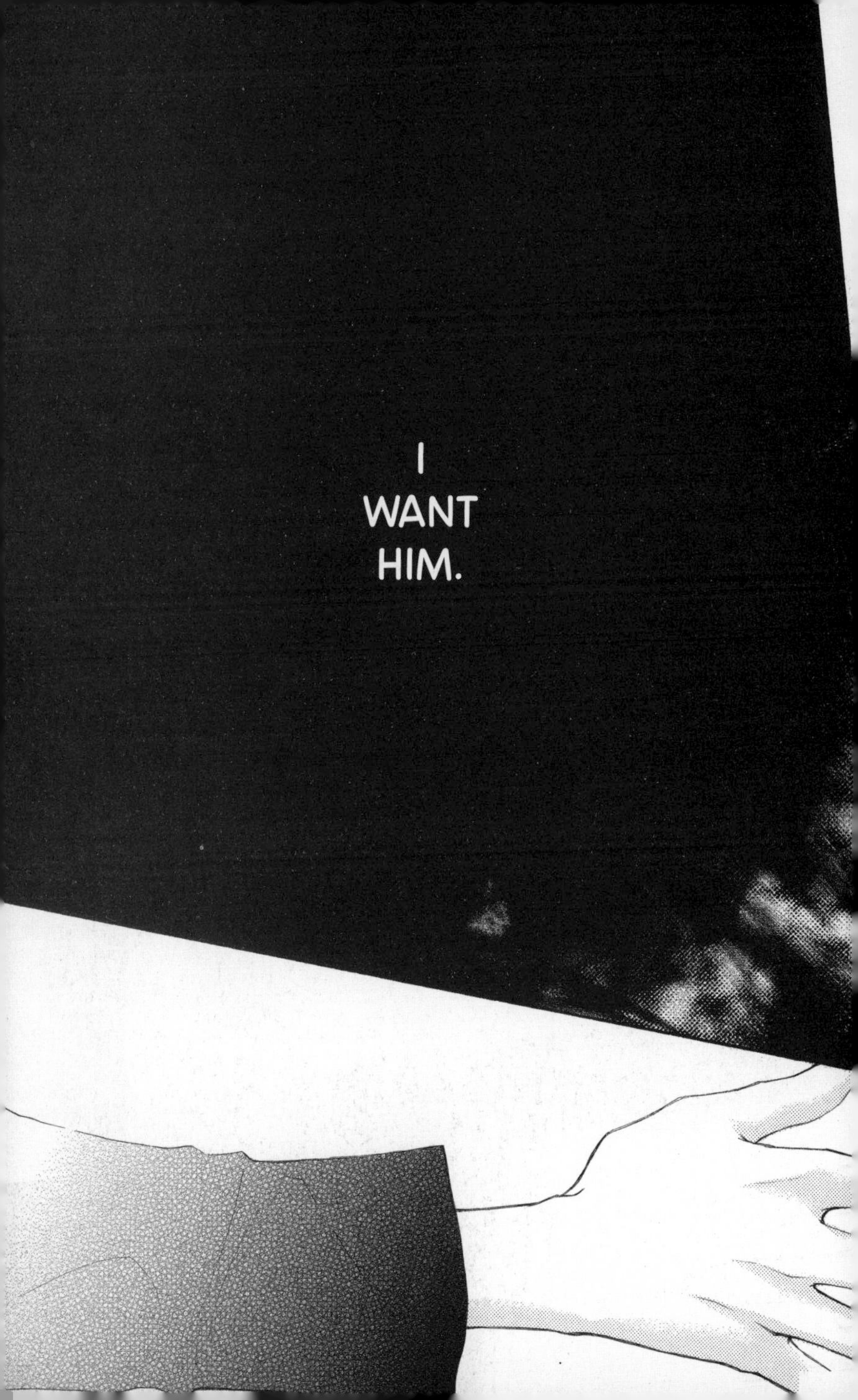
I WANT HIM.

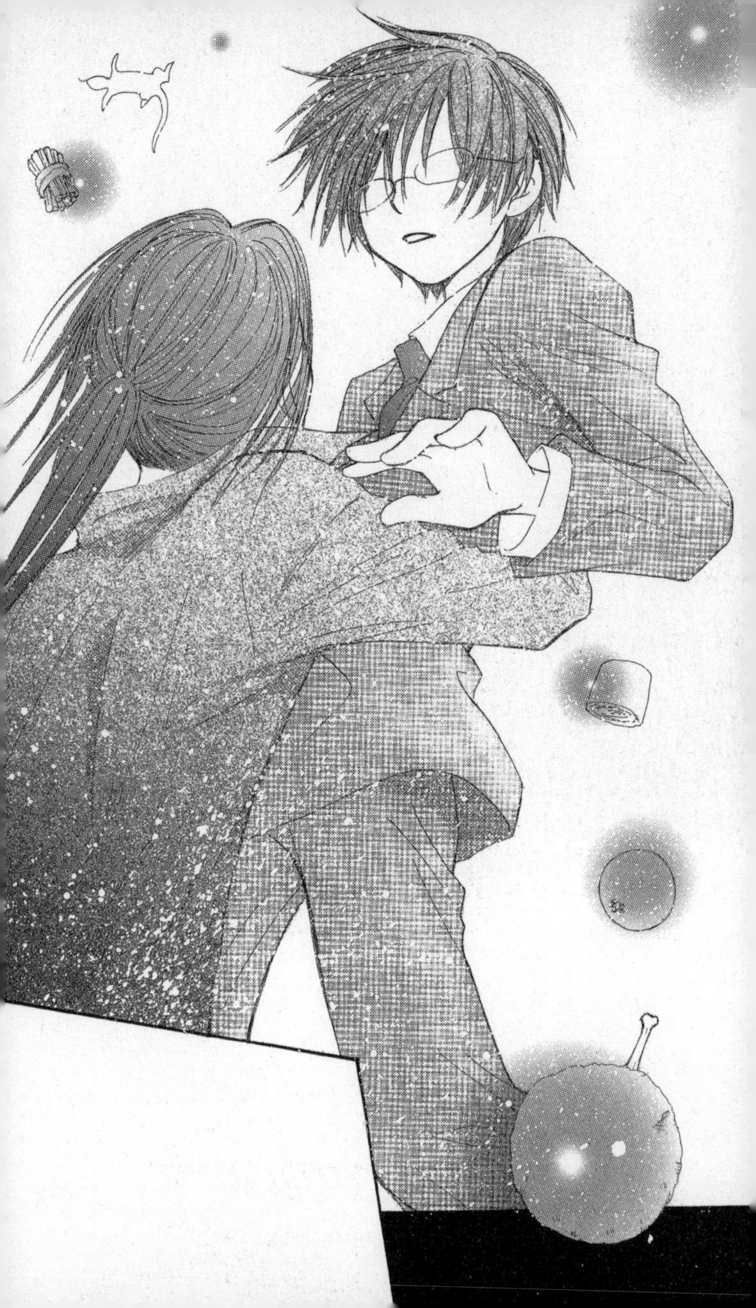

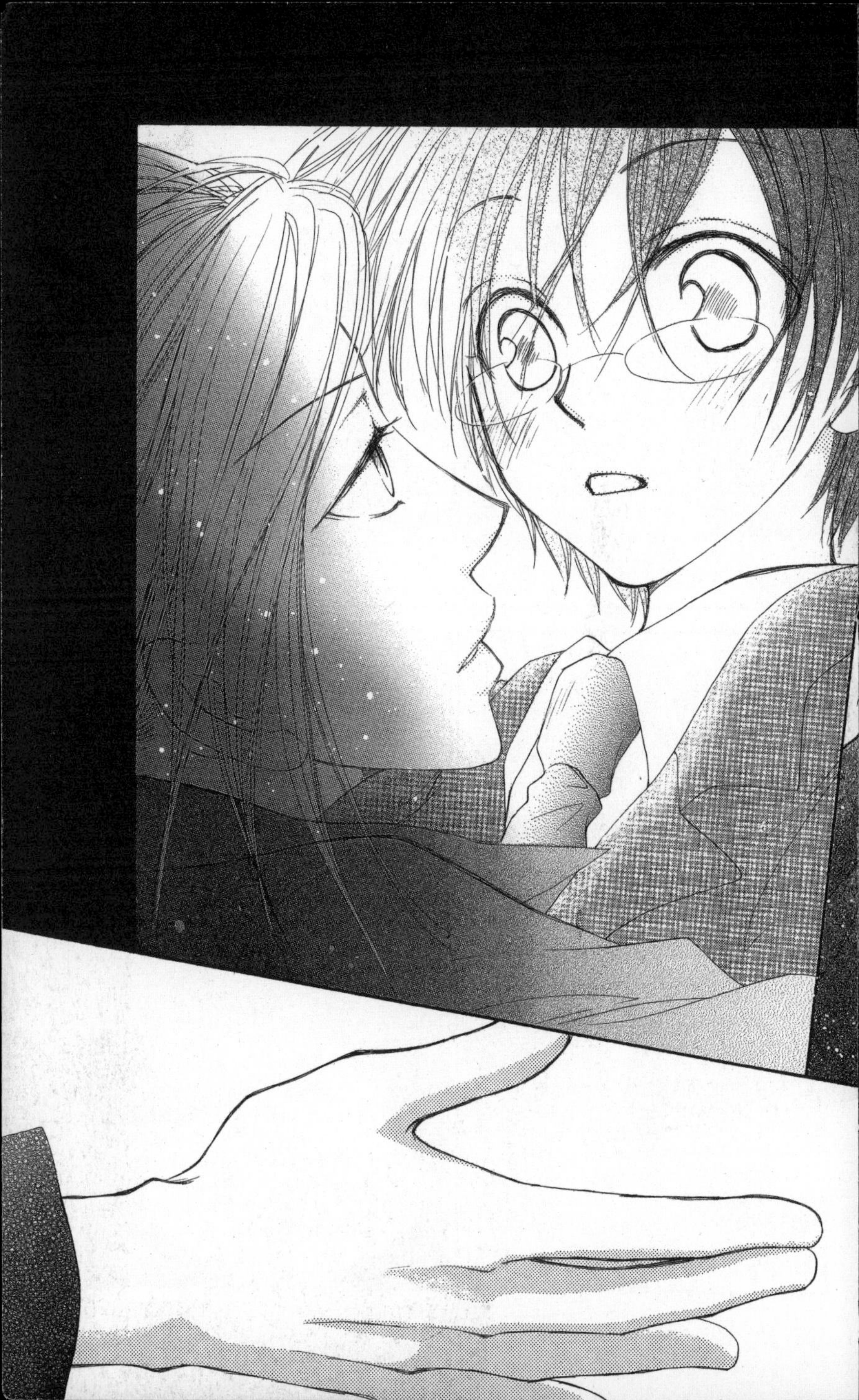

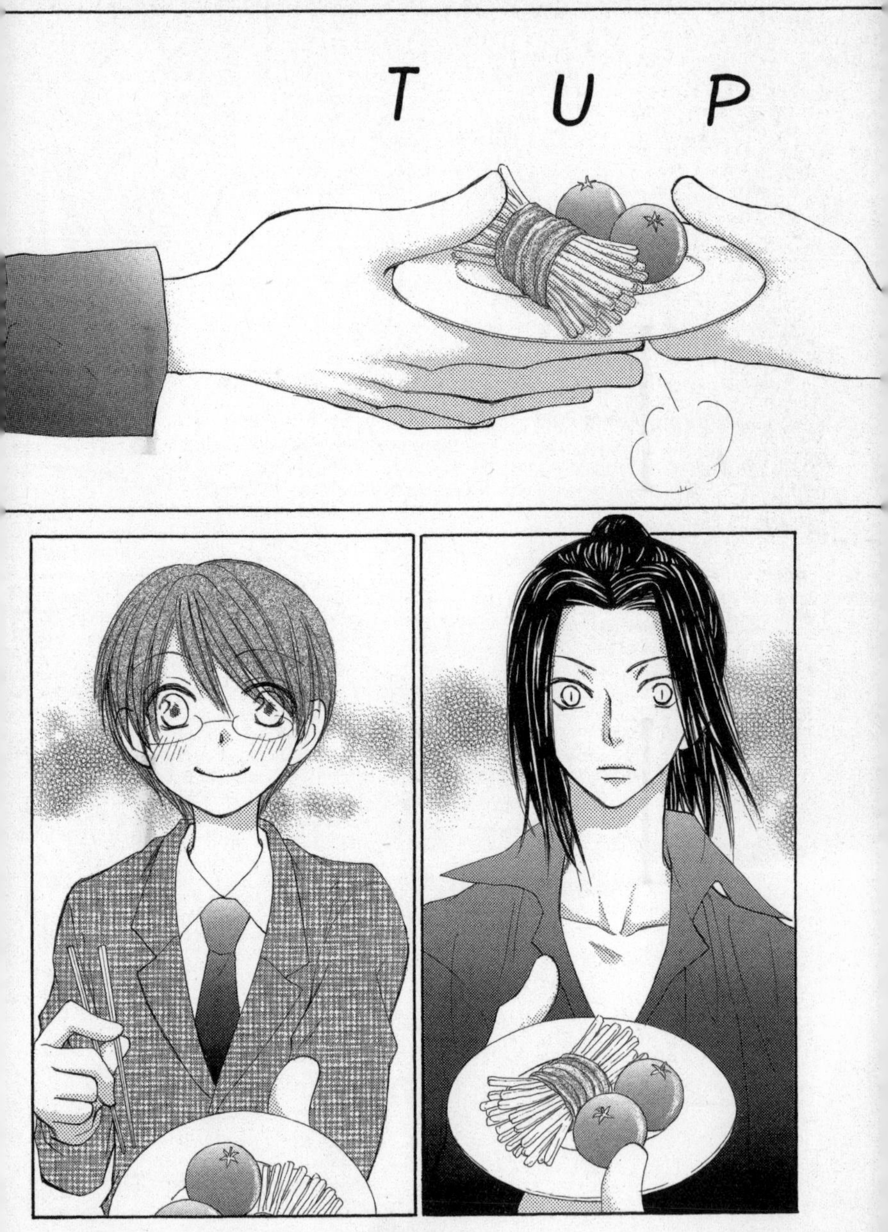
T U P

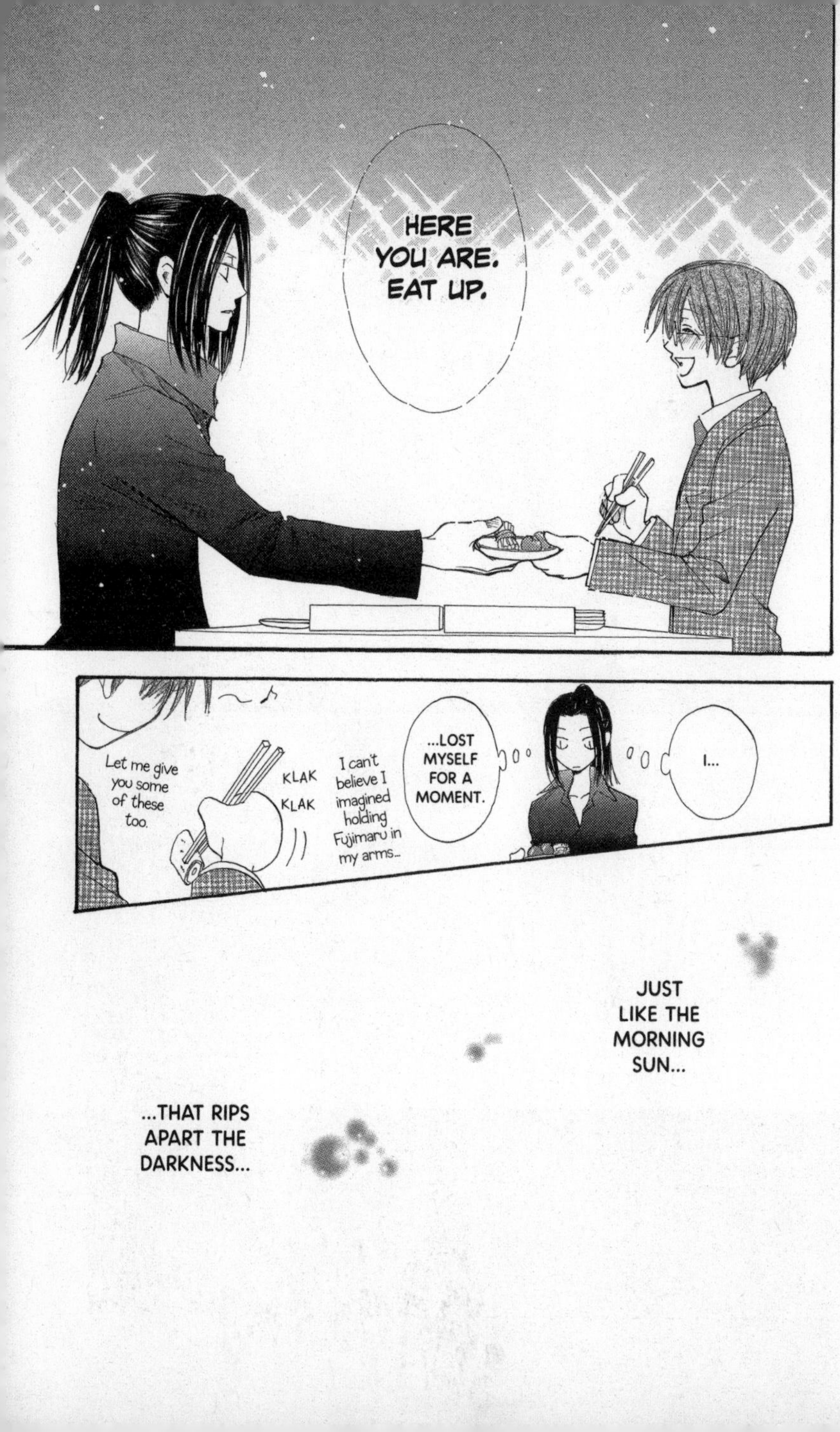
HERE YOU ARE. EAT UP.
I...
...LOST MYSELF FOR A MOMENT.
I can't believe I imagined holding Fujimaru in my arms...
KLAK KLAK
Let me give you some of these too.
JUST LIKE THE MORNING SUN...
...THAT RIPS APART THE DARKNESS...

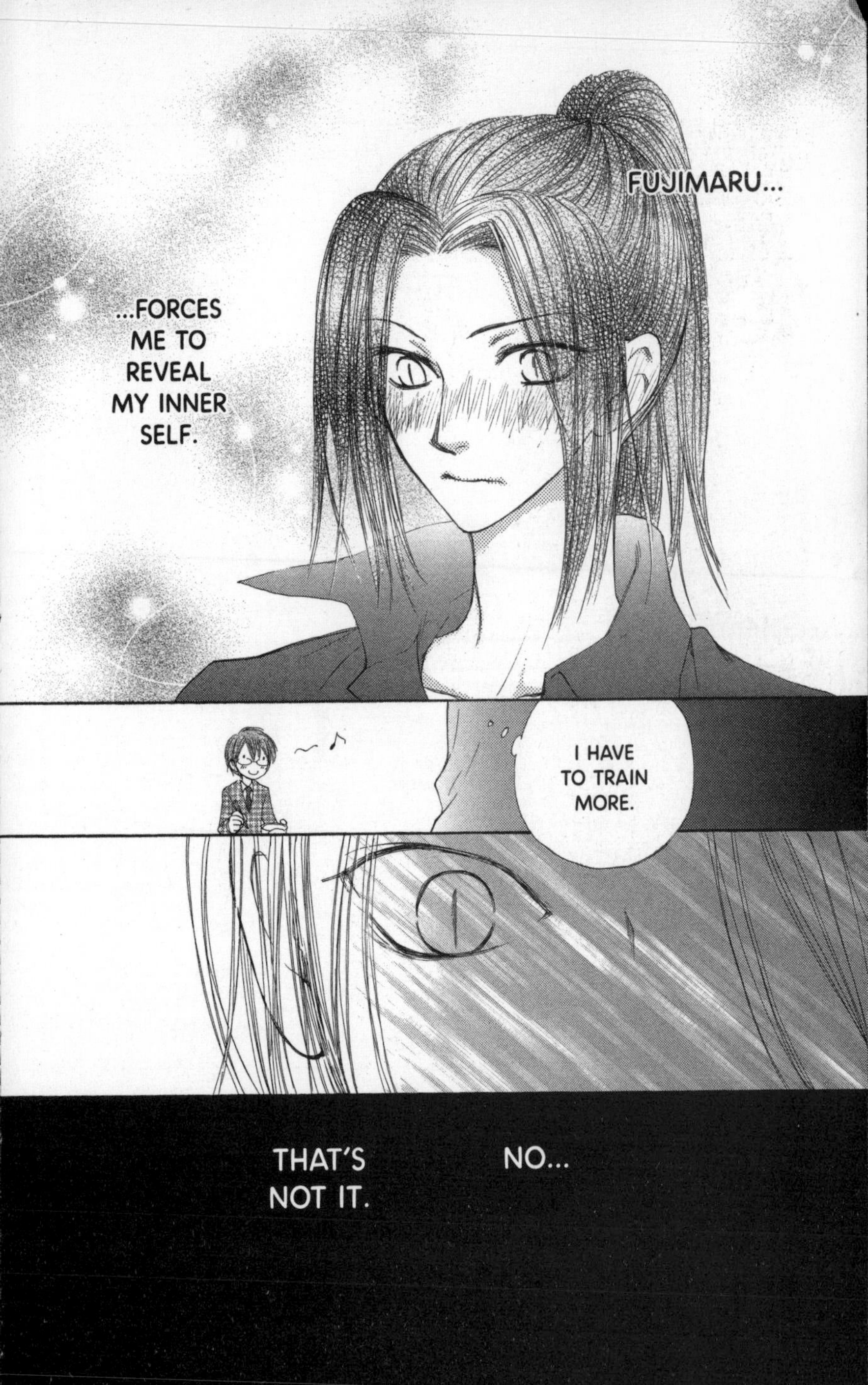
FUJIMARU...
...FORCES ME TO REVEAL MY INNER SELF.
I HAVE TO TRAIN MORE.
NO...
THAT'S NOT IT.

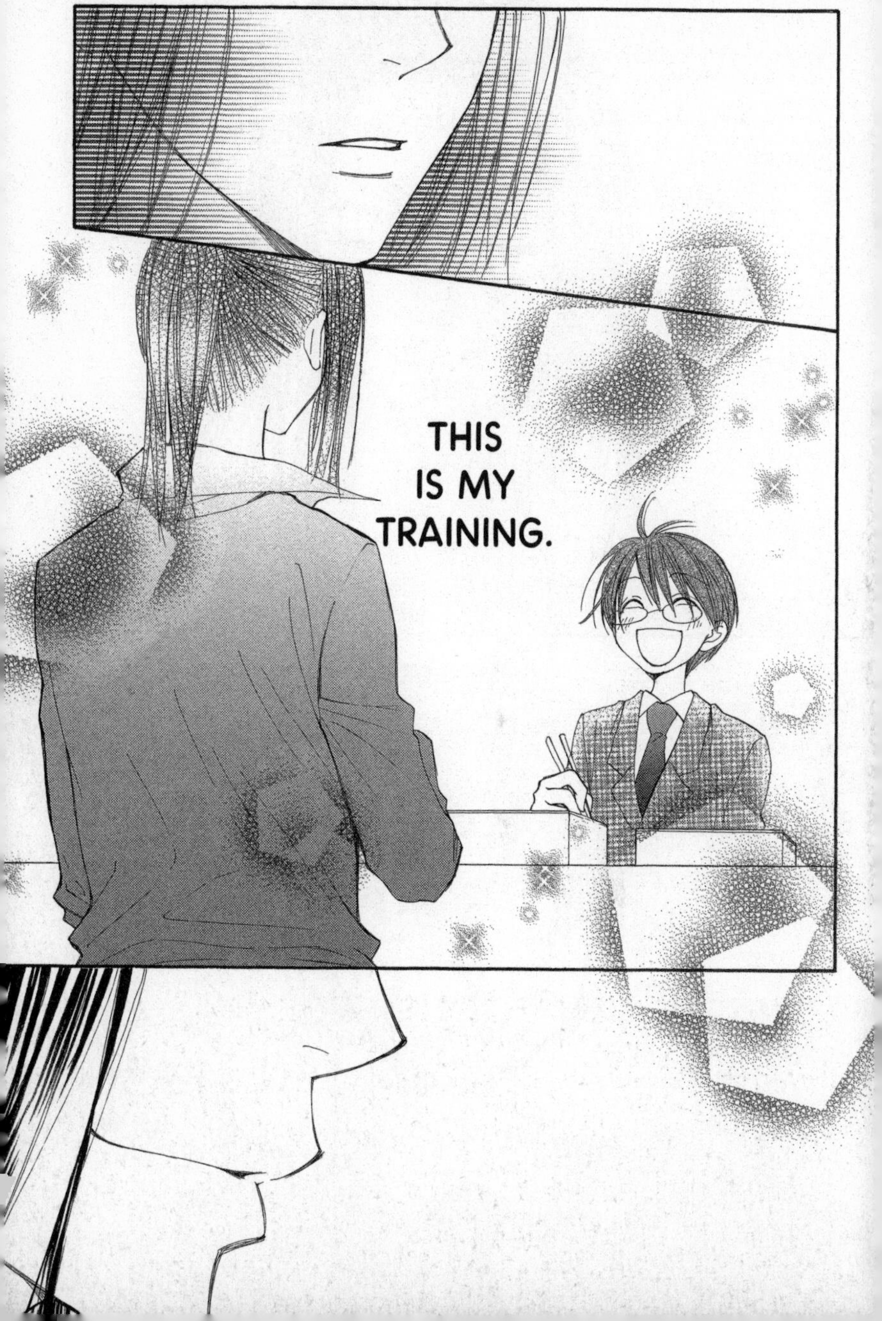
THIS IS MY TRAINING.

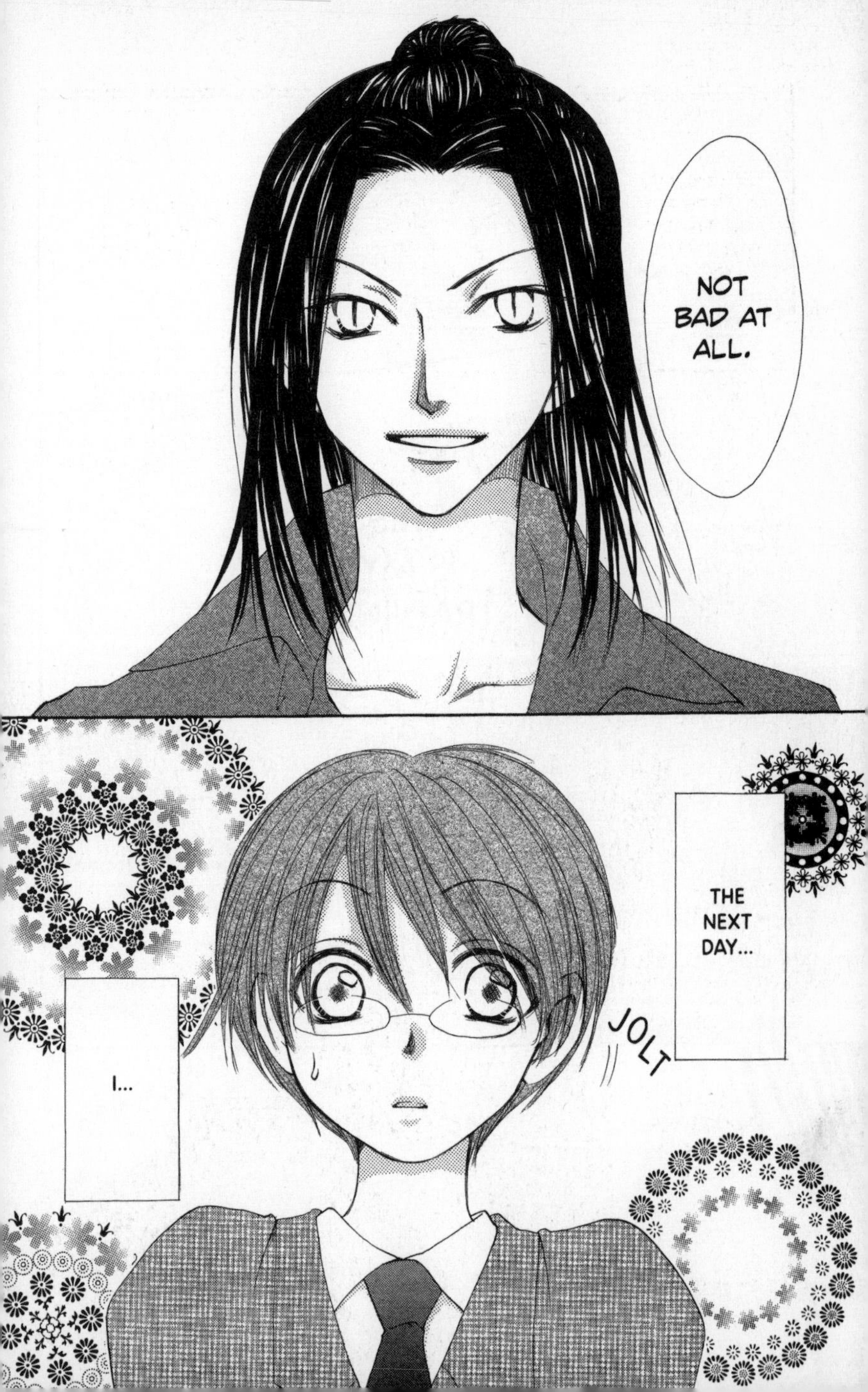
NOT BAD AT ALL.
THE NEXT DAY...
JOLT
I...

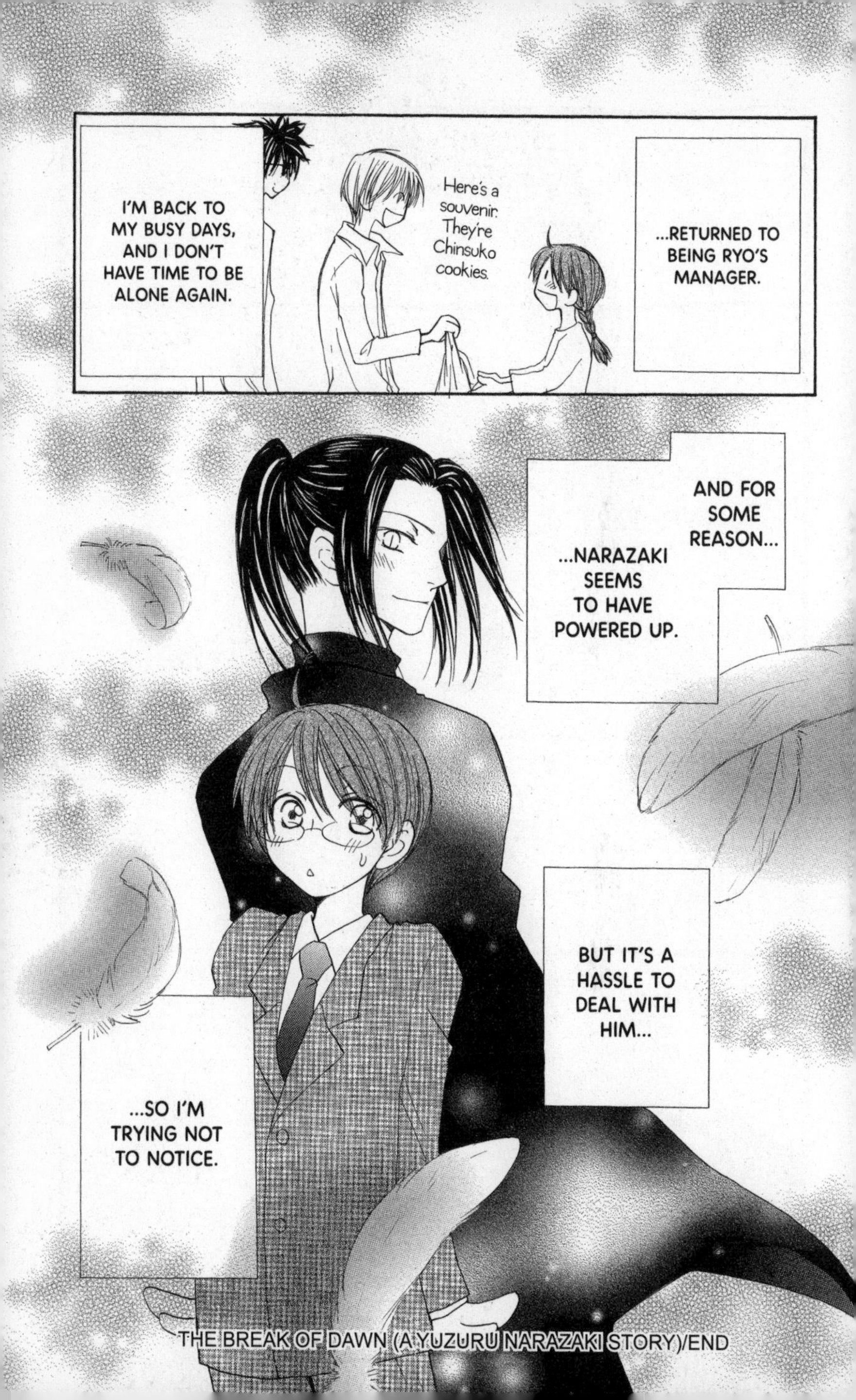
...RETURNED TO BEING RYO'S MANAGER.
Here's a souvenir. They're Chinsuko cookies.
I'M BACK TO MY BUSY DAYS, AND I DON'T HAVE TIME TO BE ALONE AGAIN.
AND FOR SOME REASON...
...NARAZAKI SEEMS TO HAVE POWERED UP.
BUT IT'S A HASSLE TO DEAL WITH HIM...
...SO I'M TRYING NOT TO NOTICE.

THE BREAK OF DAWN (A YUZURU NARAZAKI STORY)/END

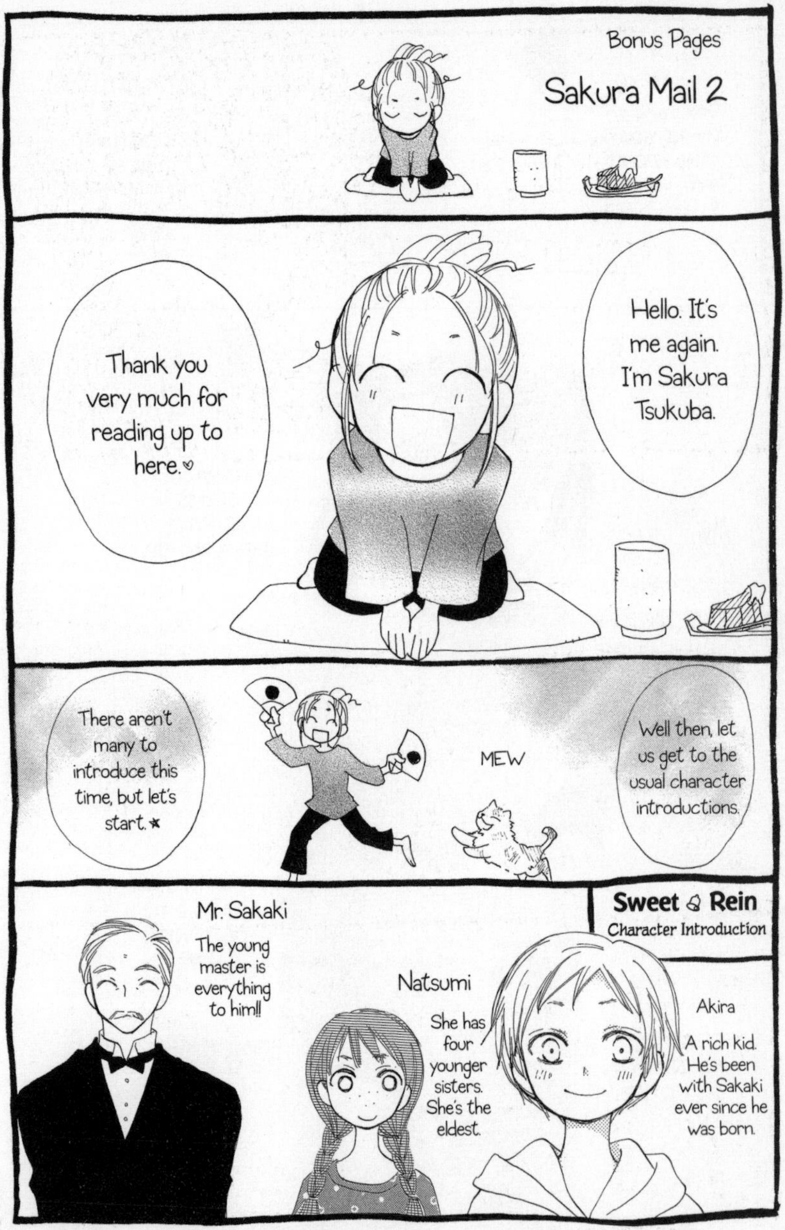
Bonus Pages
Sakura Mail 2
Hello. It's me again. I'm Sakura Tsukuba.
Thank you very much for reading up to here.♡
Well then, let us get to the usual character introductions.
MEW
There aren't many to introduce this time, but let's start.★
Sweet Rein
Character Introduction
Akira
A rich kid. He's been with Sakaki ever since he was born.
Natsumi
She has four younger sisters. She's the eldest.
Mr. Sakaki
The young master is everything to him!!

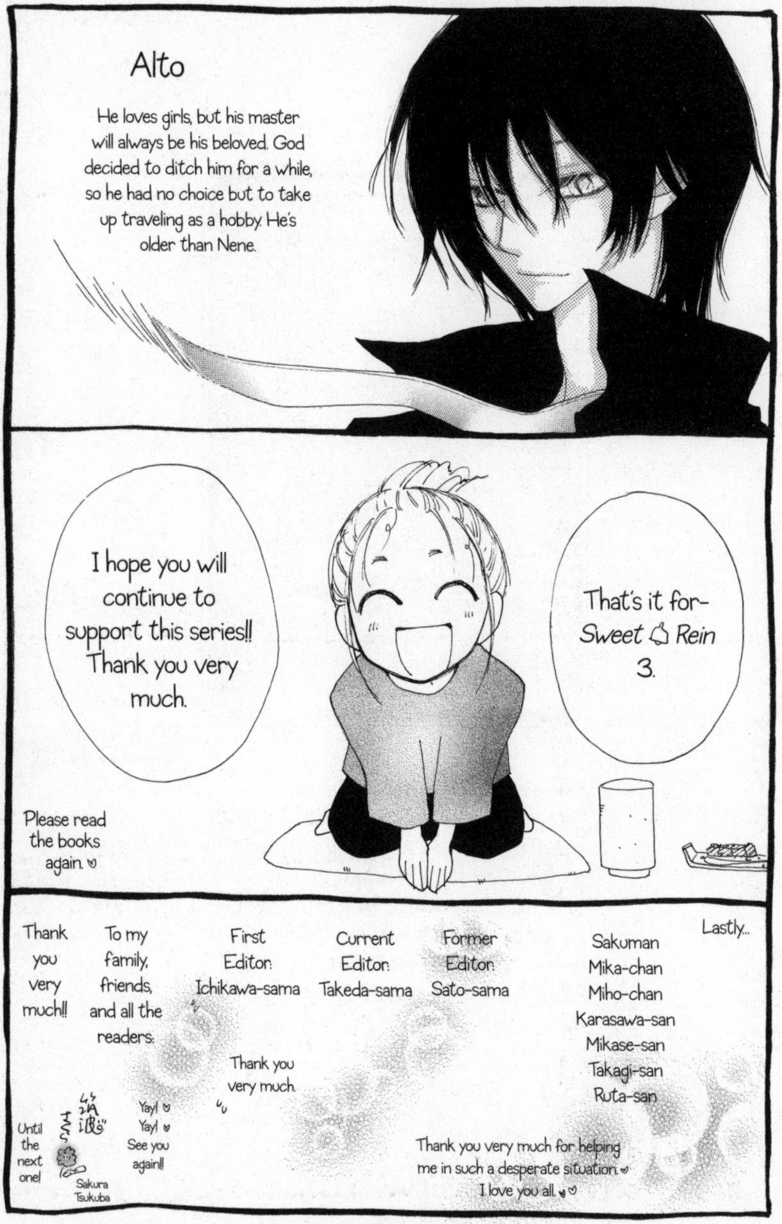
Alto
He loves girls, but his master will always be his beloved. God decided to ditch him for a while, so he had no choice but to take up traveling as a hobby. He's older than Nene.
That's it for- Sweet Rein 3.
I hope you will continue to support this series!! Thank you very much.
Please read the books again. ♡
Lastly...
Sakuman
Mika-chan
Miho-chan
Karasawa-san
Mikase-san
Takagi-san
Ruta-san
Thank you very much for helping me in such a desperate situation. ♡
I love you all. ♡
Former Editor: Sato-sama
Current Editor: Takeda-sama
First Editor: Ichikawa-sama
Thank you very much.
To my family, friends, and all the readers:
Yay! ♡
Yay! ♡
See you again!!
Thank you very much!!
Until the next one!
Sakura Tsukuba

Sakura Tsukuba is from Saitama Prefecture. In 1994 she debuted with *Hikari Nodokeki Haru no Hi ni*, a title which won the LaLa Manga Grand Prix Kasaku Award. Her other works include *Land of the Blindfolded* (recipient of the Hakusensha Athena Shinjin Taisho award) and *Penguin Revolution*.

Sweet 🔔 Rein

Volume 3
Shojo Beat Edition

Story and Art by
Sakura Tsukuba

Translation/Tetsuichiro Miyaki
Adaptation/Nancy Thistlethwaite
Touch-up Art & Lettering/Inori Fukuda Trant
Design/Izumi Evers
Editor/Nancy Thistlethwaite

YOROSHIKU • MASTER by Sakura Tsukuba
© Sakura Tsukuba 2009
All rights reserved.
First published in Japan in 2009 by HAKUSENSHA, Inc., Tokyo.
English language translation rights arranged
with HAKUSENSHA, Inc., Tokyo.

Printed in the U.S.A.

Published by VIZ Media, LLC
P.O. Box 77010
San Francisco, CA 94107

10 9 8 7 6 5 4 3 2 1
First printing, July 2014

www.viz.com   www.shojobeat.com

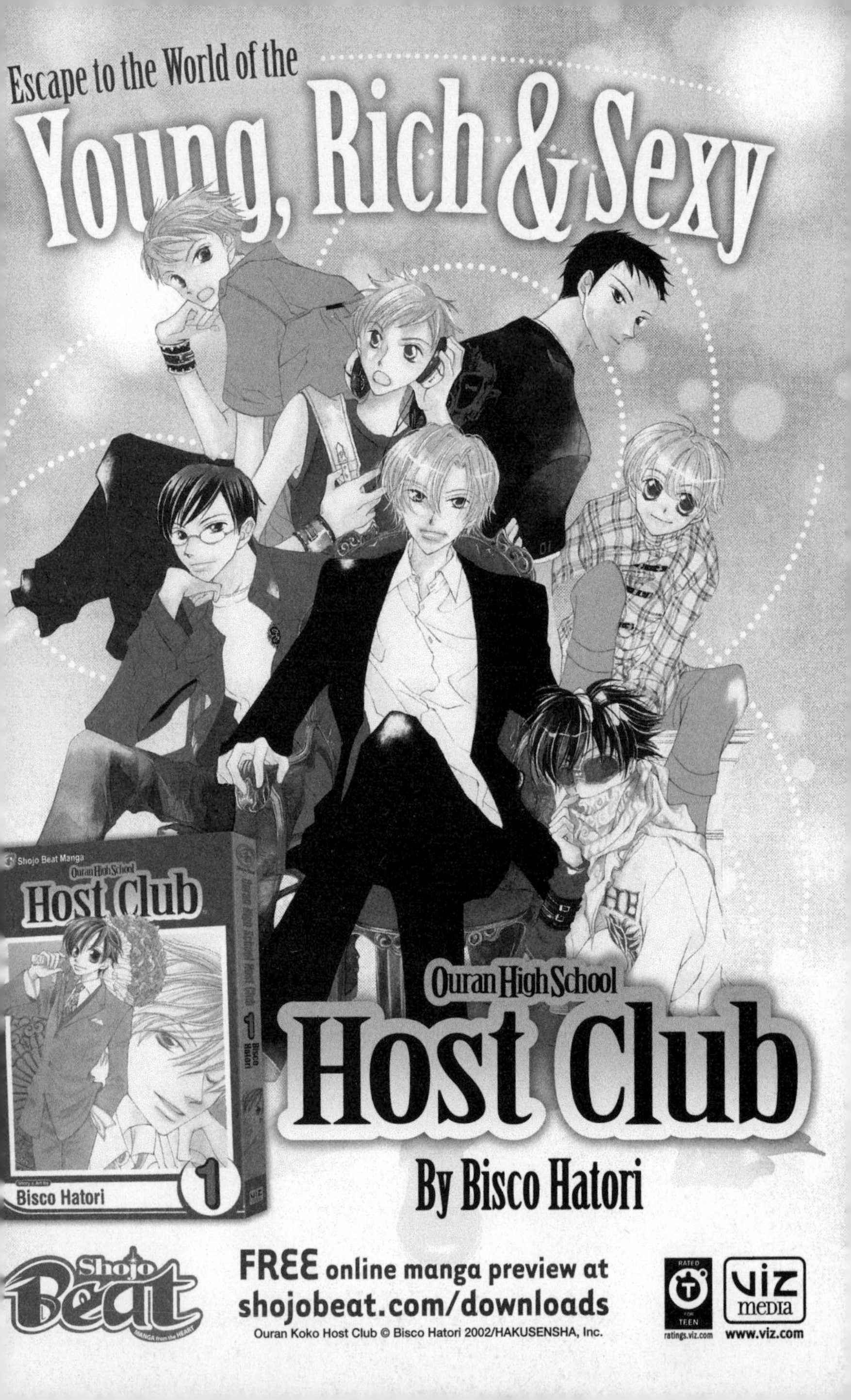

Escape to the World of the
Young, Rich & Sexy
Shojo Beat Manga
Ouran High School
Host Club
Bisco Hatori
1
Ouran High School
Host Club
By Bisco Hatori
FREE online manga preview at
shojobeat.com/downloads
Ouran Koko Host Club © Bisco Hatori 2002/HAKUSENSHA, Inc.
ratings.viz.com
www.viz.com

You may be reading the wrong way!

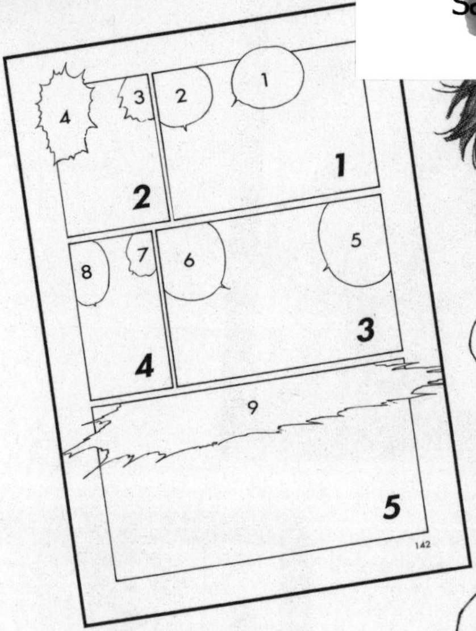
1
2
1
3
4
2
5
6
3
7
8
4
9
5
142

This book reads right to left to maintain the original presentation and art of the Japanese edition. The diagram above shows how to follow the panels. Turn to the other side of the book to begin.

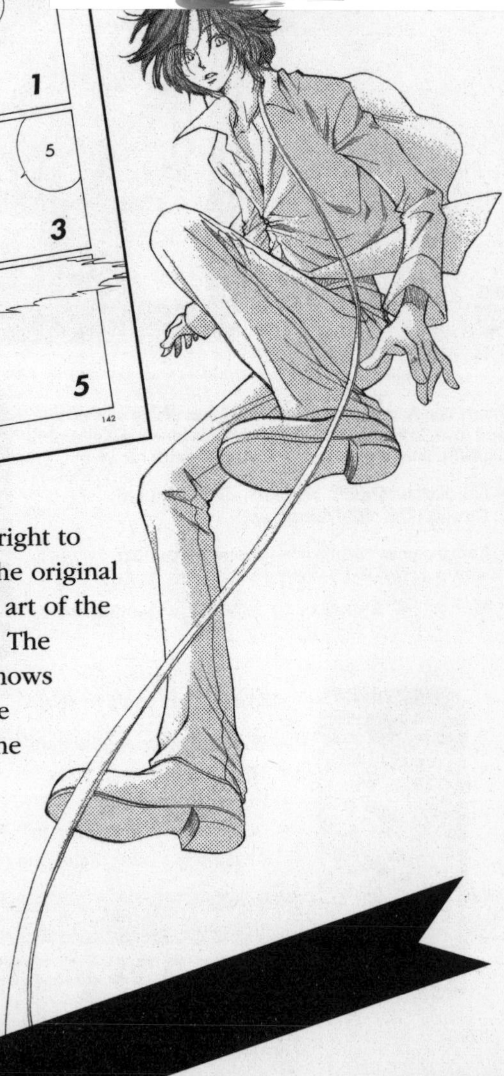